THE MAD FEAST

Also by Matthew Gavin Frank

Preparing the Ghost

Pot Farm

Barolo

The Morrow Plots

Warranty in Zulu

Sagittarius Agitprop

Matthew Gavin Frank

Liveright Publishing Corporation
A Division of W. W. Norton & Company
New York London

THE MAD FEAST

An Ecstatic Tour through America's Food

Printed in the United States of America
First Edition

For information about permission to reproduce selections from this book, write to Permissions, Liveright Publishing Corporation, a division of W. W. Norton & Company, Inc., 500 Fifth Avenue, New York, NY 10110

For information about special discounts for bulk purchases, please contact W. W. Norton Special Sales at specialsales@wwnorton.com or 800-233-4830

Manufacturing by Courier Westford
Book design by Lovedog Studio
Production manager: Anna Oler

Library of Congress Cataloging-in-Publication Data

Frank, Matthew Gavin, author.
The mad feast : an ecstatic tour through America's food / Matthew Gavin Frank. —First edition.
pages cm
Includes bibliographical references and index.
ISBN 978-1-63149-073-6 (hardcover)
1. Cooking, American. 2. Cooking—United States—States. 3. United States—Social life and customs. I. Title.
TX715.F8357 2015
641.5973—dc23

2015027864

Liveright Publishing Corporation
500 Fifth Avenue, New York, N.Y. 10110
www.wwnorton.com

W. W. Norton & Company Ltd.
Castle House, 75/76 Wells Street, London W1T 3QT

1 2 3 4 5 6 7 8 9 0

For Lu, with whom I like to eat

Contents

MIDWEST

PACIFIC WEST

GREAT PLAINS

MOUNTAIN WEST

SOUTHWEST

MID-SOUTH

Preface

THE MAD FEAST is intended to be a spastic, lyrical anti-cookbook cookbook of sorts that also may be a fun and digressive revisionist take on U.S. history. The choices of dishes herein reflect the ways in which these dishes seem leashed—in ways both real and implied—to their states' history or geography, how issues of temperature and texture, density and depth, sweetness and spice span the food and the place. The book is ordered to reflect a diverse journey around the U.S., and therefore "region-hops." After we live in one region for a while, the subsequent section is meant to offer a little vacation, in a different landscape and culture.

Each essay begins with this line of questioning: What does the state at hand mean? What does a typical foodstuff associated with said state mean? What does Alabama mean and what does hummingbird cake mean when wedged into the context of that state's history? How do state and history and foodstuff relate? What ancillary subjects will I have to engage in order to stalk both food and state toward the blurry answers to these questions?

After spending twenty years working in the restaurant industry (my first job was as a dishwasher in a fast-food chicken shack on the outskirts of Chicago—I was eleven years old), and the years thereafter often thinking and reading about all things edible and imbibable, I became interested in exploring a new kind of food writing. So much of our food writing seems interested in engaging food as "easily delicious," as a shortcut to meditations on celebration, ceremony, memory, and/or family. This is certainly one admirable, and familiar, way to engage food, of course. As opposed to treading this ground, and to seeking out the "scrumptious," I grew more interested in exploring notions of the un-scrumptious. During the writing process, these essays grew more and more preoccupied with whether an engagement of food can wrangle with the un-scrumptious while still retaining the element of sensuality. As a result, it's my hope that *The Mad Feast* embodies the forms of food writing and the cookbook while interrogating the parameters and roles of each.

Throughout the book, the character of Uncle (and sometimes Aunt, Mother, Father) makes a dominant appearance. A fairly obvious admission: the uncle is not always entirely my uncle, and the aunt is not always entirely my aunt. As I was writing these essays, I visited and/or interviewed a bunch of folks in the state at hand. Invariably, certain personal connections of mine wouldn't be able to answer some of the focused questions I had, so they would direct me to friends of friends of friends, and eventually, someone would say, "Oh, yeah! My uncle's a lobsterman who lost a finger!" Or, "Oh, yeah! My uncle used to work in a bowling ball factory and is now getting through his forced retirement by obsessing on racehorse injuries!" I made phone calls and sent emails and rented a string of cars and drove a wealth of miles until I found that someone who had worked at a bowling ball factory. In other cases, the guy who worked at the bowling ball factory serendipitously presented himself and redirected the essay in progress. And in other cases, I was lucky enough to talk to the aunts and uncles themselves, and invariably, I looked for connections between their lives—be it a manner of speech or another aspect of their personalities, histories—and the lives of my own uncles, aunts. And I looked for odd connections between other nephews across the country and me. Looking for communion. So the uncles and aunts throughout are composite characters—one part my uncle, many parts other people's uncles; are Uncle and Aunt, collective archetypes embedded within other archetypes, like America, and Food.

That said: nothing in the book is entirely fabricated. The protagonist in each essay represents a version of me and my experience, embedded within various—and real—regional histories and landscapes. The occurrences of the mothers and fathers in the book are based on aspects of my actual parents and our relationships. When my wife shows up, the character is based on my actual wife. Nonfiction is a funny genre. It's the only genre defined by what it's not. It's not fiction, but what is it then? I've applied the term "essays" to these pieces instead, as they are (as essays are, by definition) a series of attempts, as opposed to presumptions of certainty. These pieces grapple toward a larger, nebulous truth that might exist beyond or in spite of me, but for which, in order to approach it, to draw a chalk outline around it, I needed to engage various aspects of myself—via various lenses—as tools.

Though I often resist being this confessional: all of the events herein are rendered as the products of my lived experiences in conversation with research—archival, observational, interview-based, etc. (the "lenses")—with the goal of uncovering a larger, if implicit, statement about the intersection of who we are, how we live, and how/why we eat. Unless I overtly signal to the contrary, or in obvious cases (the ever-reincarnating Arkansas beaver, for instance), all of the events in this book happened in the lives of real people, or they happened to me. That's me living out of the garage in Vermont. That's me in the Illinois slaughterhouse. That's me and my wife in New Mexico, Mississippi . . .

SOUTH

Florida: Key Lime Pie

Arkansas: Beaver Tail Bouillon

Alabama: Hummingbird Cake

Mississippi: Mississippi Mud Pie

Louisiana: Crawfish Étouffée

South Carolina: Perloo

Georgia: Peach Pie

FLORIDA

Key Lime Pie in Hell

HERE, OUR CITRUS IS DWARF, the rind thinner, the acid mapping our tongues. Here, we name our citrus after our island chains, which we've named after the tiny metal code-crackers that unlock our doors. Here, our code-crackers come at us like our limes: with teeth. This is chemistry, concentration, this is a boiling down to, and a boiling down to something that will burn us, eat away at our mouths. Here, the more dessert we eat, the more we slur our speech. Here, the ear is the code-cracker, deciphering with its nodes and whirls the complaints of a lime-battered tongue.

This is lime as a halogen bulb, as something we have to squint against to see, swallow. In condensing the fruit like this, Florida offers us the kind of dare we can take only beneath an armor of sugar. Here, in this kind of heat, my uncle collects a basketful of bougainvillea flowers for his new girlfriend. They are red, or they are pink, or they are white, and they have grown between thorns and are otherwise known as the *paper flower*. These are the flowers we can record our names, and the names of our favorite desserts, on.

Here, expressions of love are condensed until too thick, until too thick to run from the fat can into whose lid Uncle has cut a triangle with a can opener with another fucking palm tree on its handle. Just east of here, tourists swim among the sea lice off of Fort Zachary Taylor Beach, wonder if the resulting itch in their crotches is more sour or sweet.

In Key Lime Pie, we temper the acid with sweetened condensed milk. This does little to keep the key lime from spoiling faster than other citrus. Just east of here, no one wonders why we name our beaches after the last president to own slaves while in office. Regardless, the hog snapper swim beneath us with the yellowtail and the grouper, never once considering the panic in our legs, the panic necessary to keep from sinking, which here, is just another kind of spoilage.

Uncle says, *we are indentured to this island.* Just east, at the Dry Tortugas, the bioluminescent algae flash their blue-green wavelengths. They are predators and they are parasitic and their protozoan neighbors had better watch out, as they are part of the dinoflagellate clan, a designation that translates as *whirling scourge.* These whirling scourges, after being eaten by aphotic fish, release a neurotoxin in such a way that it gels in the bloodstream of these fish in a reaction very similar to that of the acid of the key lime meeting the thick saccharine drool of the condensed milk that Uncle's girlfriend struggles to extract from its can.

Here, we learn to cook from the wars waged in our ocean. Uncle got fired from the Blond Giraffe (*Best Key Lime Pie in Florida 8 Consecutive Years!*), and from Martha's Steak & Seafood which serves Blond Giraffe Key Lime Pie, and from Alice's at La-Te-Da which serves Blond Giraffe Key Lime Pie, and from El Siboney which serves both Blond Giraffe Key Lime Pie and a *ropa vieja* Cuban braised beef so tender you can braid it like hair, and Key West Seafood which serves Key Lime Pie from Sysco, and he never says anything about the ways in which the bougainvillea is relatively pest-free, or about how his best friend was ass-shot last night over a baggie of cocaine in Bahama Village and is both convalescing and coming down in the hospital on Stock Island, or about how the mosquitoes here raise welts on his legs the size of stone crab claws, or about how he's talking so little these days, not sleeping at all, or about how I misinterpret his silence as the nursing of a torn-apart tongue after so much of this pie, or about how the key lime juice—so acidic—chemically reacts with the condensed milk in such a way that the filling of the pie thickens without baking, or about how this chemical reaction—responsible for *8 Consecutive Years!* of ideal consistency—is called *souring.*

The crust is graham cracker, or the crust is store-bought pastry, or the crust is homemade, or the crust is, as Uncle says, "This stupid fucking part of the earth we have to live on," even all the way out here, on a crumb of dirt in the middle of the ocean 130 miles from the mainland. He holds his arms out to his sides and spins a bit as he says this. Granted, he's been drinking all afternoon, but that does little to undo the facts: here, our scourges whirl. They're often the prettiest things in the room.

* * *

HERE, DESSERT CAN INSULT. At Key West's Louie's Backyard restaurant, head waiter Ben Harris says that purists are often "offended by the slices [we serve] . . . with a gingersnap crust and garnished with berries." Uncle slathers sunscreen on his belly, even though he doesn't plan on leaving the house today. Habit honors tradition. His tongue is rutted. His crust is homemade, if not inoffensive.

Some food historians believe that Key Lime Pie was invented by Florida Keys sponge fishermen in the late 1800s. Bound to their boats for days on end, they packed foods that refused to spoil, even in this heat, along with an easy protein source and the fruit they culled from local trees—cans of condensed milk, eggs, key limes. They would gather their catch, the seawater running into the pores and along the channels of the live sponges, the seawater responsible—in these beasts without systems nervous, digestive, or circulatory—for delivering food and oxygen, for scrapping waste. The fishermen would place their catch in tubs they called *survival pods*, and they would allow the sponges to exhale and exhale until dry, and they would open their cans, crack their eggs, juice their fruit, make their pie, their catch destined to become the padding in the helmets of our pilots and soldiers and football players, the things with which we wipe our counters and toilets, the filters for our municipal water supply and the applicators for house paint and rouge, contraceptives secreted away, the things Uncle's new girlfriend uses to augment her breasts, the purple rectangular thing Uncle uses, damp with tap

> ***The key lime says, if we don't have to cook, we can eat that much faster. The key lime says, it's hot enough.***

water, to cool down his forehead, on the couch, beneath the whine of the ceiling fan, as his girlfriend forks, from a paper plate, the precise yellowish triangular thing into Uncle's mouth that at first will make him cringe with its sourness, then, as the thick sweet asserts itself, close his eyes, forget about the ways in which he himself has dried out as if in some edge-of-a-continent survival pod, and hum as if communing with the ceiling fan, with all things pressed of the water that sustains them. Here, we absorb the poisons of the lovely lit-up things that aim to kill us. We do this, Uncle says, because we are hungry, excited, and easily seduced. He opens his shirt. His girlfriend touches the scar. Her fingers are sharp and sugary.

There is no official recorded recipe of those early Key Lime Pies because, Key West historian Tom Hambright says, a little too aggressively for my taste, "You didn't do that because everybody knows how to make 'em." In the kitchen, Uncle's girlfriend cries a little as she smashes the graham crackers for the crust. This too, for similar reasons, she will not record. Here, fickleness is a kind of survival pod, and a lime that spoils so much faster than other fruit can release a sharp, preservative juice. The key lime says, if we don't have to cook, we can eat that much faster. The key lime says, it's hot enough.

Uncle's girlfriend admires her new body, distorted in the wrung swan's-neck silver of the kitchen faucet. Uncle fans himself, feebly, with a curl of lime rind. He quotes, over and over again, the eighth essential step in the Florida Department of Agriculture's Official Key Lime Pie recipe. In the kitchen, his girlfriend substitutes her fists for the recommended rolling pin as he mutters, "Let cool, let cool . . ."

* * *

JUST NORTH OF HERE, Palm Springs Phase III Senior Living Complex opens next to Palm Springs Phase II Senior Living Complex in whose clubhouse talent show I, as a child, sang—way, way off key—Whitney Houston's "The Greatest Love of All" to a roomful of my grandparents' friends, including the obese and infamous Janette Shamus who I later found out threw herself down a flight of stairs in Vernon in order to collect the insurance money and retire, and who taught me how to hustle bingo, and who told me her purse was made out of the skin of the largest alligator ever pulled from Lake Okeechobee, and that she bought it for a mere ten bucks at the Thunderbird Flea Market on Sunrise Boulevard in Fort Lauderdale, where my own grandmother would stock up on her crumpled papier mâché earrings, plastic bracelets in every color (to match her stockings, and purse, and shoes, and eye shadow), perfume that smelled of clove cigarette and giant leopard moth-ball, where she would buy me VHS tapes of vampire movies and bathing suits that would fray at the crotch in a week, notoriously bargaining with the vendors to the point at which I had to, embarrassed, walk away and wait at a distance behind the corn dog stand. But I would eavesdrop, listen to her routine, her three most popular lines variations on "Do a little better for Grandma," "It's senior citizens day," and "Well, I hope you know I'm not paying the tax on that." Oftentimes, the bilingual vendors would tell her to go fuck herself in Spanish, she would tell them to go take a shit in the ocean in Yiddish, wagging her loose finger in their faces, and the capitalist beat went on, as the famed Thunderbird Flea Market Circus began its show, and I would watch the third-rate elephants march among the gold-plated thumb rings and stands that would carve your name cursive and seriffed into necklaces, topped by leotarded acrobats who struggled to somersault, and Cuban refugees hiding behind clown makeup and putty noses, and I would watch while sitting on my grandfather's shoulders, eating my snow cone, its paper sleeve wettening, the syrup staining my shirt front the color of this washed-out sky, pretending there really was such a thing as a blue raspberry, and watch thc drugged beasts lumber with their filed tusks beneath fluorescents and the speaker salesboys showing off the breadth of their bass, and Janette Shamus would open that purse and pull out a heat-sealed hard candy, so green beneath the cellophane, and she would whisper the flavor, *key lime,* as if doing me a favor, as if confessing a secret, as if rendering a prediction so seductive that it would send me, years later, riding with the other organic detritus to the continental country's southernmost point.

* * *

Here is the coconut, and here is the mango, and here is the banana, and here is the mamey. Here are the ways in which our tongues work and burn, our bodies rise and fall. So ancient here. So minimal in the face of *8 Consecutive Years*. Adding heat is a shunning of both tradition and chemistry. A putting of a windbreaker over a goose-down coat, a fur hat on a yak, another sunburn on top of a perfectly good sunburn. We do this only if our source ingredients become dangerous to us. Uncle holds his tongue. That's because it's bleeding.

Supersaturation undoes absorption, every time. Even my skills at hustling bingo can't argue with this. Here, the southernmost point is marked with a rusty buoy, jutting like a pimple from the concrete at the intersection of South and Whitehead Streets. Next to it, I can buy conch shells in which I can hear the ocean, and Key Lime Pie far less delicious than the Blonde Giraffe's. As I take my first bite, I'm not sure if that whirling in my ears is coming from the vulva of the giant seashell or the actual Atlantic.

Today, the Blonde Giraffe cooks its pies "to prevent salmonella." Today, Uncle curses the cruise ships, resents that the tourists can eat the same pie he does. His girlfriend says something about the sacrifice of the locals, about how, during the Depression, the Keys began to advertise their precious pie as *World Famous!*

Famous or not, Key Lime Pie compels a man to vandalize his own home. Uncle has scratched "THIS IS HELL" into the back of his bathroom door with a Phillips-head. Behind us, Hemingway beats the shit out of Wallace Stevens again at Sloppy Joe's bar, goes home to his inbred polydactyl cats who will, years later, continue to propagate a species of six-toed felines, and Stevens goes home and writes "She sang beyond the genius of the sea . . ." and Tennessee Williams has another nervous breakdown behind the jalousies of the same front door I will, years later, live behind.

The Blonde Giraffe now sells, in addition to its world famous pie, another 170 Key Lime items. These range from Key Lime Pecans to Frozen Pie-on-a-Stick (a favorite of honeymooners), Key Lime candles to Key Lime shampoo. There's even the Key Lime sponge, the flagella of which, in defense mechanism, wrap around the acidic molecules of the fruit's rendered pith in a motion not unlike that of a noose cinching itself, without the need of external executioner, around the fat neck of a man not unlike Uncle.

Though the bougainvillea that overtakes the backyard is relatively pest-free, this season it suffers from a bane of giant leopard moths who, after nightfall, open their wings to their full three-inch span and feed on the same papery flowers that now desiccate into red or pink or white sludge in the basket on Uncle's girlfriend's nightstand—the one whose drawer handle has been carefully molded and scrolled into another stylized version of another fucking palm tree. Here, the giant leopard moths are also called whirling scourges.

In the late 1700s, French botanist Philibert Commerçon, sailing under the command of explorer Louis-Antoine de Bougainville, disguised his lover, Jeanne Baré, as a man and, violating the sexual regulations of the time, snuck her on board the fluyt *Étoile*. In addition to becoming the first woman to circumnavigate the globe, Baré was also the first European to observe the bougainvillea, pluck one of its flowers, and, in the face of her masculine disguise, assertively tuck the magenta bloom behind her ear. This says little about other disguises: the acid we mask in a paste of milk and sugar, the sponges we hide, sew up into our bodies. The coconut palms say nothing, just stand like so many erections planted upside down, muse to the artists, furniture makers, bakers who, at the Blonde Giraffe, ice their souvenir pies with their ubiquitous fronds.

On the wings of the giant leopard is a collage of black spots. These spots are aposematic, meaning that they boast a lack of palatability to the moth's potential predators. Nature dictates that, over time, the predators will get over this, forcing the moths to once again adapt, develop a new disguise to transfer how revolting they are.

We have undone the key lime's natural unpalatability with milk-in-a-can. The last cow on Key West, circa 1900 (abandoned there due to a broken wagon following a delivery of fresh milk from the mainland), swallows its moo, considers eating the local citrus, before deciding against it. Uncle has adapted and adapted to the couch.

* * *

SEPTEMBER 25, 1998: Key West is evacuated due to Hurricane Georges, which is about to arrive any minute now, but many locals stay and do as they always do during these tropical storms, which is to stock up on nonperishable food and water and batteries, and especially booze and cocaine, and to board up their windows and to invite their friends, and to throw the island's famed hurricane parties/orgies, and, if they live through it, and, if their homes are still standing—at least partially—they will climb to the roofs—as I did, as my uncle did—and, either naked or in a too-small swimsuit, front-flip down into the street, which has, after the storm, become a river, on which my and Uncle's hungover and oversexed compatriots kayak and swim and fish, and in which they try and fail to make love, and they think nothing of circumnavigation, even as they try to swim around the entire island without ever crossing that submerged border between floodwater and actual ocean.

Uncle, not sleeping, carves "FUCK NOAH" into the coffee table, brushes the pie crumbs to the floor for the fire ants. Uncle's girlfriend thinks nothing of Baré, tries on Uncle's blue palm tree button-down, but doesn't dare look in the strangled mirror of the kitchen faucet. On the counter beside, the graham cracker crumbs, as if post-hurricane, are as pulverized as the Keys.

In 1965, a bill was introduced in Florida demanding a $100 fine for any establishment advertising Key Lime Pie not prepared with the juice of actual key limes. In 2006, the Florida senate and the Florida house passed "important" legislation designating Key Lime Pie the official pie of the state of Florida. In her Florida Pride T-shirt (another palm tree, more citrus), Uncle's girlfriend works her knuckles against the crumbs. To the naked eye, they can't get any smaller.

Uncle flops onto the couch in a living room full of bamboo. In the backyard, hanging upside down from the thorns, so many giant leopards wait—hungry, excited—for dark. With the finished pie, she walks all the way around the couch as if it were an island, as if this filthy floor were the sea. As if commanded by law, Uncle sits up, eats his slice without joy. He remembers that *Florida* means *feast of flowers*, imagines the lime in bloom, but is unsure as to whether this means that it's we who consume the flowers or if the flowers, eventually, will eat away at us.

Extermination festers in the petals, is secreted away into the nethers of the egg. It takes a little acid to bring it out. He goes for seconds, blows air over his blistering tongue, rubs at the burning in his chest. If his face is florid, he thinks, he's getting closer to the state that surrounds him. If his face is florid, he is either having a heart attack or becoming a flower. He is eating lime juice and eggs and milk and graham crackers. He is fattening himself for the moths.

After Hurricane Georges, the power outage. The quiet dark. The disaster that has robbed so many of their homes is the same disaster that allows Key West, finally, I think, to feel like an actual island in the middle of an actual ocean. There are the obvious things I've forgotten. There are the stars. There's the moon. There's Cuba, and there's a foghorn. There's the Blonde Giraffe still selling, though their ovens are down. They're making it the old way again. There's my uncle finally finding sleep, and his girlfriend finally finding sleep, and there are the giant leopard moths taking to the sky like the kind of plague that inspires aria. There must be ten thousand of them, eating the bougainvillea flowers in the dark. And there's a palm tree out there that I can't see, but I can hear the wind in its fronds. And I eat my pie with my hands—the old way—and listen to the fronds clack together like parrots kissing, or something even more beautiful.

Key Lime Pie

Servings: 6
Yield: 1 Pie

Graham Cracker Crust Ingredients
This makes enough crust for about 4 pies
4 cups graham cracker crumbs
¾ cup granulated sugar
¼ cup butter, melted

Filling Ingredients
2 cans sweetened condensed milk—Borden's
1 cup key lime juice—fresh
8 egg yolks

Meringue Ingredients
*8 egg whites**

½ teaspoon cream of tartar
⅓ cup confectioner's sugar

Graham Cracker Crust

Preheat oven to 350 degrees F.

Mix the cracker crumbs, sugar, and butter together.

Line a 9-inch pie tin with the cracker mix, pressing firmly to line bottom and sides.

Bake for 8 minutes at 350 degrees F.

Filling

Whisk the condensed milk with the lime juice and egg yolks in a stainless steel bowl.

Pour into the pre-baked graham cracker shell.

Set aside while making the meringue.

Meringue*

Beat the egg whites to a soft peak—add cream of tartar and continue to whip to a stiff peak.

Continue whipping and add the sugar, whipping until the meringue forms stiff peaks.

Decoratively add meringue on top of the custard.

Bake for 15–30 minutes at 350 degrees.

Cook until the meringue has good color.

Check with a wooden skewer or cake tester to be sure the custard is done.

*Be sure the bowl and whisk used to beat the egg whites are very clean, otherwise the egg whites will not form a stiff peak.

Serving Idea: Garnish with slice of lime.

—Blue Heaven Restaurant

The Ecstasy of the Beaver Tail

for Elena Passarello

WHEN THE MEN WITH bluish rifles line up along the illuminated railing of the Ozark Bridge, do not marvel at how the bridge's support cables resemble your own ribcage. Heave air into your lungs—the ones many biologists have compared to dwarf Seckel pears—turn away from the men and from the lights, the gift shops peddling postcards of your cousins, the antique shops peddling lampshades named Mulberry, murals of steamboats and murals of Quapaw chiefs, and, as you hear one shot follow another, the water spouting over your guard hairs, dive deep. Protect your ears with your valvular flaps. Allow the thin film over your eyes to act as goggles—a compensation for your poor sight. Get lost in the soft tangle of the wild celery.

You are told you don't have the capacity for love. That beating in your chest is only the extra body fat. You are semi-aquatic, after all. I'm the same way—confusing the thing that warms me for affection. This time, you will not make it. You will devote your tail to supper. A boy will complain, "Beaver again?!" and you will recognize your name, know you've heard this complaint before—many, many times. You wake up again in the Arkansas River. You have a new tail. You faintly remember the bullets, the biting. You build a dam against this.

In eating you, they take your balance into their bodies, revise, in swallow after swallow, their own internal gravities. In fullness, in satisfaction is a shift in force. You wonder if, after eating your tail, their hearts fall to the middles of their bodies—three feet from the crown, three feet from the earth. They are not semi-aquatic. They do not need tails in order to remain standing when hauling their mud.

You'll never know this: that an Arkansas blogger named Lewis&Clark will tell the world that your tail is best boiled in saltwater. That, regarding the cooking of your tail, a man whose last name is Manship will use words like *direct heat* and *open fire* and *until the meat starts to separate from the skin* and *peel off skin* and *tender.* You are smarter than all other rodents save for the Norwegian rat, though your heart is so much larger. Your three *venae cavae* are so much prettier, and your right ventricle—good Lord!—is as large as that of the seal. You've always felt that those with the capacity to love are often treasured for their extremities. Your tail is in full bloom—like a carnation, like pancake batter reaching for the edges of the griddle before the heat stops it in place.

* * *

You wake up in the river. Miles away, in Texarkana, Scott Joplin touches a piano for the first time. From the bridge, two sisters with fur hats call your name. Our spines are only remnants, essential reminders of an earlier time. Bones stacked like piano keys, if the piano were not standing but in repose. We eat your tail to remember how our bodies used to be. I can't tell if this is sweet or gamey, holy or heathen.

You remember Thomas Aquinas, but not how you got to Arkansas. Since you can't read, you remember only the crust of his knuckles, the musk of his collarbones, how he trapped you along the bank of the Seine. He had been reassigned by the Dominican order to be regent master of the University of Paris. Aquinas was not happy about this. He soothed himself by trapping the animals he found along the city's river—red squirrel, least weasel, leopard frog, mink—obsessed with categorizing which beasts were a sin to eat, and when. You remember how he studied you by candlelight in his small office at the university, which smelled of glue, parchment, ink, dander. You remember: he kept you in a cage on his writing desk, next to which he penned, "Of fishes, they were allowed to partake of the drier kinds, because thereby the moist nature of the fish is tempered." He would whistle at you, kiss the air, rule you a fish according to his new ideas about dietary law. Now, even the devout can eat your tail during Lenten Fridays.

You will die in that cage, in which Aquinas has mistakenly assumed that the maple leaf ground cover he has laid will soothe you, remind you of the river. The day you die, Aquinas will boil you with laurel and sea salt. He will share your tail with Étienne Tempier. He will write, recording the fifteen signs preceding the Judgment, "on the 'seventh' day all the stars, both planets and fixed stars, will throw out fiery tails like comets." He will not think to associate your body with anything celestial. He would consider your rebirth in the Arkansas to be heretical.

* * *

YOU WAKE UP in the Arkansas. From the bridge, two sisters whistle Joplin's "Maple Leaf Rag." You think of Thomas, the pathetic ground cover he spread over your cage bottom, his hands so careful, so flat, so balanced, the warmth of them so cosmic they could be tails. Still today, in the Arkansas towns of Lead Hill, Fountain Hill, Violet Hill, Coal Hill, Gravel Hill, Pilot Hill, towns named for water and towns named for flowers and towns named for flight, and towns named for the industries that killed their residents, in restaurants named Hog Hut and Catfish Inn, Ray's and Shirley's, Cotton's and Cove, Doc's, Whistlestop, Dee's and Calamba, it's beaver tail special on Friday with fries.

In Rectors Place, Arkansas, in 1850, a man named Beaver will build his family cabin from the local oak and hawthorn. He will build a grit mill, an inn called the Stagecoach, and a ferry to cross the White River, in which you will wake up, swim among the bloated bodies of the Quapaw. Above you, the town will be renamed Beaver's Ferry, then Beavertown, then Beaver. Confederate soldiers will find refuge here during the Civil War, when they will nourish themselves on your breast, jowl, tail, before collecting three-ring bullets into their hearts.

When felling your own oaks and hawthorns, your tail supports you, allows for the chewing. Enables your teeth, the uprooting. When swimming, your tail flips in four directions, acts as a rudder.

To the men on the Ozark, the water's surface will for a few seconds bear the mark of the cross, the crossroads. You are diving deep, but not deep enough. And Aquinas will write, "on the 'eighth' day there will be a great earthquake, and all animals will be laid low." Your tail was once six inches long, is now twelve inches long; was once four inches wide, is now five; was always three-quarters of an inch thick, from Aquinas to the Arkansas. In this thickness is a consistency that tries to wedge itself into the crevices of memory. Still, every time, you forget that your tail has been eaten and eaten.

Aquinas Catholic Church in Washington County is 77 miles from the Ozark Bridge. Aquinas University in Fayetteville is 60 miles from the Ozark Bridge. The average distance from the beaver's tail (where it meets the body) to its heart is sixteen inches. That's fourteen bites. You imagine our hearts in the centers of our bodies. You imagine, correctly, that you are swimming in a river beneath a bridge that arcs within a town called Middle.

Love is all about sustenance, excision, sacrifice, politics—allowing the toughest part of you to stew and stew until it softens.

The hill people sprinkle your tail with spicy vinegar, spread your meat with the mush of purple hull peas, and peas called black-eyed, and field, and Crowder, and Lady, soak up your juices with soda biscuits, chase your musk with persimmon pudding. You wake again to the water, fluttering with the awareness of having decorated so many mouths with the flattest end of you. Arkansas again.

Meriwether Lewis writes, "Killed . . . bever . . . near a Cottonwood tree near the river . . . Shore—the leaves of the Cottonwood were much distroyed—as were those of the Cottonwood trees in it's neighbourhood. I therefore supposed that it fed on the folage of trees at this season, the flesh of this anamal is a pleasant and whoalsome food—they resemble the slowth very much in the form of their hands, or fore feet. Their teeth and eyes are like the porcupine." This is the bulk of his day's journal entry, and though you are consumed, you consume Lewis. Clark picks his nose and wipes the detritus on a sliver of kindling. It pops in the fire. Together, they eat your tail from a platter of bark, argue over the split, who got the larger portion. Clark snores. Lewis tries to find sleep. He blinks at the sky.

His eyes are better than yours, but they don't have that wonderful film. The stars throw their fiery tails. Like Aquinas, like Arkansas, he can't stop thinking about you.

This world needs to be tamped down, thought Zeus when he enlisted Hermes to attack the arrogant beaver, who had been bragging of the beauty of his fluffy tail, declaring it more worthy of reverence than the gods. Hermes jumped into his chariot and crushed the beaver's tail, again and again, beneath the stone wheels. The beaver sank into depression, until Athena spoke to him of the sort of balance that depends on flatness. Do you still feel the weight of those wheels? Tell me, does time confuse the weight of pain with the weight of comfort, until all that remains is weight itself? Cry me a river. Chew me a branch. Dream your body aromatic with carrots.

* * *

YOU WAKE UP. This is not the river, but the lake named for you. On your way to the surface, you pass a crappie trying to couple with a spoonbill catfish. You've learned not to shake your head. You swim toward the shore, the local sheriff pacing on the deck of his pontoon boat, screaming something about security into a megaphone. Overhead, the buzzards circle, release their shit like rain into the lake. News reporters squat on the roofs of their Winnebagos, their flashbulbs exploding, focused on a family of three struggling to water-ski in the shadows of the limestone bluffs. You too stare at the gray-haired patriarch with the sunburnt belly as he calls, "Chelsea!" to his daughter, "Be careful!" His swimsuit is red with white flowers on it, hemmed just above the knee. Because you can't read, you will not know that the *New York Times* will report on August 18, 1993, of this very "Chelsea! Be careful!" or of the heat the reporters called "wilting," or the sunset swim the father and daughter shared, the lovely way his body arced from dock to water like a collapsing bridge.

They will not report on the ways in which their boat unzipped the lake like an earthquake, how you could tell that this man spent his childhood eating your tail for supper—maybe even complaining about it, about the way he stared at you, pointed you out to his daughter, whispered something into her ear. You will think he is speaking of you, and not the lake, when you overhear him tell the reporters as he's toweling off, "I just wanted to come home," muttering, "to the Beaver."

There is Aquinas misjudging you again. There is the winter when you warm yourself with maple leaves. There is Clinton, two years later, hiring an intern fresh out of Lewis and Clark College, forgetting the suppers of his youth, making policy, chasing tail. You know: love is all about sustenance, excision, sacrifice, politics—allowing the toughest part of you to stew and stew until it softens.

From the shore of Beaver Lake, you watch the family of three disappear into the house in which they're staying. The reporters have left, and so has the sheriff. They are turning off their own ovens, own TVs. They are drooling onto their pillowcases. You have outlasted all of them here. Smoke comets from the chimney. You watch the house until all the lights go out. You're longing for something, but don't have the language to take a stab at it. You have your instinct, and your poor vision. You watch the house until the planets are usurped into a greater darkness. You clean your tail with your hind feet. You gather your mud.

Beaver Tail Bouillon

Ingredients

1 adult beaver tail
4 sprigs of thyme
2 bay leaves
4 sprigs of flat leaf parsley
3 lightly bruised sprigs of tarragon
5 sprigs of rosemary
10–20 black peppercorns (whole)

Beaver Tail Preparation

1. Place the beaver tail on a grill grate directly above the coals or on a hot cast iron on the stove.

2. Flip the tail at 15-second intervals or whenever bubbles occur.

3. When scales are blistered but not burnt, place the tail in an ice bath for 5–10 seconds.

4. Cut around the perimeter of the tail to peel both sides. Discard the skin. Veins should be observable in the posterior of the tail. The tail should be gelatinous.

5. Soak beaver tail in a 10–20% saltwater brine overnight.

Bouillon

1. Fill a 7.57-liter (8-quart) Dutch oven with 6.5 liters lightly salted water.

2. Tie thyme, parsley, bay leaves, tarragon, and rosemary in leek leaves with cooking string and add to Dutch oven. Place black peppercorns in solution or sachet for easy removal.

3. Sauté one medium to large onion, two stalks of celery and two small carrots in butter to make a mirepoix. Add to oven when fragrance is robust.

4. Place brined beaver tail in oven and cook at 350 degrees for four to six hours.

—Josh Brewer

The Beginning of the End of Hummingbird Cake

IN THE PINEAPPLE is the fiber we've been looking for, the sweet yellow threadiness we'd never confuse for stitches, for wound. In the banana is the quickening rot, the rot being the softest, sweetest stage of the fruit. This is not Hawaii. There are no resorts here. We swim in no ocean, but in One Mile Creek, where there are no whales, only six partially submerged washing machines giving in to rust, a rot slower than that of the banana, more ferric than sweet.

* * *

ONE MILE CREEK: deflated footballs, downturned antifreeze jugs, skim milk cartons, dolls naked and dolls clothed. The biggest dirty diaper I've ever seen, painted, as if deliberately, with a crucifix of shit.

* * *

HISTORY IS AS CLOYING as sugar, is less prone than the banana to rot. Here, we sweeten our trash with tropical fruit, add a leavening agent, a little cinnamon, pecan. Vanilla for Tahiti. Egg for the earth. Salt. Flour. Here, we frost fantasy with cream cheese and imagine the speed required for an ultimate cleaning, a final washing away. How fast can we eat our Hummingbird Cake without getting sick? This: our skunk cabbage, our syrup of ipecac. Hummingbird Cake as a purging of the creek. How fast do we need to eat to commune with the wingbeats? The very fast wingbeats?

In Mobile, in August, 93 percent humidity. In One Mile Creek, in August, the number of discarded tank tops quintuples. There's a pink "LIFE'S A BEACH" one. There's a red one collaring an egret. The relative humidity of a human exhale is almost always 100 percent. The relative humidity of a human exhale through a mouthful of Hummingbird Cake (allowing that p = pressure, the force with which we breathe out, w = water content of the cake [averaging pineapple at 87 percent, banana at 84 percent, the pecans at 10 percent, the cake base at 30 percent, the cream cheese frosting at 75 percent], Tc = temperature in Celsius, a = enthalpy, a thermodynamic potential that encompasses everything from the origination of a substance to its final resting place in the end stages of entropy) is almost always:

$$p_w/[Pa] = RH \times 610.8 \exp\left(\frac{17.2694T_c}{T_c + 238.3^\circ}\right)$$

or smoke, or mirrors, or a language I incompletely understand. The hummingbird hovers over Mobile, knowing nothing of the things named after it, everything of enthalpy and equation. It watches the egret free itself from the tank top, bite, then reject the left shoulder strap. The hummingbird watches twelve mothers fork cake into their mouths. Watches us light our fires. It inhales and exhales 250 times per minute, each.

In our carbon is our incompletely burned garbage. In our cake, the pineapple beckons to the banana, and the banana to us. According to Aqua Lab's Moisture Migration Department, in an article not-so-scholarly titled "Fruitcake and Fruit Cereal Surprise," "Water content is nothing more than a distraction. Pay attention to that number, and the outcome feels like sleight-of-hand." That flock, a bunch of small things, looks like one big thing. History makes off with the nectar. In this, is some kind of abracadabra, some distraction that only our water can understand.

* * *

PAPER PLATES, Snickers wrappers, empty two-liters of Mountain Dew, traffic cones, cyanide.

* * *

ABOVE MY HEAD in Montgomery, circling—scouting, perhaps—as they're equally drawn to sugar, I can't tell if that's a hummingbird or a *Vespa mandarinia*, that giant yak-killing hornet, the bee whose mandible is so relatively strong (and orange) and bears a single black tooth perfect for burrowing—that tiny strength like the hummingbird to the human, Earth to Cassiopeia, our small stories about our desserts and breath and garbage able to inflame only our small, same hearts, some larger story, larger heart, forever out there bobbing like another inky blob in the rank shallows next to pineapple rind, banana peels. Dead, in rigor mortis, *Vespa mandarinia* flares out its wings to their full three-inch span, and if we dare to lift its body, it is a cross that fills our palm.

Though it had been made in countless kitchens throughout the American South, the first published recipe for Hummingbird Cake appeared only in the February 1978 issue of *Southern Living* magazine (the self-proclaimed "Southern Belle Bible of Gracious Hostessing"). The recipe's author, Mrs. L. H. Wiggins, offered no explanation for the cake's name. Everything has its waste. Even our graciousness still bears a sort of garbage.

Other names for Hummingbird Cake: Granny's Best Cake, Jamaican Cake (the hummingbird, a.k.a. Doctor Bird, is the Jamaican national bird), Cake That Don't Last, Nothing Left Cake, and the contradictory Never Ending Cake. In its nicknames, Hummingbird Cake is both nothing and forever. Other theories as to the reasoning behind the cake's name: It's sweet; hummingbirds like sweet. When you eat it, you hum with happiness. Like the hummingbird, we flock to this cake, eat it intensely and quickly, and disperse when sated.

I wonder if, humming, to the hummingbird I sound like the yak. In Montgomery, I wonder if the bird and I are equally confused about things at this point in our lives. All around me, it seems, are wingbeats—how the sounds of some birds evoke an illusion of peace, others an illusion of menace. How the sounds of all birds fool us, commune with the sounds of the insects in some romantic linguistic. How insects are birds that bite. How peace and menace are forever communing. How strangulation (by tank top, by cake) is the sibling to embrace. How each is equally intimate, drawn to sugar. How that notion is rote, so often discussed in the time of the noose. How the birds overhead are the gallows, mercifully empty of our bodies. The mouth can commune with this kind of weather, history. Sure, the hands are important, but the mouth is closer to the heart, the heart to the thing we eat with.

* * *

BICYCLE TIRES, truck tires, toy truck tires, rope.

* * *

ORIGINAL CAKE, Entropy Cake, Down to the Crumbs, Immortal. According to *World of Hummingbirds,* the hummingbird's brain is 4.2 percent of its body weight, the largest proportion in the bird kingdom. It can remember every flower it has ever been to, and how long each takes to refill its receptacles with nectar. The lower beak is flexible and widens and bends downward when it sips. When a person is hung, the lower lip drops from the upper, widens, bends downward, as if reaching for one final sweetness.

Like the hummingbird, we can remember. We try not to remember, but still we can remember. We throw our trash in a creek we know is too shallow to bury it, but still, every time we go there to swim, we're surprised—disgusted, even—to see the lids of our discarded washing machines, the eyelids of our old dolls. In Montgomery, as in Mobile, as in the core of the pineapple, the threads of banana, an egg white, a pressure, an origination, a last stage, a way-too-sweetness. A wet, fast breath. A hummingbird named Black-Chin, named Buff-Belly, named Ruby-Throat, named Rufous. *Tchup-zee-tchuppity-tchup,* they say. Behind me, the sound of glass breaking. A rickety bus—its tires, backseats. Everywhere, the tragedy of breathing. No cake in sight. Wings confusing themselves for other wings.

Because it is so rich, Hummingbird Cake, according to *Southern Living,* "needs to be served in small slices." In this is obvious metaphor, saccharine trash. So, we purify via pineapple, banana, eggsfloursugar, the kind of fork we can throw away without thinking. We eat, with plastic, like the most anxious of the birds.

* * *

BROKEN PLATES with faceless blue soldiers on them, exhaust tubes, road flares, lawn mower blades, flowerless pots, wheelless wagons, floppy disks leaking their cotton guts, AAA batteries, chicken ribs, a

"Welcome to Our Home Sweet Home" doormat, an evergreen mood ring, speakers, an empty dog collar with "*ROSA*" etched in script into the gold bone-shaped name tag.

Hummingbird Cake

Ingredients

3 cups flour

3 cups sugar

1 teaspoon cinnamon

1 teaspoon baking soda

1 teaspoon salt

6 eggs

1 cup oil

3 bananas, chopped

1 cup crushed pineapple

1 cup pecans

Mix first five ingredients in mixing bowl. Beat eggs and then add to flour mixture. Add oil to mixture followed by bananas, pineapples, and pecans.

Bake at 350 degrees for 25–30 minutes or until golden brown.

—*Something Special Deli*

Elegy for Arlo and Mississippi Mud Pie

WHEN MY WIFE CALLS the Mississippi River Valley "the other Valley of the Kings," I do my best to stay on task, to think of all the restaurants in Tupelo, and beyond Tupelo, who brag of "the Best Mud Pie in Mississippi," "the Best Dirt Cake on Earth," and I try not to laugh at dessert named for sediment wet and sediment dry, for the gooey terrestrial stuff that holds us now, as we scatter Arlo's ashes into the river, as if we are some kind of offering to some kind of god—one that holds unsteady in this washed-out sky, this awful humidity, heat indices topping 114 today, the sort of weather forecast with words like *warning* and *dangerous* and *excessive* and *extremely*—and I try not to think of Egypt, of all things mummified, of river mud as embalming-fluid-in-a-pinch, as the stuff we walk on taken inside of us, filling us, and to do this, I must take my wife's hand, kiss the old lunchtime chocolate from her mouth, before we lift the thermos of our fourth miscarriage over our heads, and, into the current of the Big Muddy, scatter and scatter.

Take comfort in the trying again: the Mississippi River Valley is one of the most fertile agricultural regions in the country. I know because she tells me without crying that in Egypt, on the west bank of the Nile, in the heart of the Theban necropolis, archaeologists excavated in 2005, in the original Valley of the Kings, the KV63 embalming cache. In this chamber, they found a wooden bed frame with lions' heads carved into the posts, broken wine jars, shards of pottery, and kits containing embalming supplies: salts, linens, natron, and mud trays. The mud was often spread over the flesh of the dead, funneled via their mouths into their bodies as a preservative measure. And now we litter the water with the thermos itself, watch the humidity shudder like a mirage at its surface. All of the earth in the water has turned the river yellow. All of this water, carrying the earth.

Also in KV63: seven wooden coffins, the smallest of which, designed for an infant, bears the worst of the termite damage. The termites the archaeologists encountered in 2005 are said to be direct descendants of the termites of the grand pharaonic era. In this, I sense some commentary on the large story inside the smallest things, but the details are lost in the river, after having been cremated with a butane grill lighter on its bank.

How much of this river would have to evaporate before we can call it *mud*? My wife tells me that the Mud Pie we ate after lunch was named after the banks of the Mississippi. It was first created, she said, by those who lived along said banks at the tail end of World War II. She shouts over the current and I can hear "simple ingredients," I can hear "chocolate and sugar and butter," and I can hear "the stuff they could find and afford, the stuff still in the supermarkets after all that war," and I know she's looking for answers, and I am too, and before I ask her how she knows so much about war and mud and pie, if she can read the code of the wavering humidity, its prisms hanging like the ghosts of the mummified in the air, she tells me, still shouting against the river, "read it on the back of the menu . . ."

We bought the grill lighter for $2.99 at the Double Quick convenience store in Clarksdale. This is an insufficient tool for heating Mississippi Mud Pie. The water berates its mud, and the water is yellow. The infant coffin of KV63 bore on its lid—also badly termite-damaged—a tiny yellow funerary mask. These yellow faces, archaeologists theorize, indicate female occupants. My wife stares into the water, trying to pick out which is the ash, which the earth. I stare at my wife staring into the water. Today, so hot it's dangerous, the river is yellow. Today, the river is wrong. Neither of us says, *Goodbye, son.*

The sheer amount of weather here communes with the sheer amount of water. Today—it's funny—the relationship seems civil. "In Mississippi, Death of Politician Marco McMillian Stirs Old Civil-Rights Fears," reads the March 8, 2013, *Washington Post* headline. The former choirboy who grew up next to the railroad tracks on the Delta knew, according to the article, that to run for mayor, he "needed the blessing of the silver-haired oligarchy that ruled quietly from church pews." This proved difficult, as McMillian was gay, African American, and, according to eighty-nine-year-old voter Bertha Blackburn, "the answer to our prayers." His body was found wedged into "the mud of an isolated stretch of levee outside Clarksdale."

Here, we wonder about the sheer amounts of things: water and hatred and earth and mourning. We wonder if this brew is a suspension or solution, homogenous or super-saturated. We wonder which is soluble in which. "No matter," my wife says, reaching for the water with her foot, "it's all still sludge, sludge, sludge . . ." Here, solution is the sugar in the butter, the burnt embryo in the Ol' Man. Twenty-two-year-old Domino's Pizza employee Lawrence Reed was charged with McMillian's murder. So far, the sheriff's department has released no further information about the case, but reported that the Clarksdale Domino's Pizza serves no Mud Pie for dessert, but a pale imitation called Chocolate Lava Crunch Cake, and something called Cinna Stix. What we also know: in the days following McMillian's death, Twitter saw its highest concentration of posts linking to a grainy video of Nina Simone singing "Mississippi Goddamn."

My wife doesn't sing. She never sings, not even in the shower. Now, she doesn't sing as she keeps the thermos lid, looped onto her belt by its yellow plastic handle. On its top, a decal of some unidentifiable bird, Any-Bird, trying to be part of all the countless species riding those awful thermals above us. The bird at her belt is as shameless as mud, but less versatile. It knows, as the chameleon knows, but will never divulge: *copying* is not the same as *being*. Our ceremony here is not original. Countless couples have done this countless times before us. We know that. It's also not original to know that.

In grieving, in tempering our grief with self-awareness, we are human, and copycats. What earned Mississippi Mud Pie an "international reputation," according to the Mississippi Tourism Association, is the "sheer amount" of chocolate in each serving. I think of all that cocoa, flour, butter, egg, vanilla, pulverized cookie, and fudge sauce heaped into piecrust, think of the chocolate ice cream melting over the top, and want to believe that by taking so much of it inside us, as salve, as salvation by saccharine, we are also preserving ourselves, if only in this state, on these banks, as if with soda ash, pickling salt, this actual mud.

The state bird of Mississippi is the mockingbird. Above us, in the great magnolias and bignonias, never descending to our mud, they sing and, in singing, dupe. My wife stares into the water. That's not a real flute. Her foot can't reach its surface. *Baby, that's not a real dirge.* When my wife was a child, growing up rural, she built an infant out of mud. She kept it "alive," she told me, by feeding it other mud.

Ankhesenamun, King Tutankhamun's wife (whose name was found inscribed on various pottery shards recovered from KV63) may have said, "Every first child is a terrestrial child . . . and mud returns to mud . . ." Florists "have been working overtime delivering arrangements" in commemoration of McMillian's death, and the bignonias bloom in the churches and line the levees, and fill the funeral service chapel at Coahoma Community College, and wilt above us, and leak the sort of yellow nectar that could be confused with neither river nor fudge sauce. My wife's childhood mud doll "died" when the rain came. She held a funeral for it, and her parents told her a story about baptismal waters and resurrection that she incompletely remembers, but even as a child, identified as insufficient consolation.

The bignonia was named for the seventeenth-century French ecclesiastic and writer Jean-Paul Bignon, who penned an early version of the classic "Beauty and the Beast," the only known version in which the Beast yanks a revered book (thought to be the Bible) from Beauty's hand "and tosses it into the mud as he proclaims his love for her." My wife tells me that Bignon was an unrepentant sexist who believed (as indicated by this scene) that women should neither read nor think, but remain busy bearing large male children and preparing filling desserts with plenty of chocolate. And below us rushes fluid, fluid, fluid, and my wife says that in preservative is every oxymoron, the immortalization of the dead being only one. Arlo, she says, lives forever in silt, in war, in levee and lock, in all steam belched from the steamboats, and the notion that ghosts move not like the humidity at all, but, like all hunter-gatherers, are stressed, rushing, fluvial.

According to the Mississippi Tourism Association, "Versions of Mississippi Mud Pie vary wildly in interpretation and mean many things to many people. Most are encased . . ." My wife assures me: the ghosts know what it's like to be mud, bi-elemental, neither here nor there, earth mixed with water until it flows, sometimes, into our mouths. We know: the Mississippi is the world's fourth largest drainage basin, but as we lose the ability to distinguish sediment from dessert, ash from sugar, the river from all that blood, we think nothing of outflow, discharge, watershed . . . Mighty, mighty. We try to remember all the nicknames for the river, but this is the best we can do.

Here, the pie hides its menace in its chocolate. Here, the pie, as ghost, embalms-cum-steels us for the moving on. Here is the fusion of brownie and soufflé, dense and light, the knock-knock joke at the burial, the river that, in this weather, cools our ashes. The river is yellow. My wife wants to find a motel with a kitchenette. She hands me a note written on the napkin stained with this afternoon's Mud Pie. I read: *180 beats per minute, small human muscle, gnats lifting from the sludge, the angry child as the rat's nest in the lily, the weak child ballooned with yellow milk, named after a flower I could never pronounce, the mud in the mouths of the bees, the mud in our hearts like detergent and birdseed, the bird who answers our questions with questions, our good manners in the face of this mud, and please, please, remember what we've done here in butter, sugar, chocolate . . .* and all differences between eulogy and shopping list dissolve into the extremity of the weather and the river that drowns out even the best imitations of the bird of this state.

Other names for Mississippi Mud Pie: Beautiful Pie, Best-Ever Pie, Dirt Cake, Baby Cake, Funeral Pie, The Holy Grail. Here, face down in an isolated stretch of levee, we breathe out the molecules of our final dessert into the mud. The thermos lid, in the hot wind, clicks like a metronome against her pant snaps. Like the water, the sky in this heat goes yellow, the way of some fat ceiling. We say nothing of shafts or chambers, of the tiny things who survive by eating into the things meant to encase us. We think nothing of their bloodline, and of all the lives taken by the sort of mud we can only compartmentalize via association with sugar, and fork and plate.

The sort of mud so heavy, the fork can't be plastic, the plate, paper. Finally, we turn from the river to each other. Soon, we can't bear to look, so we look up, to sky, the clouds stretched there. Like metronomes. We know: though we can't see them, there are stars hiding behind all of this day and heat, and we wait for them, as if to excavate us from the thick of this place.

Mississippi Mud Pie

For the Chocolate Cookie Crust

Nonstick cooking spray
16 ounces chocolate sandwich cookies such as Oreos (35 to 40 cookies), crushed
5 tablespoons unsalted butter, melted
½ cup toasted, ground pecans

For the Flourless Chocolate Cake

4 tablespoons (½ stick) unsalted butter
6 ounces good-quality dark chocolate (60 to 70%), chopped
2 tablespoons plus 1 teaspoon instant espresso powder
¼ cup strong coffee, at room temperature
¼ teaspoon salt
1 tablespoon pure vanilla extract
6 large eggs, separated, at room temperature
1 cup sugar

For the Chocolate Pudding

¾ cup sugar
½ cup dark unsweetened good-quality cocoa powder
¼ cup cornstarch
¼ teaspoon salt
4 large egg yolks
2½ cups whole milk
3 tablespoons unsalted butter
2 teaspoons pure vanilla extract
3 ounces good-quality dark chocolate (60 to 70 percent)

For the Whipped Cream Topping
1¼ cups heavy cream
2 tablespoons granulated sugar

Directions

Make the Chocolate Cookie Crust: Preheat oven to 300 degrees. Lightly spray a 9-inch springform pan with nonstick cooking spray. Line pan with parchment paper and lightly spray parchment and sides of pan.

Place cookies in the bowl of a food processor; process to very fine crumbs. You should have about 3½ cups. Transfer to a small bowl. Add melted butter and, using a spatula, stir until well combined.

Pour crumb mixture into prepared pan and press evenly with the back of a spoon into bottom and up sides, leaving about ½ inch between the top of the crust and top of the pan. Transfer to freezer until crust is set, about 10 minutes.

Transfer crust to oven and bake until dry to the touch, about 10 minutes. Transfer pan to a wire rack and let cool.

Make the Flourless Chocolate Cake: Increase oven temperature to 350 degrees.

Place butter and chocolate in a heatproof bowl set over (but not touching) simmering water to melt; stir to combine. Remove from heat. In a small bowl, whisk together espresso powder, coffee, salt, and vanilla; set aside.

In the bowl of an electric mixer fitted with the whisk attachment, beat egg yolks with ½ cup sugar until light and almost doubled in volume, about 5 minutes. Add melted chocolate mixture and beat until just combined. Scrape down sides and bottom of the bowl and mix on low speed for 5 seconds. Add coffee mixture and beat until just combined. Scrape down the sides and bottom of the bowl and mix on low for 5 seconds.

In the clean bowl of an electric mixer fitted with the whisk attachment, beat egg whites until foamy. Gradually increase speed to high and slowly add remaining ½ cup sugar, beating until soft peaks form.

Transfer 1 cup egg white mixture to chocolate mixture and, using a rubber spatula, gently fold to combine, about 30 seconds.

Add remaining egg whites and continue gently folding until they are almost completely combined; do not overmix. Pour into cooled cookie crust and transfer to oven. Bake until cake is set but still jiggles slightly, 38–42 minutes. It may not appear completely cooked. Transfer to a wire rack to cool completely. Cake will deflate in the center as it cools. Tightly wrap cooled cake with plastic wrap and refrigerate at least 3 hours and up to overnight.

Pudding: In a medium saucepan, whisk together sugar, cocoa powder, cornstarch, and salt. Add egg yolks and whisk until combined. The mixture will look like a thick paste. Slowly pour in milk, whisking constantly.

Place saucepan over medium heat and bring mixture to a boil, whisking constantly to prevent it from burning on the bottom of the pan. Boil for 30 seconds and immediately transfer to a medium bowl. Add butter, vanilla, and chocolate; whisk until combined. Continue whisking until mixture is cooled slightly. Let stand at room temperature for 15 minutes. Press a piece of plastic wrap directly on the surface of pudding to prevent a skin from forming. Transfer to refrigerator until chilled, at least 3 hours.

Stir pudding to loosen and pour on top of cake, making sure to stay within the cookie crust border. Using an offset spatula, spread pudding to form an even layer on top of the cake. Transfer to refrigerator for 30 minutes.

Prepare the Whipped Cream Topping: In the chilled bowl of an electric mixer fitted with a chilled whisk attachment, beat cream until soft peaks form, about 1 minute. Sprinkle sugar over cream and continue whisking until stiff peaks form. Spread whipped cream over chilled pudding layer, working all the way out to the sides. Garnish with chocolate shavings and toasted pecans.

Unmold cake and serve immediately. The cake can also be kept, covered, refrigerated, for up to 2 days.

—Heather Ries, The Ladybugg Bakery & Cafe

The Sad Autoerotica of Crawfish Étouffée

WHEN THE OLD WOMAN WITH no upper lip tells you, in the Faubourg Marigny, that to pluck a crawfish from the bayou is akin to tying a silk scarf around one's neck, that, as these little freshwater crustaceans asphyxiate in our air—the breeze of which carries sassafras and olive spread, desiccated peppers, powdered sugar, greenish decoctions called herbsaint and Mississippi, drizzle begetting rain begetting flood—their feathery gills flex, the twenty segments of their bodies clatter like castanets, their eye stalks extend, antennae dance, and, most importantly, she says, their sperm ducts roil, gonads quake, the females, releasing their aphrodisiac urine, flare their oviducts in anticipation of the males' reaching swimmerets, one desperate and futile stab at (literally) breathless procreation with, as is typical, a mere fishing net, or the unresponsive human hand, you believe her. When she tells you we all want one more go at ecstasy before the final smothering in the chocolate roux, the shellfish stock, the onion, the celery, the bell pepper, the garlic, she says, the butter, she says, the lemon, the cayenne, the thyme, you, hungry and horny, humid and sad, believe her.

Though the English translate *étouffée* as *stifled*, the French speakers know better. There's more violence to it than that, more action, premeditation. They know: *étouffée* means *smothered, suffocated,* the sort of violence that's allowed to titillate, that inspires us, here, to die with our genitals, like our lungs, gasping. You know, because the old woman tells you: Louisiana is just compacted sediment washed down the Mississippi River. "No matter how much land," she says, "no matter how high the walls, all that biota will get inside. We've made a state here. So many parishes. But we can't choke out the water." You know, because she tells you: so many things living in the river drown in our air.

Louisiana—literally, Land of Louis—is named for Louis XIV, who, according to the old woman, may have said *the world goes pink with buffoonery, billions of crawfish running away.* And he may have been speaking of the visions elicited by his penchant for autoerotic asphyxiation, some hallucinatory crawfish speaking equations into his fat ear that it would take only a stocking to solve. And the old woman stares at her hands as a brass band starts their set in a bar up the street, shakes her head and whispers, "Canicula. Ligature." And you wonder about the fate of a place named for a king who took his orgasms without oxygen, if a name can bear a clairvoyance—if only of the meteorological kind, if, in *Louisiana,* is both a dish that reminds us of identifying fetishes, and the sort of weather that will sweep our houses, if not our breaths, away.

"I am going," Louis spoke on his deathbed in 1715, "but the State shall always remain." That his lips were slick with spittle, most historians can agree. On whether he was speaking of this mass of compacted sediment, or of suffocation, or of the weather, or of orgasm, the jury's out. We chop through our celery without thinking of Louis's ribs. Stir our roux dark and thick without thinking of all that riverbottom sludge collecting in so many throats. In it, so nutrient-rich, in the bodies of the drowned, the Louisiana orchids still flourish. If we have the sexiest of flowers growing from our mouths, does that mean we can talk our lovers into the scarf, the stocking, the coital étouffée?

"My own aunts saved themselves from drowning by hauling their bodies out onto enough of that sludge," the old woman says, undoing and redoing the clasp of her bracelet, the center of which bears an amulet of the Louisiana flag—a mother pelican crouching in her nest, staring down at her three chicks, their mouths begging at her bill. And from her bill, three red droplets fall, the viscera of whatever she's smothered to feed them. We stuff our mouths full of crawfish and take in a little less air. Things, you think, taste better this way.

If desperate, the pelican, the state bird, will prey on seagulls and ducklings, holding them underwater, drowning them, before eating them headfirst. Unless the storm is too strong, they will open their bills and drink rainwater, their mouth-bags able to hold thirteen liters at capacity—seven more than the human lung. Beneath the pelican—on flag, on bracelet—whatever has been eaten looses its blood over words like *Union, Justice, Confidence . . .* , not a single one of which occurred to Louis as he shuddered like a crawfish into the stocking.

". . . that sludge," the old woman says. "But they didn't breathe for so long. It affected their brains, their limbs. They had to have their legs cut off . . ." The swimmerets of the crawfish, laced along the ventral side of the abdomen, are often mistaken for shorter walking legs, though they are much softer, used not only to carry sperm, but to carry the subsequently fertilized eggs. When preparing our étouffée, these are the parts most of us cut from the body first, discard into the nethers of the muddying stock. The tubas up the street crush themselves out like cigarettes. "When the saints are legless," she says, "no one marches in."

Author John Curra, in *The Relativity of Deviance*, writes, "The carotid arteries (on either side of the neck) carry oxygen-rich blood from the heart to the brain. When these are compressed, as in strangulation or hanging, the sudden loss of oxygen to the brain and the accumulation of carbon dioxide can increase feelings of giddiness, light-headedness, and pleasure, all of which will heighten masturbatory sensations." And author George Shuman, in *Last Breath*, writes, "When the brain is deprived of oxygen, it induces a lucid, semi-hallucinogenic state called hypoxia. Combined with orgasm, the rush is said to be no less powerful than cocaine, and highly addictive."

Autoerotic asphyxiation was the first documented treatment used, in the seventeenth century, for erectile dysfunction, the idea having been bestowed upon witnesses to public hangings who noted that executed males often developed persistent "death erections." Early morticians noted that females who were executed by hanging exhibited engorged labia.

Peter Anthony Motteux, editor of Britain's *The Gentlemen's Journal*, died of autoerotic asphyxiation, as did the composer and virtuoso double bassist Frantisek Kotzwara (who played for the King's

Theatre, and who, after a prostitute refused his request to cut off his testicles for two shillings, tied one end of a silk scarf to his neck and another to a doorknob, leading to a demise that the *American Journal of Forensic Medicine and Pathology* could call only a "sticky end"), as did Kichizo Ishida (whose lover, Sada Abe, then excised his penis and testicles with a razor blade and infamously carried said souvenirs in her purse for weeks afterward), as did Stephen Milligan, British political Conservative, as did the actor David Carradine, and Reverend Gary Aldridge of the Thorington Road Baptist Church (who was discovered some 300 miles from New Orleans, hog-tied, wearing two wetsuits, a head and face mask, diving gloves and flippers, and rubber underpants, and with a dildo the coroner called "modest" in his anus the coroner called "unremarkable"), and Michael Hutchence of the band INXS (whose death in 1997 inspired you to buy your own silk scarf, powder blue . . .).

* * *

Overheard dialogue in Coop's Place on Decatur Street: "Oh my God, this étouffée is soooooo goooooood . . ."

* * *

The old woman tells you that many crawfishermen uphold the superstition that a good étouffée depends on a good catch, and a good catch often depends on the superior quality of a single crawfish (not necessarily the largest, she stresses) who imposes this quality (sweetness, softness) onto the remainder. This one is often referred to as *l'écrevisse super*, or Super Crawfish.

Long before it became the slogan of the U.S., Motteux used the phrase *E pluribus unum* as the motto for the *Gentlemen's Journal*, translating it himself as "one chosen among many." Though they're not quite as snag-resistant as the football jig, many Louisiana crawfishermen still prefer the traditional roundhead jig, even along rocky bottoms. Though you believe the connection to be tenuous at best, you can't help your titillation when reading the "rocky bottom" of Stephen Milligan's obituary in the *Independent*, the last line of which reads, "If politicians can be divided into cavaliers and roundheads, Milligan was very much a roundhead."

And Carradine said, "You know, I've never actually really believed that death is inevitable . . . there's always an alternative. There's always a third way," and Michael Hutchence said, as if in response, "We'd have to suck away at oxygen canisters . . . just so that we can keep playing. I'm the smallest fish." And you hold your breath—right there on Frenchmen Street—in mimicry or empathy, and you know that in a lack of breathing is a rush of blood, is *engorged*, is a shattering, perhaps final, orgasm, and if something shatters, that means it's broken.

* * *

August 29, 2005, a Monday. Some one thousand crawfish seep through a crack in the levee. One of them is the smallest. In mimicry or empathy, the old woman sneezes twelve cherries of blood into a peach monogrammed handkerchief.

When the female crawfish releases her urine, it drives the males into such a frenzy that, depending, it can be interpreted equally as an invitation to sex or to battle. Thomas Breithaupt, the behavioral psychologist, believes that the female crawfish is most able to gauge a male's size and strength (read: his suitability as a mate) only by inspiring him to aggression. And here, the Spanish killed the British who killed the French who killed the Acadians who killed the Creoles who killed the Plaquemines who killed the Caddoan Mississippians who killed the Tchefunctes who killed the earliest documented archaic-period mound-building culture in North America, whose mounds still exist and have been variously interpreted by archaeologists as being a neighborhood, a trading center, and a ceremonial religious complex, and perhaps it's because we can't determine exactly what this place is, or perhaps it's because we think this may be the earliest example of a civil war battleground, or perhaps the earth here has been so compacted that when we press our lips to it, we can siphon no air, or perhaps it's because there are no crawfish here, or perhaps it's because the old woman tells you, "Those who have the money needn't worry about the water," or perhaps it's something else that inspired us to name this historic monument Poverty Point.

You know, because the old woman tells you: the batons of Baton Rouge are red because there's blood on them. She tells you: Here, we call our counties *parishes.* That doesn't mean that our food is always incantatory, our sex lives bored, ecclesiastic. Because of this weather, this history, we smother our water-dwellers with the good land vegetables. In this way, we retain the breath required to blow our étouffée cool enough to stuff our mouths. In this way, we fight back. We serve it over rice—anything to soak up the roux, the sludge, the agent of the smothering.

The hurricane, the old woman tells you, wiped out two-thirds of the city's trees. Certain wards lost every one. You imagine the trees she once told fortunes under—the Southern magnolias and live oaks, the cherrybarks and sawtooths, the overcups and cows—trees you will never get to see. In the aftermath of the hurricane, she tells you, in regard to the decimation of New Orleans' urban forest, Tom Campbell, spokesperson for the Louisiana Department of Agriculture and Forestry, summed it up with all of the gentility a non-native Louisianan could never muster: "It looks like the dickens," he said.

Winding among the aboveground vaults of St. Louis Cemetery Number One—so many thousands in just one square block—you watch a group of congregants alternately grieve and celebrate. So many bury their faces into the necks of their loved ones, take in, for just a moment, no air—as if a momentary lack of oxygen is honoring the sort of sadness that, if left unchecked, if taken out of context, can kill us too. Another vault, so little room . . . You watch the congregants—mothers and fathers and sons and daughters and aunts, uncles, cousins, grand-this and grand-that. There is something huge about them, and uniform—in their clothing, their grieving, their once-in-a-while laughs. They accumulate like clouds, and you speak this aloud as if incantation: *You accumulate like clouds.* Though you're not exactly sure what it is you're trying to summon, you do know that, taxonomically, crawfish belong to Astacoidea and Parastacoidea, and you know that these classifications are known as superfamilies, and you want to interpret this as something as heroic as the weather, but you know it has more to do with prefix, dominance, missionary, *on top of* . . .

What else can we do to secure our place here than to make of the *super* the *sub*, the meat over which we spoon the thickest of our sauces? You watch them stifle their crying. You wonder about the intersections of grief and sex, grief and the body, the body and violence, the hanged man and the hanged woman, the poor beast that doesn't know whether to fuck or to fight, that carries its eggs in its softest, safest parts, that drowns so we can eat. You wonder about the parts of us to which so much blood rushes when we die by asphyxiation, as if searching a blind alley for any escape. You wonder what role the weather plays. The earth, you think, is the mouth-bag. The old woman would like that, would say something constellar about all of these faces smothered in all of these necks. As ever, it's the neck that does the smothering. As ever, and ever-odd, we're hung by these parts of us and our pants and our dresses can do nothing but jump up.

Like the crawfish, we sometimes don't want to be heard. If the weather—like Louis, like Land of Louis, like St. Louis, like the comforted and comforting in St. Louis Number One, like all things for which our homes are named—can't hear us, maybe they won't find us. Like the crawfish, like every lover really, we wonder if we're not breathing, enough.

Crawfish Étouffée

Ingredients

1 pound crawfish tails (packaged with fat)
1 medium onion
½ bell pepper
1 rib celery
2 cloves of garlic
3 green onions
3 sprigs parsley
¾ stick butter or margarine
1 tablespoon flour
2 cups chicken stock
2 dashes hot sauce
2 cups cooked rice

Instructions

1. Chop bell pepper, celery, garlic, onions, parsley and green onions.

2. In a large skillet, heat butter over medium heat and add a tablespoon of flour. Let flour cook until it stops foaming.

3. Add onions, bell pepper, celery and garlic. Cook until translucent.

4. Add crawfish tails, parsley, and green onions and cook for 3 minutes.

5. Stir in chicken stock, a little at a time, to allow the roux to thicken until it is the consistency of a thick soup.

6. Add hot sauce to taste.

7. Serve over rice.

—Darren Chifici, chef/co-proprietor,
Deanie's Seafood Restaurant

SOUTH CAROLINA

A Reception for Perloo

RAPT ARE THE INDIGNITIES of perloo, pale-faced as they are before the emerald earrings and red lipstick and clove purses of Charleston, and the racist white men who make the state's best barbecue sauce. Here, even our most deliciously prepared rice is sister to this, brother to that. A version of another original, born in destitution, its oozy starch never empowered to whip like hair from the passenger seats of Charleston's 1,001 convertibles in the sort of wind that rises like ghosts above the low country.

Sister to jambalaya, brother to pilaf, cousin to paella, to risotto, biryani, our perloo becomes itself in one bastard pot, the wider the better. Here, we lard our rice with shrimp, watch the pinkish meat try to stretch itself straight like some arthritic old ballerina, listen to the hunched joints crack themselves young again, breach the shell, which tries, in all of this chicken broth, to soften. The shrimp tells us about the good ol' days, when the body responded to our commands without hurt, when the cows were wholesome and celibate, the clamshells ever shut tight, our secret horrors trapped in the nooks of perfectly working kneecaps, the bogs of our once-good eyes, and tight-lipped bivalves, escaping only when we turn the heat up to medium—right in the middle of the knob—and coax the quiet simmer from the pan with our sexiest of broken fingers.

Here, we wonder about the point at which shell becomes skin, the softer thing easily punctured, the quickest journey of the fork to the blood. Or we lard our rice with clam, with oyster, anything with a hard shell from which we can scoop meat so cottony soft, with pinkies, into our mouths. Sure, we'll add our diced country ham, our onion, garlic, tomato, chili pepper, and oregano. We'll ask to see ghosts in the steam, listen, in the simmer, to stories of King Charles II naming our state with a booming voice and absolutely no chest hair; stories of lakes named Strom Thurmond, hurricanes named Hazel, earthquakes named Intraplate. We'll ask this joining of history and ingredient in a single pot to be more metaphor than meal, though, when we finish our bowls, it's only our stomachs that are full.

* * *

THE HAZEL IS the tree that gives us hazelnuts, the nut most often related to our eyes—the size of the iris, the murkiness of color and cataract that even the best optometrists in Charleston describe only as "in-between." Our perloo straddles land and sea, chicken and shellfish, shit like batteries and shit like bridal veils. In the steam, we think we see our dead aunts trying again for this world, for this state, in which, not so many years ago, we solicited our slaves especially from the rice-growing regions of Africa, and, with the aid of irrigation and weather and blood and family, made of this low country something we dupe ourselves into believing is our culinary birthright.

* * *

HERE, IN DEATH, we grasp for any kind of matrimony. Here, fertility is a false inheritance. We cook it all down in one wide pot, and feed the entire family. It's popularly believed that the Bessinger family makes some of the best barbecue sauce and best perloo in South Carolina at one of their many restaurants, though supping one of their meals has become, recently, a political act. Just after noon on July 1, 2000, after the state legislature took down the Confederate flag from the Capitol dome in Columbia after the long protests of the NAACP, Maurice Bessinger, in full Colonel Sanders regalia (facial hair included), stormed from his plantation (which he named Tara), past his original barbecue pit (which served as South Carolina's "Pat Buchanan for President" headquarters in 1996), and responded by hoisting the loaded flag outside each of his nine restaurants. Red-faced, he publicly called the politicians who voted to take down the flag "turncoats," and proceeded to weigh in on "slave gratitude," since, after all, he maintained, they were "blessed" to move from Africa to America. In this wake, national chain stores began to pull Bessinger's sauce from their shelves. Melvin, Maurice's brother, tried to stop this backlash and to strip the "racist" label from his family name, declaring, in the *New York Times,* "I don't say anything about black people, as long as they're educated and do right." In spite of such rhetoric, and in spite of Melvin's son David's declaration that "I'm ashamed to use my last name," Bessinger's remains one of the more popular barbecue outposts in the state, appearing in guidebook after guidebook, on TV show after TV show. We eat with heavy hearts and happy mouths the good sauce and the good meat and the good perloo, as if our morality divorces itself from our mouths, if only in half-hour intervals, lunch breaks, and becomes briefly estranged—cousin, sibling, ghost, the old woman, hunched like a shrimp, who, in dream, allows her body to pirouette like a hurricane.

* * *

If our eyes are hazel, it's due to an elastic scattering of light—a misrepresentation, a fistful of rice grains dropped to the linoleum. Our eyes, like our brains, like our wooden spoons, struggle so desperately to do right. Still, once in a while, our perloo burns onto the bottom. Some South Carolinians are fond of saying, *You can eat your perloo when the pan starts to moo,* referring to the low drone that emanates from the concoction at the intersection of the simmer and the burning-onto-the-bottom-of-the-skillet. To us, though, this sounds less like a cow speaking, than a cow crying.

* * *

April 27, 1991, in Waltersboro, a deluge nearly foiled the annual Rice Festival. In spite of the rain, a record number of people turned out to witness the famed morning Rice Run, during which the mayor repeatedly conducted a mass prayer for better weather. According to the *Post-Courier,* "The clouds parted halfway into the parade just as Sen. Strom Thurmond, R–S.C., waving from the back ledge of an open convertible with umbrella in hand, rode past . . . Damp head looked skyward . . ." Other major events at the Rice Festival: the soapbox derby ("It was a wet experience," said one participant) and a communal perloo cookout in the World's Largest Pot of Rice.

Here, our dead aunts swim together in a really big pot. Our uncles, ever shed, float to the top like shrimp shells. This is both elastic and scattered. Diffuse, and snapping back on itself. "In perloo," our uncles tell us, "juxtaposition is of the utmost importance. Shrimp's gotta go with ham. If you do chicken, you also oughta do oysters. It's not just a junk pot. This isn't North Carolina." We stare out the kitchen window screen, and the wrens, singing *Dum spiro spero*, thread the hazel. In the living room, to the lullabic simmer, our uncles have fallen asleep again on their couches, their drool collecting like ink blots on the pillows, dreaming again, briefly, of fish.

Watch the pinkish meat try to stretch itself straight like some arthritic old ballerina.

Juxtaposition: flanking the *Post-Courier*'s Rice Festival article, these headlines: "Liquid Asphalt Spills from Ruptured Tank," "Mt. Pleasant Man Found Dead in Home," "Mt. Pleasant Man Held in Rape of 9-Year-Old." The perloo knows: beneath the broth is the bottom of the pan. We rupture and rupture like oyster meat to the boil, and only then do we become tough, still edible, lifted to the mountains of one another's mouths, where we cool, spill our terrible pleasantries.

Strom Thurmond conducted the longest nonstop filibuster ever by a lone senator—at twenty-four hours and eighteen minutes straight—against civil rights legislation and African American voting rights, and in favor of the maintenance of segregation. "All the laws of Washington, and all the bayonets of the Army," Thurmond said, "cannot force the Negro into our homes, into our schools, our churches and our places of recreation and amusement," and our uncles, speaking now in sleep, wonder how such a mind-set adapted to the Senate elevators in which, not too long before his death at one hundred, Thurmond was infamous for groping African American women, or how such a mind-set adapted to the Thurmond family maid, a sixteen-year-old African American woman named Carrie Butler, and her bedchamber, in which Thurmond conceived with her a mixed-race daughter who would only come to national attention after the senator's death in 2003. The perloo can only simmer, unable to deny, in sound and smell, any ingredient suspended within it. The rice soaks up the evidence but lets it loose in our mouths, compels us to speak poison, until we can enable someone else to speak truth.

* * *

Who is beating my child?
Is it sleep?
Is it hunger?
Is it sickness?
—traditional African lullaby

* * *

HERE, WE PUSH ourselves toward dream with reminders of starvation, coughing, dream itself. The perloo says nothing of state history, or of flags, even as the clams open up creaking like basement doors. When a heifer goes into estrus, she becomes more talkative, wandering and wandering the pasture in search of a mate, nuzzling the vulvas of the other cows as she passes, her tail skyward, her back hair spiky, singularly focused, unable to untangle acts of love and acts of violence, sexual hunger and sexual sickness, the history of the rice in her mouth, from the history of those who sowed it, *so rapt are the indignities . . .*

According to BessingersBbq.com, under the tab marked *Our Story* and the subtab marked *History*, "THE LEGEND: THE BESSINGER'S LEGACY is being updated. Check back later." The rice is there to vacuum all this up. Spit it back to us so we can feel full of something. Lake Strom Thurmond was man-made for the purposes of "power production and incidental flood control."

* * *

THE FLAG'S DOWN in Columbia. More cheers than boos. Wrens choking on the sort of nuts that resemble the cloudiest colors of our eyes. Non-colors. One thing morphing into another, depending on the light. Yellow jessamines open their blooms, split like peaches. The honeybees, flying in from the Atlantic and Sassafras Mountain, finally get to open their legs to the sounds of waves crashing, of the earth trying to get up and stretch. Incidentally, and obviously, water finds the path of least resistance. We need to add rice, and an awful bastardized name, to foil its drive for power, its desire only to flood. The late poet James Dickey, professor emeritus at the University of South Carolina, said of Columbia, "[It's] halfway between the ocean and the mountains. The soil here will grow anything. There were lots of flowers and birds. They're all blood kin. I particularly like the cooking."

In a single pot, man-made, perloo is both the flood and the dam. The rice is burning. The pan makes an in-between sound. Something like a moo. None of this done. We must be patient, wait for updates, check back later.

Perloo, a.k.a. Pilau

Charleston has been a melting pot since its inception, and our pilau owes as much to French and Persian traditions as to African. One of the great American rice dishes, the trick to a light and fluffy pilau is allowing it to rest, covered, after cooking. Then fluff it with a fork or Charleston rice spoon so each grain of rice stands independently.

Ingredients

One 3–4 pound duck
1 pound Andouille, or smoked sausage
2 quarts water
1 stick butter
1 large onion, peeled and diced
2 cups chopped celery
3 large tomatoes
1 tablespoon chopped fresh thyme
To taste, salt and pepper
2 cups Charleston Gold rice

Method of Production

Place the duck in a pot, cover with water and simmer for 1 hour, skimming any fat that rises. Remove the duck and allow to cool, but reserve the cooking water.

Skin the duck, and pull the meat from the carcass. Set aside. In a heavy pot, sweat the onions in the butter until translucent, then add celery. Stir, and allow to brown lightly. Add in the tomatoes and sausage and reduce liquid by half. Add duck, season, and add rice then cooking liquid. Cover and cook on low for 30 minutes. Allow to rest for 10 minutes, fluff with a spoon, and serve.

—Forrest Parker, chef, Old Village Post House

GEORGIA

Peach Pie on Badstreet

DON'T SAY A WORD about the fuzz, or any of the soft coverings that evoke delicacy, and other things babyish. Here, the peaches we use in our pies are mutants, and sometimes these mutants flower. This does nothing to make them juicier, does, in fact, make them less palatable. Here, desirability lies in plainness rather than ornamentation, and the sort of skin that reminds us of our own, before we became these awful adults. Your mother has started grafting desirable cultivars onto dwarfing rootstock. This makes for little peaches, their flavor concentrated like bouillon cubes. You catch your father scoffing at their size, flexing his own biceps in the garden, finally happy to compare his own body to the state's natural, and famous, forms. You wonder about the point when that which has been cultivated becomes natural. In the kitchen, sifting, your mother mutters to herself, "She walks in beauty, like the night . . ."

Here, the flour is all-purpose, and the pearl tapioca is instant. The two flow together like pyroclasm. Your mother chews her fingernails to their beds, stops just short of the blood. Her secret is the peach vinegar in the crust, the ooze of the tapioca that binds the peaches (each one severed into twelve even crescents, she insists), to the lemon juice, the vanilla, the sugar. When the peaches release their juice, she says, the tapioca will catch its run, freeze it into position. The tapioca will stop the peaches.

In the living room, your father watches a documentary on Pompeii. When he's about to switch the channel back to the wrestling matches, it's the image of one ashen hand arrested on its way to a lover's ashen breast that stops him. There's a volcanism in this pie, your mother believes. Something of the lahar, of disaster narrowly averted. It's the tapioca, she says, that contains the bursting of the peaches, that allows our state both its explosion and restraint.

Your mother knows: the first artistic representation of the peach was unearthed from the rubble of Herculaneum, Pompeii's neighbor, following the Vesuvius eruption of 79 AD. She imagines, in the painting, a clingstone peach, the flesh holding desperately to its pit in some kind of final embrace, as if the art itself predicted the eruption, as if the ancient drawn peach is somehow responsible for her award-winning pie. Peaches open to heat, whether mediocre or not.

The painting of the peach survives the disaster. The real peach turns to dust. Your mother wonders, which one is at the heart of Georgia; if the pie protects the peach, allows it legacy. Your father would wonder this, but he's changed the channel to the professional wrestling matches. He's watching Michael "Pure Sexy" Hayes slip a razor blade from his trunks. Your father would wonder this, but he's shouting, "Cut his fucking head open!"

In the peach pie are both the fire and its extinguisher. Her crust is a lattice. In this way, a single strip of dough can be a shroud, even as it's buried. Your father keeps his army knife on the coffee table, next to the bowl of boiled peanuts. He often calls Vietnam "Georgia without the peaches." Your mother bakes, she says, to remind him again that he's home.

In 1924, Georgia allowed for the formation of Peach County, the last in the state to be incorporated, a county that self-defines as "the heart of central Georgia." Your mother wonders: what's the difference between the heart of central Georgia, and the heart of all of Georgia? When she finds out that they also self-define as the Peach Capital of the World, she rolls her eyes, thinks of China and Iran, and the Romans who originally named the fruit *persica,* from the Latin *malum persicum, Persian apple.* She tells your father, "I know more about goddamn peaches . . ." but he's back in televised Italy, staring at a petrified dog kicking its legs at the sky.

If the heart is *middle*, the heart is mediocre. Your mother knows, peach pies cook best at the heart of the oven, where the heat is most evenly distributed. Your mother flips on the oven light, stares at the juice bubbling, but not boiling over, noosed in the thickening tapioca pearls. She thinks of the fuzzed and the fuzzless varieties, the nature, here, of breeding. She sighs and lets the oven go dark again. Before your father takes up the remote, he decides the dog is a golden retriever.

You watch wrestling with your father. His favorite triple tag team, the Georgia-based Fabulous Freebirds, dominate the ring, led by Michael "P. S." Hayes, his long Barbie-blond locks whipping, your father says, "like the peach trees of Peach County in a tore-oh-nah-doe," and you know, because your father told you, that the "P. S." stands for "Pure Sexy," a designation that he himself tries to evoke for you on the couch by flexing his biceps again, trying and failing to get his pectorals to quiver beneath his red Georgia Bulldogs T-shirt, the flesh of his face reddening, as if moving dangerously close to his own pit.

Even from the living room, you can hear the peaches screaming in the oven. This is the last step, your mother says, before their ultimate softening. The other two Fabulous Freebirds are the decidedly unsexy Terry "Bam Bam" Gordy, whose finishing move, the Iron Spike (read: digging his thumb into opponent's neck skin/accessory nerve) and oafish bank robber's sidekick demeanor make him one of your father's favorite "loves to hate," and the nondescript everyman Buddy "Jack" Roberts (the "Jack" referencing his adoration of Mr. Daniel's whiskey). With a mouthful of boiled peanuts, still half-heartedly flexing, your father sings the lyrics of the Freebirds' entrance song (penned by Hayes), "Badstreet, USA" (Hayes's reference to the rough neighborhood in which he grew up in Atlanta, a city whose peaches your mother deems soulless, bruised from the truck ride over from counties named Bacon and Baker, Coffee and Butts, Early, Long, Liberty, Peach, and Worth, and Worth), and your father spits peanuts at the screen.

And outside, twelve peaches fall from the tree, and your mother, from the kitchen, shouts back at your father, her own mouth clean, about the difference between a clingstone and a freestone, the difference between the kind of flesh that sticks to its pit and the kind that easily peels away, and your father jabs his finger into your chest, and "which one are you, which one are you?"

Somewhere, on another channel, one petrified corpse kisses another, but here, just as the peaches quiet, your father swallows his mouthful, allows his pecs to relax and fall, and on the screen, one beautiful man headlocks another, and it looks as if neither can escape his destiny. As always, he has nothing else to say about sexiness, or purity, beyond his eating of a hot peach pie. Which is the beauty that burns our mouths, that forces us to exhale even as we swallow, the kind that demands we cool it with our breath?

* * *

IN PEACH COUNTY, less than a year after its incorporation, and over one hundred years after the white settlers pushed the Creek Nation off their hunting lands in order to sow their peaches, local farmer Samuel Henry Rumph developed a unique variety of peach that he named Elberta, after his wife. Immediately revered by the locals for its sweetness, high content of juice, snappy skin, and culinary adaptability (excellent raw, excellent baked), the Elberta peach soon breached Peach County's borders, and the remainder of the state claimed it, and renamed the variety after itself.

Still, the county served as the headquarters for the communal manifestations of "peach fever," such as the Peach Regional Rodeo (a standard rodeo at which peach pie is sold), the Peach Blossom Festival (which, as early as the mid-1920s, attracted tourists "from all over the world"), and the Georgia Peach Festival (at which Elberta drowned her sorrows over the mass combing out of her name with slice after slice of the newly dubbed Georgia Peach Pie). Your mother wants this original Georgia peach to be a clingstone, a peach that loves itself, hugs all of its parts together as if in some futile stab at survival. But she knows better. Even as your father howls at the blood on the screen, she knows it was a freestone. She knows: a name can be easily excised, the identity of an entire state imposed on the fruit named for only one woman. In this way, intimacy can be shipped from coast to coast. All it takes is breeding. Your mother wonders if the peach takes more than it gives. She takes off her sweater. Her undershirt is red; it says "Property of the Georgia Lady Bulldogs" in a neat, rainbow arc.

According to the Georgia Peach Council (operating today out of the University of Georgia's College of Agriculture and Environmental Sciences), after inventing a box mounted on casters that held six crates of peaches plus ice, Samuel Rumph, "unselfish, disregarding the many prophets of failure, created an attractive peach with good carrying qualities . . . and gave these ideas to the world." Your father, as if caught, as if skipping, hits the remote's "last" button again and again, and, as the images on the screen flash from blood to ash, blood to ash, a man's long blond hair to a girl's petrified mouth, a man's pure sexy crowing to the girl's silent scream, your father finally gets his left pectoral to bounce against his right, and you wonder about the ideas in his head, afraid that he wants the rest of the world to have them.

The stuff at the stone will never know the fuzz, the sun, the feel of your mother's fingers, until the fruit that surrounds it is eviscerated. In the addition of the tapioca is a desire to allow these things to gel, to become one decent thing . . . and Lord Byron says, "Give me a sun, I care not how hot, and sherbet, I care not how cool, and my Heaven is as easily made as your Persian's," and you swear to God he's saying something about our peaches, as preservative, you hope, or gateway out of here. Blood and ash, blood and ash. The living room begins to smell like peaches. Your father is not okay with his weakening, but he's fine with idolizing a wrestler who has hair, he says, "like a woman's."

Eulogizing Samuel H. Rumph, the Georgia Peach Council says:

> *Some men are remembered because embarking on a public career they connected themselves with great political movements or filled some high office. Others achieve fame through military, or naval exploits, "amid the tumult and the shouting and the thunder of the guns." Here is one who deserves to be remembered and who will be remembered for the gift he made to his fellow man. One can scarcely ride along the highways and see the beauty of the trees in peach blossom time, or later in the season look upon long rows of them bending under the weight of their luscious fruit, without calling to mind this modest, efficient man who had a vision. His name will ever be associated with that queen of all varieties and the creation of a new industry.*

Your mother, oven-mitted, bends like the Creeks under the weight of her pie. It's the tapioca. The fruit that wants to find its earliest name. It's the cling that wants to be free, and the free that's starving for intimacy. It's the fuzz as the ash, and the ash that will allow so many future generations to see us exactly as we are. The cooked peach, ever modest, gives its juice to tapioca and crust, though it cares nothing for the relationship between efficiency and flavor.

Your father cuts his slice down with his army knife. On its blade, decades-old blood, a little rust, and the hardened syrup of so many former peach pies. In this knife is efficient, if immodest, storytelling. Your father falls asleep on the couch. Hayes wins. Vesuvius wins. You rise with your mother, careful not to disturb him. You watch the couch cushion slowly rebound from your weight.

Outside, you stand with her, holding your basket. One tree, she says, does not make an orchard. The light is waning. The sky is the stone. If the sky is the stone, you're not sure if you're the flesh, or the peachtree borer, the insect named for the crop that it kills. The peachtree borer can eat through bark, eat through ash. The peachtree borer seeks out the wounds, the weakest parts of trunk and fruit. Its wings are clear. We can see through them, the peaches distorted as if in a funhouse mirror. Through the wings of the things that kill us, our fattest fruits are made skinny, and our softest of fuzz predicts its own aging. Above you, one drupe huddles against another, evolving: these incredible soft skins, the moth that finds its way in, to fruit. Here, we don't need to be peeled to be eaten, under a roof to find heat.

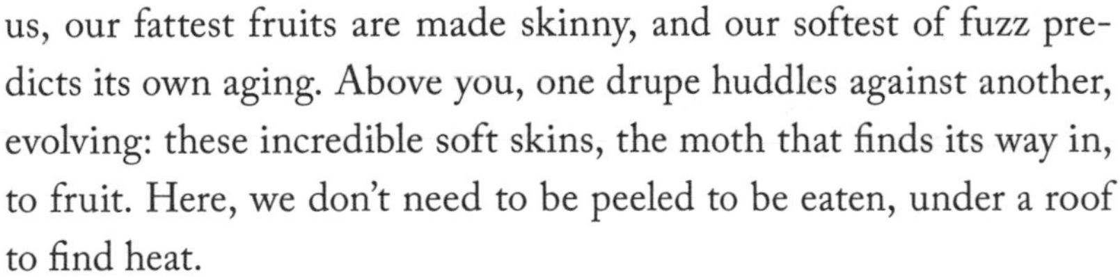

In this wind, you can't tell if it's the peaches, her body, or the whole county that's beating. In this wind, a landlocked county named for peaches can be *coast-to-coast*. You reach for the fruit, wait for the fruit to reach back. Your mother uses a butane lighter so she can see the bruises. She sighs. She picks the ones she thinks are the ripest.

Georgia Peach Pie

Yield: 1 9-inch pie

For the Pie Dough

Butter (cold, cubed)	*6 tablespoons*
All purpose flour	*1¼ cup*
Salt	*⅛ teaspoon*
Baking powder	*⅛ teaspoon*
Cream cheese (cold)	*¼ cup*
Ice water	*1 tablespoon plus 1 teaspoon*
Apple cider vinegar	*1¾ teaspoon*

For the Crumb Topping

All purpose flour	*1 cup*
Dark brown sugar	*1¼ cups*
Pecans (toasted)	*½ cup*
Salt	*¼ teaspoon*
Butter (cold)	*6 tablespoons*

For the Filling

Peaches (peeled and pitted)	*2 pounds*
Sugar	*½ cup plus 2 tablespoons*
All purpose flour	*3 tablespoons*
Salt	*¼ teaspoon*
Heavy cream	*⅓ cup*
Egg yolks	*2*
Whole egg	*1*
Vanilla extract	*½ teaspoon*
Nutmeg	*½ teaspoon*
Cinnamon	*¼ teaspoon*

Preheat oven to 350 degrees. Have ready a deep 9-inch pie pan.

To make the dough: cut butter into small cubes and refrigerate. Place the flour, salt, and baking powder in a food processor. Pulse a few times. Cut the cream cheese into four pieces and add to the flour. Pulse briefly until you no longer see the cream cheese. Now add the cold, cubed butter and pulse until sandy. Add the ice water and cider vinegar and pulse until large clumps begin to form. Remove from the processor, shape into a uniform disc, wrap in plastic, and refrigerate for at least 30 minutes.

To make the crumb: place pecans on a baking sheet and toast in oven for 5 minutes, or until fragrant. Chop finely and set aside to cool completely. In a medium bowl, whisk together the flour, dark brown sugar, salt, and chopped pecans. Cut cold butter into small cubes, add to bowl and coat with the dry mixture. Now work the mixture gently with your fingertips until it is no longer sandy, the butter softens and small crumbs begin to form. Place bowl in refrigerator.

To make the filling: cut the pitted and peeled peaches into ¼-inch slices. Place them on a baking sheet lined with parchment and greased with cooking spray. Sprinkle peaches with 2 tablespoons of the sugar and bake until softened, edges are lightly browned and juices released, about 30 minutes. Flip peaches halfway through baking. Set aside and let cool. Combine remaining ½ cup of sugar, flour, salt, and spices in a bowl. Whisk in cream, whole egg, yolks, and vanilla until smooth. Set aside.

Sprinkle some flour on your work surface and roll the pie dough into a large circle. Fit dough into pie pan, crimp decoratively and freeze for 20 minutes. Remove from freezer, and line with a 12-inch sheet of parchment. Place dry beans or pie weights on top of parchment and blind bake pie shell until light brown on the sides, about 15–20 minutes. Remove the beans and continue baking an additional 5–10 minutes until evenly golden brown. Let cool.

Place the roasted peaches on bottom of baked pie shell. Pour the filling on top, and then cover completely with the reserved crumb. Bake for 45–50 minutes until the crumb is well browned, the top of pie is puffy yet firm to the touch, and peach juices are starting to seep out. Remove from oven and let cool completely before serving.

—Eric Wolitzky, South City Kitchen

NEW ENGLAND

Maine: Whoopie Pie

Vermont: Maple Creemee

Rhode Island: Clear Clam Chowder

New Hampshire:
New Hampshire Corn Chowder

Massachusetts: Boston Cream Pie

Connecticut: Connecticut Clam Chowder

James Earl Jones Eats Whoopie Pie

IN WINTER, WE BEAT the cream in steel bowls, and our wrists are hurting, and we call out in voices too high-pitched to be called masculine. We think little about our state, about its geographical tumor-ness, about our father's hands, the old net scars there, trying, and failing, to wedge the whisks from our own. To the football game on TV, Dad screams "Fuck a duck!" while Mom, in the kitchen, tells you why brown sugar is brown. When she calls molasses *viscous,* you will think she's mispronouncing *vicious.* Her hands are shaking, but she never drops the whisk.

In 1984, your third cousin, your dad tells you, tries to hang himself with a length of cassette tape—*The Empire Strikes Back.* Dad uses words like *pussy.* You begin wondering about the feel of the tape—the crackly smoothness of it. You begin wondering about magnetism and particles, and you read somewhere that ferric oxide is inorganic, and chemists consider it an ill-defined material. The throat, in contrast, is very well-defined. You touch your Adam's apple with two fingers and swallow—this beautiful up-and-down.

In the whisking is both the whisking away and the whisking toward. How the air makes the cream solid. How the air, this cold, sweetens the chest. The secret is in the air, and therefore, invisible, and infuriating. Here, we work hard to make the liquid of things go away, apply strength and heat, coagulant and the kind of voice called *bedside manner.*

In 1984, three teenage boys threw Charles O. Howard over the State Street Bridge in Bangor. Howard drowned in the Kenduskeag Stream as the boys, from above, hurled homophobic slurs, attacking, among other things, the pitch of Howard's voice. When we're ill, the most comforting vocal pitch to the ear is bass. When we're well, as when we're drowning, the jury's still out.

In many Maine hospitals, Whoopie Pie, the official state treat, is "liquefied" and chilled, and given to patients who've just had their tonsils removed. It is coagulant, sealant, replacement for both the standard ice cream and the cut-away parts of us. In the Whoopie Pie is every Amish woman's broken leg, tendinitis, farmhouse mastectomy, the slowness of the horses. The slowness of horses to hospital. Is the chocolate cake buns your mother describes as bosomy, the oven cracking their tops. In Maine, we know: it's the heat that fissures us. It's the cool of the cream in the middle that holds our parts together, keeps our insides inside.

Dad feels that the eel is a masculine animal, for obvious reasons. For less obvious ones, he calls the Whoopie Pie *bitch food*. Dad knows: rivers meander. He does not think of metaphor when he talks of weirs, the barriers he used to install in order to alter the river's flow, hinder the passage of the fish. I went fishing only once with Dad. He was not happy that I was afraid of the rainbow trout.

In this kind of winter, we stay inside as much as we can. The ocean's there, close now. But we never think of it as roiling. Your father, or my father, hides Bowie knives in his underwear drawer. Mother thinks differently of knives now, thinks of the things we must cut from ourselves in order to live. Here, in excision, is the extension of a life. Here, we fill in the blanks with sweetened cream. No one whisks it to soft peaks faster than Mother. She whisks. Nothing of her body shakes.

In 1717, the Great Snow decimated Maine. Horses froze and livestock froze and our vocal cords constricted and we all tipped more toward soprano. In cold, and in high-pitched voices, panic. We kept warm, and alive, by whipping. It wasn't until years later that we associated whipping with cream, 25-foot snowdrifts with dessert. In winter, we write our names on the windowpanes with our tongues. We name the sweetest, softest stuff after ice.

Father likes masculine names, single-syllable names. Masculine voices. In bass, he says, is power. In the eel is power. No other animal, he says, maximizes its muscle output more. Mom takes a cookie sheet of chocolate buns from the oven. Your father, or my father, says, "a good strong name." You don't tell him—just like I don't tell him—that telemarketers often take you for the lady of the house.

Other names for Whoopie Pie: Gob, Black Moon, Big Fat Oreo, Big Fucking Oreo, Bob. A whirring sound: you can't tell if that's the snow, the electric mixer, the football audience complaining on the television. You can't tell if the pitch of your voice is the smallest of something, the largest of another.

In 1717, a record number of pirates raided vessels along the Maine coastline. The popular pirate boat of the time was a two-masted ship called a snow. The world's largest Whoopie Pie was slapped together in South Portland in March 2011. The ground was still soggy. The pie weighed 1,062 pounds and was sold by the slice, and the proceeds went to the mailing of smaller Whoopie Pies to Maine soldiers in Iraq and Afghanistan. Your mother says something about philanthropy and treats. Your father says, "It's all a big fucking something."

When Maine's blueberry farmers and potato farmers and sweet corn farmers and dairy farmers found that their wives had, in their lunch pails, wrapped in linen a small chocolate cookie sandwich with a sweet cream filling, they reportedly shouted, "Whoopie!" That they were eating cake batter leftovers did not diminish their excitement. That Father considers such an exclamation less than masculine did not slow their eating, compel them to wipe the cream from their chins. Father is conflicted about farmers.

In 2011, Maine legislators launched Proposition LD 71, "The Act to Designate Whoopie Pie as the State Dessert." The Pennsylvania Dutch and the New Hampshire German tried to intervene, claiming that the dessert belonged to them. Regardless, the proposition received full bipartisan support and Father asked what the fuck this had to do with the dropping lobster prices, and Mother began whisking not only for her body, but for the state.

My father says that James Earl Jones is the most masculine man he can think of. It's his deep voice, he says. I don't tell him what I've read: that it takes greater vocal strength for a soprano to sing alto than it does for a bass to sing baritone. It's harder to go lower. On the telephone, when he's around, I try to sound more like a man.

The bottom bun of the Whoopie Pie is the same as the top, except wetter. The breastbone of the dove is relatively stronger than that of the elephant. It's cold outside. I thumb through the atlas. I think of names written in snow, names drowning in thick streams. I think of how my father says he's beaten many people up, sure, but he's never thought to drown anyone. Of how *Bangor* means *monastic enclosure,* or *the sharp upper rods of a wattle fence*, or *horned*. Of how *whoopie* means *sex*. Of how our entire state resembles a growth that demands excision.

My mother talks of ghost itches, and whisks. My father has stopped talking. I've started doing push-ups. James Earl Jones says, "My stutter was so bad, I barely spoke to anyone for eight years." MaryAnne says, "We use gelatin in our cream." My mother says nothing to her of cheating, of shortcuts, of sugar as the sweetest thing that will kill us. Nothing of: The stuff inside of us, whipped. Perfectly mixed. One thing dissolved into another, our wrists making it happen. Contradiction is: my feminine voice, and the strength of the muscles required to produce it. In the pasturage outside of Bangor, the hoofless horse notices no flies, makes no sound. That doesn't mean that neither is there, and ready to bite.

Is my voice the voice of my body? Is a one-thousand-pound cookie sandwich the voice of the new war bond? My mother looks at a picture of herself young and her voice does something I don't like. Contradiction is. So, we eat two Whoopie Pies. One for comfort, one for the identity of our state. These two reasons are not the same, will never be the same. We are one out of fifty, and we are the extremity. We temper extremity by moving toward the cream in the middle. We need to do this so desperately, we legislate it.

Father sleeps on the couch. Our mothers are making Whoopie Pie to bring to the neighbors'. They know, but won't admit, that hers is the best. They know that, after she got sick, her Whoopie Pies got better. Like the cassette tape, this is also ill-defined material. We are swagger and insecurity. We wonder which is the cream, which the sugar. We know: *Kenduskeag* means *eel-weir place.*

We are body and voice, pectorals and castrato, the Force and the Dark Side, we are the horse in the mild winter, our names frozen on windows. We look through our names and see the horses shiver. We are ladies of the house. We are Bob. We are father and son.

Whoopie Pie

Cake

In a large bowl, cream:

1½ cups sugar
2 eggs
1½ teaspoons vanilla
½ cup butter
Just under ½ cup oil

Add 1½ cups milk slowly.

Separately sift:

3 cups flour
½ cup & ⅓ cup cocoa
¾ teaspoon baking powder
1½ teaspoons & ¾ teaspoon baking soda
½ teaspoon salt

And stir into batter.

Drop batter by spoonful onto a greased cookie sheet and bake 15 minutes at 350 degrees.

Cool. Sandwich filling between two cakes.

Filling

1 cup milk
½ cup oleo

6 tablespoons flour
1 cup sugar
½ cup shortening
2 teaspoons vanilla

Cook milk and flour in saucepan until thickened. Cool, and beat in remaining ingredients. Beat until filling is light and fluffy.

—Sue Moody, Moody's Diner

VERMONT

The Scabbing of the Maple Creemee

BECAUSE THE CAR can't talk, it leaks. The oil seeps into the concrete floor of the garage, and he names the droplets after this year's most popularly named babies in Vermont: Rhett, Morris, Maya, Emma, Zoe, Miles. *These are mice*, he thinks, oil stains as fat-bodied mice flattened, he thinks, by the same sort of heavy-handed sweetness that slicks his mouth, that has slicked his mouth now for days, as he falls asleep and wakes up on a garage floor next to a LeBaron, ice cream cone crumbs ever stuck to his lips, as he notices the oil stains joining together into something larger—something decidedly not-baby, not-rodent—something evoking the crescent and the blade, the sickle and the moon. *Smile*, he thinks, and then says, "Smile," as if naming the child he will never have, as if naming the gathering shape loosed by a failing car. He has no place to live but here. Still, it never occurs to him to use the word *homeless*.

Again, he eats a breakfast of three Maple Creemees—the delicious faux-vanilla soft serve larded with the thick syrup of the state's best trees. His mouth is a crescent—pathetic and lunar. The sound that should be coming out of it remains trapped in his cold esophagus. This is what he gets for surviving on polysorbates and maple syrup. There is nothing laughable about this.

This family has gone on vacation, left the garage unlocked. When they return, he will move into the trees. He tries to take comfort in state history. Tries to find the comedian mouse—the one who hides beneath the chassis and wears a bow tie, or beneath his sleeping bag. The one who will try to make the sickle laugh, make all of this a little less dangerous, a little duller. It's late, time for bed. He devours the last Creemee of the day—the one from Morse Farm, the one local papers refer to as "top-class." He bought it from a man named Burr, and thought nothing of the flora that attaches itself to his collars and cuffs and pillowcase. He bought it and stared at the banner behind the counter—*It's Sugarin' Time!*—and thought nothing of his failing wristwatch, the second hand unable to make its sweet and sweeping rotation, instead hiccupping in place in between the 3 and the 4. He lays his head next to the rear passenger tire and licks the maple-infused calcium sulfate from his inferior labial frenulum. He swears he can hear the air leaking out. Here, the secret is one of deflation. Something in this garage is in need of a pump.

Walking along the road from garage to Creemee stand, he passes a pasture through which gallops a horse without a tail. He knows: there's something synthetic about amputation here. The laryngitic horse who mourns the sound of its own whinnying. He knows: the calcium sulfate allows his Maple Creemee to hold its swirling shape. It is desiccant and coagulant. It allows for the drying, the clotting. In this way, his ice cream can be the scab, the bandage. He thinks of ways to put all that oil back into the car.

He knows: calcium sulfate is perfect for repairing drywall, and for making casts. One lick at a time, he thinks, he will build himself a house, will make his limbs strong again. He closes his eyes and cries and dreams that he is laughing. He will move into the trees like a tapping in reverse, like the sap creeping back into the trunk. But he knows: once the blood has left the body, it's poisonous to put it back inside.

* * *

WABANAKI LEGEND credits maple syrup production to Glooscap, a cultural hero whose name translates as Man Who Came from Nothing, or Man Born Only of Speech. Some communities tell us that Glooscap was created by the Great Spirit himself, while others claim he was the product of a human mother who died in childbirth. Either way, Glooscap is a transformer, changing evil monsters into benign forest animals. But he's also a diluter. When he came to a native village that had gone to ruin, and found that its inhabitants had grown fat and lazy, gape-mouthed beneath the maple trees and suckling from the trunks, the Great Spirit instructed him to temper the sweet sap with water, so that the people would have to work hard to extract it via hours upon hours of boiling. Legend dictates that this story was originally told to the Wabanaki by Glooscap himself, but it's tough to know what to believe, as Glooscap's name also translates, in certain communities, as Liar.

* * *

HE SPRINTS THROUGH the forests of Vermont, the rats fleeing like the split of water at the head of the ship. They unzip the forest floor, collect the burrs with their belly fur, knock the buckets over. He's almost certain: once, they were monsters. Burr Morse told him that the leakage of sap from a maple is called a *run*. Here, even the stuff inside the trees flees the body that tries to hold it.

Home state pride: In a tiny lab in Georgia, Vermont, in the early 1840s, Gardner Quincy Colton, a man with sensitive ears, tried to eradicate pain, and the human expression thereof. He believed he had solved what dentists at the time called "the screaming problem." Playing the roles of both showman and medical student, Colton became the first person to apply nitrous oxide, or laughing gas, to the practice of tooth extraction. After fleeing Vermont and failing to find gold in California, he devoted his life to traveling the countryside in a wagon, performing on-the-fly tooth-pullings from coast to coast. Though many of his patients succumbed to infection, and many others had trouble stopping the bleeding, they felt no pain, and laughed and laughed into the gas mask, inhaling the "alluringly sweet" taste of it. Here, we fuse the decidedly chemical with the sweetest thing that spills from our trees. Here, we call this dessert, and we misspell its name so as to be cuter than we actually are. When pressed through lips numb with anesthesia, *maple* becomes *apple*, becomes *male*, becomes *map*, *Maya*, *Miles*, *impale*.

He buys his breakfast Creemee, and Morse taps it out on the counter: *It takes forty gallons of maple sap to make one gallon of pure maple syrup. Into that two-hundred-year-old tree, we drill exactly one tap hole . . .* He licks, and thinks of dentistry, of the nerves of incisors screaming into the sponge of the cracking cone. Ojibwe legend credits the production of maple syrup to Nanabozho, a shape-shifting spirit who could sweet-talk the trees into giving up their essence. His mother also died in childbirth. In his mouth, as in the trees, the natural and the invasive braid themselves thickly. He leans his elbows on the counter. He is feeling a little woozy. Morse may, or may not, tap out the words *Sole hole*, with a thumb that's sheathed in syrup.

* * *

IN ALGONQUIN CULTURE, "every part of the tree has a designated use—from shelter, transportation and weapons, to tools, clothing and art . . . spectacular totem poles, dramatic masks . . ." According to *History House* magazine, Colton saw the use of laughing gas in public tooth extractions as "entertainments," and his "sole occupation." He will move into the trees like a shadow, or the word *shadow*.

* * *

AGAIN, HE CAN'T SLEEP. He is squatter and hungry and sweet-toothed and chemical. The polysorbate 80 is constricting his throat, rocketing his body toward some saccharine infertility. The maple in him tries to fight against this with words like *rich* and *mellow* and *full-bodied*, *B2*, *B5*, *B6*, and *niacin*. He knows: the Algonquin called maple syrup *sinzbukwud*, or *the stuff that's drawn from wood*. If we are tapped, we are emptied. He wriggles into his sleeping bag. He's filling something. He closes his eyes. He's lost his toothbrush. Something inside his body keeps wriggling. And the running sap leaves such a skinny silhouette. With it, the dumb squirrel thinks it can hang itself, and become a monster again.

* * *

COLTON SUPPORTED the practice of bloodletting for ailments ranging from insomnia to stroke to manic psychosis to malnourishment. He dreams of flaccid trees surrounded by squashed apples. When he wakes up, it seems as if, during the night, someone has pumped the tires. He tells himself that his diet of Maple Creemees means that he's living off the land. Algonquin legend credits the production of maple syrup to the squirrel, who, etymologically shadow-tailed, tapped the trees while the rest of us were sleeping next to a stranger's vehicle.

According to Thomas E. Keys's *The History of Surgical Anesthesia,*

> *The gas used in these lectures by Dr. Colton was contained in a rubber bag, and was administered through a horrible wooden faucet, similar to the contraptions used in country cider barrels. It was given in quantities only sufficient to exhilarate or stimulate the subjects, and reacted upon them in diverse and sundry ways. Some danced, some sang, others made impassioned orations, or indulged in serious arguments with imaginary opponents, while in many instances the freaks of the subjects were amazing . . .*

* * *

HE BRUSHES his teeth with his pinkie, spits an amalgam of maple syrup and magnesium hydroxide onto the rear passenger tire. He knows: magnesium hydroxide is a fire retardant, a smoke suppressor. Maybe he's eaten too much soft serve. His throat's gone cold. The spit runs from the tire as if keeping time in some nonlinear code, some crescent sort of way. He wonders about the point at which a *freak* becomes *amazing*, *death wish* becomes *Creemee.* Like oil, the syrup seeps into the soft serve. And the tailless horse accommodates the flies . . . He knows because the maples tell him: winter's coming. This morning, he could hardly finish his cone when a robin fell dead from the sky into a pile of yellow leaves. Dropped by a raptor, he thinks. The single lines of sap have dried on the trunks. He thinks of boundaries, old surgical scars, bodies halved by the sorts of coagulants that we have to boil and boil and boil to make sweet.

Sap boils to syrup at 220 degrees Fahrenheit—eight degrees hotter than the boiling point of water, and blood. The bark receives the drill. Into our holes, the birds will flock and make their nests. The sap Vermonters use to make maple syrup is called the xylem sap. That *xylem* refers to the transport tissue in vascular plants is merely factual. That his favorite vascular plant is a living fossil called a horsetail is also mere.

In shadow is the shifting of a shape. All syrup eventually hardens. When baby female mice were injected with some of the same chemicals that allow a creemee to coagulate, their bodies began ejecting the lining of the womb. He drops his eyes. He names the new oil leaks, before they're usurped into the sickle. His lips are freezing. He doesn't think of distance, of forbidden fruit, of sex or infertility, or widowers, or wives, even as *maple* becomes *Miles, apple* . . .

He's tired. He knows, even now, that the best he will be is *Uncle*. He speaks into this role, as if it's the hole in the trunk. He listens for the echo, the ghost. He says, "nothing, nothing, nothing," and tells himself he's performing a countdown. He eats his Creemee, watches the planes coming into Burlington revise Cassiopeia. He is about to faint, or fall asleep. He thinks of her that summer, her ivy dress stretching for the sun, her knees flashing like defingered castanets. This is the memory as the squirrel doused in syrup—rife with sugar, but unable to run.

The first snow. Before tapping his last tree of the day, Morse tells him with his fingers: Vermont legend dictates that bad weather originates in the wing pits of the birds. He thinks of her that summer, covered in snow. The maple has gone off in his mouth, like spoiled milk; like a firework. He closes his eyes, tries to remember her smell in the face of the LeBaron. Colton would have described it as *pulmonary, digestive, patina, sap*. He would have put it into a mask, ceremonial or otherwise. He closes his eyes. His sleeping bag constricts, arterial, around him. He will wake to tires and drops of fresh oil from which he will fashion children and pets. He imagines squirrel piñatas dropping headless over so many people dancing among the maples. He imagines planning a birthday party for a daughter or a son.

Somewhere, beyond such garages and deformed horses, a flood of sap pours from the trunks. The birds shake whole storms from their feathers. With ice cream, he thinks he can get her back. With all the double Es he can muster. "Cree," he says. "Mee," he says. Like the mountains here, he is so green.

Maple Creemee

Ingredients
3 cups heavy cream
1 cup whole milk
½ cup VT maple syrup
1 tablespoon vanilla paste
8 egg yolks
½ cup sugar

1. In a medium-sized sauce pot, combine cream, milk, vanilla paste, and maple syrup.

2. Bring cream mixture to a light simmer. Remove from heat.

3. In a mixing bowl, whisk egg yolks and sugar until fluffy, about 1 minute.

4. Slowly whisk in cream mixture, do not stop stirring the mixture until all of the cream is added. This will prevent the eggs from scrambling.

5. Return the mixture to the sauce pot and steep on low heat for 3 to 5 minutes, stirring constantly. The mixture should start to thicken a bit. Remove from heat.

6. Pass the custard through a fine mesh strainer and chill for at least 2 hours.

7. Once mixture is cool, add to soft serve machine or add to your home ice cream machine and follow manufacturer's instructions.

—Bluebird Vermont

The Clouding of the Clear Clam Chowder

THOUGH HE CAN'T SEE too well, though his perception has given up on breadth as well as depth, though *deep* is something he applies now only to his favorite gaping soup bowl—the one once etched in red, "HAPPY AS A CLAM," now missing in age the ultimate M—or the flavor of the clear broth inside it, Uncle is able, in our state, to count the coins of carrot that outnumber the chopped bellies of the bivalve, and curse his chowder clearly, as if his mouth, angry, but hungry, is the thing on his face that can best see what's really going on. We wonder: the smaller the thing, the less there is to see, the more clearly we can see that thing. We wonder if clarity has more to do with the size of the observed thing, or the time it takes us to observe it. The gull with the short attention span dive-bombs the littleneck, considers the cherrystone. There's little sustenance in consideration.

Clearly, we are the smallest state in the union—its Adam's apple, or kidney stone, the belly of one small thing in the throat of another. The Beavertail lighthouse, protecting sailors from Narragansett Bay's aggressive rocky coastline since 1749, is illuminated twenty-four hours per day, seven days per week, and makes a full counterclockwise rotation every six seconds. In 1779, during the Revolutionary War, British soldiers destroyed boats and morale by burning the lighthouse down, and making off with the optics and foghorn, drenching the coastline in darkness for the remainder of the war. To make the night as navigable as possible, various soldiers took shifts maintaining small shoreline fires. To boost their spirits, they roasted clams until their shells blinked open, and, dry-mouthed from the fires, swallowed their gills, their adductors, their retractor muscles, their feet, their mantles, their labial palps, their necks and anuses, their gonads and intestines, their kidneys, their mouths, their hearts, with the aid of the bloody seawater only.

How many parts per million of blood cells can be suspended in the water before that water becomes something else, before we stop calling it the ocean? We eat all of the clam. We call it only *the whole belly*. We are not seeing these things clearly. Because our shorelines, historically, have been muddied with our insides, we revise with our chowder. Uncle holds his cloudy fist in front of his face, cheers for Rhode Island's Clear Clam Chowder, which shuns the tomato and the cream, the red and the white, in favor of the briny astringency of pure clam broth, larded with onion, carrot, celery, thyme, and potato. Uncle drops his fist, nearly misses his spoon, slurps a mouthful, and couldn't care less whether the orange thread of meat was once an anus, or a heart.

Either we see, or we break our bodies onto the rocks. Rhode Island legend has it that Beavertail Lighthouse's first keeper, Abel Franklin, was a pathologically responsible man. After the lighthouse was first destroyed by accidental fire in 1753, Franklin reportedly lit a lantern at dusk and held it aloft all night long. The shipping vessels, as a result, never crashed during this period of destruction, but also never imagined that they were guided by a strange skinny man, holding a flame above his head, whirling on the beach in six-second intervals, alternately talking to himself, singing to himself, whooping, and falling silent.

Though it's the oyster that commonly makes pearls, that doesn't stop the clam from trying. We so call our state (fully named the State of Rhode Island and Providence Plantations) because the explorer Giovanni da Verrazzano, in 1524, believed it to resemble, from the water, the Ottoman island of Rhodes. When the Pilgrims arrived, it was unclear to them which "island" Verrazzano was referring to, so they took a stab at it. At best, Uncle says, we are named after the loopy guesswork of a bunch of exhausted, sea-diseased, starving evangelicals. "We're a hallucination, boy," he says, as he swallows the last of his bowl, which allows him to see the bottom more easily.

Or we so call our state because explorer Adriaen Block, in 1610, passed by Rhode Island and, without even landing, wrote in his journal (loosely translated from seventeenth-century Dutch), "Today, I can see it through the fog: an island of reddish appearance." The red, historians guess, was due to the red autumn leaves, or the clay close to the shoreline, and early Dutch cartographers took him at his distant word and began to include a Red Island (in Dutch, *Roodt Eylant*) on their maps, one that the sea-diseased, starving evangelicals, with an apparent penchant for phonics, nonsensically renamed after nothing.

We are not quite Rhodes and not quite red, but, full of clear broth, we can see to the bottoms of our bowls even when full; we can determine how many spoonfuls, how long it will take us to finish, even before we start. With this much of the clam to hew through, we're often wrong. In clarity, is an easy admission of fault, mistake. Pretty trees. Robust clay. In the early seventeenth century, before the lighthouse was built, before it could tell us what we were really seeing, so many scalps of the Wampanoag, the Narragansett, and Pequot littered the rocky shoreline where 130 years later, Abel the Human Lighthouse would all night dance with fire.

Though the surgery was deemed a failure, and the doctor told him that blindness was unavoidable, Uncle asked to keep his excised cataract, called it the Foreskin of the Clam. He keeps it—this pinkie nail of caul fat—in a tulip of seawater on his nightstand, hopes it will grow—like some sci-fi brain, like something he once ate and now longs for—to befriend him. Here, we must think like the clam, allow brain and mouth not only to communicate, but to merge.

Our name is a mistake, and so Rhode merges with gibberish. Narragansett means *People of the Small Point*. In the article "Structural and Molecular Interrogation of Intact Biological Systems," Kwanghun Chung states:

> *I was trying to understand how migrating cerebellar granule cells find their way through the developing brain. This involved dissecting hundreds of tiny brains from chick embryos into slices and label-*

ing some of the cells with a fluorescent dye. I'd incubate the slices for a week or so and embed them in a gel. Then, I'd use a machine called a microtome to shave each one into dozens of sections, each thinner than a human hair, mount those onto glass slides and, finally, examine them with a confocal fluorescence microscope.

A new method of injecting brain tissue "with formaldehyde and hydrogels . . . [alleviated this] time-consuming and laborious process . . . by making samples of the biological tissue completely transparent." The method is known as CLARITY, and "CLARITY gives a clear view of the brain."

* * *

CATARACT DERIVES from the Latin *cataracta*, meaning *waterfall*, meaning *the descent of the water*, meaning *a downward gush*. In this way, blindness is akin to drowning. In this way, the sort of broth that renders clear all that floats in it can obstruct, can clog, can deafen, can asphyxiate.

During the 1938 hurricane, whole colonies of upside-down Cassiopeia jellyfish swept up the U.S. East Coast from Florida, oftentimes finding themselves cold and confused along Rhode Island, where they hugged the awful rocks of the red Narragansett Bay shoreline for any kind of warmth. Because, according to Matt Berryman's *Marine Invertebrates*, Cassiopeia jellyfish prefer areas saturated with sunlight, we can easily tell that their bodies are transparent, that their intestinal tracts are tied into orchid shapes, that they have tiny bells for hearts, ringing so quietly against displacement, as our houses collapse and collapse.

Uncle says he knew Abel's great-great-great-great-great-great-grandson, also named Abel. "A ballet dancer," Uncle says, "and a pyromaniac." You wait for him to laugh, but he just picks clam from his teeth, sucks the clear broth from the sponge of it. Strange: the blinder he becomes, the less you can distinguish if he is lying or not. Here, if we can see through something, that means we can also see inside it. Here, even clarity is confusing: we can't tell which is the shit, and which the flower. And Cassiopeia says, "I am so much more beautiful than the nymphs of the sea," a vanity which aroused the wrath of Poseidon who, as punishment, tied her upside down to a chair in the heavens and flooded her terrestrial queendom in a falling curtain of water.

The chowder finished, Uncle applauds his broth. Though he can't quite see it, his palms redden like the gooeyest earth at our shoreline. Because we can see more of it—into it—our chowder is prettier than yours. And in Rhodes, in 478 BC, local forces cut off the heads of Persian invaders, skewered them on pikes and lined them up along their sunniest shore as a beacon of warning. Even from a distance, no one confused the clarity of its redness. Uncle fills in the gap on his favorite soup bowl: HAPPY AS A CLAN, A CLAP, A CLAW, A CLAY.

* * *

Other etymologies of *cataract*: *to dash down, to strike down, to assassinate.* According to Zahra Etebari Goharrizi's *Blindness and Initiating Communication*, blind people are often more talkative than those with sight. "Blind people," she asserts, "make up for the lack of visual cues by directly asking for the personal information they were interested in. Blind people, far from avoiding the personal dimension, confront it directly and ask for the missing information in words. Also were the blind–blind conversations more spontaneous and contained more utterances."

* * *

Here, according to the Beavertail Lighthouse Museum Association, sailors, blinded by the weather, asked their questions over and over again, and "a great gun at Beavertail was provided to answer ships in the fog." Here, the less we see, the more noise we have to make, wave our fires around. Here, clarity is an excuse not to talk.

Sometimes, the sun was so strong, the heads burst into flame. Sometimes, the children were so bored, they danced with them. This much is clear: here, like the conversations of the blind, weather is impetuous, and we need to be warned. For shards of shell: transparent broth. For the fog: the horn. The hemoglobin in the Atlantic, the clams in our mouths . . .

According to *The Lighthouse Log*, when Abel Franklin died, he left his sons land and ferries. "Each daughter received 1200 pounds. His wife Sarah received 500 pounds, all household goods, a riding mare, a cow, and a slave named Margaret." We know: *clarity* and *certainty* are two different things. It's clear that there's a light at the shore. We're not certain if it's a house, or a head, or an entire man that's burning. There's Abel as Cassiopeia. There's Margaret, meaning *flower*, meaning *pearl*. This much is clear . . .

So, we boil our chowder clear as consommé, but like so many of our drowned, we shun the raft. And the flower, and the pearl: *I'm here, I'm here, can't you see me . . .?* Uncle knows: if the broth is the thing we're steeped in, all of this sea air, these rocks, this horrible red clay bears our savors, essence, story. In it, as long as we're swallowing, we can continue to make it up, layer it, make of our bodies the ocean at night, wonder, exploratory in all this darkness, what's on the other side of us, finally associate soup with state, fire with safety, broth with *smallest*, every window with the perfectly working eye.

Clear Clam Chowder

Rhode Island Broth Style Clam Chowder

8 ounces bacon, medium to fine diced
8 ounces lightly salted butter
1 cup celery, medium to fine diced
1 cup Spanish onion, medium to fine diced
1 cup Pinot Grigio or dry white wine
1 teaspoon black pepper
2 quarts ocean clam juice
1 pound chef's potatoes, peeled and medium diced
1 quart chopped sea clams
¼ cup fresh chopped parsley (not dried)

In a 6-to-8-quart stockpot on low heat, cook bacon until fully cooked and lightly brown.

Add butter, celery, and onion and cook until the vegetables are just beginning to soften.

Add white wine and cook for 1 minute.

Add black pepper, clam juice, and potatoes, increase to a simmer and cook potatoes until just barely soft.

Add chopped clams and bring back to a simmer for 30 seconds. You just want to cook the clams through but lightly.

Add chopped parsley for great color and vibrant flavor.

Serve immediately to only your closest friends and family. Rhode Island Broth Style Clam Chowder is a special treat!!!

—Scott Cowell, Melville Grille

Coming of Age with New Hampshire Corn Chowder

IT'S EVENING IN CONCORD, and the husks pull shut over dying yellow meat, blushing and modest as the debutantes of Old Hampshire. Soon, we will sleep and wake and pulverize kernels for the chowder, and we will wear T-shirts with the image of an ear of corn superimposed over our state at our chests, underlined in script with slogans like "Nebraska who?" and "Proud to be a New Hampshire Aztec," and the blackflies will hatch at our windowsills, and we'll scratch at our necks—at their rising bites—and we'll tell ourselves that we're *awake!*, that it's civic duty that compels us to press the germ of the kernel from its hull and fiber, and we will whisper with the other boys the thematic dirty jokes about the endosperm and the gluten, and we will touch ourselves in circles, while the chowder simmers, to vaginal diagrams of corn, and we stir and we touch long before our mothers die and our fathers die and our rearing is overtaken by drunken widower uncles who move us around the country in search of odd jobs like *corn detasseler*—a job that will temporarily send us back here, to the smells of the cob's milk and the blackflies copulating in the defunct woolen mills, and we will still have to convince ourselves toward wakefulness, and we will again mechanically stir the chowder as if this is our bodies' primary inheritance, and we will forget that *Concord* means *peace, a covenant*, and we will stir more sleepily, and we will dribble our pathetic cream into the stockpots of the world and read—on another T-shirt, no less—for the first time in our lives, that the nickname of the city of our birth is the City in a Coma.

We stir beneath the whir of the most peaceable of the ceiling fans and don't hear the blackflies at the window who, in their crazed flying, crush their eggs against the heat of the pane. This is what we do in New Hampshire, according to the blog "In Our Grandmothers' Kitchens": "blend warmth and comfort, chunkiness and creaminess." To our pressed kernels, we add bacon and potato and onion and bell pepper ("preferably not yellow," so as not to compete with the corn!), chicken stock and cream. We compel these things to release their juice and fat, and we let the flavors reduce and concentrate and marry, as Uncle himself reduces and concentrates and marries and remarries and loses concentration and gets fat, and we pretend that the blackflies are releasing their eggs in a beautiful process, rather than the sort of birth that feeds from us with teeth, that first stretches our skin so thin before penetrating to the blood.

* * *

Other names for the blackfly: buffalo gnat, turkey gnat, river blinder, blood meal. Other names for our state cities: Space Town, Granite Town, the City that Trees Built, the Crutch Capital of the World.

* * *

"Discard the cobs," say our grandmothers' recipes, and find another crutch. We stir and the corn usurps the bacon, the plant again takes the pig down, and we stare out the window through the curtain of flies and there's a disturbance in the sycamore that's either the wind or something more menacing. We stir and Uncle mutters something about 163 businesses in New Hampshire named for Marco Polo—Marco Polo Unique Gifts boutique in Portsmouth, Marco Polo Garden Chinese restaurant in Keene ("Really good General Tso's chicken") . . . We stir and allow the steam to obscure the kitchen, the window, the fan, Uncle, allow ourselves to think of all exploration as mapping one thing onto another, as closing our eyes in the shallow end and allowing the voices of our first girlfriends to lure us toward the deep.

Again, we close our eyes and imagine bodies as hard as the corn. We imagine the amount of stirring and simmering required to soften them. We imagine we have what it takes. We stir and stare through flies at a skyline as slack as the grasses, pathetic in the face of such virile corn, and we think of all the comatose things in our city, and read, in *The Patch*—the local paper—that "Of course Concord is no Boston (or even Portsmouth) but if you keep your eyes and ears open various activities do appear."

We know: all blindness is exhilarating before it becomes debilitating. We know: the blackflies kill cows and blind farmers who sometimes fall into their pitchforks while reaching for the immature ears. We try to keep our eyes and ears open. Look: appearing there, over that ridge, before the cornrows, is an activity.

This is corn as aphorism, as—in a horseless county—the gift-fly whose mouth is too small to peer into. This is cream as garish adolescence, as the bell pepper disappearing into the broth, as all ingredients whose names dupe us into believing that they can ring, musically. Uncle drums on his thighs with the discards. We try, and fail, not to associate the muted whumping sound of cob on denim with a body going flaccid before dropping into the grave.

* * *

WE STIR and remember our first kisses beneath the Loveland Bridge in Rumney. We try to fabricate bad metaphors about memory: how the bridge was named for Lewis H. Loveland, Jr., who beneath its arch in the late nineteenth century built a crutch mill and manufactured more than 3,000 pairs per week, exporting to Australia and Africa and the battlefields of World War I, earning Loveland the nickname "the King of Crutches" and Rumney "the Crutch Capital of the World," and we stir and remember cold lips and we stir and think of all productivity as hobbling on bad legs toward all misremembered joy.

In death is only more loam, Uncle says, and you know: the corpse is good for the crop—all of our parents can whisper their rebukes again in the steam of the corn chowder. We stare at our stirring hands and become ashamed at what they've done, where they've been. "A cob in the palm . . ." Uncle says crudely, before muttering about the Norman Conquest, the Iron Age, the model he himself built as a child of Stonehenge, out of the corncobs his own grandmother stripped for a New Hampshire sort of chowder.

So what if Uncle got fired from New Hampshire Industries Mechanical Motion Parts (market leader in pulleys, sheaves, and sprockets) for touching himself on the line? Innocently, after three rums-and-Squamscot Diet Maple Cream Soda, he tells us he was thinking only of the corn. Empathy is a kernel.

* * *

My father never washed his sleep shorts, cleaned his ears with the waistband. He didn't believe in tampering with hearing, the drums, the hammers responsible for height. He admired tall buildings, slept for an entire year next to the Tallest Cornstalk in Nashua. October was best, he said. No flies. Now, he wonders if all wives creak in age, go bald in the face of needles and the healing things they carry. If all husbands tear their rotator cuffs like husks (just another kind of leaf), the dough of something besides bread, a thickening soup. When he put his ear to the windowpane, the blanket of the blackflies, he swore he heard tiny sawmills. Maybe this is responsible for the softness of his ears, wet as paper before it becomes paper. Maybe he heard my mother coming with a blond rolling pin and the end of lymphoma. Regardless, I now know that he lied. Here, even in October there are bugs who will drain us.

* * *

IT'S TOO OBVIOUS to say that the ingredient for our state dish had to be domesticated like a dog. Too obvious to associate food with leash. We feed our chowder because it will feed us, clean its shit, take it out for a walk and it pulls us wherever it decides to go. Today, our chowder walks us past the hospital where all of the patients who are not in comas eat corn chowder for lunch. Not a single one thinks that it reminds them of their grandmother's.

In an ear of corn, the silk is the stigma of the female flower, catching the pollen that falls from the tassels—the male flower. Each silk is capable of birthing one kernel of corn. Each silk sheet is capable of softening the sleep of Uncle, who blinds himself into believing that material equals luxury, or Aunt. Each blackfly larva, having been laid in running water, attaches itself to the substrate via tiny hooked silk threads at the end of its abdomen. In this way, it is the spider. Outside of itself. Each bowl of chowder fills us before another insomniac night. We have the silk to thank for so much here.

* * *

In December 1940, two earthquakes rocked New Hampshire at Ossipee Lake, and were felt in all six New England states, plus Pennsylvania and New Jersey. Residents counted over 120 aftershocks, which lasted until the following February. Houses crumbled and businesses crumbled and cows died and pigs died and people died, and one bull was decapitated by a falling chimney, and the monuments in the cemeteries shifted their positions, and the corn, and the Corn Chowder, was just fine.

* * *

If our mothers and fathers embraced the coma before dying, what else can we do but stay up late, pinching ourselves awake, finding those parts of us most like the cobs, or the suggestive diagrams of childhood, and shove all our best innuendo beneath the thin husks as if fly-teeth through silk, and close our eyes and think of eggs or kernels and call out the names of our old girlfriends who shout back from graves of their own, and though we're lying down and it's just the ceiling fan that rebukes us, we convince ourselves that, in this creamy hour, we're moving toward them; we'll win this game.

Lou's Corn Chowder

Serves: 50

Ingredients

1½ gallons water

1 #10 can creamed corn

One 40-ounce bag of frozen corn kernels
2 gallons heavy cream
1 gallon whole milk

1 celery stalk diced small
3 medium onions diced small
10 potatoes peeled and cubed small

5½ tablespoons seasoning salt
1 tablespoon black pepper
2 tablespoons garlic powder
2 tablespoons veggie base

6 cups roux
5 cups chopped, smoked bacon

Boil potatoes till slightly soft and drain, set aside.

Sauté onions and celery in large 6-gallon pot with a couple tablespoons oil.

Add water to pot and veggie base.

Add cream and milk and heat to almost boiling.

Heat roux, add to pot, and stir in till thick.

Add potatoes, bacon, and spices.

Heat to serving temperature and season with salt and pepper to taste.

Note: We make roux in large quantities, we use 4 pounds of butter to 2 quarts of flour and cook till lightly boiling while stirring. After it is put in the chowder we simmer to the thickness we want for the chowder. Some people make their roux at the start of their chowder, we choose to add it at the end to get our desired thickness,

—Shawn Nelson, Lou's Restaurant & Bakery

The Material Consequence of Boston Cream Pie

LET'S TALK LOGIC. If Boston, then Paul Revere, then tea, then colony, then revolution, then city, then Cream Pie. If tea, then the sugar in the Cream Pie steeping. If steeping, then invading. If sugar, then parasite, and parasite dissolving into sweetness. If *colony,* then *like the colon,* then the chocolate in our stool, and the birth of all schoolyard playground jokes in the aftermath of the Independence. If c*olony,* then like England's asshole, and no wonder why we wanted to be named something else, like a state, as if of matter.

If solid, liquid, gas, cream, egg, sponge, vanilla, the steaming away of the excess liquid in the oven, then it's hard to tell, considering the whole pie, which is the colony, which the state, which the proper way to move through streets of dust, then cobblestone, then asphalt, which the proper way to navigate a pie that's all soft. If the pie gives no resistance to the fork, then it's hard to tell which part of it is the most important. If resistance, then *résistance.*

If October 23 is National Boston Cream Pie Day, then I'm not sure if this is mere celebration, or holiday—a term that evolved from a rigorous devotion to a special religious practice, to a day off. If the latter, then let's eat our pie in pews–cum–chaise lounges. If sponge, and frosting, and cream, then it's hard to tell which is the holiest part, hard to know when my tongue is closest to God. If holiday, then the pie relaxes, prayerfully, into our mouths.

If Massachusetts is named after the indigenous Massachusett population, and translates as *near the little big hill,* then the entire state is confused as to the size of the thing it's closest to. If a revolution goes around, then it comes around. If revolution, then cliché—

after eating Boston Cream Pie, I am as happy as a clam. If I am as happy as a clam, then I am using cliché to make Boston Cream Pie sound disgusting. If a city goes with a state, then a bivalve reference goes not with chocolate.

If Revere, then reverence, and all other ill-defined, creamy things. If we call it a pie, then chef M. Sanzian of Boston's Parker House Hotel will roll over in his grave, once again agitated in death that his 1856 dessert creation—vanilla-flavored *crème pâtissière* (a custardy filling comprised of egg yolk, milk, cream, sugar, and flour) sandwiched between two discs of sponge cake, and frosted with chocolate ganache—which is a cake, *a cake!*—is once again being called by the wrong name. If rolling over in his grave is too much of a cliché, then chef M. Sanzian will instead flop inside it like a fish at boat-bottom, or ooze from its confines like cream from the two layers of sponge, or open his legs to the shower of dirt like a clam to the sun, whatever inner meat still left, glistening like morning dew, smoke on the water, the sweetest cliché, and all other attractive things that resist our desire to bite them.

If Puritan, then our pie, if not our lust to eat it, is clean. If our pie is good, then our pie is Sarah Good, the first to be executed at the Salem witch trials, and whose famed historical scream, just before she was lynched, inspired, if implicitly, our practice today of dying the sponge cake orange for Halloween and calling it Boston Scream Pie.

If little big, then good bad; then the frustration elicited at the definition of a single thing via opposing adjectives; then the disproportionate number of women with "Good" in their names who were executed in Massachusetts for witchcraft—besides Sarah: Goodwife Bassett, Goodwife Knap, Goodwife Greensmith, Dorothy Good, Goody Glover (who cast spells on the children of John Goodwin), and the trials of these women were described by Robert Calef (who, in the mid-1690s lost his standing as "a good Baptist citizen" after he wrote a book denouncing the trials): "And now Nineteen persons having been hang'd, and one prest to death, of which above a third part were Members of some of the Churches of N. England, and more than half of them of a good Conversation in general . . ."

If to be prest to death is to be executed by crushing, then we must realize that this term has been variously interpreted, and methods have ranged from crushing by elephant (once popular in Southeast Asia), to crushing by boulder (once favored by the Romans, the Vietnamese, the Aztecs . . .), to crushing by *peine forte et dure* (an old French method involving the placing of heavier and heavier stones on the convicted's chest until either suffocation ensued or the skeleton collapsed, whichever came first)—no matter the method, the disposal of these corpses has been described by historians as a "sloppy mess."

If early recipes for Boston Cream Pie often require that the two layers of sponge cake be "prest" to the custard, then I'm happy M. Sanzian pursued a career in pastry rather than in the courts. If travel writer Debi Lander describes the Boston Cream Pie as "perfect for a pie-throwing contest; firm enough to throw and not fall apart, but gushy enough to make a sloppy mess," then pardon me if I ask, politely, for a diminutive slice. If M. Sanzian was French-Armenian, then he belonged to an ethnicity that comprised less than 0.0001 percent (a percentage so low, that some sources document the population at 0.0 percent) of his adopted state at the time he invented what was to become, exactly 140 years later, the official state dessert of Massachusetts.

If the bill to recognize Boston Cream Pie as the official state dessert of Massachusetts was initially sponsored by a civics class at Norton High School in 1996, then one may propose that the teacher devoted far too little class time to the discussion of Confucius and legalism, electoral reform and human development theory, eco-anarchism and kleptocracy, and way, way too much time to sweets. If the Boston Cream Pie returned the favor to its sponsors, then the Boston Cream Pie is both delicious and pedagogically sound.

If Mrs. Beaudreau's third grade class at the Charlton Street School in Southbridge collectively compiled a PowerPoint presentation called "Massachusetts Favorites," and if said PowerPoint includes seventeen slides, and if we can assume that the favorites are ranked (slide one being most favorite, slide seventeen being least favorite), and if Boston Cream Pie ranks second, then the Boston Cream Pie—at least to these third-graders—is better than the cod, is better than the chickadee, is better than the Boston terrier, and the *Mayflower*, and the right whale (the official state marine mammal), and Plymouth Rock, and the chocolate chip cookie (the official state cookie), and Johnny Appleseed, and Benjamin Franklin. If Mrs. Beaudreau's class is right, then the only thing about Massachusetts that's better than Boston Cream Pie is the official state insect, the ladybug.

If we listen closely to the ladybug flex its wings while digesting the sixty-some aphids it eats in a given day, their dome-shaped bodies crackling like campfire, then we may close our eyes and we may be listening to castanets, or the applause of palm fronds, and we may be far away from Massachusetts, and revolution, and crushed girls, and any sort of secretive dessert that gives to our mouths without sound. If Boston has a continental climate with maritime influences, then our meteorological character can be described as humid subtropical, and then palm fronds are not such a stretch.

If another name for the ladybug is God's cow, then we can assume that we are conflicted about this insect. If Mrs. Beaudreau writes, under Class Announcements, "Dear Parents, Thank you to all who have contributed to our classroom over the year by sending in tissues, pencils, food etc.," then we can assume that the school had an insufficient supply of all three, and we can worry about the potential next year, should the parents be less generous, for the wayward sneezing, the giving in to permanent ink, the hunger, the hunger, for the dwindling supply of our second favorites, for, at recess, the ladybug gorge-fest. If the Boston Cream Pie runs out, then the aphids will thrive.

If John Winthrop, Massachusetts Bay Colony's first governor, was right in 1630 when, aboard the ship *Arbella*, Anne Bradstreet (the New World's first recognized female poet) by his side muttering a litany of thick-tongued *Amens!*, he delivered his famed and seasick "city on a hill" sermon, which surmised that, among other things, Boston, and everything named for it, had a special covenant with

God, then we can assume that Boston Cream Pie is some serious ambrosia delivered to our holy plates not by doves (as in Greece), or by chickadees (they're the eighth favorite), but by swarms of those sexy red beetles strong enough to bear it.

If Boston Cream Pie is the food of the gods, and if, today, the Parker House Hotel's price range is listed variously as Expensive, Luxury, and $$$$, then Boston Cream Pie's origins are pricey, if not divine, not at all the original proletariat dessert that "official state" would have us believe. If the Parker House Hotel had the same reputation in 1856 as it does today, then only the wealthy could afford to eat Boston Cream Pie.

If tea, then imagine the harbor dammed with sponge cake. If we are to trust in names and aliases, and if, in Boston Harbor, the ladybugs of Calf Island are smaller than in the city, then the ladybugs of Little Calf Island are smaller than that.

If, in the mid-nineteenth century, Boston's social and cultural Yankee elite named themselves the Boston Brahmins, then one can assume it strange that they did not adopt the Brahmin practices of eating only vegetarian when not fasting, and of cremating the bodies of their dead on a riverbank, the ashes immersed in the water; and one can assume it even more strange that the two primary Boston Brahmin families were named Bacon and Coffin.

If our water supply, derived from the Quabbin and Wachusett reservoirs west of Boston, is so pure as to be one of the only in the nation to be exempt from federal filtration requirements, then *purify* and all of its puritanical derivatives are now obsolete. If this tells us something of our history, then this telling resides either in some commentary on the statute of limitations, or in some other atrocious cliché. If we scattered the embers of our dead in the harbor instead, then we could have drunk all that tea.

If massacre, then the custard bleeding out. If Bunker, then the custard safely inside. If we eat the Boston Cream Pie with closed eyes (*castanets, palm fronds . . .*), then love, like history, is blind. If all's fair in love and war, then let's eat the entire pie. If siege, if Siege of Boston, then real civics, then overused fairness spilling its banks carrying tea and the dead, tea and the dead, then kleptocracy, then rule by thieves, then (if Mrs. Beaudreau is right, and children are the future) the third-graders of Massachusetts will never go hungry again, they will take all they need from Expensive and Luxury, they will wipe their noses and trace turkeys from their fingers and eat cake-confused-for-pie until the cows—or at least the God's cows—come home, the home being the closest to the little, biggest mouth of this state.

Boston Cream Pie

Serves: 4 to 6

Ganache

4 oz / 115 g semisweet or bittersweet chocolate (56 to 62 percent cacao), chopped, or ¾ cup semisweet or bittersweet chocolate chips
½ cup / 120 ml heavy cream

Pastry Cream

1¼ cups / 300 g milk
½ cup / 100 g granulated sugar
¼ cup / 30 g cake flour
½ teaspoon kosher salt
4 egg yolks
1 teaspoon vanilla extract

Sponge Cake

4 large eggs, separated, plus 3 egg whites
1 cup / 200 g granulated sugar
2 tablespoons freshly squeezed lemon juice
¾ cup / 90 g all-purpose flour
Pinch of kosher salt

Cake-Soaking Syrup

⅓ cup / 80 ml hot brewed coffee
⅓ cup / 70 g granulated sugar
1 cup / 240 ml heavy cream

Instructions

1. Special equipment: 13 x 18 inch / 33 x 46 cm rimmed baking sheet, parchment paper, stand mixer with whisk attachment or handheld mixer, sifter or sieve, offset spatula, clean cardboard

2. ***To Make the Ganache:*** Place the chocolate in a small, heatproof bowl. In a small saucepan, heat the cream over high heat until scalded; that is, until small bubbles form along the sides of the pan. Pour the hot cream over the chocolate and let sit for 30 seconds. Slowly whisk the chocolate and cream together until the chocolate is completely melted and the mixture is smooth.

3. Let cool to room temperature. The ganache can be stored in an airtight container in the refrigerator for up to 1 week.

4. ***To Make the Pastry Cream:*** In a medium saucepan, heat the milk over medium-high heat until scalded; that is, until small bubbles form along the sides of the pan. While the milk is heating, in a small bowl, stir together the sugar, flour, and salt. (Mixing the flour with the sugar will prevent the flour from clumping when you add it to the egg yolks.) In a medium bowl, whisk the egg yolks until blended, then slowly whisk in the flour mixture. The mixture will be thick and pasty.

5. Remove the milk from the heat and slowly add it to the egg–flour mixture, a little at a time, while whisking constantly. When all of the milk has been incorporated, return the contents of the bowl to the saucepan and heat over medium heat, whisk continuously and vigorously for about 3 minutes, or until the mixture thickens and comes to a boil. At first, the mixture will be very frothy and liquid; as it cooks longer, it will slowly start to thicken until the frothy bubbles disappear and it becomes more viscous. Once it thickens, stop whisking every few seconds to see if the mixture has come to a boil. If it has not, keep whisking vigorously. As soon as you see it bubbling, immediately go back to whisking for just 10 seconds, and then remove the pan from the heat. Boiling the mixture will thicken it and cook out the flour taste, but if you let it boil for longer than 10 seconds, the mixture can become grainy.

6. Pour, push, and scrape the mixture through the sieve into a small, heatproof bowl. Stir in the vanilla and then cover with plastic wrap, placing it directly on the surface of the cream to prevent a skin from forming. Refrigerate for at least 4 hours, or until cold, before using. The cream can be stored for up to 3 days in an airtight container in the refrigerator.

7. ***To Make the Sponge Cake:*** Preheat the oven to 350°F / 180°C, and place a rack in the middle of the oven. Line the baking sheet with parchment paper.

8. Using the stand mixer or the handheld mixer and a medium bowl, beat together the egg yolks, ¼ cup / 50 g of the sugar, and the lemon juice on high speed for at least 6 to 8 minutes if using the stand mixer or 10 to 12 minutes if using the handheld mixer, or until thick and doubled in volume. Stop the mixer once or twice and scrape down the sides of the bowl and the whisk to ensure the sugar and yolks are evenly mixed. Transfer to a large bowl and set aside.

9. Clean the bowl and the whisk attachment or beaters (they must be spotlessly clean) and beat the egg whites on medium speed for 2 to 3 minutes with the stand mixer or 4 to 6 minutes with the handheld mixer, or until soft peaks form. The whites will start to froth and turn into bubbles, and eventually the yellowy viscous part will disappear. Keep beating until you can see the tines of the whisk or beaters leaving a slight trail in the whites. To test for the soft-peak stage, stop the mixer and lift the whisk or beaters out of the whites; the whites should peak and then droop. With the mixer on medium speed, add the remaining ¾ cup / 150 g sugar very slowly, a spoonful or so at a time, taking about 1 minute to add all of the sugar. Continue beating on medium speed for 2 to 3 minutes longer, or until the whites are glossy and shiny and hold a stiff peak when you slowly lift the whisk or beaters straight up and out of the whites.

10. Using a rubber spatula, gently fold about one-third of the whipped whites into the yolk mixture to lighten it. Then gently fold in the remaining egg whites. Sift the flour and salt together over the top of the mixture and fold in gently until the flour is completely incorporated. Pour the batter into the prepared baking sheet.

11. Using the offset spatula, carefully spread the batter evenly to cover the entire baking sheet. Concentrate on spreading the batter toward the corners and edges of the pan. The center will be easier to fill once the edges are filled with batter. Don't worry about the top being perfectly smooth; it is more important that the batter be spread evenly so that the cake is the same thickness throughout. Bake the cake, rotating the baking sheet back to front about halfway through the baking, for 18 to 24 minutes, or until the top is pale golden brown and springs back when pressed in the center with your fingertips and the cake doesn't stick to your fingers. Let the cake cool in the pan on the wire rack for about 5 minutes.

12. Line a large cutting board with parchment. Run a paring knife around the edge of the still-warm cake to release it from the sides of the baking sheet, and invert the cake onto the parchment. Carefully peel off the parchment and allow the cake to cool completely. Using a chef's knife, cut the cake in half crosswise and then in half lengthwise. You should now have four cake layers each about 5½ x 8 in / 14 x 20 cm. Cut the cardboard so that its dimensions are just slightly larger than the cake layer dimensions.

13. ***To Make the Soaking Syrup:*** In a small bowl, stir together the coffee and sugar until the sugar has dissolved.

14. Using the pastry brush, brush the top of all four cake rectangles evenly with the soaking syrup, using up all of the syrup.

15. Place one cake layer, syrup side up, on the prepared cardboard rectangle. In a medium bowl, using a mixer or a whisk, whip the heavy cream until it holds very firm, stiff peaks. Fold in the pastry cream until well combined. Using the offset spatula, spread about one-third of the cream mixture over the cake layer. There is a tendency for the cream to mound in the center, so be sure to spread the cream out to the edges of the cake. In fact, to make the best-looking cake possible, it is better if the cream layer is slightly thicker along the edge than in the center.

16. Place a second cake layer, syrup side up, on top of the cream layer and press down gently so the cake layer is level. Using the offset spatula, spread about half of the remaining cream mixture over the cake layer. Again, you want to spread the cream a bit thicker along the edge of the rectangle to prevent the final cake from doming.

17. Place a third cake layer, syrup side up, on top of the cream and press down slightly to level the cake. Using the offset spatula, spread the remaining cream mixture over the cake, again making it a bit thicker along the edges than in the center. Top the cake with the final cake layer, syrup side up, and press down gently so that the top layer is flat. Lightly wrap the cake with plastic wrap, place in the freezer, and freeze for about 8 hours or up to overnight, or until it is frozen solid. (At this point, the cake can instead be put into the freezer just until it has firmed up and then it can be well wrapped and frozen for up to 2 weeks.)

18. At least 3 hours in advance of serving, remove the cake from the freezer and place it on a cutting board. Using a chef's knife dipped in very hot water, trim the edges of the cake so that they are neat and even. (These trimmings make for great snacking.) Dip and wipe the knife clean several times as you trim to make sure you get a neat, sharp edge on the cake. Trim the cardboard underneath so it is flush with the cake.

19. Place the cake on its cardboard base on a cooling rack set on a baking sheet. Pour the warm ganache over the top of the cake. Using the offset spatula, spread the ganache in an even layer. It will begin to firm up right away when it hits the cold cake, so work quickly to even the surface. Let the excess ganache drip down the sides of the cake, leaving some parts of the cake exposed. Let the ganache set for several seconds, then transfer the cake to a serving plate. Let the cake thaw at room temperature before serving.

—*Annabelle Blake, Flour Bakery and Café*

Connecticut Clam Chowder Screams Bloody Murder

IT'S NOT FAIR, this regional bullying, this bloodying of the knees of a bivalve, the stealing of its salty lunch money. Let's split its hinged parts with nothing but our tongues, imagine the sediment we find there to be code that, once cracked, will finally tell us the difference between a region and a state.

When your uncle speaks of Connecticut Clam Chowder, he may also speak of sagittal planes, of gills that have become ctenidia—deluxe organs that allow these headless filter feeders to feed and breathe, of all things who bury themselves in a seabed. He will say nothing of New England, or of domineering mothers who steal recipes from their children, call them their own.

Here, orange is an air-raid siren, and green are the spruce needles that clog its megaphone, overtake its warning. Your uncle tells us that the ocean's getting bigger, but you're not sure yet what he means.

Yes, we use potato, onion, celery, possibly corn, certainly salt pork (*never bacon, never bacon*). Your ancestors, and mine, traveled to this country with the pigs. Because of the rain, the winds, the hurricanes, because our houses are destroyed and rebuilt, because in 1897 (a date your uncle still talks about while cursing this ocean, muttering about the superiority of the Pacific—something his own father would have dismissed as blasphemy punishable by the lash), the weather *prevailed with uniform severity throughout Connecticut,* and July 13 and 14 were no longer known as Tuesday and Wednesday but as *the 30 Hours Rain,* and because *crops are ruined* and *the highways are dangerously washed,* and *all rivers are greatly swollen,* and *factories have been compelled to shut down,* and *railroads have experienced considerable trouble*, because of all of this, and because of your uncle's "weakening mind, awful hands" (as your aunt calls it), he tells us loose stories of folks who lost their acres of potato and onion and possibly corn, folks who couldn't receive their processed pigs by road or their clams by train, folks who lost their sons and daughters to rivers named Pawcatuck and water named Oxoboxo, and water named Little and water named Hope, and it's all we can do to listen while waiting for the chowder to come to the kind of simmer we can believe in. The kind that whispers the name of our state, that reclaims, in the face of all this climate, the things we've—and not the whole fucking region—invented.

Because the ocean is milky gray and the sky is milky gray, and because your uncle's eyes are giving in to cataracts and he can no longer tell a quahog from a surf, an Atlantic jackknife from a grooved carpet shell, we add carrot for color, and parsley for a different kind of color. In spite of the narrative, neither does your uncle's eyes any good. Your uncle is getting frustrated. He is not happy with the "New Englanders." He tells you—and you tell me—that he's beginning to feel murderous. He's stopped caring about the clams. He calls them the food of the poor. He begins reading everything he can about Charles Manson, searching for any connection between mania and Connecticut.

Your aunt shells forty clams, palms the window glass over the kitchen sink. She says something about how we all need to clean ourselves of the sand, or whatever it is we choose to bury ourselves in for warmth. She says something about the seabed as down blanket. The down blanket as the thing we stuff into our ears when the pigs are screaming in the cold. Our bodies, she says, are seabed to our blood. Outside of us, our blood freezes as water does—at (for this time of year) a downright balmy 32 degrees Fahrenheit. Our skin is a thermal barrier. It keeps our soup warm. Your aunt stirs the soup, chops, neurotically, the parsley. Your uncle tells us that Charles Manson once believed his blood to be clam chowder, that he had rubbery things floating within him, intermittently slowing and speeding the electrical impulses in his body. In this weather, water freezes, and the stuff inside us thickens noticeably, becomes a little crazy.

Many argue that the Connecticut Clam Chowder, the obvious

basis for the New England variety, differs now from the popular, all-encompassing, dumbed-down version. Connecticut Clam Chowder still honors the early colonial preparation—made with milk and not cream, and never any thickening agents. The role of the milk is one of fortification—is blanket and thermal barrier and salve (to say nothing of mother)—not one of flavor enhancement. As such, there needs to be twice as much clam stock as milk. Your aunt is careful about this. We can see her own hands beginning to shake as she downturns the cardboard container into the stockpot—the container that your uncle, in spite of the instructions, opened from the wrong side.

Connecticut Clam Chowder should bear a thin consistency and a grayish color—not that of the ivory goop that calls itself after New England. Not that of your uncle's iris as he laments that he no longer has the eyesight to be an efficient killer. Your aunt stirs, sighs. It's she who has to slaughter the pigs now. Craziness thickens.

Always salt pork. Never bacon. *Never* as a rule to be broken. *Never* as the banks of a river that, year after year, break their promise. Connecticut keeps trying, your aunt tells me, to make its clam chowder "bigger" than the New England variety, in spite of the thinner broth. "More clam flavor," she says, as the 2 percent spills across the Formica. Your uncle licks the clamshells for their calcium carbonate, tries to calm the burning in his chest. Outside, a pig is orphaned, and the rain confuses itself with snow, the ocean with the river, trying to run, like any old tributary, into the widening spaces of a loved one's brain. Your uncle tells us, these clams have been around for 500 million years, but there's no honor in longevity anymore—not in the face of our blades. You confess you don't know if he's talking about Manson again, or the way we so easily scoop the meat from the shell with the soup spoon—so much duller, but so much more convenient here than the knife.

The Algonquians named the state Quinnehtukqut, or *beside the long tidal river.* Your uncle tries to bullshit me, gives me some line about *connect* and *cut*, about how the state, if in name only, is confused as to whether to bind or to sever. It's the I, he says, that joins these two parts of our state. It's the state as schizophrenic. It's the self as another kind of bivalve, protecting another nickel of rubbery meat.

The bind, the sever: From 1978 to 1987, the Connecticut River Valley was plagued by the Connecticut River Valley Killer. Your uncle picks the *brunoise* of carrot from the broth with his fingers, works its softness against the roof of his mouth with his tongue. He still remembers these numbers. Seven homicides—all women, all by knife. The first: twenty-seven stab wounds. She was watching the birds when the first one hit. Watching the birds, your uncle says, through all twenty-seven. In their tweeting, an awful catastrophe given in to aria. A washing away of the seabed. A grayish sky. The music of the simmer. A soup spoon ringing the lip of a bowl with moose on it. The burnt tongue. The split valve. A region usurping a state. The state bleeding the thinner soup.

In our blood running away from us is retreat. In our blood freezing within us is some greater permanence. Your aunt is the one who tells us: the salt pork cuts more easily when frozen. How many spoonfuls, batches, narratives does it take until we are finally solid? Like winter, craziness thickens blood to blood.

The final murder: January. A terrible snowstorm. 11.4 inches. A snowplow driver discovering her abandoned car. Her body frozen at the base of an apple tree. The cores yellowing. The skins soft and red. The flesh grayish as our chowder, the juice thinner than our shock.

The white of an apple is essentially an enlarged floral hypanthium, a fusing together of the bases of the organism's sepals, petals, and stamens. According to Elizabeth A. George's and Margaret Pieroni's *Verticordia: The Turner of Hearts*, this violent fusion of flower parts often involves the usurping of a stamen with a "fringed anther appendage clasping in the front, somewhat resembling a clam." In this, you wonder about the body dump, the message therein, the communication between human anatomy and that of the apple, and that of the dish your aunt stirs with such an undulating delicacy that it can only be called *loving*. The state as the apple, the region as this whole fucking orchard.

Sometimes, the hypanthium of a flower can be so deep within its anatomy, can have such a narrow top, that the flower can trick us into believing it has an inferior ovary. These are programmed to attract the attention of a very narrow and specific audience, by duping said audience into believing that they are like-minded, like-bodied. Orchids, for example. Our chowder to the residents of our state, for another. Lover to lover. Which the killer, the victim?

Holding the wooden spoon, her wrist moves like a river that has never claimed a life. The Connecticut River Valley killings remain unsolved. And we're still looking for a way to identify our own soup. Your uncle kisses your aunt for the first time this month. She looks shocked as the ant who, accustomed to lifting such large things onto its back, finds its first too-heavy fruit.

The chowder as too heavy, as the opposite of distillate. As obscuring the original seabed. As a fight to stake our claim by any means necessary. As the commingled saliva drying on your aunt's lips. As usurping our beautiful confessions. Murder as a delusion of grandeur. For both parties. This chowder as inadequate bandage for such bloody knees. Which Darwin's orchid, and which the moth with the 33-centimeter proboscis?

Somewhere, a river is still liquid, runs into the Atlantic with a sound like an early boiling. You tell me that Connecticut lunch laws demand that an employer provide a thirty-minute break only after an employee has worked 7.5 consecutive hours. Your aunt tells me that it takes a good four hours to prepare a proper Connecticut Clam Chowder. You tell me that it's best after it sits for at least two days.

Your uncle cries himself to sleep, drops his book to the peach shag. Your aunt tells us that clams are miracles—they respire by means of siphons, they shoot their breaths like stars, their shells used by the Algonquians as money. She tells us this, then sits next to your uncle on the couch. The chowder cools in the stockpot, develops itself for tomorrow and the next day, and the day after that. You know: Connecticut was the fifth state accepted into the union. Your uncle is on his thirteenth *sorry*. Your aunt reads a book on whales.

Creamy Cape Cod Clam Chowder

On Cape Cod, clam chowder means quahog chowder. Quahogs are large hard-shell clams, also known as chowder clams, and they are abundant on the Cape. Quahogs have a wonderful flavor that results in distinctive chowder. Chowder is a dish of humble origins and it often relies on "found foods" like fish that you catch yourself or clams that you dig. Clam chowder is like apple pie, everyone has his or her concept of what it should be like (usually people like their mother's version best). In the spirit of true home-style chowder making, this recipe depends on potatoes to lightly thicken the chowder; no other starch is added. My version uses salt pork, which adds a mild richness to the chowder; you can substitute bacon for a smokier flavor. This chowder can be served in small cups as a starter or in larger bowls as a main course. Serve toasted Common Crackers, Pilot crackers, or oyster crackers on the side for a little crunch.

For equipment you will need a 4-to-6-quart pot with a tight-fitting lid, fine mesh strainer, wooden spoon, and a ladle.

10 pounds small quahogs or large cherrystone clams
4 ounces meaty salt pork, rind removed, cut in small (⅓-inch) dice

2 tablespoons unsalted butter
2 medium yellow onions (about 12 ounces) cut into ½-inch dice

2 cloves garlic, finely chopped
2 stalks of celery (4 ounces), cut into ⅓-inch dice
5 to 6 sprigs fresh thyme, leaves chopped (1 tablespoon)
1 large dried bay leaf
2 pounds Yukon gold, Maine, PEI or other all-purpose potatoes, cut into ½ to ¾ inch dice

2 cups heavy cream
¼ cup chopped fresh Italian parsley
Freshly ground black pepper
Kosher or sea salt

Making Ahead

All chowders improve after they are cooked, so allow at least an hour from the time the chowder is cooked until it is served. You can make this chowder 1 or 2 days in advance. Reheat it slowly; never let it boil.

1. Scrub the clams and rinse well. Place them in the large pot with 2 cups of water and turn heat to high and cover. After you see a little steam escape, let them cook for about 5 minutes. Quickly remove the lid and move the clams around in the pot so they cook evenly. Cover and cook for 5 minutes more, or until the clams open. Pour off the broth and reserve. After it has settled a bit, strain the broth, leaving the very bottom (½ inch) of broth in the container. You should have about 4 cups. Pick the clams from the shell and place in the refrigerator to chill, before dicing them into small (⅓-to-½-inch) pieces.

2. Heat a 4-to-6-quart heavy pot over low heat and add the salt pork. Let it cook until crispy and brown. Add the butter, onions, celery, thyme, and bay leaf. Sauté, stirring occasionally, with a wooden spoon, for about 10 minutes, until the onions are softened but not browned.

3. Add the potatoes and 4 cups of the reserved clam broth as well as an extra cup of water. The broth should just barely cover the potatoes; if it doesn't, add more broth or water. Turn the heat to high, cover the pot, and boil the potatoes vigorously for about 10 minutes, until they are soft on the outside but still firm in the center. Smash a few potatoes against the side of the pot to assist in lightly thickening chowder.

4. Remove the pot from the heat and stir in the cream and diced clams. Season with black pepper; you may not need salt (the clams usually add enough of their own). If you are serving the chowder within the hour, just let it sit and "cure." Otherwise, refrigerate it and cover it after it has completely chilled.

5. When ready to serve, reheat the chowder slowly over a medium heat. Do not let the chowder boil. Ladle into cups or bowls and sprinkle with parsley.

Makes 3 quarts: serves 12 as a first course or 6 to 8 as a main course.

—*Jasper White's Summer Shack*

MID-ATLANTIC

New York: Bagel

Maryland: Blue Crab

New Jersey: New Jersey Ripper

Pennsylvania: Philly Cheesesteak

Delaware: Dover Cake

At the Center of the Center of the New York Bagel

THIS IS AN ILLUSION of roundness, a flattened sphere, the rotund world squashed, as if beneath a loafer. At its middle, either a gaping zero, or the zero squashed—a flattened sphere within a flattened sphere, an eye swollen shut, having once seen the beautiful constellations in a stockpot of boiling water—as if something umbilical had been excised: our tether, perhaps, to every conflicting narrative in this state.

This is Homer and Aristotle finally compromising on the shape of the earth. We eat our bagels because they are not necessarily anything, not necessarily sweet, or savory. They are not trapped by the doughnut's severe identity, by our expectations of grease and confectioner's sugar. Here, we further the narrative by choice: Garlic? Cinnamon-raisin?

Today, this is who we are: circular, without origin or end; flat, so we can't roll easily away from our centers. Does this make us heliocentric? Geocentric? This is the bagel as a bumping-and-grinding of astronomical theory to theory . . . Who would say the bagel is ponderous? Who would say it is incantatory?

According to the American Academy for Jewish Research, the scriptures the Midrash and the Talmud and the Targum do "not think of a globe of the spherical earth, around which the sun revolves in 24 hours, but of a flat disk of the earth, above which the sun completes its semicircle in an average of 12 . . ." and one of the old great secrets of the Torah is that "the earth is usually described as a disk encircled by water."

In the bagel is zero, and its origin story—its rebellion against the other numbers, its refusal to behave like a 2 or an 11. Like zero, the bagel commands a strange reverence, belief or lack thereof. Aristotle liked to say that he did not believe in zero, and he would swagger as he told people this in one outdoor arena or another, the rainwater, susceptible to the cold and to Celsius's measurement of it, becoming ice in his beard.

Here, the zero—believe it or not—is geocentric. Just look at that manhole cover on Broadway, and that man popping from it, poking his head through the firmament, the hard hat reflecting our sun and neon advertisement, a fat bagel sandwich in his clean hand. Into this nothing, we shove everything; everything being blistered onion, garlic, caraway, poppy seed, sesame seed, and salt.

Into this narrative of everything comes dissent, belief and lack thereof; as if the pre-Socratic philosophers were jockeying with Columbus about the parameters of the planet: according to SeriousB, on the "Serious Eats" blog: "No, no, no—never caraway! It ruins it. Overwhelms the other flavors with its nastiness, and is a pain to chew too." Buffy agrees, as does BaglFreek, though HungryCristal just plain loves caraway and for some superlative reason refers to the everything bagel as the Hypertension Special, as if, in this flattened sphere, overly decorated, is some commentary on our quickly beating hearts.

* * *

HERE, WE SUSPEND the bagel in the sort of water that so opposes its shape, it cooks it, makes it ready for our mouths. In this is some treatise on the homogeneity in all repulsion—the perfect relationship of round and flat, of zero and the agent that boils it.

New Yorkers like to say that it's our water that makes our bagels taste so different, so good. Manhattan's early settlers siphoned their water from shallow, privately owned wells. According to NYC Environmental Protection:

> *In 1677 the first public well was dug in front of the old fort at Bowling Green. In 1776, when the population reached approximately 22,000, a reservoir was constructed on the east side of Broadway between Pearl and White Streets. Water pumped from*

wells sunk near the Collect Pond, east of the reservoir, and from the pond itself, was distributed through hollow logs laid in the principal streets. In 1800 the Manhattan Company (now The Chase Manhattan Bank, N.A.) sank a well at Reade and Centre Streets, pumped water into a reservoir on Chambers Street and distributed it through wooden mains to a portion of the community. In 1830 a tank for fire protection was constructed by the City at 13th Street and Broadway . . .

Here, the bagel is born in a fluid between Pearl and White, tries its damnedest to be immaculate, pure as hunger or crystal, to Collect its debated flavorings like burrows or boroughs, to cloak us from the rats who Chase other rats in the hollow logs, the wooden mains, themselves trying their damnedest, under our feet, to eat and couple and propagate their species as, birthed from the water that decorates their back fur, the bagel presses from the Chamber, defying fire by boiling, by wetness, emerges sleek and saturated, the testimony of its journey written silent in the gaping surprised zero at its Centre.

* * *

WHAT ELSE CAN we do but open our mouths in the sort of way that confuses hunger for communion? Today, the homeless man on the corner of Pearl and White, doubly all-inclusive, shouts about having had sex this morning with an everything bagel.

* * *

"THE THREE WATER collection systems," says NYC Environmental Protection, "were designed and built with various interconnections to increase flexibility by permitting exchange of water from one to another." Here, the embryonic bagel stretches its dough—the yeast, the little bit of sugar, little bit of salt, high gluten flour, and the room-temperature water—flexes its paste toward its fellows, considers the stack of ingredients that will soon top it or embed themselves within it, and soon, if we are patient, we can bite in the name of connection and exchange and flexibility, and take these things inside ourselves via the sort of breakfast we mistakenly dub as simple.

Here, we eat while walking. Escape is essential. Here, escape is both a slave to, and a salve for, pain. The hole in the bagel's center, it is believed, was created so that many bagels could be threaded onto a length of string and carried for great distances as sustenance to the persecuted cultures that had to flee the wrath of those who wished to destroy them. Here, zero accommodates the string, and feeds us. All it takes is a boiling point.

Bagel comes through Yiddish from the Old German, meaning first *to bend or bow*, then *a stirrup or ring*. Here, the bagel is so weighed down, we confuse, if only linguistically, its collapsing for genuflection. Which the weight of the narrative, which the sesame seeds? Here, we allow such a confusion to become a ring—the very thing that entraps us, becomes the symbol for a sacred union. It's easy to associate said confusion with the Jews and the Old Germans, harder to determine why the bagel, in seventeenth-century Krakow, was the most popular gift given to women in childbirth. Amniotic, umbilical, the bagel passes from one vessel into another . . .

* * *

In the 1970s, a New York Bloomingdale's began selling shellacked bagel jewelry, igniting what briefly became known in the city as the Poppy Seed Anniversary. Says Milton Berle, "We used to buy day-old bagels. They were so hard we had to hammer the butter on. Then my uncle came up with a brilliant idea. He went to Israel and made a fortune selling Cheerios as bagel seeds. If you believe either of the previous, there's some border property along the Golan Heights I'd like to sell you."

* * *

Every minute, enough Niagara River water pours over the Falls to make 640 million cups of coffee. This helps to wash down the 3 billion bagels eaten last year in the U.S. alone. New York City's water supply, in its long and storied history, has been contaminated by rodents, sewage, industrial waste, petroleum, Diet Mountain Dew bottles, Cheeto bags, Cheerio boxes, Genesee beer cans, rat shit, cat shit, dog shit, my shit and yours, rotting fish, steaks, pork chops, cellophane, guns, fertilizer, pesticides, glue, human bodies, and an "underground oil leak bigger than the *Exxon Valdez* spill," all coupling into a sludge that environmental scientists have dubbed "black mayonnaise," that includes, like our bagels that supposedly depend on this water for their goodness, "just about everything . . . seemingly just about everything."

"It's never going to be pristine," says Walter Mugdan, EPA official, and says John Lipscomb of the Riverkeeper clean water advocacy group, "It's a by-product of our society," and says environmental writer Verena Dobnik, "On the Queens side, the cries of seagulls fill the air as they swoop over a junkyard that sells scrap metal to China . . . and nature survives—just barely."

According to bagel expert Maria Balinska, in the Middle Ages,

> *Christians insisted that any kind of bread, given its connection with the person of Jesus Christ, should be denied Jews. The Christian mob began attacking any Jew with the temerity to continue to buy or bake bread. However the local ruler was a wise man and, having been petitioned by the local Jewish community, announced that it had been ruled that it was only what was baked could be properly called bread. The Jews promptly took the hint and departed to seek out a way to prepare wheat without baking. What they decided on was boiling and what resulted was the first batch of bagels ever made.*

As the Jews further became scapegoats for any sort of calamity (including the Black Death plague of 1348–9, during which Jews were hunted and murdered as a sort of sacrifice to the disease), they loaded their boiled bread rings onto rope and sticks and lit out for what they only believed would be greener pastures.

* * *

The homeless man on Pearl and White screams, "Fuck the pretzel!" and we hope he's not really going to do it.

* * *

In the 1970s, New Yorkers, deciding en masse to make sandwiches of their bagels, demanded a new recipe, a softer consistency, in order to "domesticate" what were often then colloquially known as "cement doughnuts" or "Brooklyn jawbreakers." According to *New York Times* writer Mimi Sheraton, "We became too lazy to chew," much less flee the city with only a string of bagels to sustain us.

Knead the dough for ten minutes until it is smooth and elastic. Let rise in a warm place for one hour, until the dough has doubled in size. If the dough rises too quickly, move it to a cold area (this process is called retardation). Punch the dough down . . .

Here, if we plunge into water either toxic or boiling, we can briefly leave this earth. Maria Balinska says, "The hole itself has intimations of eternity in the way it goes from being a finite space in the middle of the dough to an infinite space once you have finished eating the bagel! Heady stuff."

* * *

Materialists! You lack all sense. Your brain is maimed.
Do you think the bagel's more important than its essence?
Are you running from the spiritual idea? Its presence
Is indeed the central core and cause of every entity
Even of crude brass
So rude and crass
Just out of curiosity
Cut the brass in pieces and then with care
Slice the smallest sliver thin as hair
Then slowly further subdivide it like one divides the year
To months and days, hours, minutes, seconds. Isn't it quite clear

That now you're at the bagel hole, the rounded zero.
Do you grasp the thesis? Think! Now you have a mere 0.
Its profundity assess and cogitate!

—from "The Bagel Hole and Two Brass Buttons" by Yiddish poet Eliezer Shtaynbarg (1880–1932)

* * *

According to Encyclopedia Americana's *Cosmology*, "The Hebrews saw the earth as an almost flat surface consisting of a solid and a liquid part, and the sky as the realm of light in which heavenly bodies move."

In 2008, astronaut Gregory Chamitoff, on his space shuttle mission to the International Space Station, became the first person to take the bagel into outer space. He also shunned the caraway, and packed eighteen sesame seed bagels for the three-day trip. He did not load them onto rope or stick. Biting into his first, in zero gravity, ever-rising, he did not consider how the sun, reflecting from the surface of the Space Station, allows the structure, to us back here on terra firma, a brightness sixteen times greater than that of Venus. He did not consider the weightlessness of a single bubble of trapped air making for countless surfaces as the stockpots of the earth began to come to their boil.

In Manhattan, "95% of the total water supply is delivered to the consumer by gravity. Only about 5% of the water is regularly pumped to maintain the desired pressure."

This is the bagel as everything in need of a tether. This is the prayer that one day, all pressure can be determined by desire.

* * *

. . . cool on a wire rack.

* * *

According to the Food and Drug Administration, "there is no legal standard of identity for bagels in the United States. Bakers are thus free to call any bread torus a bagel, even those that deviate wildly from the original formulation."

According to John Mitzewich, in his article "Taking Things to a Hole New Level," the greatest mystery in the universe is "how people can eat un-toasted bagels."

Maria Balinska may wonder if *baker* and *boiler* can ever be the same thing again. In complex dynamics, a mathematical set of points whose boundary is a distinctive and easily recognizable shape, like a circle, is called a Mandelbrot Set.

If the toasting of the bagel is a shunning of its origins, the cutting of the cord, what other sorts of persecution can we forget via the addition of a second form of heat? How much temperature is required before we can double back on ourselves like a ring, until we can return to zero?

According to Camille Flammarion's *L'atmosphère: météorologie populaire*, the engraving on page 111, by an unknown artist, portrays a "cosmic machinery [that] bears a strong resemblance to traditional pictorial representations of the 'wheel in the middle of a wheel' described in the visions of the Hebrew prophet Ezekiel. One of the most significant features of the landscape is the tree, which some people have interpreted as the Kabbalistic Tree of Life." The caption beneath the engraving in Flammarion's book reads: "A missionary of the Middle Ages tells that he had found the point where the sky and the Earth touch . . ."

We bow and bow and run away. This means we're not yet broken. This means we're touching something. We look around and around for a filling meal, with people.

At the funeral home, spread on the table, apricot *rugelach*, chocolate-chip *mandelbrot* cookies, pyramids of bagels, lox flushed with shock, three different kinds of cream cheese and white plastic knives with which to spread it. If we are to spread it, we must first halve our bagels, but, like zero, they don't behave. Like zero halved, a halved bagel remains a bagel. We rebuild it with cream cheese and say nothing of brick or mortar or *haroset*, of building a harder purity from the sewage. All it takes is redefinition, as we turn from the dead to the food, tell ourselves *shhh* and *I'm sorry*, and speak of cycles and full circles and clear boundaries, the flatness of the face in death, the flatness of the lid that seals us in, and we chew, and through mouthfuls of bagels and everything on them, we say it again: *shhh* and *I'm so, so sorry* and *a better place*, and *it'll all be okay*, and we chew in cycles and circles and the minced onion is cooked so soft it hardly makes a sound against our teeth and this is good and this is ample and this is sufficient.

Bagel

Total Time: 2 hrs 15 mins
Working Time: 35 mins
Yield: 24 bagels

Ingredients

3 cups warm water (110 degrees F)
½-ounce packet active dry yeast (about 5 teaspoons)
8 cups bread flour
4 tablespoons malt syrup
4 teaspoons kosher salt
5 teaspoons fine sugar
Vegetable oil to coat bowl
Sesame seeds, poppy seeds, kosher salt or dried onions

Instructions

1. Place the warm water in a bowl and dissolve the yeast completely; set aside. Combine flour, malt syrup, and salt in the bowl of an upright mixer fitted with a dough hook attachment. Add yeast mixture.

2. Mix on low until the loose flour has been worked into the dough and the dough looks shredded, about 2 minutes. Increase the speed to medium low and continue mixing until the dough is stiff, smooth, and elastic, about 8 to 9 minutes more. (If the dough gets stuck on the hook or splits into 2 pieces, stop the machine, scrape off the hook, and mash the dough back into the bottom of the bowl.) The dough should be dry, not tacky or sticky, and somewhat stiff.

3. Shape the dough into a ball, place it in a large oiled bowl, and turn it to coat in oil. Cover the bowl with a damp towel and let the dough rise in a warm place, until it springs back when you poke it, about 20 minutes. (It will not rise that much.)

4. Heat the oven to 425 degrees F and arrange the rack in the middle. Fill a large, wide, shallow pan (about 3 to 6 quarts) with water, bring to a boil over high heat, then reduce heat to medium low and let simmer. Cover until you're ready to boil the bagels. Line a baking sheet with parchment paper greased with oil or cooking spray. Place a metal rack inside a second baking sheet and set aside.

5. Turn the risen dough out onto a dry surface. Divide the dough into 24 equal pieces, about 3 ounces each. (While you work, keep the dough you're not handling covered with a damp towel to prevent drying.) Roll each piece into a 9-inch-long rope, lightly moisten the ends with water, overlap the ends by about 1 inch, and press to join so you've created a bagel. As necessary, widen the hole in the middle so it is approximately the size of a quarter. Cover the shaped bagels with a damp towel and let rest 10 minutes.

6. After resting, stretch the dough to retain the quarter-size hole (the dough will have risen a bit) and boil the bagels 3 or 4 at a time, making sure they have room to bob around. Cook for about 30 seconds on each side until the bagels have a shriveled look, then remove to the baking sheet with the rack in it. Adjust heat as necessary so the water stays at a simmer.

7. Brush the bagels with water then sprinkle with toppings as desired. Arrange the bagels on the baking sheet lined with parchment paper about 1 inch apart and bake. Rotate the pan after 15 minutes and bake until the bagels are a deep caramel color and have formed a crust on the bottom and top, about 10 minutes more. Remove from the oven and let cool on a rack for at least 30 minutes so the interiors finish cooking and the crusts form a chewy exterior.

—Evan Giniger, Kossar's

MARYLAND

The Dawning of the Blue Crab

LIKE THAT OF the Cassiopeia jellyfish, the Maryland blue crab's intestinal tract ties itself into an orchid. Your uncle, on indefinite leave from the day-boats, squirts ointment over the net scars on his hands, tells you that thc orchid, our sexiest of flowers, has nothing to do with femininity or, more specifically, your aunt in the kitchen, dressed in what she half-jokingly calls her "uniform," as she drops crab after crab into the kind of steam that reminds you more of industry than clouds.

Your aunt knows more about sexual dimorphism than she'd care to admit. She hums the song she learned in school so many years ago, the one about the difference between male and female blue crabs:

The belly of the male
is skinny and stale
like the Washington Monument, no less!
The belly of the girl
is rounder than a pearl
like the Capitol Dome of the U.S.!

You wonder if the crab is more patriotic or blasphemous. If those crabs necklacing the shore of Isle of Wight Bay are only lying dormant, like the orchid—its flowers fading, the petals falling from the stem—or are really dead. Since his days off, Uncle, your aunt says, likes to be as inactive as possible. She tells you that the jellyfish, by the way that they float, see our world as upside down. You watch the blue crabs rise to the top of the water. You watch Uncle stare at the ceiling. You wonder if, to the jellyfish, *belly-up* means *alive.*

Over the pot, your aunt's hands redden like the crabs from other states. Here, our crabs evoke ocean, sky, your aunt's throat jeweled in her wedding sapphire, the bodies of the scab watermen found littered along the shore with too much ocean in their lungs. Your aunt doesn't say, *serves them right,* doesn't think of sexy flowers that fake their own deaths, of nets that tear the limbs from men like your uncle. She flexes her fingers into the kitchen light. The red fades from her palms. You know: no one tears a blue crab leg from its body like your aunt. To commune with the crabs, and to avoid jealousy of what your aunt calls "their uncomplicated lives," according to familial mythology and superstition she eats blueberries while cooking them, wipes the juice from her lips with a red sponge in the shape of a claw.

Here, to be boiled is to be uncomplicated. Uncle dozes on the yellow couch, having the nightmare again about the Blue Crab Crisis of 2009—the declining stocks of female crabs, the deep-catch restrictions, the $7.5 million in federal disaster aid that went, as Uncle says, "more to the watermen who agreed to quit crabbing, who snuck into the yards at night and hauled away our fucking pots"—his snoring sounding to you less and less oceanic as the dream progresses.

Your aunt smooths her "uniform," the image of the cross-eyed crab wandering too close to the pot, the bubble-lettered "Don't Bother Me, I'm Crabby" bunching at her middle. She says nothing about *a child of her own,* never calls you *my sister's kid.* The crabs cool, right side up to a Cassiopeia, on a bluer dishtowel next to the sink. Your aunt knows that, whether male or female, the belly of the blue crab is called an *apron.* In Maryland, we all know the apron is inedible.

Maryland, with the blue crab, is one of only three states to name a state crustacean (along with Louisiana's crawfish and Oregon's Dungeness crab), state officials convening over the course of a week in 1989 in order to determine this, make it official. Soon after this declaration, after the fanfare and festivals, bandstands and carnival rides, the blue crab catch dropped from an estimated 126,000 tons to 27,000 tons, with revenue subsequently dwindling. While the blue crab, as state crustacean, got a new title, so did the equipment of the crabbers. The abandoned traps piling up on the docks and shorelines of Maryland became known as *ghost pots*.

* * *

HERE, WE BOIL or steam our blue crabs in seawater and in white vinegar and in a half-cup of Old Bay seasoning, at least. The Old Bay mission statement declares that "Blue crabs are our raison d'être (ask your French philosopher friends)," which means that, as your aunt says, "Old Bay assumes we're stupid."

You can tell by his snores. Uncle is dreaming again of fishing with Frantz Fanon, the French-Algerian philosopher and existential humanist who wrote on the "colonial subjugation of people identified as black," who died in Maryland, and who ate, Uncle insists, a last meal of blue crab. In spite of your uncle's insistence, your aunt says that Fanon was not speaking of the resurgence of the Maryland blue crab industry when he said, in a 1959 speech, "Certain ochres and blues, which seemed forbidden to all eternity in a given cultural area, now assert themselves without giving rise to scandal."

* * *

IN BINOMIAL NOMENCLATURE, the Maryland blue crab is *Callinectes sapidus*, or *beautiful, savory swimmer*. Like anything, we define it for its looks, actions, flavor. You wonder how to define this: throughout the past decade, the U.S. has seen over five hundred commercial fishing deaths, with over a quarter of these documented in the waters around Maryland, and over half of these involving the fishing of crustaceans, state or otherwise.

Scandal: In 2009, much of that $7.5 million in federal disaster aid went to the scab watermen of Maryland, who earned as much as $400 per day cleaning the docks and shorelines of the dead fishermen's washed-up ghost pots. In 2010, Maryland received another $2.5 million in federal aid to help out-of-work crabbers start oyster farms instead. In 2011, twenty-five out of every twenty-six oyster farms failed due to, according to the *Baltimore Sun*, "a slow start," "a cumbersome approval process," and "red tape." According to the *Chesapeake Quarterly*, "only five companies are listed as currently growing and selling oysters in Maryland's Chesapeake Bay." Your uncle, in dream, spits toward the ceiling. Your aunt, cooking, dries her hands on her apron. At her belly, only a cross-eyed crab, a stupid phrase. Not that it matters in this kitchen, but Maryland is the wealthiest state in the nation. In this way, even the state that encompasses us seems so far away.

* * *

MARYLAND IS NAMED for Queen Henrietta Maria of France. The slave ship the *Henrietta Marie*, which in 1700 deposited 191 captive Africans in the "New World" before sinking on its return trip to England, was also named after the woman we sometimes call Our Maryland Queen. When he wakes up, Uncle says that a starving blue crab will often eat its own excrement. You imagine the catch of the dead fishermen, hungry, waiting in their traps for the federally employed "crisis" watermen to dispose of them. You imagine the few still living, their hepatopancreases flashing yellow in their intestinal tracts. Tangled like this, they can't tell which is ocean, which sky. You think that, in this state, if they could summon the energy, any comparison of their bodies to the stupid hibernating orchids should make them angry.

Your aunt wants to say something about the crisis in the body. How in delicacy is some awful prediction, a future doing without. Your aunt bites her lip. You can't tell if this is anger or sadness. She speaks of eating so much of this hepatopancreas as a girl, when she called it, as most Marylanders do, the blue crab's *mustard*, once a coveted delicacy of Chesapeake Bay. That this part of the crab, if eaten in high doses, has been found to be responsible for countless miscarriages and cases of infertility among the women in Chesapeake Bay is something neither your aunt nor your uncle wishes to talk about at the supper table.

You know, because you've watched it hundreds of times. Though you haven't yet eaten, you know that, once you've finished your meal, your aunt will retain the crab shells and bodies for stock. You know: when she scoops, with two fingers, the mustard into the trash can, she will bite her lip, close her eyes, hold her breath.

Because the blue crab mustard contaminates the boiling broth, the Maryland Department of Health, neurotically and redundantly, says, "These liquids should be discarded. Do not use the cooking liquid. We want to protect people." Even the most erudite of your French philosopher friends may be baffled by Old Bay's declaration that the cooking liquid can be retained for its Maryland Crab Soup.

* * *

Our Maryland Queen said, "If the wind is favorable, I shall set off tomorrow . . . I am hazarding my life, that I may incommode your affairs . . . If I die, believe that you will lose a person who has never been other than entirely yours, and who by her affection has deserved that you should not forget her." Twenty-eight years later, we named a slave ship after her.

Your aunt watches the steam freeze onto the kitchen window, the ice collect on the pots in the yard. Strange, she thinks, how we turn red when we both burn and freeze. The steam will fade before the ice melts. We will remember no details about either.

Up the road in Crisfield, the residents prepare for the 66th Annual Hard Crab Derby. This year's events include a crab cooking contest, a crab picking contest, an arm wrestling contest, a hard crab derby race, an open air religious service, and "Fireworks!!" Offshore, the escapee blue crabs begin to regenerate their lost legs. Your aunt says, "And they don't have to pray to do it."

* * *

Besides the steam and the snow, other things that redden your aunt's hands: a childhood sting from the Cassiopeia jellyfish; an allergy to the orchid and an addiction to its beauty. The one thing that turns a blue crab red is cooking it. Here, *red* is when something blue is done, and *done* is when something is ready to eat.

* * *

Here, you learn in school early, the process by which water becomes steam is called the enthalpy of vaporization. If further heat is applied, the substance can reach the critical temperature at which distinct liquid and vapor phases no longer exist. Though you're no expert on thermodynamics, you imagine the resulting substance, which is said to "effuse through solids like a gas, and dissolve materials like a liquid." You imagine the stockpot and everything in it, your supper and everything your supper reminds you of: the venom of the Cassiopeia, the sapphire at your aunt's throat, the sepals of the Coerulea orchid, the seasoning, the broth, the crab . . . At the critical temperature these are all one thing.

Uncle says that when something blue burns, it turns red. When something red dies, it turns blue. In this, you sense a nebulous commentary on both Maryland priority and the last meal of the day. In this, you know that *nebulous* and *critical* can be the same thing.

Like your hands and your uncle's, your aunt's hands will bleed when she eats blue crab. Your uncle will measure his net scars against the viscera of the blue crab, say nothing about capitols or monuments, but, as if reaching for anything sweeter and thriving, mutter, "honeycomb, honeycomb," between bites.

According to the K–12 Education: Blue Crab online resource, "The outside parts of a blue crab are hard. Inside the crab, are the soft parts. Crabs must shed their shells in order to grow." Luckily, Uncle says, we're soft on the outside too. If he shed his scars, he knows: that means he's decomposing. Your aunt knows, even while trying to commune. When carrying fertilized eggs, the female blue crab is called by marine biologists and fishermen alike a sponge crab, or a berry crab. Your aunt wipes the juice from her lips.

"Why are blue crabs blue?" ask the K–12ers. They ask the same of the sky.

* * *

"It was dawn," Frantz Fanon said (and Uncle believes he was predicting his own journey to, and subsequent end in, Maryland), "The combat between day and night [and Uncle imagines the heyday, the boats knocking against one another like castanets, squealing like the boiling crab]. Exhausted from the struggle, the night slowly breathed its last sigh [and your uncle sighs and tucks his napkin into his collar, and your aunt sighs and picks up a knife]. A few rays of sun heralding the victory of daylight hovered timid and pale on the horizon [and the ocean out the window is thinner than our blood] while the last stars slipped under the bank of clouds [and the steam and the steam] the color of flame trees in flower."

On the dish towel—the bluest you've ever seen, you now think—the crabs drain. The seasoned water meanders from their bodies into wet loops on the cotton. Your aunt tries to whistle but no sound comes out. There is nothing floral about this.

Blue Crab

Bring water to a boil in steamer pot

Add live crabs and J.O. crab spice (the spice is available from J.O. Spice Company, Inc., 3721– 25 Old Georgetown Road, Baltimore, Maryland 21227: Phone: 410-247-5205)

Steam crabs 12–15 minutes

It's that simple for one of Maryland's finest foods

—Jimmy Cantler's Riverside Inn

The New Jersey Ripper according to Google

NEW:

- *Breaking news*
- *Fox News*
- *ABC News*
- *The New York Times*
- *Daily News America*
- *New York Post*
- *Deliver Peace of Mind. Make customers happy by protecting their purchases. NEW is the industry leader in extended service plans.*
- *The New Yorker*
- *New Hampshire*
- *New Testament (*Although Christians hold different views . . .*)*
- *New World*
- *What is Newton's Second Law?*
- *New England Journal of Medicine*
- *New College of Florida (*Top-ranked, located in beautiful Sarasota . . .*)*
- *New girl on FOX (*. . . is an offbeat and adorable girl in her late 20s who, after a bad break-up, moves in with three single guys. Goofy, positive, vulnerable, and honest to a . . .*)*
- *Dallas Morning News*
- *What is Newton's First Law?*
- *New Advent (*I can't really say the new movie 42 is about Jackie Robinson. The movie never really gets into the heart and soul of the man . . .*)*
- *New Museum (*respected internationally . . .*)*

- *Newgrounds: Everything, By Everyone (*Club a Seal, Teletubby Fun Land and Pico*)*
- *Astrophysics Authors/Titles (*We present new high-precision measurements of the opacity of the intergalactic and circumgalactic medium (IGM, CGM) at <z>=2.4 . . .*)*
- *New Relic (*Pinpoint and solve performance issues in your Ruby*)*
- *New Jersey (*New Jersey voters initially refused to ratify the constitutional amendments banning slavery and granting rights to the United States' black population . . . In 1962, the world's first nuclear-powered cargo ship, the NS Savannah, was launched at Camden . . . race riots . . . no income tax . . . assassination . . . Telugu spoken prominently in Middlesex County . . . approved casino . . . Jersey oak has been used extensively in shipbuilding . . . turnpike . . . Faulkner Act . . . downgrade the Death Row prisoners' sentences from "Death" . . . Born to Run . . . is said to be haunted by strange, ghostly people who jump out from behind trees at cars traveling down the unpaved portion of the road . . . ground penetrating radar . . . Teamsters . . . Lenape tribe slaughter . . . Lenape means "Human Beings" . . . and the SS Morro Castle beached itself near Asbury Park after going up in flames while at sea . . . State Bird: Goldfinch . . . State Insect: European Honey Bee . . . State Dance: Square Dance . . . State Soil: Downer*)*
- *What is Newton's Third Law?*
- *Hacker News*
- *Discovery News*
- *New limited color diversity in fleshy fruits on local and global scales*
- *Is news the plural of new?*
- *New is the new old*
- *New is not news*
- *Who is Newton?*
- *"SHOPPING" FOR* **NEW**
  - *New Balance Minimus*
  - *New Moon Book*
  - *New Phones*
  - *New Skylanders*
  - *New iPad*
  - *New Saxophone*

- *New Versailles Vinyl Raised Garden Bed*
- *New Hunter Fan 21434 Sonora 52 Inch Ceiling Fan with Whisper Wind Motor*
- *New Kryptonite U-Lock Fahgettaboudit Mini with Sliding Dust Cover*
- *New Age Pet Rustic Style Lodge XL*
- *New Trophy Ridge Sure Shot Pro Rest Large Black Left Hand Apache Drop Away Arrow Rest Super Quick with Whisper Quiet Operation, no matter what*
- *OvaCue New Fertility Monitor*
- *New Prescription: The New Morning-After Pill*
- *New Miscarriage Therapy: When Grief Becomes Depression*
- *New Baby*

✦ *SEARCHES RELATED TO* NEW

- *New synonym*
- *New songs*
- *New DVD releases*
- *New movie releases*
- *New movies*
- *New C++*
- *New balance*
- *New definition*
- *New sounds like No*

JERSEY:

✦ *Jerseylicious*

✦ *Jersey Mike's*

✦ *Jersey Boys*

✦ *In Jersey, Pop Tarts are Crazy Good*

✦ *Jersey Shore Season 6 (*The roommates describe how their trademark acronyms can also be used as "Guido Math . . ." The roommates worry about digging a hole on the beach . . . JWOWW says her final goodbye in the Confessional Room.*)*

✦ *New Jersey Commission on Holocaust Education (*EXCITING NEWS: Ceremony at Cumberland County College, Vineland, New Jersey commemorating the contribution by the Raab family toward providing materials to the Holocaust/Genocide Resource Center*)*

- *New Jersey Lottery: Give Your Dreams a Chance*
- *Official Jerseys*
  - *MLB*
  - *NHL*
  - *NBA*
  - *FFA (*Preparing young people for leadership and careers in agriculture: Lapel Slogan [replete with sun and dove]: Soar to New Heights*)*
- *Jersey Grown Shrubs*
- *The Real Housewives of New Jersey*
- *Throwback Sports Jersey: Orlando Cepeda*
- *New Jersey State Bar Association (*Attend Hurricane Sandy Response Program or Experience the Westin Excelsior Rome at Mid-Year Meeting*)*
- *Jersey Jack Pinball (*We are committed to exclusively building full-sized, full featured commercial arcade pinball machines and we are the only current manufacturer of Pinball Machines in the United States with that Mission . . . The most important role Jack can be is our customer, a Pinball Player. To take the root of what is best loved, true mechanical action married to the latest technology where we build our games with Passion, not with a Calculator*)*
- *New Jersey Redevelopment Authority (*Our mission is to provide a unique approach to revitalization efforts in New Jersey's cities [According to the NJRA Board Minutes dated October 25, 2012, the sole duty accomplished at that meeting was the approval of the minutes of the June 26, 2012, meeting and Cosmo Iacavazzi abstained even from that]*)*
- *Jobs4Jersey*
- *Edible Jersey*
- *Jersey is a Knit Fabric. It Was Originally Made of Wool But Is Now Made of Synthetic Fibres*
- *What is Jersey Jerusalem?*
- *Who is Jersey Green?*

- *New Jersey Future*
- *New Jersey Heroes*
- *New Jersey Cultural Trust*
- *New Jersey is:*
    - *"a valley of humility squeezed between two mountains of conceit." —Ben Franklin*
    - *"having tomatoes growing in your backyard." —Tony Ciavaglia*
    - *"the idea of hitting a jackpot." —Jerry Schneidman*
    - *"tired of being the brunt of jokes." —Jerome Premo*
    - *"picking up the garbage, trimming trees." —James Keyes*
    - *"one hell of an attractive combination." —Malcolm Forbes*
    - *"humble no more." —Richard McMullen*
    - *"Cheaper." —Leslie Walten*
- *Jersey Equine*
- *Jersey Cows*
- *Channel Island of Jersey: High Butterfat Content*
- *New Jersey Drought*
- *New Jersey Academy for Aquatic Sciences*
- *Best Hospitals in New Jersey*
- *New Jersey Herald Birth Announcements*
- *New Jersey Infant Car Seat Laws*
- *New Jersey Infant Feeding Guide*
- *New Jersey Infant Toddler Credential*
- *New Jersey Infant Adoption*
- *New Jersey Infantry + Civil War*
- *New Jersey Infant Mortality Rate*
- *New Jersey Dad Guilty in Baby Bridge Death*
- *New Jersey Couple Admit Causing Teething Infant's Death By Rubbing Heroin on Her Gums*
- *Where is Jersey now?*
- *Worst Hospitals in New Jersey*
- *"RECIPES" FOR* **JERSEY**
    - *Jersey Flashlight (*a classic mixed drink of apple whiskey, lemon peel, Angostura bitters, and hot water that is set on fire while mixing*)*
    - *Buttered Jersey Royals with Parsley, Mint, and Chives (*Made

with the first young Jersey Royal potatoes, or some well-flavoured mainland variety such as Pentland Javelin*)*

- ✧ *Jersey Summer Salsa (*Tomatoes, peaches, and corn . . .*)*
- ✧ *The Jersey Lightning (*Death & Co. Applejack, Tea-infused Vermouth, lemon juice, sugar cubes, soda water . . .*)*
- ✧ *The New Jersey Ripper (*Deep-fried hot dog, so named because its skin tears when pulled from the oil bath*)*

- ✦ *SEARCHES RELATED TO* **JERSEY**
  - ✧ *New Jersey Devils*
  - ✧ *New Jersey Zip Code*
  - ✧ *Miniature Jersey Cow*
  - ✧ *Lord Love Jersey*
  - ✧ *Jersey Sex Tube*
  - ✧ *New Jersey Roach Infestation*
  - ✧ *Trimester Obsession Jersey Skirt: Miracle Maternity*
  - ✧ *Made in Jersey*
  - ✧ *New Jersey Death Fest*

RIPPER:

- ✦ *Jack the Ripper*
- ✦ *The Yorkshire Ripper*
- ✦ *The Rostov Ripper*
- ✦ *Atlanta Ripper*
- ✦ *John the Ripper*
- ✦ *Joel "The Ripper" Rifkin*
- ✦ *Tim "Ripper" Owens (*Heavy metal singer*)*
- ✦ *Kirk "The Ripper" Hammett (*Heavy metal guitarist*)*
- ✦ *"The Ripper" Paul Burchill (*Professional wrestler based on Jack the Ripper whose finishing move is the C-4*)*
- ✦ *Ripper mutant kangaroo–human hybrid*
- ✦ *Ripper the bulldog*
- ✦ *Ripper the miniature chainsaw*
- ✦ *Ripper the circular razorblade launcher*
- ✦ *Sterling Hayden as Jack D. Ripper*
- ✦ *Who is Ripper in the Hunger Games?*
- ✦ *Remove broken slate with our new ripper*

- *Ripper for your bulldozer*
- *How Jack the Ripper worked*
- *Ripper: a generic name for a strip club (*may be a truncated form of "stripper"*)*
- *Walk the Jack the Ripper Walk*
- *Ripper—A New Musical (*Just might make a killing*)*
- *The Infamous Quack The Ripper Genuine Taxidermy Duckling: Despicable Display (*Looks like this little guy has been a bad Ducky*)*
- *Judas Priest: The Ripper*
- *Ripper Street*
- *What is Ripper Street rated?*
- *Why is Ripper Street not available on iPlayer?*
- *What is Ripper mode in Metal Gear?*
- *Operation Ripper*
- *Miscarriage of Justice: The Real Yorkshire Ripper Story*
- *Ripper hot dog variety*
- *Ripper is colloquialism for flatulence*
- *The Ripper*
- *Was Jack the Ripper a Woman?*
- *"PATENTS" FOR RIPPER*
    - *Modular Impact Ripper Assembly*
    - *Ripper Shank*
    - *Hydraulic Ripper*
    - *Ripper Tip*
    - *Ripper Boot*
    - *Linear Impact Ripper Apparatus*
    - *Ripper Blade*
    - *Grader and Ripper Thereof*
    - *Ripper Shoe*
    - *Ripper Tooth*
    - *Sewed Seam Ripper*
    - *Power Shingle Ripper*
    - *Cable Ripper*
    - *Road Ripper*
    - *Counter-Rotating Knife Paper Tail Ripper*
    - *Boiled Eggshell Ripper*

- *Ripper Vibrator*
- *Impact Ripper*
- *Breast Ripper:* Add your own comments—this instrument reserved for women accused of conducting a miscarriage or adultery.
- *Sonic Earth Ripper Bar with temperature Gradient Control*

✦ *SEARCHES RELATED TO* **RIPPER**

- *Ripper Slang*
- *Mac the Ripper*
- *Ripper Urban Dictionary*
- *Ripper Ruby*
- *Ripper Vampire Diaries*
- *I'm in Love with a Ripper*
- *Baby Paper Ripper*
- *Ripper Hot Dog Actress*
- *Ripper Dead Space 2*
- *Ripper farm implement*
- *Ripper game*
- *Ripper depression*
- *Ripper anorexia*
- *Ripper "sexually insane"*
- *csection and ab ripper x*
- *Did you mean* stripper?
- *And my wife and I cry together again and vow the trying again, and we're so far from Newark and Elizabeth and that Portuguese bar where, after a few drinks, we first said* son *and first said* daughter, *and ate our New Jersey Rippers, and burnt our tongues on the fat, and we don't say* biological *or* running out *or* father *or* mother, *or anything about the insufficiency of aunt-and-unclehood, of cat ownership, will not say* broken, *and so we say* ripped *and* ripper *and hope that will help should the heart need restitching, and when we hold hands it's like an interview, and it's so important to try to answer these questions, fresh from the oil, without ripping.*
- *I did not mean* stripper.

The New Jersey Ripper

Note: Rutt's Hut, the Clifton, NJ, hot dog stand famed for the Ripper, hung up on me four times before I was able to get hold of the current owner, who was willing to identify himself only as "Johnny."

When asked for the Ripper recipe, Johnny told me, "No disrespect to you and your book, but it's a true delicacy. I'll take the recipe to my grave, brother. It's a skilled art. A family secret."

After about five minutes of online research, I found a discussion board on the Jersey Ripper, on which folks recommend filling a 5-quart saucepan half-full with oil, and heating it to 350–375 degrees. Jersey locals insist on using a dog specially made to withstand the heat of deep-frying—specifically, a Thumann's Beef and Pork Natural Casing Frankfurter (reportedly the same dog used by Rutt's Hut).

Rutt's Hut offers as its recommended topping a house-made relish of carrot, cabbage, onion, and mustard. According to Serious Eats.com, "If you want to get exotic you can ask for a 'cremator' which is hammered in the deep fryer until it turns black. Not really my thing—I was almost turned off to deep-fried dogs completely by some well-done dogs a few years ago, but a lightly deep-fried dog—at Rutt's a 'ripper' or the barely fried 'in and out'—can be really terrific. For the truly adventurous order your ripper 'dipped' in the same brown gravy they use for fries and roast beef platters."

When asked if he could at the very least describe the method of preparing the Ripper, Johnny said, "It was created by the original owner, Royal Rutt. My dad and uncle then ran the place, and now I do. The method? We deep-fry the dog. If anyone else does it, all you'll get is a long black tube. Ours? It comes out and it rips open."

When Johnny finds out I'm originally from Chicago, he says, "Whenever Chicago wants a real dog and not a salad dog, I'll be happy to oblige."

Then, he hangs up on me.

—*MGF*

A Heartfelt Engagement of the Devil, Joe Paterno, and the Philly Cheesesteak

(NOTE: The italicized segment headings come from the University of Pennsylvania's song "The Battle Cry of Penn.")

Hang Jeff Davis from a sour apple tree . . .

JEFFERSON DAVIS—SOON TO be the U.S. Civil War–era President of the Confederate States, and owner of seventy-four slaves on his sprawling Brierfield plantation in what is now known as Davis Bend, Mississippi—sat, eighteen years old and, therefore, excitable and horny, on his whining mattress in his bunk at West Point, sniffing the earthy, chalky—and almost swampy—black and gray granite stone walls—the smell itself some bastion to neo-Gothicism, though young Jeff did not yet have that word at his disposal—twiddling, perhaps, his thumbs, or something more volatile; hungry, perhaps, for the sort of sex that he also had few words for, or the sort of sandwich that had yet to be invented—that wouldn't be invented for another hundred years in Philadelphia by brothers Pat and Harry Olivieri—a sandwich that best described the frenzy in his chest, an egg bursting with canaries or mosquitoes, and Jeff Davis felt abuzz and stung and blood-sucked from the inside, and closed his eyes and twiddled, and imagined a beef so thinly shaved it could be diaphanous, could be lingerie, could be the skin over his future wife's throat before she succumbed to malaria, could be simultaneously masculine and feminine, free and enslaved, North and South, could be the sort of beef that we'd later call *frizzled*—meaning *fried until crisp and curled*, meaning *fried noisily*, meaning *scorched*, meaning *the ribbed steel plate forming the part of the gunlock that receives the blow of the hammer*, meaning *a lock of hair*—and perhaps the teenaged Davis considered all received things as gifts or blows to the head, considered all locks to be binding or silken, and he heard Christmas songs drunkenly sung out the window, and he stood and forgot his own body, forgot his sexy dream sandwich, as he joined his fellows, and helped, that night, to launch the infamous Eggnog Riot (sometimes called the Grog Mutiny) of West Point, wherein he imbibed the smuggled-in (and forbidden-at-West Point) booze, broke some windows, punched some officers, shot a few bullets into the barracks' neo-Gothic ceiling and walls, screamed profanities, screamed in pain, earned a house arrest wherein, bored and hungover, he had not the energy to twiddle a damn thing, but had energy enough perhaps, to predict the addition of melted cheese and scorched onions to his fantasy sandwich, to predict his role in the collapse of the Confederate economy by printing more and more paper money to cover his Civil War expenses, to predict the accusations of treason, his resistance to Reconstruction, his sociopolitical insistence on "a democratic white polity based firmly on dominance of a controlled and excluded black caste," his insistence that his "inferiors"—whether militarily or racially—call him "father," his death in his own bed just after midnight on Friday, December 6, 1889, his legacy of presidential libraries named after him, holidays honoring his birthday in Florida and in Texas, in Kentucky, Louisiana, Tennessee, in Alabama, in Mississippi, a transcontinental Memorial Highway named after him (from which many states since stripped his name, save for Virginia, both Carolinas, Georgia, Alabama, Mississippi, Louisiana; many other states renaming portions of the old Jeff Davis Highway after Martin Luther King, Jr.); energy enough perhaps to predict the abolition, how newly freed slaves would use his name in a song sung to the tune of "John Brown's Body," and how white Southerners "believed it was [their] responsibility to help defend the 'honor' of Jeff Davis by 'drowning' the 'ornery'" singers, and how the University of Pennsylvania would later adopt the first line of that revised song as "The Battle Cry of Penn," and students would at football games bellow their lines about an ironic and fantastic lynching, a dreamed comeuppance, their own mouths full of the sort of sandwich that Davis himself could only imagine, their own young mouths filled with frizzled things, and the hair of their lovers, taken into the cold Pennsylvania wind, unable to tell which thing over their tongues, which thing hatching in their chests, is the cheesy melted thing, and which the unrepentantly sour.

* * *

The Malus tree (pronounced *malice tree)* is also known as the wild apple, the crabapple, the crab, the sour apple. Since it is self-sterile, it depends on bees to propagate its species. In certain cultures, it is known as the *food of the butterflies*, sustaining so many Lepidoptera, that most diaphanous of insect orders, taken into the wind, beautiful hungry species named Brimstone and Gothic and Hebrew and Dagger, named Emperor, named Satellite, named the Engrailed, named Brown. In orchard emergencies, a bucket or drum bouquet of flowering sour apple limbs is placed directly beneath beehives as sexual bait. The wood is difficult to carve by hand and burns hot and slow, without producing much flame—perfect for frizzling, without charring, our beef. The branches are relatively thin, also easily taken into the wind, and therefore, often bend to breaking if asked to support the weight of a hanged man.

* * *

While launching, in 1930, a Philly hot dog stand at the intersection of 9th, Wharton, and Passyunk, cheesesteak innovators Pat and Harry Olivieri had to hold down other jobs, as sled-makers. Pat claims that the sort of cheese that should accompany a true Philly Cheesesteak should be able to glide, like a sled on snow, over the bread, and therefore began using an early version of Cheez Whiz—that processed yellow paste—as well as provolone. Legend dictates that Pat gave away half of his first cheesesteak to a cab driver, who then spread the word to his fellows. Today, Pat's is proud of its "fascist" ordering process. In order to be served, a customer must order via shorthand as stipulated on a laminated sign next to the window. The ordering begins with the number of sandwiches desired, the type of cheese (Whiz or provolone), and the desire, or lack thereof, for onions (represented as *Wit* or *Witout*, in honor of the Philadelphia accent, and some romantic linguistic inherent in all blue collarism). So, an order sounds something like this: *Four Whiz Wit*. Customers are not permitted to ask questions, and are discouraged from saying things like *Please*. Across the street from Pat's is Geno's, a rival cheesesteak restaurant that, due to former owner Joseph Vento's outspoken xenophobia, bans non-English speakers from ordering a sandwich. "[These immigrants] don't know how lucky they are," Vento says, "all we're [Geno's Steaks] asking them to do is learn the English language." The late Vento hung a sign next to his window too, directed, he says, mostly at the Mexican immigrants in the surrounding neighborhood, bearing the images of an eagle and Old Glory, declaring, in all-caps, and strangely mispunctuated, "THIS IS AMERICA: WHEN ORDERING 'SPEAK ENGLISH.'" Pat's current owner, Frank Olivieri, responded by purchasing ad space on ESPN Deportes, stating that he does not care which language a customer speaks "when ordering cheesesteaks." "No problemo," Frank says, "we're Spanish-friendly," and outside the city confines the hive empties into the bucket of sour apple viscera, and behind the counters of Pat's and Geno's so many shavings of beef, in noisy whisper, go the way of the hanged man's hair, nested with sunlight, apple feathers, taken into the wind, the thing on the dead body that's most alive.

I, the Devil, ask permission to acquaint myself . . .

. . . is not how Joe Paterno, Penn State football coach from 1966 to 2011, introduced himself to a new crop of players, instead preferring, "Believe deep down in your heart that you're destined to do great things," and the Devil said, "I have a different nature . . . I am blameless and sinless [and] . . . receive different judgment than man," and Paterno said, "Losing becomes a habit," and the Devil said, "I am full of wisdom," and Paterno said, "Disaster is just around the corner," and the Devil said, "I am perfect in beauty," and Paterno said, "Publicity is like poison; it doesn't hurt unless you swallow it," and the Devil said, "My heart became proud on account of my beauty," and Paterno said, "Heart is the key to all locks," and the Devil said, "My pride is self-generated," and Paterno said, "Throw," and the Devil said, "No," and Paterno said, "Satisfy your hunger," and the Devil said, "I was thrown to this earth."

When Paterno was accused in 2011 of concealing defensive coordinator Jerry Sandusky's forty instances of child sexual abuse spanning 1994–2009, and when former FBI director Louis Freeh reported that Paterno concealed Sandusky's actions in order to "protect publicity surrounding Penn State's celebrated football program," public reaction bore various strains of outrage. According to Sullivan Monroe of Cheesesteak Sports,

> *Many of you have requested that I remove Joe Paterno's statue from my Cheesesteak Sports banner. The statue stays. None of you haters' comments deserves even the simplest of responses, but my patience has been overruled by my heart. I knew there were alot of jealous envious haters out there. Always has been. But this many? There is no way Joe would allow a child to be hurt or harmed. At ANY cost. Let me say it again: There is no way Joe would allow a child to be hurt or harmed. At ANY cost. He did not understand the severity of all that was happening. Gov. Tommy C (one-term-Tommy) [Pennsylvania governor Tom Corbett, who initially assigned only*

one investigator—a disempowered state trooper—to the Penn State child molestation cases] is the next one who needs to be investigated. And castrated. You are all as much to blame, if not more. You all suck. Big time.

And the Devil spoke in big-time tongues, and Paterno said nothing. He said nothing.

Down went McGinty to the bottom of the sea . . .

AND WE SING and we sing for touchdown and tackle, for the mouthguard evicted from the mouth, for the blood in the eye, the loss of breath, the twitching of the hands, all constriction, by rope or by water, of the other side . . .

Joseph Flynn, Pennsylvania songwriter and steelworker, cashed in in 1889 during a surge of Irish-bashing in popular culture. In his song "Down Went McGinty," a foolish Irishman drinks too much, falls off a wall into the ocean, and drowns to death. The song, says critic Sigmund Spaeth, was "naive . . . because we had by no means outgrown the unsophisticated simplicities of behavior. Love still expressed itself in a kiss . . . Right was still right and wrong was still wrong with special . . . corresponding antagonism toward infidelity, dishonesty . . ." which we are compelled to asphyxiate with melodic accompaniment. If we are singing about it, it's not happening to us.

And McGinty could have been John McGinty, who landed penniless in Allegheny County in 1836, or Owen McGinty, who landed penniless in Allegheny County in 1874, or T. Joe McGinty the bootlegger, or Joe McGinty the composer whose songs include "I Wanna Sleep with You," "So Run Down," and "No Tears," or Every McGinty, or No McGinty who ever crossed into Pennsylvania legally or ill-, where the service of water into the lungs is guaranteed no matter the language you speak, at least within the context of a song whose title includes both *Cry* and *Battle.*

What else can we do but shave our meat down to a nightgown

to remind us of our own fragility, and that we have the power to devour it between slices of bread? Here, our sandwiches remind us: sometimes, without generals, we need signs to order us, we have to hold our breaths until we pass out to sympathize, we have to hold and hold down, make music of violence, keep quiet, and quiet, we have to learn to live *witout.*

The McGinty family motto, originally (and oddly) a battle cry, as emblazoned beneath the coat of arms: *Felis demulcata mitis—A stroked cat is gentle.* In the cheer, as in the cry, as in the frizzle, is the drowning out of the mindless celebration of atrocity, in weep or whoop. Here, it's easy to sympathize with horror, to apologize for it in sandwich and song. Just ask those painted-faced kids with the pompons. Here, the ocean strokes the lung, and like all cancers, our awful, wonderful Whiz, easily spreads.

The Devil identifies himself as masculine, rich, and cultivated . . .

LATIN, ENGLISH: How *Paterno* is the anti-father, means *not father,* a *don't-look-at-me-I'm-not-your-daddy-hood*—more of an uncle. How Paterno insisted on the fatherly, imposed upon himself and his players the roles of father and sons, via the enforced nickname JoePa. Here, bad things taste good, and this is how the hearts of all false fathers give out, drop into troughs of ice reserved for the swollen knees of college boys, the fluid there yellow as fall, the fall leaking from the sandwich of our state. Can something be both enforced and endearing?

Latin Vulgate: How *Lucifer* means *light-bearer, morning star, bringer of the dawn.* How luciferase is the enzyme that allows a firefly to ignite, to signal out into the lonely dark for a mate. How the Devil has pouty lips and lingerie, a diaphanous heart, is a moony romantic, an early riser, watching the sun come up in the sour apple tree, is a wish inherent in an enzyme, the reminder that, in all of our chests is a charring, a shorthand, a revised song, a quiet treatise on timing, the processing of the cheese.

She's my Annie, and I'm her Joe . . .

JEFF DAVIS IN SONG, lynched: we swear we can hear him tick. Or maybe that's the bees. Context changes everything, except the thinness of the beef, and we all just want to be pet until gentle . . .

Annie is Little Annie Rooney, a character in the same-named song written in 1890 by the British composer Michael Nolan. Soon, the American singer Annie "The Bowery Girl" Hart ripped off the song, called it her own, and began performing it around the States, compelling the bitter Nolan to retire from composing as she stuffed her pockets. The song went on to inspire a comic strip character, herself ripped off from Little Orphan Annie. Little Annie Rooney is also an orphan who travels about, all-too-trusting, getting into misadventures with her dog, Zero. The original song includes the lines:

Ev'ry evening, rain or shine,
I make a call twixt eight and nine,
On her who shortly will be mine,
Little Annie Rooney.
She's my sweetheart, I'm her beau;
She's my Annie, I'm her Joe,
Soon we'll marry, never to part,
Little Annie Rooney is my sweetheart!

Which tells us little about the origins of the Scottish phrase "She's having an Annie Rooney," which means someone is expressing a violent act of rage. Patricide is often an Annie Rooney, but not always.

Says Marian Zeiset, Goodville, Pennsylvania, farmer and cashier, "I've been driving a horse and buggy since I was eight or nine. I was out driving a tractor around this morning—a diesel, on steel wheels. Our Mennonite church doesn't allow rubber wheels. I quit school when I was fifteen. Our church only goes to eighth grade. We studied writing, math, spelling—not science."

Bastards. Songs. Sandwiches. School. Bastards. Here, the fireflies make us angry while we're waiting in the hour-long line for our cheesesteaks. We practice our lines, the pronunciation of them. Here, *Joe*—Joseph—can simply pine for Annie, no longer signify a duplicitousness or treason, a brief loyalty to the oppressive Pharaoh and all slavery, sexual or otherwise, no longer mean, in Hebrew, *he will add*, spawning tasteless joke after tasteless joke as we wait in line to butcher the word *with*, according to the rules.

There's only the illusion of science to this. Here, Joe will add onions to his sandwich. Here, a brilliant insect dies virginal in the Cheez Whiz that we order in English, in code.

The Devil tells us he has existed as long as we have . . .

ACCORDING TO Simon Singh's *The Code Book: The Science of Secrecy from Ancient Egypt to Quantum Cryptography*,

> *cryptanalysis [is] the science of unscrambling a message without knowledge of the key. While the cryptographer develops new methods of secret writing, it is the cryptanalyst who struggles to find weaknesses in these methods in order to break into secret messages. Arabian cryptanalysts succeeded in finding a method for breaking the monoalphabetic substitution cipher, a cipher that had remained invulnerable for several centuries. . . . Cryptanalysis could not be invented until a civilization had reached a sufficiently sophisticated level of scholarship in several disciplines . . .*

Perhaps the answer to Paterno's silence is more complicated than the protection of a football legacy. We can only hope. We can only search the borders of the secret, notice what surrounds it, attaches itself to it by proximity and static. What else can we do but cryptanalyze song and sandwich, pray that all that yellow goop conceals a key of which, as yet, we have no knowledge? We sing, we bite, we feud to find out . . .

The thin beef and processed cheese: each conceals the poor quality of the other, and they are thereby delicious together. At best, this is confusing to the mind. After all, as Singh says, "the science of secrecy is largely a secret science." At best, the mouth, as always, couldn't give a shit. It only wants to take in, do its own processing according to its own savage code.

Like all desire, hatred rarely remains a secret for very long. Pat's hates Geno's openly. Hidden in this—beneath that baby-tooth mound of charred onion, waiting on the griddle for *wit*—is the key to infatuation, dependence, irresistibility, compulsion, if not quite love.

* * *

Oh, listen to my tale of (Whoa!)
Any ice today lady? No. Gitty-up!

Not all concealment here yields deliciousness. In rivalry is electricity, and each lives to make sandwiches another day. We wait in long lines. We smell exhaust and listen to neon sputtering in its cursive tubes. We bite. We *mmmmmmmm* . . . Somewhere else, in secret, a locker weakly closes. The beef, the cheese: which the rubber, which the steel?

"Any Ice Today, Lady?" is a song written by Troy, Pennsylvania, native Pat Ballard in 1926. In the song, a desperate ice salesman on horseback (a common trade in 1920s' Troy in the warm weather seasons) attempts in vain to peddle his wares. He begs, he lowers his price, he worries, correctly, that the heat will hasten the melting. Still, in spite of his impassioned pleas and ratcheted-up anxiety as the song progresses, it becomes obvious that his potential customer is losing interest, yet still the salesman persists. By song's end, he is shouting like a madman in the streets, interrogatively and repetitively chanting the word, *Ice? Ice?* Soon, our defeated protagonist gallops away on a horse named Napoleon, bound for some exile to starvation, a diet of frozen things. Maybe the key to all of our epidemic secrets lurks in Troy, in the belly of that fucking Trojan Horse that's immune even to the best of our *Whoa!*s. Today, 30 percent of Troy's population still lives below the poverty line.

We stop and we start again. We *whoa* and *gitty-up*. Such is the way with most guilty pleasures. We want to tell our stories. Oh. We want to tell them, make someone listen. Woe. Whoa. We eat and our hands shake with the weight of it, and we confuse a great sadness, the condition of sadness with a vocalization of surprise, which doubles as a brake. The horse pulls up. We look down from our mount and make our pathetic offers to whoever is willing to briefly listen. Of course, "The Battle Cry of Penn" truncates the desperation and equates the flight from failure with some victory charge. This, of course, is not logical, is running with blinders on, is a huge thing made trivial, is processed, at best.

It's tough to call something this skinny *steak*. In this way, associations with lingerie conceal the cow. In this way, the noise of the postgame showers doesn't clean, but obscures the horrible filth . . .

In *gitty-up!* is our restarting, the beating of our animal as we ride off toward another state to which we can make our tragic pitch.

"Losing your sense of excellence or worth," Paterno says, "is a tragedy," and Simon Singh answers, "No, [it is a] tragic execution . . . Anybody sending an encrypted message had to accept that an expert enemy codebreaker might intercept and decipher their most precious secrets," and all we can do is look away to something else—to sandwich rules, to the sandwich itself, and the furnaces whisper their steel secrets, and the bees can't stop their fucking the flowers—it's in their code—and how can we still keep our eyes open? Our mouths? And Paterno once again gives an answer that isn't an answer, "I don't want to miss anything."

The Devil admits to having stolen from us . . .

The rope conceals the throat, restricts the swallowing and the song. The water, the entire body. Body usurps body. If only it were ice. If only we had the money to buy it. (*Print, Jeff Davis, print!*) Here, even our fighting spirit songs tell us: your secrets will be the death of you. Have faith in our song, its bastardy, collage. Have faith that it's the key, will tell us something about all sin, the secrets written in the ghosts rising from the griddle, about the wispier versions of ourselves, about the personality of an entire state. In this way, we drown and asphyxiate to the galloping of the varsity team, the inhales and exhales of the marching band, the cheerleaders, the *crowd*. This tells us nothing about microcosm, the representativeness of atrocity. "If no symbol appears more frequently than any other," Singh says, "then this would appear to defy any potential attack via frequency analysis. Perfect security? Not quite."

. . . and lynching, and drowning, and sweethearts, and ice, and sexy singers in spandex pants delivering their dramatic monologues to bongos, and horses, and the apple, the apple, the apple . . . On the playing field, lynching is not only musical, but composed, orchestrated, *orchestral;* is Jeff Davis, wishful thinking, is sport, is a Hail Mary, is *athletics*.

Thank you, Simon Singh, for your retention of faith, and maybe even your soul. Thank you for saying that "A ciphertext still contains many subtle clues for the clever cryptanalyst." "Traits," Singh assures us, "can still be discerned even if the encryption is by homophonic substitution." Still, we fail, still, we can't tell which *woe/whoa!* applies: how Lucifer conceals the beautiful dawn in fire, the bucket conceals the crabapple flower, as the quilt of bees conceals the bucket. If we try to listen to the secret here, discern the inherent relationships and substitutions, our own poor hands may plump with venom, and shock.

* * *

Pennsyl-Pennsyl-Pennsylvania!
Pennsyl-Pennsyl-Pennsylvania!
Pennsyl-Pennsyl-Pennsylvania!
Oh Pennsylvania!

Our state name means *Penn's Woods*, not after founder William Penn, but after his father, Admiral Sir William Penn, with whom the son had a complicated relationship. King Charles II owed a debt of £16,000 to the Penn patriarch, and since this repayment went toward establishing our state's land grant, it was Charles who lent us our name and wouldn't change it, despite the desperate protests and embarrassment of the younger Penn, who was still carrying around some serious daddy issues. Even our state's abbreviation represents the dominance of the father. Still, Penn the son went on to establish "freedom of religious conviction for all," save for the Delaware, Susquehannock, Eriez, Shawnee, Cayuga, Mohawk, Oneida, Seneca, Tuscarora, Iroquois . . .

* * *

"THIS IS AMERICA: WHEN ORDERING 'SPEAK ENGLISH,'" loosely translated into the Mohawk language: *Ontiaten:ro' America, Tiohrhen:sa sata:ti.*

* * *

THIS IS a lynching state. A drowning one. Check your whistle at the door. We can hear ice at the window. The snow is cheering, almost cheerful. We join hands as we cross the state line, wondering if we should feel fatherly or overheated, frightened or in love. It's corny to say, *Father, no.* So, let's not say it again. After all, our own hearts only want to touch down in some mathematic of healthy grass, some secret celebration spray-painted orange and spiked hard into any zone that's less terminally named.

Cheesesteak

Ingredients

4 thinly sliced slices of rib-eye
1 tablespoon canola oil
3 to 4 pieces American cheese
Salt & pepper
One 7-inch-long Italian roll, cut in half lengthwise

Directions

1. Heat a skillet on medium high. When it reaches 275 degrees F, add canola oil to the pan.

2. Add 4 slices of sliced steak to the skillet.

3. Spread meat apart and cook for one minute. Flip the steak, season with salt and pepper.

4. Continue to cook until the steak is no longer pink and the internal temperature is at 160 degrees F.

5. Add 3–4 slices of American cheese on top of the steak. Once the cheese has melted, remove the steak from the pan.

6. Place the steak and cheese onto the roll. Top with your favorite toppings (we love sautéed onions), close the roll, and enjoy!

—Tony Luke's

Qualifications on Things Said about Dover Cake

(It's just cake, really. Regular cake.)

* * *

(This is a choice between butter and margarine, between what your mother would call a weeping cow, your father [when referencing any udder, or, as your girlfriend would say, *every* udder] would call the squeezing of the dregs of AquaFresh over the Tynex® Classic Standard Round Nylon Toothbrush Filaments he helps to manufacture at the DuPont factory over in Wilmington, Delaware, a fifty-four-minute commute from your house in Dover, where there's still a half slice of Dover Cake left in the fridge [you ate the other half last night after smoking the sort-of decriminalized medical marijuana your girlfriend jokingly calls Freon Lycra after the chemicals/polymers her own father helped to manufacture at the DuPont factory over in Wilmington—a mere fifty-one-minute commute for him—before he started getting the nosebleeds, and before he self-diagnosed—only half-jokingly—as having haloalkane poisoning, which you and your girlfriend searched to no avail on the Internet before she began to cry all over your Adam's apple—the one your father called an Adam's crabapple, another example of his passive-aggressive feminizing of you after you quit the Dover High wrestling team because you were sick of being a Dover Senator and didn't give a shit about a letterman's jacket and, even though your father ranted and raved, ever reminding you that you have now sullied the names of famed athletic DHS alumni like Carl Ergenzinger who went on to play for the Houston Astros and Renie Martin who went on to play for the San Francisco Giants—teams whose names your father associates with Real Men, with outer space and propulsion and barrel chests and swinging dicks—you still got in his face and told him you wanted to draw and that you wanted to act and *you* reminded *him* that R. Crumb was also a DHS alumnus to which he responded, "*That* pornographer?!" and that Teri Polo also graduated with honors from DHS, to which you assumed your father's reply would include the word "bitch," but instead was relegated to a wrinkled forehead to which he held his hand in such a way that you noticed, in the light of the refrigerator, the lattice of scar tissue mapping his wrist to his fingernails, so you felt obligated to feel bad for him for the few seconds it took him to muster, "Teri *Po*lo? Teri fucking *Po*lo?!"—and you wiped the tears from your girlfriend's face with the back of your own unscarred hand, and smoked three drags each from the Freon Lycra in the backyard beneath the dead white oak that your mother implored your father to cut down because "It's bound to hurt somebody," to which your father refused because "It's the biggest fucking tree in Delaware, Margaret," and as the weed anchored itself into your bloodstream like a Classic Standard Round Nylon Toothbrush Filament into a Classic Standard Molten Plastic Toothbrush Base with Classic Standard Injection Port—which your father also helps to fabricate—she buried her face into your neck again, but this time was laughing and licking and you felt so big and so good, as if you had Ergenzinger and Martin *and* Crumb *and* Polo inside of you, allowing you to feel like a *Senator!* and allowing you to flip the bird in a direction you mistake for Wilmington but are quite certain is the bedroom window of your sleeping parents—your Dover Cake contest–winning mother and toothbrush-making father—and allowing you to know—just *know*—that your destiny lies outside of Dover, and maybe even all of Delaware, in a place where fathers are defined beyond their chemical/polymer of specialization, and cakes are defined by more than a shaving of mace into the batter] that your father now calls "a measly, lousy half slice of motherfucking cake?!" before shoveling said measly lousy half slice into his mouth in a sound that reminds you of an asthmatic chainsaw struggling to turn over but only burping blue smoke, of every tool that can't cut a fucking thing down—not anymore.)

* * *

(This is what the locals called the Delaware River 348 years after it was named after Sir Thomas West, the 3rd British Baron De La Warr, thirty-seven years after it was nicknamed the Acropolitan Sinkhole when the *Corinthos* tanker upchucked 11 million gallons of crude oil into it, and one year after it was nicknamed DuPont's Outhouse after the company was fined for dumping hydrogen chloride, titanium tetrachloride, iron chloride, titanium ore, overflow wastewater treatment chemicals, and various other substances whose molecules your father has inside of him, into the current that Henry Hudson once, in 1609, called, "Great.")

* * *

(This is how your mother refers to the stiff peaks of the egg whites before she asks them to accept the flour, the sugar, the butter [or margarine], the milk, the mooing of the cows—a sound she fears will make the cake fall, will make your father angry if she does not win the contest this year, does not come home with the check for $125.)

* * *

(This is how she refers to the mace, which makes you think of evergreen trees, and the dry, lacy, reddish things that cover its seeds. To make this cake, she says, we have to undress all things egg-shaped. We have to pulverize the thinnest of our clothes, trust that the cake will keep our bodies warm. This is also why you think of your girlfriend's favorite bra, and why you think that it's your favorite too.)

* * *

(This chemical/polymer on which DuPont makes over $250,000/day was said to have been invented by the nineteenth-century French chemist Chevreul, who accidentally "discovered" a fatty acid with such a lustrous appearance that he actually swooned in his laboratory, ran his hands beneath his lab coat, and cried, *"Margarique!,"* a word he knew derived from the Greek *margaron*, or *pearl*. This pearly spread soon became the butter substitute that lent its own name to other things pearly [actually or metaphorically]—the flower marguerite, the cocktail margarita, and Margaret, your mother, who curses the complaining cows now, threatens to slaughter them all and start using the margarine again.)

* * *

(Because Delaware seems so flat on an otherwise spherical earth, your mother bakes her Dover Cake in a single round loaf pan, just to remind herself where she really lives.)

* * *

(Your father wonders why you're so cold, why you need the three blankets. He will fake-punch you, arrest his fist an inch from your face. When you flinch, he will say, "Two for flinching," then real-punch you twice on the arm, right where you just got your allergy shots.)

* * *

(You will tell him nothing of how you plan [and will fail] to self-asphyxiate with said blankets after he goes to sleep.)

* * *

(The mace is the aril of the nutmeg. The aril is known as the *false-fruit*.)

* * *

(This, because she had a heavy hand with the sugar today. That, because your father came home from work with half a left pinkie and a nosebleed she tried to stanch with paper towels printed with roses.)

* * *

(You wonder if it's the flower or the blood that does the lying.)

* * *

(If the one ingredient that distinguishes your state's cake is *false*, no wonder we expect the picture of the flower to have a beautiful smell.)

* * *

(Dover Cake is disappointing.)

* * *

(You think this only because your girlfriend shows you the original recipe she ripped from the already overdue Dover Public Library book *Seventy-Five Receipts for Pastry, Cakes and Sweetmeats* [1832], authored by the semi-anonymous Miss Leslie, a recipe that includes in its ingredient list many things which neither your mother nor any of the other contest regulars use: things like one glass of brandy and ½ glass of rosewater and, your girlfriend's favorite, ½ teaspoon of pearl-ash dissolved in a little vinegar. You imagine briefly, your mother on fire.)

* * *

(The oil from the nutmeg and its mace is also used as a major ingredient in cough syrups and toothpastes. You wonder when these will become the new state dessert. Your mother wonders, briefly, if Dover Cake is medicinal, if all of those prisoners who smuggled the spice into their cells ingested it for the flavor or the euphoria.)

* * *

(Your girlfriend performs this act while whispering vinegar names: rice, sherry, apple cider, champagne. By the way your mother screams in the kitchen, you know she's burnt herself on the element again.)

* * *

(You scream this together into the wind coming off the Delaware. Afterward, she tells you that, compared to other spices, ground mace is the least likely to clot.)

* * *

(You won't notice, until tomorrow, that someone has penciled "FUCK DOVER" into the bottom left corner of the recipe's page, just beneath the imperative, "Wrap it in a thick cloth and keep it from the air.")

* * *

(You erase this, just to rewrite it in your own hand.)

* * *

(Here, cake, and those who prepare it, suffocate and burn. Here, we forget that an entire people were massacred or enslaved so others could steal their nutmeg and mace, shave it down to its dust over our cakes.)

* * *

(You scream alone into the river wind. She's not here to tell you that the process by which butter is pressed from nutmeg and its mace is called *expression.*)

* * *

(Because of this polluted river, our unlacy coverings, we must find our autoerotica in the eating of cake, and the subsequent shunning thereof. Through the walls, you hear your father's sharp cough, your mother's electric mixer speed to a whine. You wonder what it is exactly that your father is choking on.)

* * *

(Because of this year's contest theme, your mother decides to frost her Dover Cake with the earth's continents. It cools on the counter and you swear that the bellowing cows make the steam dance like an aurora.)

* * *

(Myristicin poison is pronounced *my wrist is in poison*. For this reason, your mother never eats raw mace, compulsively checks her pulse. For this reason, it is recommended that one not feed Dover Cake to dogs or to livestock.)

* * *

(By this, you mean, *blood*. By that, you mean, *in Elizabethan times, it was believed that mace could ward off the plague . . .*)

* * *

(She takes second place to a woman from Magnolia, another woman named Margaret. The last thing your father thinks about is flowers. Your mother sits at the kitchen table, trying not to hear the cows. It's late. You wait for your girlfriend to call. Your father flops facedown onto the lemony tabletop. His body heaves. His left hand—the one with the bad pinkie—reaches forward for the half-eaten cake, desiccating beneath the plastic wrap he also helped to fabricate. His fingers reach across hard batter and frosting for the east coast of North America, but don't quite make it. This ocean once had brandy and rosewater in it, you think—only the delicious things we meant to spill into it.)

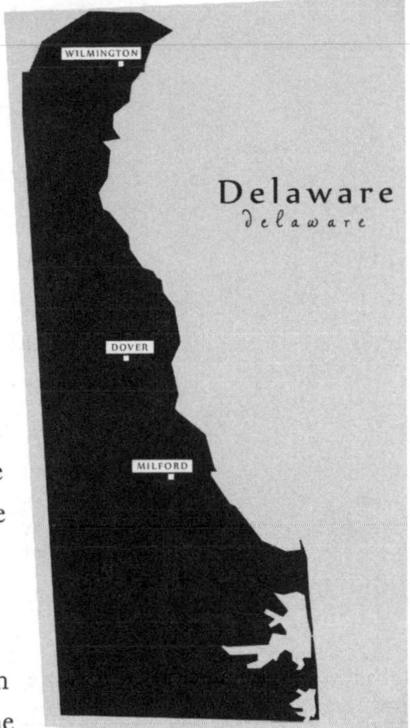

* * *

(But, of course, if we ingest too much of it, mace can have psychoactive effects. We can succumb to the delirium. Those may not be real cows.)

* * *

(By *toxicity*, you mean, *this landscape.*)

* * *

(Because of this, she reaches for his hand, then thinks better of it. His body heaves, waits for the blood, or for the batter to resoften. His hand is lost at sea. There's a storm coming to this cake. You're waiting for something too, but neither one of them says anything about family, nor about how much mace is too much mace. You hold your breath. You think of history joining with the living room, the factory, library, high school cafeteria where dessert every Friday is Dover Cake, of roses meeting eggs, the commingling of cows and chemists. You do not let your breath go. *Together,* DuPont says, *we can feed the world.*)

Sugar-Free Red Velvet Dover Cake

Ingredients

Vegetable oil for the pans
2½ cups all-purpose flour
1¾ cups SPLENDA®
1 teaspoon baking soda
1 teaspoon fine salt
1 teaspoon cocoa powder
1½ cup vegetable oil
1 cup fat free buttermilk, at room temperature
2 large eggs, at room temperature
2 tablespoons red food coloring (1 ounce)
1 teaspoon white distilled vinegar
1 teaspoon vanilla extract
Crushed pecans, for garnish

Directions

Preheat the oven to 350 degrees F.

1. Lightly oil and flour 3 (9-by-1½-inch round) cake pans.

2. In a large bowl, sift together the flour, SPLENDA®, baking soda, salt, and cocoa powder.

3. In another large bowl, whisk together the oil, buttermilk, eggs, food coloring, vinegar, and vanilla.

4. Using a standing mixer, mix the dry ingredients into the wet ingredients until just combined and a smooth batter is formed.

5. Divide the cake batter evenly among the prepared cake pans and place pans in the oven evenly spaced apart.

6. Bake, rotating the pans halfway through the cooking, until the cake pulls away from the side of the pans, and a toothpick inserted in the center of the cakes comes out clean, about 30 minutes.

7. Remove the cakes from the oven and run a knife around the edges to loosen them from the sides of the pans.

8. One at a time, invert the cakes onto a plate and then re-invert them onto a cooling rack, rounded sides up. Let cool completely.

Cream Cheese Frosting

1 pound fat free cream cheese, softened
3 cups SPLENDA®
1 stick unsalted butter, softened
1 teaspoon vanilla extract

Directions

1. Cream the cream cheese until smooth and then add the softened butter.

2. Next add the SPLENDA® and the vanilla extract. It's ready to use.

3. Note: do not overbeat cream cheese as it will become too soft.

Frost the cake. Place 1 layer, rounded side down, in the middle of a rotating cake stand. Using a palette knife or offset spatula, spread some of the cream cheese frosting over the top of the cake. (Spread enough frosting to make a ¼-to-½-inch layer.) Carefully set another layer on top, rounded side down, and repeat. Top with the remaining layer and cover the entire cake with the remaining frosting. Sprinkle the top with the pecans.

—Chef Dana Herbert, Desserts by Dana

MIDWEST

Minnesota: Hotdish

Wisconsin: Sheboygan Bratwurst

Iowa: Loosemeat Sandwich

Michigan: Pasty

Missouri: St. Louis Barbecue

Illinois: Deep-Dish Pizza

Indiana: Hoosier Cream Pie

Ohio: Cincinnati Chili

The Hotdish Muddies the Water, or, Those Poor Drowned

THIS IS DESPERATION, imagination, blowing bubbles into our cream of mushroom soup not because we're feeling playful, but because, in this cold, the snow fine as dust, it hurts to take air in, so we extend our exhales as long as we can, pretend that *history* and *nostalgia* are the same thing.

This has everything to do with a tater tot crust as blanket in our Hotdish, as some golden brown storm cloud cresting the baking pan, yanked from failing oven after failing oven in the church basements of Arrowhead, along the shores of Lake Superior, in International Falls, Minneapolis, St. Paul.

This winter has depth, layers. This is winter as *casserole*, as the French word for *saucepan*. This is a season so freezing, it doubles back on itself, and simmers. Sometimes, our bodies get so cold, they burn. Sometimes, we overflow the pan's lip, stiffen on the element. Sometimes, like the drowned with ice in their lungs, we stick to the bottom.

In this weather, unlike the tater tots in our Hotdish, we don't golden, but redden.

* * *

UNCLE TALKS of his years harvesting sugar beets, raising turkeys in Todd County ("Now the poorest goddamn county in the state," he says) before he was forced by General Mills, Cargill, Hormel, and Schwan to retire, these same companies now producing the processed hamburger and frozen string beans and potato buds we heap into our Hotdish, use to feed congregations. He lost so much of his body to the cold and to the thresher, he has a single finger left, "the important one," he says, as he struggles to wrap it like a boa over the stem of his fork, sink it into the hottest middle part beneath the tater tots.

According to Hallie Harron's article "Heating Up the Heartland": "Minnesota's signature hotdish combines heartiness, great taste, and adaptability"; our state casserole retains no official recipe, or rules, beyond economic and gustatory desperation. As such, we have our hamburger-mashed-potato-string-bean-cream-of-mushroom-soup-La-Choy-fried-onion Hotdish, and our Hotdish made with canned tuna and Kraft macaroni 'n' cheese, with canned peas or canned corn, topped with potato chips crushed to dust, or shoestring potatoes, or anything crunchy and sharp enough to remind us that we still have some fight left, even in all of this cold, that we're not all—just mostly—soft.

Harron says, Hotdish was birthed out of hardship when "budget-minded farm wives needed to feed their own families, as well as congregations in the basements of the first Minnesota churches," and she says that the cream of mushroom soup soon became so favored, so ubiquitous, that it became better known, in early Hotdish circles, as *Lutheran binder.*

* * *

Uncle finishes his Hotdish, keeps breathing out. He stares at the palms of what he once called his "big Minnesota mitts," at what once killed so many turkeys without additional weapon, and if he permitted himself an inhale, however cold, surely the obscenities would drown out Martin Luther, proselytizing from the Great Beyond, "I have held many things in my hands, and I have lost them all." Somewhere beyond this town, Lake Superior roars over a record number of drowned bodies this year, and its icebergs—even the little eyelet ones—creak against one another in the sound of steam escaping through some thick blanket of potato product. Uncle cracks his knuckle against the casserole dish, burns himself, finally breathes in, as, over his head, above the couch, the print of Matisse's *Goldfish,* painted in 1911, shudders against the sheetrock.

We imagine the goldfish are the peas. All of those poor drowned as the mushrooms with cream in their gills.

* * *

UNCLE MENTIONS hanging something from every fruit tree in the yard that now, in this kind of weather, bears no fruit. He wants, we think at first, to remind himself of bounty. But, because he's muttering through a mouthful of Hotdish, we can't tell if he wants to hang a can of soup, or a can of corn, or the last piece of unground meat he saw years ago, or the last fresh potato, or his own dumb body from the boughs of the tree that once bore things named Lady and Delicious.

In 1911, Minnesota abolished the death penalty. The Republican representative from Gaylord, George MacKenzie, championing the abolition bill, said, "Let us bar this thing of Vengeance and the Furies from the confines of our great State; Let not this harlot of judicial murder smear the pages of our history with her bloody fingers," and Uncle says, "What does blood have to do with any of this?" and we don't know if he's speaking of Hotdish, or ovens failing in so many cold Lutheran basements, or of Lake Superior, which, in 1911, sensed perhaps a disruption in equilibrium and subsequently claimed more lives that year than it ever had before.

Martin Luther says, "Even if I knew that tomorrow the world would go to pieces, I would still plant my apple tree." Uncle stares out the window, and the land is untilled and overgrown and undergrown and white, and there are no birds, and the goldfish on the wall breathe neither in nor out, and Uncle says, in the presence of no birds, swallowing the thick last of the amalgam, a crumb of perfectly gold tater tot holding to his bottom lip, "That's because that motherfucker never lived in motherfucking Minnesota."

* * *

IF THERE ARE no birds, the only song here is the steam escaping our Hotdish, freezing in the air even before it can get to our windowpanes, blind us to the weather outside.

Uncle says, here, blindness is another kind of protection, and we think he means a kind of warmth, another sort of blanket, until we see something coagulating in his eyes, and remember that there are no rules to Hotdish, that casserole is variously defined by necessity, that iris and ice have only an R to separate them, the letter that's desperate to evoke a kind of growling, but here, today, in this living room, this winter, can only groan, overfull, digesting, but still so far from warm.

We think he's sleeping with his eyes open when he says, "Boy, you never think of Minnesota when you think of the Dust Bowl, but think of it now. Two fucking decades of no beets. All our farms cinders in the summer, frozen cinders after. Ha! That was the rotation." So, of course, the canned, the bagged, the processed. The tubers now reduced to buds in a box, which sounds to us like some funeral for something floral, but which sounded to all those Dust Bowl "farm wives" like the perfect ingredient for a basement resurrection.

Uncle mutes the television—the program perpetuated by the Minnesota Historical Society: a vaudevillian brew including this hour Yo-Yo Tricks with Dazzling Dave, Fancy-Dancing with Larry Yazzie—Member of the Sac and Fox Tribe, and Magic with Brodini. The show is newly called *The Big Wow Family Variety Show* (formerly known as *Global Hotdish*). Historical Society executives credit the renaming to a flood of viewer letters wherein countless Minnesotans expressed that naming a variety show after the state dish was either a trivializing of their culinary cultural inheritance or setting the bar too high.

* * *

THE MINNESOTA WINDS blew continuously from 1934 to 1936. These winds whirled so violently that residents couldn't tell if they were coming off the lake or from the land. Approaching winter, cold snaps were so abrupt that this pulverized dirt froze in midair. The winds were so fierce that, according to some locals—especially farmers whose properties were flat, uninterrupted by building or landscape—the frozen earth blew all winter long, pelted crops and windows and faces, pocked hands. This *black snow*, during blizzards, embedded itself in the actual snow and collapsed roofs, industries.

The federal government paid Minnesotans to kill their emaciated cattle, encouraged the afflicted to hang wet sheets over their homes to protect themselves from the plague. But in Minnesota, wet sheets freeze, the ice sloughs to the ground in the sort of shards with which so many Minnesotans—desperate, imaginative, dirty-mouthed, and destitute—took their lives.

In this way, federal advice becomes mercy killing. In this way, we retreat to the basement and pour everything we have into our one remaining dish.

* * *

WE KNOW: ten thousand lakes is bullshit. An inefficient number. Here, in winter, we know: in these lakes, goldfish or fish otherwise colored—fish imperfectly baked—float not belly-up to the sky as we'd like to believe, but sink toward the bottom, to the depths that have so far frozen incompletely.

Here, the lowest of the church basements remains, if only in narrative, the last thawed-out thing.

We know though, in the Eastern Dakotan Sioux dialect, *Mnisota* means *sky-tinted water*, the Sioux did not mean that the water was blue. Given the weather here, Uncle says that's obvious, and is a common mistranslation. In the Santee subdialect, the name more accurately translates as *somewhat clouded water* or *snow in the water*. We look out the window, the trees hunched under the weight, our breath producing on the glass the sort of frost that reminds us, when scraped off, of the white middles of the potatoes, the soft stuff beneath gold crust. If farm wives, we think, then farm mothers, and stare into the window-frost and wonder why, in this house, it's just us and our uncle.

We know because Uncle tells us. The Sioux demonstrated *Mnisota* to the settlers by dipping a hollowed gourd into a lake, then pouring, drop by drop, milk into the water. According to state legend, when one could no longer see to the bottoms or sides of the gourd, when the water was sufficiently unclear, the Sioux would nod to the settler, who wouldn't know what to expect when the weather finally turned, and whisper the name of our state.

* * *

HERE ARE FREEZING rain and snow and sleet and storms we call Alberta Clippers and Panhandle Hooks, and the tornado embedded in the blizzard, the graupel in the rime. Here, a front blows us from behind. Here, snowflakes cry into our ears and we can't tell if they are killing us or pleading with us. It is all we can do to swallow, as if thermodynamically, our meat and starch and canned this and frozen that, to empty our bodies.

To appease the black snow of Minnesota, children were deployed to kill bull snakes and fox snakes and rat snakes and racers, garter snakes and milk snakes and hognoses and smoothies. We hung their skins from rafters and clotheslines, next to frozen hornets' nests, and frozen blouses, tied them to bedposts, and to the middles of our kitchen oil lamps, by the orange light of which we ground the last of the snake meat. In summer, the skins would blister, crisp. In winter, they would retain their moisture, often freeze. Uncle, perhaps really sleeping now, speaks of Hotdish and snakes, wet heavy centers, crumbly toppings. How the weight of all things varies with the weather. Occasionally, in winter, Uncle says, someone would try to hang himself with a length of snakeskin, and occasionally, the skin would be strong enough and he would succeed.

Here, success is convincing ourselves that heat is enough. Failing that, the snakes overtake us.

"Pray," Luther said, "And let God worry."

* * *

UNCLE, IN SLEEP, convinces us. Gravity is only weather, the inevitable sinking into the baked sludge beneath, and electricity is the closing of the oven door. Listen, he says, for the hiss in the blizzard, the rat sewn up, like all libido, in its belly. Listen for that ultimate drop of milk.

All toppings sink and become soggy. All heat dissipates and becomes the frost on the window. In this way, everything can become smaller, mute, as if televised. We look at all that white sky. All those dead beets. Let's stand naked as potatoes, the puddle for the hail, become so agitated we have to leave the state, unzip the last things left on our bodies. Let's close our eyes and imagine obvious things inside of us—blood and fire and poverty and family, and something even hotter than that.

Bulldog NE Tater Tot Hotdish

Serves: 6

Roasted Mushroom Bechamel 1.5 qt

4 ounces yellow onions, small diced

6 garlic cloves, minced

¼ pound butter

6 fluid ounces all-purpose flour

4 cups whole milk

2 teaspoons kosher salt

1 teaspoons white pepper, ground

3 cups cremini mushrooms, small chopped

Braised Beef Brisket 1 to 1½ lbs cooked weight

3 pounds beef brisket

2 sprigs rosemary

5 stems thyme

1 medium-sized red onion, sliced

1 garlic head, cut in half

2 cups of any chocolate stout beer

1 cup red wine

3 ounces brown sugar

2 cups beef stock reduction

2 cups water

3 tablespoons black peppercorns

1 bay leaf

Caramelized Brussels Sprouts 1.5 quart

2 quart Brussels sprouts, stem removed, cut in half, and blanched until bright green

1 pound whole butter

2 cups brown sugar

1 tablespoon salt and pepper

4 fluid ounces black truffle oil

3 cups grated fresh Parmesan cheese

½ cup minced chives and parsley equal mix

6 cups baked tater tots

Method

To make the Roasted Mushroom Bechamel: Sweat the onions, mushrooms, and garlic in butter until translucent and the mushrooms brown. Add flour and heat through, cooking until it slightly browns. Slowly add milk and cook over low heat until it thickens, should reach but not exceed 140–145 degrees F. Season and refrigerate until later use.

To make the Braised Brisket: Cut the brisket into large chunks. Season with 2 teaspoons kosher salt and 1 teaspoon black pepper. Sear in a large pan until browned on all sides. Remove meat from pan and set aside. Sauté the onion, garlic, and herbs in the same pan and deglaze with red wine. Reduce to au sec then place everything into a roasting pan. Foil wrap and put in the oven at 275 degrees for 4 hours. Remove meat and strain liquid. Shred the beef and reduce the liquid by half. After the liquid reduces, add enough reduction to the beef to cover the meat by an inch. Store until ready to use.

To make the Caramelized Brussels Sprouts: Melt the butter in large round and shallow pot until it starts to brown slightly. Add sprouts and turn heat down to low. Cook sprouts until they start to brown. Add sugar and cook until completely caramelized and sticky. Should be slightly crispy. Season with salt and pepper, store until later use.

Assembly

In a large bowl, combine the freshly baked tots, black truffle oil, and 2 cups of the parmesan cheese, and toss until thoroughly mixed.

Place the tater tot mixture into baking dish and spread evenly. Top the tots with the cooled braised brisket and juice. Spread the caramelized Brussels sprouts evenly over the beef and tots. Pour the cooled mushroom bechamel over to cover most of the already layered ingredients. Sprinkle the last cup of parmesan cheese and herb mix on top of the Hotdish. Cover and bake in the oven at 375 degrees for 30–35 minutes until slightly bubbly. Pull the foil and bake 5 minutes more. Place the Hotdish on a cooling rack or towel for 7–10 minutes before serving.

—Kevin Kraus, executive chef, Bulldog, NE Minneapolis

WISCONSIN

Endnotes for the Sheboygan Bratwurst

THOUGH THE SHEBOYGAN bratwurst was brought to central-eastern Wisconsin by German immigrants from the Nuremberg area, it is the French, after whom so many Upper Midwestern towns are named, who claim ownership of its invention by claiming ownership of the invention of all sausage.

* * *

DEPENDING ON the various pronunciations based on syllabic stresses, *Sheboygan*, loosely translated from the Chippewa, means *a needle,* or *anything that perforates or pierces,* or means *send through,* or *drum*, or means *a great noise coming from beneath the river,* or means *pipe stem,* means *hollow bone*, means *ascension*, or *resurrection*, *birth, rebirth,* means *fuck you and your tarragon.*

* * *

THOUGH THE ACT of smoking meats as a preservative measure was initially popular solely with the Romans, the French claim ownership of the salting method responsible for the first hams and sausages. According to the text *Heptaméron*, by Queen Marguerite of Navarre (1492–1549), a poor Pyrenees pig stumbled over its trotters and fell into the headwaters of a natural salt spring on the outskirts of the town Salies-de-Béarn. The clumsy beast drowned, its body rescued by a team of herdsmen and eaten by the townsfolk during an impromptu feast. Blown away by the flavor the salt spring imparted to the meat, the locals began to mimic the salting procedure, and word, as they say, got out, all the way to Nuremberg.

* * *

HERE, ALL perforations bleed alike.

* * *

IN THIS WAY, not only were the horses saved, but the first European to reach the Wisconsin River, Père Jacques Marquette himself, without the spices the explorers used to savor their sausage, would have bled out that night.

* * *

WISCONSIN means it *lies red*, which means that even our blood withholds its truth.

* * *

HERE, WE GRIND the veal with the pork, we shun the hog casing or, if already cased, rip the meat from it. We think nothing of evisceration. There's too much snow for that. We flatten it onto the griddle with diced onion. Here, our meat can't be contained, and therefore, goes cold so much the faster.

* * *

HERE, IN THE WINTER, those who descend from Nuremberg take their sausage with red wine similarly spiced with clove, cinnamon, anise . . . We make no jokes about the season, or any sort of trial.

* * *

THOUGH BRATWURST'S origins have been traced back some six thousand years, the art of sausage-making really gained a foothold during the Western Roman Empire, when the ruling class's palates demanded a more refined cuisine (they went so far as to legislate ways of preserving pig joints), and was elevated to operatic status in France and Germany after the empire's fall in the fifth century. Originally, as now, the sausage dealt primarily with pork, which, according to Galen, a second-century Roman doctor (of Greek origin), first entered into the human diet via cannibal cultures, as the meat of the pig most closely resembles that of the human in flavor.

* * *

In hot climes, we eat each other traditionally; in cold ones like this, we do so only desperately.

* * *

Here, we must question the nature of *true* in *The Last True Wilderness of the Midwest* (a name that often refers to the grouping of Wisconsin, Michigan, and Minnesota), implying the falsity of other trees, trees elsewhere, Indiana trees and Illinois trees. The trees in Ohio are bald-faced liars and the Iowa trees are imported. Somewhere, beneath these, the first true wilderness shades the silkworms, and, should they have dined on beet greens, their red thread, and the rainwater going rank in the shells of their halved cocoons.

* * *

The cocoon predicts the casing. Rebirth predicts its ripping open.

* * *

The poplar, in the worst of its dreams, is of the people, but not of Sheboygan.

* * *

Sheboygan is a coat made of sheepskin.

* * *

A parka stuffed with the feathers of so many dead birds. One may wonder, heart-burning past midnight with too many bratwurst sandwiches, where all the birds' meat went. All of the bills, blood, brains, feet.

* * *

So much depends on the grain of the grind.

* * *

Coarsely, we squeeze into our jackets and our brains tell us that we're warmer.

* * *

We are ready for this world, and its towns and restaurants and trails and bicyclists and old drunk men with dead wives named Dafne or Tannhäuser, Isolde, Salome, or Elektra, and Lake Michigan to poach us beyond grief and trichinosis.

* * *

This is the true wilderness of the Midwest.

* * *

Encasing a region in a slogan helps to make its winter more bearable.

* * *

We remember the Bavarian–Austrian Salt Treaty with hot tongues and freezing lips. In Sandee's Pub, Heinrich throws a dart at Fritz.

* * *

Because this is a small town, the meth lab, by definition, is close to the Walgreen's.

* * *

The Sheboygan Bratwurst Company's customer testimonials, for example: *Phenominal [sic], shouted grease, fat bursting, so addicting, excited, exited [sic], wonderful, amazing, thank you, thank you, thank you, don't shrink . . .*

* * *

Here, size is a plea.

* * *

In Wisconsin, I saw a cauldron of considerable size only once. In it, a grad student of mine was boiling the head of a doe. "Preparing it," were the words he used. The cauldron's feet were held in place by the ice. The fire couldn't melt all of it. I think he detected my shock, but mistook its source and suggested we go have some lunch. I ordered the Sheboygan brat on a hamburger bun with poppy seeds and coleslaw. He had the whitefish sandwich with sweet potato fries. I put both meals on the university credit card.

* * *

SOME PATRIOTS mistakenly believe that *Sheboygan* is an endearment for Scheibenberg, a Saxon hamlet whose population has been steadily decreasing since 1951.

* * *

SHEBOYGAN BRATWURST as cute exodus, as babyfied exile to a seven-month winter.

* * *

WE FLATTEN our bratwurst in resigned camaraderie. Today's *Minneapolis City Pages* headline reads, as written by Hart Von Denberg, "Minnesota Ranks 28 in U.S. Penis Size. The Good News? We're Ahead of Wisconsin."

* * *

THE SHEBOYGAN brat as indifference toward equality.

* * *

SHEBOYGAN BRAT, the addition of.

* * *

ACCORDING TO Sheboygan's Brat Days "History," "The idea of Bratwurst Day goes back as far as six decades B.C." Fast-forward:

> *Mayor Edward C. Schmidt's proclamation, which designated the 13th as Bratwurst Day read, in part: Whereas, this community has achieved national fame and recognition for the exclusive manufacture of a special kind of roasting sausage, and Whereas, it is a known and established fact that the production and distribution of bratwurst has increased year by year to a*

point where it has become an industry of vital importance to this community—all citizens and visitors are to refrain from roasting bratwurst on their own grills and will attend and enjoy the 'Bratwurst Festivities' to be held on the main street in the City of Sheboygan.

Streets were renamed Bratwurst Boulevard and Onion Oasis . . . Nowhere else in the world would you find a scene like this at 8 a.m.

Fathers shove their daughters forward, hoping, every year, that they will be driving home with this year's crowned Bratwurst Queen seatbelted into the passenger side.

* * *

WHEN ASKED why she ate over a dozen miniature brats, cooked, according to the *New York Times*, "over an open beechwood charcoal fire and lined up with Teutonic precision on a paper plate, [a Sheboygan woman named Betsy] later explained, pitcously, 'I was cold.'"

* * *

SAY "SHEBOYGAN" in Germany, and no one will understand you. It is ours now, the last true ours of the Midwest.

* * *

GREEK MYTHOLOGY further details the importance of the pig, citing that Zeus, as an infant god, was sustained by the milk of a prominent sow.

* * *

"A COARSE grind is fine."

* * *

ACCORDING TO the *New York Times*, "In Sheboygan, [bratwurst] is an object of veneration, taken as seriously as a lock of some medieval saint's hair."

* * *

I OVERHEARD someone say that the smell of uncased bratwurst cooking is "celestial." Juice spitting freely. Her comment predicted the aurora borealis that drew green lassos over Lake Michigan. The story of the aurora borealis, as rendered on the *Channel 3 Nightly News*, included the line, "went missing . . . last seen on his snowmobile at the Old Plank Road trailhead," which predicted the commercial advertising "Two-buck Ladies' Night brats." The frost on our bedroom window looks churchly.

* * *

WE MUST be careful.

* * *

TWO BRATWURSTS are usually squeezed onto one bun. Says Charles K. Meisfield III, fourth-generation Sheboygan bratwurst manufacturer, "It's a mortal sin here if you order a single."

* * *

OF THE *She* in *Sheboygan*, we say, and define: *used in place of* it *to refer to certain inanimate things, such as ships and nations, traditionally perceived as female,* as in Anne Sexton's verse, "The sea is mother-death and she is a mighty female," or "Is the cat a she?"

* * *

IN SANDEE'S, someone calls the Sheboygan brat "Caesarian," then throws a bull's eye to end the game.

* * *

IN ITALY'S Emilia-Romagna region, a hush falls over the village of Ferrara. Talk of its indigenous *salamina da sugo* rarely breaches its borders, though this anarchic sausage is seen by many as another precursor to the Sheboygan bratwurst. Perennially crowning the Christmas tables of the Ferrarese, the mysterious and controversial dish remains out of reach for the rest of the world, allowable only via reinvention in another last true wilderness.

The salamina cum Sheboygan style of sausage was first documented in a fifteenth-century letter from Lorenzo il Magnifico to

Duke Ercole II d'Este. Apparently, the first to produce the product were the *porcaioli* of the Trentino and Bormio mountains. Eventually, they migrated into the Po valley, and then into the area that was to become Ferrara. Not a single discovered document mentioned salamina da sugo again, until 1722.

Capturing the artistic heart and palate of writer Antonio Frizzi, salamina da sugo became the object of his poem "Salamoide."

Frizzi writes, "I mix the pig's liver with its meat, put an iron on top, and step on the iron."

Frizzi went on further to speculate that the pigs destined to become salamina are born carrying the spirits of all dead women. In tasting it, he wrote, one has difficulty separating flavor from verse.

Often invoked as a reliable aphrodisiac, the salamina (or salama, as it is often called) was a popular meal at wedding banquets and brothels. The dish was reputed to soften the skin and add life to the blood of newlyweds, as well as prepare the ladies of the night for their customers.

The Slow Food movement, which, among other revolutionary tasks, takes it upon itself to rescue "endangered" foods from the jaws of overregulation (from governmental departments of "health"), flies the salamina da sugo as one of their primary flags. This is, indeed, a nearly extinct breed of sausage, stirring the Slow Food movement to educate the masses via protest in an attempt to lift it from certain death.

Today, the salamina remains commercially illegal, reserved for back-alley gourmands and cultish, hooded dinner parties, and those of us Upper Midwesterners who take it in numbed form, lifted from the frozen food tubs at the Piggly Wiggly.

The dish begins with the grinding of the "less noble" but more flavorful parts of the pig: liver, tongue, belly, shoulder, chin, top neck, throat lard, cheek, thigh. The ground meat is then coupled and cured with an array of spices—types and amounts differ with each producer. Typical spices include salt, pepper, nutmeg, cinnamon, clove, and garlic. Red wine (approximately two liters per ten kilograms of meat) is added to the mixture—usually a Sangiovese, Barbera, or semisecco del Bosco Eliceo. Certain producers also add rum, grappa, or brandy.

The mixture is packed into a pork bladder, tied with twine, and traditionally divided into eight segments. In a well-ventilated, dark chamber, at about 50 degrees Fahrenheit, the salamina is hung to ripen and age for at least one year. During this time, the salamina is periodically brushed with olive oil and vinegar.

Once sufficiently aged, the salamina will bear a protective coating of white mold. Prior to preparation, the mold is rinsed away and the cased meat is soaked in lukewarm water for at least twelve hours. After the soaking session, the salamina is placed inside a cloth bag, which is then tied to the center of a long wooden stick. The stick is draped across the top of a large cauldron, so that the salamina bag is hanging in the middle, away from the pot's bottom and sides. The cauldron is filled with water, and the salamina cooks for about four hours at a low simmer. Once ready, the salamina is cut from the bag and gently removed from its casing with a spoon. The salamina's wine is released during the cooking process, yielding a viscous and spicy sauce.

* * *

Like our wilderness and our winter and our sausage, we are barely legal and stubbornly clandestine. We are the Culinary Underground, gathering in windowless spaces, camps in the woods, reading by candlelight, ancient farmland recipes, and passing samples of banned foodstuffs. We, and the salamina, and its Sheboygan brat offspring, will survive in the coldest attics of the world.

* * *

This part of the world is confusing and beautiful.

* * *

Try it with mustard.

Sheboygan Bratwurst

In Sheboygan, Wisconsin, the famous brat sandwich is cooked on a charcoal grill then finished in a sauce of beer, butter, and onions. It is served on a Sheboygan hard roll with butter, ketchup, brown mustard, raw onion, and pickles, or any combination of those. You can order a single or double brat (one or two sausages on the roll).

—Harry Ljatifovski, owner,
Harry's Diner and Harry's Prohibition Bistro

The Fata Morgana in the Loosemeat Sandwich

IT TAKES A TORNADO named Orbit, or Target, or Moss, or Thurman to rip Iowa corn kernels from their cobs. It takes the sky doing the can-can, showing off its thick gray thigh, waving around the grayer slip. So much wind here this season, you wonder if any kernel has a chance, if the cob can hold on to one, two maybe, tighten its silk in the face of what meteorologists are calling a final loosening, *loose* being the more wonderful, expressive version of *loss.*

This flat landscape plays tricks on us. We're not really seeing what we think we're seeing; eating what we think . . . This is state as sorceress, siren, the Vulgar Latin for *fairy*; as the untwining of our optic nerves; the curvature of the light rays over the cornfields in this kind of wind is stronger than the curvature of the earth. This is Iowa as bullying the planet.

What else can we do but name our state sandwich after this coming apart? If we anticipate the separation, the severing of arm from body, body from earth, ovule from its little bedchamber in the cob, and, more to the point, roof from house, beef from its bone, we can brace ourselves for this wind, we can be loose, noncommittal, just freewheeling enough to come easily undone. Here, it's better to shed than to shatter.

My uncle orders his second Loosemeat Sandwich, tells me that these have nothing on the originals, the ones Abe Kaled created at Ye Olde Tavern in Sioux City in 1934. My uncle ate these unformed, uncompacted burgers at Ye Olde until 1974, when the place closed as Bertha's—Abe's wife's—health went south, and none of their children showed any interest in continuing Abe's tradition of steaming, then heaping a molehill of crumbly ground beef onto a steamed white bun, topping it with ketchup, mustard, sautéed onion, and pickle, and serving it—for a dime—not on a plate, but on a neatly folded square of wax paper, the children instead preferring to uncouple from Sioux City, a town that so revered its corn, it built five "palaces" to honor it.

Ye Olde stayed open from 7 a.m. to midnight. Seventeen daily hours of meat falling from other meat. Uncle and I bite easily through the Loosemeats. Uncle and I swivel on our stools, chewing, the mess of our futures all over our shirtfronts. We know: things here are loose by design. If we are more easily wiped away, we are more easily rebuilt. In this, we may be misguided, but, still, our sandwiches are softer than yours, which means they have more heart.

If the stool has no backrest, that is an uncomfortable stool, but, still, we can come down off of that stool that much faster. Uncle and I argue whether the Loosemeat is more or less evolved than the hamburger. Whether its looseness—what Uncle likes to call its ABC-ness (Already-Been-Chewed-ness)—indicates an evolved state or an entropic one. If the Loosemeat is easier to chew at the start, we have to do less work. Here, the more broken-down we are, the more evolved we are, the closer we are to the end state.

The Loosemeat Sandwich, as compared to the hamburger, begins its life closer to being chewed and swallowed. Uncle says, this is appropriate to Iowa, as the tavern windows convulse in their frames.

* * *

Along the crossroads of I-35 and I-80, the wind farms pluck energy from the sky, which is darkening. Uncle calls these farms Ballerinas with Blades, drives off the road, hypnotized. Stanching his nosebleed with the steering wheel's wool cover, he comes up with another description, but it is loose, at best. We name the wind here Whispering Turbine, and we name it Alberta Clipper, and we think that the same thing that can cut us down can also tell us the secrets we mistakenly believe are the most precious. In the Loosemeat is the sober embracing of our inevitable, hair-whipping lives. In this sloughing off is the illusion of the fresh skin beneath the old.

If the cornrows sometimes seem like passageways out of here, this is, at best, a loose stab at escape. Get real. Getting lost is not the same as getting out. That elevator at the end is not really a palace.

Some Iowa historians claim that Abe and Bertha Kaled created the Loosemeat Sandwich because, dually arthritic, they hadn't the strength in their hands to form the meat into a decent patty, one that would hold itself to itself. So, they used the ripped-apart corn as excuse, and said that the sandwich, born in stubborn weakness, was a tribute to the fields after the weather.

In 1900, Iowa had more residents than California. In 1887, Sioux City was home to the 1887 Corn Palace, which encompassed more than 18,000 square feet and housed a roller rink named Goldie. In 1888, a new Corn Palace was built which included such architectural flourishes as a "huge main tower" and several "sub-towers." Every square inch of the exterior, except for the wood of the flagpoles, was covered with glued-on grain culled from the local elevators, which, in all of this flatness, from the interstates look like main towers themselves.

The flatness, Iowans say, allows the grain elevators their majesty. We're convinced sometimes that they are mirages, swimming loosely in the watery heat haze. We drive toward them, faster and faster, but still, they're so far away. Here, the fields are these everlasting foothills. Here, we tighten our grip on the wheel. Uncle knows: distance is distorted by the stuff that blows through the air—the ripped silks, the grain that, in the winds of 1888, tore from the facade of the Corn Palace and, in the whirling Whispering Turbines and Alberta Clippers, stayed with us, right here in this state, where they know, as we do, as does the Loosemeat Sandwich, that we call our towers *elevators*, even when they're going down.

* * *

Even as I think *swimming*, and *watery*, I know: Iowa is the state whose residents are least likely to own, or ever board, a boat. Even our descriptions for mirages are sort of mirages, and thereby some of the loosest language in the country. Soil loosens, leaves, in this weather, the earth for the sky. Though satellite photos still today depict the gutters carved into the earth by the wagon wheels of the passing-through pioneers, these ruts are not as deeply planted as the 1848 headstones that flank them, reading BELOVED, reading STARVATION, reading UNMATCHED, DETATCHED, THE WIND TOOK HER . . .

"If this land were correctly built," Uncle says, "all this shit wouldn't blow away," but that's too easily apocalyptic for me, so I gum my sandwich and wonder about the difference between *away* and *around*, a swallowing throat, and a tightening one. "If you tie a knot too well," Uncle says, wiping the mustard from his chin, "you'll never get that knot undone." Up the road, a turbine that looks miles closer than it is loses a screw, and all things permanent become damnable, embarrassing.

In 1889, the Sioux City mothers and fathers decided that not enough people yet recognized their hometown as the Corn Palace City, so they sponsored the Corn Palace Train to travel to and along the U.S. eastern seaboard. Like the Corn Palaces themselves, the train cars were decorated with stuck-on cornmeal, most of which detached in the wind when the train traveled at high speeds, dusting the coastline with this strange new pollen from the country's middle. Still, and though it threatened the town with bankruptcy, the Sioux City mothers and fathers "all considered it a good investment."

We know: it's tough to invest in a sandwich we know is going to disintegrate. Better to make it slapdash from the get-go. We know: if it's already broken, it can't break.

* * *

OTHER NAMES for the Loosemeat Sandwich: the Tavern, the Maid-Rite, the Sloppyless Sloppy Joe, the Canteen, the Tastee, the Charlie Boy, the Nu Way, the Wobble, the Slump, the Clogged (read: Broken) Heart. We don't name our tornadoes anymore. They're too common. And that's putting them on the same level as our sandwiches.

Between bites, Uncle speaks of a phenomenon he calls the Iowan Inversion. In this flatness, he says, it's tough for us to process distance. If we stare long enough at the tornado on the horizon, "loosen our eyes," he says, it will appear to flip itself and attack, instead, the cosmos.

We know: in the funnel is a tapering, a breaking-down. It's easy to mistake this for a tightening, but we know better: *funnel* derives from *fundere, to pour.* We know: the pouring requires a severing—one thing leaving its source. Roof from house, beef from bone . . . If this meat is loose enough to pour from our sandwiches, can we more easily dominate it, claim ownership? Can we tell ourselves that this kind of weather needs us? That the wind needs to pour over our bodies? Like the wind, or any poured thing, the Loose-meat splatters to the counter. Our bodies, the poured-from things, stand shocked in this new, quick emptiness. To stay grounded, to return, we fill ourselves with anything not tied down.

The medievalists know: the inverted funnel is a symbol of madness. The paintings tell us this: Bosch's *Ship of Fools, Allegory of Gluttony and Lust.* This is a callous sort of insanity, one which tries to convince us not to prepare for the weather, one which tells us that the tornado touches down in the sky, one which tells us, our homes are well-anchored, formed, as if into patties a quarter-inch thick. "Look at the Tin Man's hat, even," Uncle says, "and we all know that motherfucker was heartless."

The tornado struck the hospital in Creston, buried Fremont County in I-beams and plastic pipes and skylights. Dogs watched their own eyes go out in shards of old bathroom mirror, the glass and their bodies now collecting the rain, differently, but both collecting. In the mirrors, the distorted reflection of deluge sopped into the kind of fur that, from a distance, in all of this flatland, when our own heads are bleeding like this, can be a cornfield undulating in a wind so nonthreatening we call it a *breeze.* In this way, we can make even the most unwieldy, light. The invisible, reflective. If the corn moves, we can see the wind. If the soil rises above us, this land is fall-off-the-bone.

This is state as the farmland according to the *Physiologia Epicuro-Gassendo-Charltoniana,* "bent into arcades," rising like "innumerable palaces, which divided into towers . . . a sweep of windows, then pines and cypresses . . . mountains . . . and a beautiful expanse of water, reflecting its cultivated shores, and the cattle that were grazing on its banks."

We forget that both *mirror* and *mirage* derive from the same root: *to wonder, to admire*, both acts made real in the mathematic of flatness and wind. Boasting no desert, mountain, sea, forest, volcano, canyon, Iowa is so flat, it's been called the country's missing tooth. A gap. Uncle knows, for a tooth to go missing, it must first become loose.

* * *

IN 1890, Sioux City built the "biggest Corn Palace yet." Dwarfing the grain elevators, the Palace featured a 200-foot-tall main tower, six 100-foot-tall sub-towers, and an obese dome decorated as a globe, the countries mapped with kernels of corn. On this globe, both Iowa and, in turn, Sioux City were outsized and dominant and central. According to the *Sioux City Journal*, the Palace housed an auditorium that could accommodate 1,200 people, and a miniature valley bearing "far distant mountains clothed in pines" from which "came a stream of water, leaping over rocks, winding across a meadow, and falling into a lake below where palmettos were growing." Uncle bites into his Loosemeat and you, and I, can't help but become heavy-handed, watch the loose meat flop onto the wax paper like so many airborne palmettos halved by the turbines that, no matter how long we drive off the interstate, it seems, in this flatness, we'll never reach.

We don't have mountains here. We can see everything. We have to fabricate out of fiberglass, and dream of the kind of land that has the power to obstruct. This is, of course, wishful thinking made manifest, and manifest destiny, like actual destiny: another sort of optical trick.

If the turbines become unhinged, blow toward that silo, we can, briefly, until impact, see the *wind* . . .

* * *

"THE MATHEMATICS of excess of loss," says mathematician Yoong-Sin Lee, "involves heavy algebra . . . the heavy algebra is often a great mental burden. [These] ideas have geometric as well as symbolic interpretation."

There's a house rendered to triangles. A Palace, a heap of arcs, nodes of grain that once served as siding. Let's work at this. Graph it. Let's make the triangle stand for *evergreen*, and then, *immortal*. Let's redefine the axis as the point at which all things will eventually come apart.

We know, in permanence is the one-note, the stubborn tree that only, just to see what it feels like, wants to turn red. Ye Olde Tavern and Abe Kaled's Loosemeat were lionized in 2011 on an Iowa radio program titled *Pickles and Ice Cream*. I want to say something about the sour and the sweet as equally delicious, about the loosest things that can still sustain us, but this is obvious symbolism at best, so heavy—like loss—that we can only drop it.

Here, it's better to shed than to shatter.

The year 1891, according to SiouxCityHistory.org, was the last in which the Corn Palace was "active." In reverence is the preservative brine evolving toward the melting-away. Our sandwich tells us that regression is the obvious next step forward. If something's coming loose, that means it's still active.

Let's take only loose things into us. If it has a definite shape—corners, edges—it can cut us. It can be the fiberglass in our lungs. Let's cut it down first.

* * *

In a lack of action is petrifaction. A crusting-over, a tightening of the molecular structure. The original pore spaces fill in with minerals, grain. And we eat so many sandwiches. The Corn Palace of Sioux City is petrified. That doesn't mean it's afraid of the weather. That doesn't mean it will survive it.

In all mathematics, Morris Kline says, is the loss of certainty. That's how the discipline moves forward. Bertha Kaled, dying, says, "I would have to carry most of the responsibility because [Abe] didn't know anything about cooking . . . I was kind of a mother."

"And the sunsets," Uncle says, "rip the sky open." We lose our homes, and our Olde Taverns, and our drive to call tornadoes by human names. Our mothers and fathers and husbands and wives. We lose the energy to break through anything that's tightly bound to itself. That's the wind's job. We can fight by recovering. By corn. By making our world looser the next time around.

"Mountain, headstone, sunset, gut," he says. "It's amazing what we call pretty." In mothering, Uncle says, is the drive to make things coalesce. Though I don't think he really knows what he's talking about, he's right when he says, "All restaurants close." He orders his third Loosemeat, stays on his stool, says something about *not how it used to be.* Outside, the clouds stitch together, become this beautiful gown, cinched so tight, the sky, dying again for nakedness, can't take it off. It's yanking at its collar. Uncle knows: the turbines will scream, the sirens will scream, the air will turn the color of the mustard on his chin. Things will become unmoored again, fall easily from their buns. I will imagine that it's the weather Bertha Kaled was talking to when she spoke her last public words: "Thank you. I'm very glad to know who you are. I've seen you, but didn't know your name."

Loosemeat Sandwich

My name is Melissa Freidhof-Rodgers and I am the general manager of Ross'. My grandfather started out his restaurant career by purchasing one of the original Maid Rites. He later developed his own concept and started Ross' Restaurant. Safe to say that we have been serving up the loosemeat for 75 years in one form or another. It is definitely a Midwestern food item. I will never forget when we prepared food on the Rachel Maddow show, my favorite moment was of her laughing when I used the term "loose meat." Which in my upbringing was quite a common term.

A little bit of history on our place: operating since 1938, Ross' Restaurant has been serving up great food in Iowa for ¾ of a century. We are still family owned and operated, and have been featured on CNN, MSNBC, NBC, Iowa Public Television, the *New York Times*, and even internationally in Europe on EenVanDaag. We have served presidents, vice presidents, and celebrities, and everyone remarks about feeling right at home at our establishment which we love. It's fun to do new takes on the classics. I am not sure that my grandfather would have liked the idea but am sure he would have enjoyed the taste once he tried it.

Sriracha Rossburgers

1½ pounds of fresh ground beef, local and grass-fed is ideal
⅛ cup of soy sauce
2 teaspoons freshly ground pepper
3 cloves of fresh garlic, finely minced
½ cup chopped onions
½ teaspoon seasoning salt
5 tablespoons Sriracha sauce

Mix by hand or in standing mixer with paddle all of the above ingredients and cook in a large cast-iron skillet. Start with low heat and use a metal spatula to break down meat as it cooks, this can be done by smashing the meat against the bottom of the skillet and turning often. The end result should be a crumbly meat (similar to Sloppy Joes).

Bacon Caramelized Onions

2 tablespoons unsalted butter
2 medium onions sliced paper thin (about 4 cups)
Kosher salt
Freshly ground black pepper
6 pieces of cherrywood bacon, chopped
¼ cup brown sugar

Melt the butter in a large frying pan over medium low heat (we like to use a cast-iron skillet), add the bacon and onions and let them cook, stirring rarely, until they are deep golden brown and caramelized.

Sriracha Blue Cheese Sauce

4 ounces blue cheese crumbles
⅓ cup sour cream
⅓ cup buttermilk
¼ cup mayo

1 tablespoon vinegar
¼ teaspoon Worcestershire sauce
4 teaspoons Sriracha sauce
2 teaspoons granulated garlic

Putting together your burger: Slice a hamburger or brioche bun grilled both sides with butter, put 5 ounces of your cooked ground beef on the burger and top with caramelized onions and a slice of Swiss cheese, dress the burger with spinach, tomato, Sriracha blue cheese dressing, and add a sunny-side-up egg on top of the cheese. Enjoy.

—Melissa Freidhof-Rodgers, Ross' Restaurant

MICHIGAN

Elements of the Pasty and Its Relation to the Lake

IT'S NOT LIKE this with cream of mushroom soup and La Choy fried onions. In the pasty, in the singular shell, dinner shares space with dessert, as if a calzone with conjoined fillings. We start with dinner and eat downward. It's not like this with Hotdish, with casserole, with pizza with a saltine crust. In the pasty is an eating toward—a sinking into the bottom of food. Eating mimics drowning. In the pasty—a baked pastry shell, half of which includes a savory dinner of stewed meat and root vegetable, half of which includes dessert—is difficulty breathing, eyes adjusting to the mine-shaft dark and to the daylight, anticipation, harbinger, a whole new world beyond the chuck and the rutabaga, apples-and-cinnamon, an eating toward, and an eating toward sweetness.

It's not like this with backyard swimming pools, the facedown hair fanning the surface, the beach ball rolling pink over green. In Lake Superior, drowning is an expected tragedy. It's dark at the bottom of a lake. According to the Great Lakes Surf Rescue Project (GLSRP), "Overall since 2010, 210 people have drowned in the Great Lakes (74 in 2010; 87 in 2011; and 49 to date in 2012).

"'Just unbelievable how these drowning numbers just keep rising week after week,' said Dave Benjamin [GLSRP Executive Director of Public Relations]. 'At this rate we could see well over 100 by the end of the year.'"

* * *

AFTER DAYS in mineshaft darkness, my uncle, or somebody's uncle, or so many of our uncles, swear by backstroking in Lake Superior.

It has to do with currents, tides, whitecaps. It has to do with everything wet and huge and cool enough to float on. If a body of water this large isn't killing us, Uncle says, it's supporting our weight.

Like the dessert section of the pasty, the number 100 is something to reach for, to attain. 100 is a milestone. A goal, sweet and morbid. A perfect, even number. Nothing is more even, more steady, than the hands of the drowned. Not even 100. Like the mine, Lake Superior supports its own agriculture. Off the shore of my hometown, in 2010, the body of Rod Nilsestuen, Wisconsin Secretary of Agriculture, was found floating in Lake Superior.

My uncle has a bumper sticker that says "FUCK CORNWALL, THIS IS MICHIGAN." If my uncle doesn't have this bumper sticker, then he has black lung, and if he doesn't have black lung, then he's depressed due to a lack of light, and if he's not depressed due to a lack of light, he can call this only soul-sickness, can only lament the ways in which we're not jacketed in pastry dough brushed with egg yolk, a crust that will protect us from birds who scream from the dark, from the lack of air that, in the beginning, seemed to exhilarate.

"Animals Drown at Lake Superior Zoo," reads the headline, and Uncle laughs. It's his one day off. He's just come back from his swim, for lunch.

* * *

THIS IS GOAL-ORIENTED eating. The meat as a means to an end. Macerated plums on Thursday. The brake to a shaking hand. In the bath of the headlamp is the pasty and the hand that holds it. The batteries here are strong. Once we bite through the crust, release the steam, the heat, the wet, something of the ghost and something of the future, things begin to go cold, dry, the batteries here are the only things that are strong. Tomorrow, I want to lie in bed all day. I wish I lived closer to the lake. I want to lie in bed all day and listen to whitefish court other whitefish. I want to hear people swimming safely. It's good to have a goal.

In Michigan's Upper Peninsula, from 1843 through the 1920s, pure native copper just about leaked from the earth, exploded from it, and towns were established and boomed, and folks ate food and drank liquor and men spread their legs and women spread their legs and with food and liquor and spread legs made descendants who can visit these towns in the name of communion and reunion and union and none, and we call these gatherings *heartfelt* and we call these gatherings *historical*, and we use words like *ancestry* and *inheritance* and we stand on the rock piles and bluffs and tailings of Central Mine and Gay and Mandan and Cliff and Delaware and Phoenix and we eat pasties not because we need to, but because they are some sort of souvenir, some kind of shaft that leads, definitively down, toward something like heritage or lakebed, something makeshift, but geologic and collapsible, and we pretend that these towns are not popularly preceded by the word *ghost*.

The old Phoenix church, in 1858, was called St. Mary's. Later, it was disassembled and rebuilt and renamed the Church of the Assumption. We assume there are meanings in names. *Superior* derives from the Latin *superiorum* or *superus*, meaning *situated above*, or *upper*. Lake Superior has the greatest depth of the Great Lakes, which means something to a miner. It's something to one day descend into. It's a milestone. Lake Superior has the highest elevation of the Great Lakes, though Uncle backfloats upon it. To the drowned, Lake Superior lives up to its name. Here, to float upon is better than to float within. The upper implies the angelic, though implication is often misleading.

The Ontonagon Boulder, of the Upper Peninsula's village of Old Victoria, is a 3,708-pound massif of native copper. It can now be found in the Smithsonian Institution's National Museum of Natural History in Washington, DC, where, should a tourist decide not to read the exhibit's plastic three-by-five placard, he or she will wonder about the specialness of this big, ugly rock. Ontonagon, in the Chippewa language, translates as *lost bowl*. Regarding the pasty, I'm not sure what this should mean. Regarding the lake, this is convoluted metaphor at best.

According to a travel brochure titled "Visit the Upper Peninsula of Michigan's world famous 'Copper Country,'" Old Victoria is "a very picturesque ghost town."

* * *

THE ATOMIC WEIGHT of copper is 63.55 g/mol. The atomic weight of iron is 55.85. The atomic weight of sulfur is 32.07. The atomic weight of gold is 196.97. The average pasty weighs two pounds. The average human lung weighs about 14 ounces, so much heavier than this underground air, so much lighter than the pasty. Lake Superior is comparatively obese, but not lazy.

While many immigrant miners in the Upper Peninsula were from Cornwall, many more were Finns, Austrian, Croatian, Italian, Canadian, and Swedish. Each group impacted the pasty's regional evolution, with seasoning, with ingredient. Culinary arguments were fierce. Regardless, each version varied little (those who lived near Superior often used lakewater in the dough), and each version was easily portable, heavy and hearty, but clutchable in one hand, and each version, in the cold of the deep, could be heated up on a shovel held over the candleflame of the miner's headlamp. The pasties are cooking. The canaries are screaming. Someone coughs. That means they've not yet drowned.

The U.P. pasty, when compared to the Cornish variety, contained larger chucks of vegetable, a higher ratio of vegetable to meat, encased in a thinner crust. The U.P. pasty as thin-skinned, even in all of this winter, the weather, and the water, closer to the blood. The U.P. pasty as a little of this, a little of that, as Yiddish, as Fanagolo, as Esperanto, and the language through which we all can communicate up here/down here, as a means to understanding, as overused symbology, as cliché, as Kumbaya, as all things savory sharing space with all things sweet. As reminder. As anchor. As something even a really big lake can't wash away.

* * *

OFTEN, a homestead requires leaving home, and then never leaving the homestead. For the subsequent generations, it requires never leaving home in the first place. The pasty as perspective, encased in a hard crust. As riding a snowmobile before you can walk. As backfloating over 100 bodies. As your great-grandson doing the same thing.

An 1861 proverb proclaimed that the more ingredients one crams into the pasty, the more protection one has from the Devil, as the Devil may fear that he may end up as just another ingredient for the filling. In Superior National Forest, over two dozen attractions—islands, campgrounds, inland lakes, waterfalls, trails, jumps (the Devil's Washtub jump, while technically outside of the forest's boundaries, claims lives each year as folks attempt to leap from a cliff, over a series of jagged rocks, into Lake Superior)—are named after the Devil.

On the playgrounds of the turn-of-the-century U.P., schoolboys would sing:

Matthew, Mark, Luke and John
Ate a pasty five feet long,
Bit it once, bit it twice,
Oh, my Lord, it's full of mice.

* * *

THE PASTY sits fixed in the hands of the miner, poised, poisoned. The lake unfixes itself, runs from the hands we eat with. Regarding the Quincy Mine Shelter, from the aforementioned brochure, "Hopefully this historic site will be restored." An eating toward. Before we die, we take the elevator up. As with surfacing from the lake, it takes a few seconds to recognize the sun.

In the candle-shadow of the pasty and the birds and the shovel, coughing, we can't tell where umbra becomes penumbra becomes antumbra. We can't tell hands from feet. We can't tell if that's a shadow dying, or a man. We can't tell if the body is broken, or celestial. We can't tell that Lake Superior has been called the earth's youngest major feature—at only ten thousand years old, a side effect of the last retreat of the glaciers. We can't tell that the lake is tantrumming like a little sister, can't tell that *retreat* is sometimes an answer and, to a superior lake, a Big Bang. We can't tell that our uncles, still young, look so old.

So, we eat. And, in swimming after eating, test our ability to stave off the drowning. On the beach, the smell of cooking dinner. Of greasy wax paper unwrapping from pastry shells. In them, the sounds of lakes masquerading as oceans. Sometimes, the sun is out. In it, we must come up to the surface of the earth. We must retreat to the shore. It's lighter there.

Pasty

Makes: 12 Pasties

Crust
12–14 teaspoons water
1¼ teaspoons salt
1⅓ cups lard or shortening
4 cups flour

For bread maker: Combine all four ingredients in order and use the dough setting on bread maker (add a touch of water or flour depending on dough consistency).

For dough mixer: Combine all four ingredients in reverse order and mix until good dough consistency (add water or flour as needed).

Filling
1 pound ground pork
1 pound ground beef
4–5 large brown potatoes (peeled and chopped in ¼-in cubes)
2 yellow onions (finely chopped)
1 small rutabaga (peeled and chopped in ¼-in cubes)
Salt
Pepper

Combine all filling ingredients in large mixing bowl and season generously with salt and pepper. Mix filling with gloved hands until everything is held together with meat.

Cut the dough into 12 equal pieces and use a rolling pin to roll each one into about a 6-to-7-inch circle. Then put 1⁄12 of the filling onto one side of the rolled-out dough, fold over, and seal the edges.

Bake at 400 degrees for 1 hour or until middle reaches 165 degrees.

Serve with ketchup or gravy.

Enjoy!

—Jacob Taylor

A Blow to the Head for St. Louis Barbecue

HERE, I KNOW, like you know, because of simple things—light and shadow, day and night, yet another engagement of yet another horizon: once again, there's the plains meeting the sky; once again, Andromeda loses a star to the trough, the voices in the sty go mad and fast into the dark. Here's what we know: the pigs' ribs don't remind us of the xylophone. Here, there's no music when, with the sledgehammer, we strike them.

In St. Louis, at a table covered in newspaper (the headlines reading "Missouri Named Murder Capital of America" and "Retired Couple Found Murdered in Missouri," and "Stone County Deputies Find Twelve Bodies" and "State Bird—The Bluebird—Named Nation's Most Insectivorous") twelve bodies hunch over an upturned trash can lid bearing slab after slab of pork ribs sauced in a tomato-based brew that only the heathens from outside the state dare call "heavy-handed."

Across North Market Street, in the tallgrass median fronting the Louis Maull barbecue sauce company, a girl with fibrodysplasia ossificans progressiva pretends that a can of tomato paste is a doll, gives it a voice like a pig. Inside her, another confused muscle goes the way of bone. On a farm outside the city, another cow collapses from its mother, screaming into calfhood. In the next stall, a pig yawns, unsurprised, into the hammer.

* * *

IN 2006, the Kingsford charcoal corporation, in conjunction with Sure Fire Grooves (a division of Kingsford responsible for digging mini-trenches into the briquettes in order to "provide air channels that increase airflow, causing the coals to heat up faster than before") named St. Louis, Missouri, "America's Top Grilling City." According to Kelly Burke, Kingsford's "Charcoal Expert," "Places with bitter winters have catapulted to the top 10 in just one year, showing us that Americans are grilling out year round, no matter what the weather."

February 21, 2013: St. Louis received, according to the National Weather Service, a "treacherous mix of snow, sleet, and freezing rain." The result of an unstable air mass, this precipitous brew coalesced into what meteorologists refer to as *thundersnow*, which often falls in regions of "strong upward motion within the cold sector of an extratropical cyclone," or, as weatherman Scott Truett says, "Instead of pouring rain, it's pouring snow." Such a downpour allowed the snow, in St. Louis, to acoustically dampen the sound of the accompanying thunder and, since the cumulonimbus layer was lower than usual, it was tough to see the lightning from the vantage points of our grills, the fire struggling to assert itself in all of this storming, the grooves in our briquettes hyperventilating, snow up to our boot-tops in under ten minutes.

Uncle says, a pig's blood will freeze faster than that of a human because a pig has no soul to keep it warm. He heads into the barn without a jacket, and the pigs yawn, and he does it with the sledgehammer and the ice pick, and there it is, all that soulless red freezing so quickly, surefire, onto the cement. I'll say nothing here of Adam or of apples or of the way Uncle's neck waves like the Missouri River when he swallows, blows his red hands warm, excises from the pig all the parts that don't remind us of xylophones.

February 21, 2013, suppertime: In St. Louis, two fatal car accidents, an urging by Governor Jay Nixon not to leave our houses, travelers pouring into roadside Econo Lodges and Super 8s, a rash of cabin fever spreading throughout the city, wheat farmers catching the thundersnow in their mouths, whirling, asking, "Is the drought broke?" and "Is this what we've been praying for?" and two more fatal accidents, and Nixon declaring a state of emergency, and Kansas City International Airport shutting down, and Lambert Airport cancelling 340 flights, and the University of Missouri cancelling classes for the second time in 174 years, and St. Louis Walmarts selling out of sleds and alcohol, and so many of us losing our fingers and toes, and pieces of our cheeks and lower eyelids, and the tips of our noses, because we wanted to cook our ribs outside in it—in this thundersnow—and because we sacrifice small bits of ourselves for small bits of the pig, our barbecue is that much smokier this season, and Kingsford calls us number one.

And the girl playing on the median slowly turns to stone. Her doll tries to say *oink*, but is arrested at *oi*. The tomato paste, so quiet inside the can, doesn't care that it's in St. Louis, doesn't care that we only want to mix it with a little water, apple cider vinegar, brown sugar, cayenne pepper, onion powder, garlic powder, and yellow mustard, spread it over our city's style of ribs from which we've diligently removed the sternum bone and cartilage, from which we desire a softer chew, softer smoke, perfectly rectangular shape (the shape actually formalized by the USDA as "Pork Ribs, St. Louis style," or *PRSLS*), the bones beneath the meat so simple and straightforward and individually intact, and before the little girl's heart ossifies, the snow collecting in her hair, we will say the sort of cold-lipped grace over our ribs that has nothing to do with mallets moving over xylophone tiles, or the pirouette of a ballerina whose muscles are not—have never been—this confused.

A pig's blood will freeze faster than that of a human because a pig has no soul to keep it warm.

* * *

According to the 1970s' era jingle for Maull's Barbecue Sauce:

A fire's a fire,
a grill's a grill,

what makes that meat
a culinary thrill

is what you do
when you barbecue—

You gotta Maull it! (Spread that great sauce on!)
C'mon and Maull it! (Sizzle that flavor in!)
And when you Maull it (appetites go wild!)

Don't baste your barbecue—
Maull it! Maull it! (Five fantastic flavors!)

Maull it!

The pigs know: a maul (the term derived from the Latin *molere, to grind*) is a war hammer, a sledgehammer, a railroad tool used for driving spikes, a wood-splitting axe, a semi-automatic shotgun, a comic book character who derives strength from rage . . . Here, this is how we add flavor, turn all weather, blood into a thrill. All it takes is a little fire, and a basting brush, a trip to the pantry to see the five fantastic flavors, the three sizes of Maull bottles: small, medium, and patio.

Another argument of definition: here, a pig is a crop. The pigs know: a maul is used to drive a wedge into any hard substance. Uncle hangs his head, watches the small fire carve trenches into the meat as, less than thirty blocks away, a Subaru Outback folds itself into a snowbank, its hubcaps flying like Frisbees into the thundersnow, its steering wheel finding its way into another ribcage.

Other staples of St. Louis barbecue: pig shoulder and crispy snoots, the latter of which is prepared by excising the pig's nose, removing the nostrils and nasal passages, and shaving the remaining meat into strips which are then fried until crispy and dredged (or, according to Maull's mission statement, "slathered") in sauce.

According to culinary writer Steven Raichlen, the residents of St. Louis consume more barbecue sauce per capita than any other place on Earth. Also according to Steven Raichlen, "You can grill in anything. [In St. Louis] I saw people grilling in hubcaps, and the barbecue was great."

Slather may derive from *slath*, an early Norse fishing basket used to collect excised, inedible viscera, a derivation that remains unreferenced in Maull's jingles, including the one that cryptically confesses (to the image of a father and son catching Frisbees between their legs), "There's something out of the ordinary going on here . . ."

In the meatpacking plants of St. Louis, circular saws complain through bone. We will cook our meat over indirect heat. The cold, this winter, like the saws, will not be as subtle.

* * *

Missouri's nickname, the Show-Me State, is attributed to Representative Willard Vandiver who, in an 1899 speech, declared, "I come from a country that raises corn and cotton, cockleburs and Democrats, and frothy eloquence neither convinces nor satisfies me. I'm from Missouri, and you have got to show me," stressing that the state's residents should take a stubborn pride in their "devotion to simple common sense."

We know: in order to believe anything here, we need to see what's behind the curtain. We have to take off our clothing to prove the frostbite. Still, even then, the skin only serves to obscure what's inside us. We know: the cocklebur, unlike most members of the *Asteraceae* family, doesn't have seeds bearing the silky hairs that enable them to ride the wind like little parachutes, but instead has stiff hooked spines that latch onto fur and clothing and hair and skin and are difficult and painful to extract, and are poisonous to "less discriminating" "simple common" animals like pigs who will eat the plant, and will sicken with nausea, the twisting and hardening of the neck muscles, and asphyxiation, before dying.

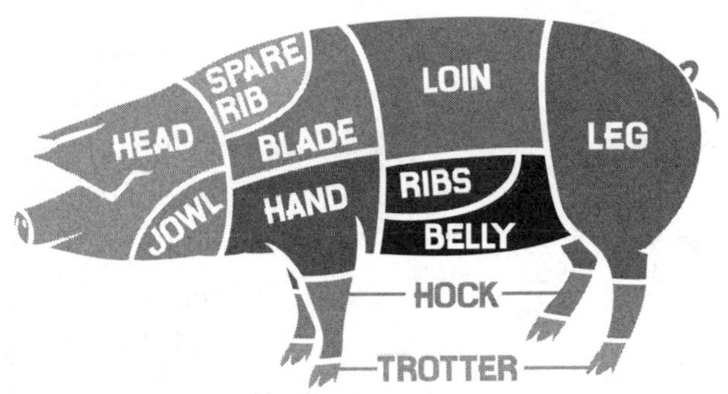

Getting to the heart of the matter often requires getting to the heart, which often requires the cracking of the ribcage.

* * *

In 1821, as part of the Missouri Compromise, the Missouri Territory was admitted as a slave state in order to balance the number of slave and free states. As such, before the "Show-Me" designation, Missouri's nickname evolved from "the Gateway to the West" to "Little Dixie," the latter of which, until 2006, still designated an athletic conference made up of seven local high schools, not a single one of which has the pig as its mascot.

Missouri is named for the Missouri tribe, who, in the Sioux language called themselves *ouemessourita*, or *those with the dugout canoes*, and who, unlike Sure Fire Grooves, never thought to patent the idea of increasing speed by the digging-into-and-away. In 1780, the population of the Missouri tribe was about 1,000 people. In 1805, it was about 300. In 1821, the year of the Compromise, it was about 80. In 1910, about 13. All of these headlines, stained with sauce.

* * *

MASCOTS: bulldogs, panthers, eagles—those from whom we don't often excise ribs, Indians—another story.

* * *

THE GIRL on the median screams as the muscles in her hands ossify. She drops her doll into the tallgrass. It becomes an ingredient again.

We are braided: we are pig and bone, sauce and fire. The simple, the devoted, the out of the ordinary. Here, both hot and cold things burn us. What else can we do but situate ourselves between the showing and the mauling, give ourselves purpose and name, one being more flavorful than the other? After hugging the girl on the median—like hugging a statue, I hug the last of the season's rib pigs. I know there are so many bones in there, but can feel only a hollowness, like a zeppelin made of dead leaves.

In this sort of ice, so many species thrive—grasses and worms and insects and swallows. We skid and skid on all this fertility, and wake up in a snowbank with our ribs on the outside.

Show me compromise, dream, a slow-cooked rack of spare ribs. Show me the sort of mauling that allows our skin to remain unsplit. Show me flavor without blood, the pig who knows what's coming. When the girl walks away, she sounds less like a xylophone than castanets. Still, because she lives here, she knows how to light the grill.

Uncle says that there's always a war on somewhere. In-body, out-of-body . . . He says the bones of the girl's ears—the little hammers there—will eventually fuse together, and she will, on top of everything else, go deaf. He says it's our patriotic duty to cook these ribs, and to cook these ribs outside, and to listen to the dirge-hiss of the snow falling into the fire.

Which usurps the other: the patriotism of the state, or that of the body? "Show me that it's too cold to grill," he says with so many others. Without these bones, we can't breathe, or hear. We can't hear the breathing. Without these bones, we are not Missouri . .

On the couch, fingers red from the freeze and the pigs, Uncle, after supper, unzips his snores. He tells me, in his sleep, that when Auntie was alive, she would play the violin "for groups of deformed children." When she would finish a song, he mutters, one of the kids would invariably be laughing. Sometimes, he says, she would play for the animals, believing that it helped them to grow, plump up. The pigs would hold back their yawns and snorts, listen to her aubades, potbellied and rapt.

St. Louis BBQ Ribs

Our STL ribs at Hendricks BBQ is as follows:

We skin our STL Ribs 24 hours prior to cooking.

They are coated in 3 ounces of our Hendricks BBQ pork rub.

(Our Pork Rub consists of brown sugar, paprika, dehydrated onion and garlic, dry molasses, and chipotle powder along with salt. There are also other ingredients that I myself can't even get from our manufacturer.)

After Rubbing they are placed on our smoker at 225 degrees for 4½ to 5 hours. (We use a 50/50 combination of Hickory and Apple Wood.)

After the first 2 hours of the smoking process they are mopped with a liquid consisting of our pork rub, apple juice, and our house bbq sauce and every hour thereafter until finished.

(Our House BBQ sauce is a ketchup/apple cider vinegar/sugar base. It is seasoned with chili powder, cumin, cayenne, garlic powder with Worcestershire and hot sauce. This in combination with the apple juice and pork rub creates a nice caramelization and color to the ribs as they are mopped during the smoking process).

When checking our ribs they are complete when ⅛th inch bone is showing from the center of the rack.

—*Marc Rollins, Chef, Hendricks BBQ*

The Biblical Rheology of Deep-Dish Pizza

IF FROSTBITE IS just another kind of scalding, then let's imagine this earth as a dish, or—even better—a platter, something capable of containing the thickest of our dinners, the cold cut, as if geologically, by the orange grease of the mozzarella, the pepperoni's fat char. Let's pretend that all winters can be spatula'd into our mouths in easy triangles, that, if we take too big a bite, if we don't blow the world cool, our mouths will fall lame, and we will make only weather sounds.

Uncle sprinkles crumbs of parmesan and crushed red pepper over his slice. Outside, on the window, a child leaves his hand in the frost, and the pizza whines as Uncle bites it. You think of crying, of fallow fields, of—just south of the city—some awful crow choking to death on some kernel of frozen corn. Here, in Illinois, our corn is better. Better even than the birds.

The crust uplifts the sauce. In this is some kind of offering, sacrifice. The pizza cries for its mother. The ovens gasp. "This," Uncle says, tracing his pinkie over the imprint of the child's thumb, trying to measure up, "is what your aunt and I used to call baby-making weather."

* * *

IN 1943, CHICAGOANS were desperate for anything substantial. Something to stand up to war and weather. To commemorate perhaps the launching of the city's first subway, or the Bears' winning of the Super Bowl (then known more humbly as the league title), or the way the light poured through the newly refurbished triangular windows of Union Station and pooled over the floor—the travelers in top hats and topcoats, the lit-up arrow sign boasting "TO TRAINS"—in such a way that it resembled a pie and its steam, an unnamed chef at Pizzeria Uno on Ohio Street (it could have been owner Ike Sewell, the former football player, or Ric Riccardo, the World War II hero, or Rudy Malnati, then mere line-cook, or it could have been all of them, or none of them) decided, on a legendary whim, to beef up the crust, to ladle the tomato sauce on top of the cheese, to wedge sausage into its heart, and to look through the frosty windows of that kitchen, to know that by morning 24.3 inches of snow would be on the ground, predicting, in just a few months, what would become known as the Summer of Midwestern Flooding, and Ike or Ric or Rudy or none would have taken the pizza from the oven, the crust somehow able to support the weight of all laid on top of it, never sagging, never cracking, and Carl Sandburg may have stood under the gas lamps outside in the weather, *under the smoke, dust all over his mouth, laughing with white teeth,* and before he even took a bite, as if humming some lullaby to the snow, as if estimating the weight of the thing it took both his hands to lift to his mouth, as if speaking the sole language of the city, he said *mmmmmm* . . .

Here, we call this kind of weather a *storm*—an onset, a tumult. We have to dupe ourselves into luxury, warmth. Here, we call this kind of restaurant, a *parlor.* Tom Skilling says we're getting another 13 inches overnight—so much shallower than Lake Michigan, deeper than our pizza. The ice sheaths the cattails, and Uncle, with a mouthful of sausage patty, mutters something about the elm's branches as a downed crystal chandelier, about the snow that makes us taller when we walk on it, closer to the gray of the sky and the red light of the Sears Tower blinking like the tumor that will take us all out.

In depth is move toward elegance. Parlors, platters, chandeliers, the kind of icy light that reminds us of rhinestones, even as it takes from us our fingers and toes. Neither Uncle nor Skilling says anything of snow as altar, of crust as the sacrificial stone. In depth, Uncle says, we can go back in time. He unearths wet dough from the sauce, the cheese, the sausage. He calls this layer the Urban Paleozoic. He calls Chicago "the alien bursting from the chest of Illinois."

You wonder if, within the context of your state, you are alien. You wonder why the food you require is heavier.

Sandburg may have warned you: at the word *Illinois*, its Frenchified-Algonquin-ness, bearing the migratory weight of rivers Mississippi, Illinois, Des Plaines, and Chicago, Lake Michigan and the railroads, blues and jazz, John Deere's steel plow and dirty inland creeks carrying green foam, poisonous trout, and cans of Old Milwaukee, you will sigh and feel like running, away and through stockyards to cornfields, getting lost in the very soil that's beneath both your fingernails and this snow, reinventing it, maybe even renaming it Uno—as if this state is just one thing; as if, in this place of domesticated wildness, in the middle of the fields, the tassels way above your head, bearings lost, the crows of Champaign and Chicago still alive and feasting together on the kernels, you can help locate yourself, foster some kind of bridge between thin-crust and deep-dish. Somewhere above the rows, some braggart archaeologist announces, in your uncle's voice, his discovery: that the pre-Columbian copper plate carvings he unearthed from burial sites near Collinsville, Illinois (formerly Cahokia, the central regional chiefdom of the indigenous mound-building Mississippian culture) bear an uncanny resemblance to bug-eyed pepperoni atop cheese, atop crust, and once again, you're bewildered, and once again, you wonder if this pizza has always been here, is older than the state, and you want to ask your uncle, *Where am I?* but your mouth is full.

Here, all it takes is one bite to fill the mouth. Like the snow, the sediment, the narrative, the toppings accumulate until they bury. Eight inches and counting. You eat a second slice, armor yourself from the inside. When we press the still-cooking pizza with the spatula, the layers panic. The language of this pizza, like that of our state history, is deep. That doesn't mean it has yet hit bottom.

* * *

Sandburg, if not Uncle, knows: linguists believe that the name *Illinois*, in the Algonquin Algic language, means *man*, which means that you have no idea what that means. You watch your uncle eat from his half as the child's frosty handprint gets lost in the gathering cold, and window shudders in its frame, and your chest seems to swell from the inside—perhaps you've eaten one slice too many—and Uncle's eyes go glassy, and you know exactly how long it's been since he last kissed someone, and you know that you're supposed to react as a *man*, be a *man*, a *man* beyond biology, and you swear to God or Sandburg or Malnati that you have no idea how to do that, in spite of being born in Chicago, Illinois, the biggest city in the state of Man.

You're not sure if it's the cheese or the pepperoni, or the entire depth of this deep-dish, that reminds you of your first kiss in a slaughterhouse in Urbana—a slaughterhouse that bragged about selling its sausage in bulk to places like Uno, and Due and Lou Malnati's and Gino's East. There, in the cornfields, the simmering stench of cow shit, the sewage of it carried away by a creek named the Boneyard, you take the hand of your first girlfriend and watch the lead slaughterer, a tall, thick-glasses'd man in a floor-length white smock (miraculously free of blood and fat), the name Lazerus stitched misspelled over his lapel in green cursive, blowtorching of the hair from hanging pig halves. She drops your hand when you tell her, also bragging, that these pigs will be processed a second time for the pizza in the city of your birth.

Here, we try to excise the danger from depth. Try to pretend that it's just as easy to drown in the shallow end of things. Nothing, Uncle says, asphyxiates the earth like this weather. Nothing stops the voices in our throats like this pizza. In deep-dish is overdraft protection. It keeps us from saying the things we shouldn't. Into the soft wood of the table, Uncle, with his butter knife, carves "BREADTH IS A PUSSY." You wonder if *breadth* is just *bread* spoken through a mouthful of deep-dish. You wonder if the crust is as strong as it thinks.

Ten inches. So many years ago it could have been Paleozoic, you reach again for your girlfriend's hand, as Lazerus threads two steel hooks through a pig's hind ankles and hoists it upward, the snout pointing down toward the white tile where a boy intern hoses the blood into diluted pink rivers, running his small thumb over his lips, as if reminding himself of the substantiality of his own body amid all of these larger pigs. Lazerus stands on a platform with a chainsaw, his goggled eyes rising from between the animal's spread hind legs, and with his gurgling orange ripcord Stihl, the chainsaw gasoline of it coupling with the smell of the blood, halves the hanging animal from crotch to snout. After gutting the pig into a plastic brown trash can, Lazerus yanks a thick cable as if closing window blinds over all of the state's frozen handprints, and the pig halves slide like dry cleaning along a ceiling mount toward the blowtorch station. The boy has his hose. That's something. You say nothing of pizza or Chicago, or how an entire animal can be rendered to one of twenty toppings, but while you stand separated by a hanging curtain of rosy, and now hairless, pig, you take her hand, larger than yours, and, wondering which the slaughterer and which the slaughtered, which the cheese—so used to being the top layer, closer to mouth and to sky—and which the sauce, kiss her on the lips and, desperate for any comfort, she kisses you back, and somewhere—not too far away—a pizza is pulled from an oven, a groom-to-be is late for his wedding as, with his own uncle, he gigs for frogs in the snake-infested river of Peoria, and the largest frog of the day, the thickest legs, the one demanding the full depth of the blades and their plunge, deflates on the end of the spear, and your uncle consoles himself with the comfort of pizza, filling himself with its temperature, and you listen to chainsaws and torches and popping frogs, and think of cheese and sausage, and you move to kiss her again, harder this time, believing, like an idiot, that the greater the depth, the greater the sympathy, and she's crying now, and she's lost her appetite, and you keep trying, and keep trying to thicken yourself against all rejection—romantic and regional—and this is blood, and this is bone, sauce and crust, and this is not the right thing to do.

* * *

No matter how far down our food goes, we will eventually hit the pan. We will be hungry again. Uncle worries about the roads, the drive home. You stab your fork into the pizza, think of frogs, of depth as an entrance, and invasion, a getting to the bottom of things. *In* depth, you think. Depth as something to get into. Uncle wrings his hands. Eleven inches at least. He tells you, or himself, to turn into the skid. In the skid is a loss of our bearings, our hold on the earth. In entering, we can right ourselves again, uncover all the once delicious things that burnt to the bottom of the pan.

The physicist in the kitchen scatters a fistful of cheese. He deduces that in depth is a slower speed. Like the bullet fired into the lake, the more space we traverse, the closer we are to coming to a stop. The physicist in the kitchen says, "Alternative operationalizations of depth variables result in very similar findings," as the sous-chef, as requested, cuts the pepperoni extra thick.

This pizza as the altar we raise to our mouths. This pizza allows for no substitutions. Uncle says that the enzyme responsible for a firefly's light is called luciferase, that *Lucifer* means *Light-bearer.* That his mouth is burning on sausage when he says this is appropriate. "Hell is deeper than this pizza," he says, but, in name only, so much brighter than Chicago.

The deeper we go, the hotter it gets. Hell as core, as sub-skyline, as salve against winter, as down jacket, as postcard from Cozumel to Chicago. The spiciest pepperoni wishes you were here. When you stab into the pizza like this, the heat screams from the center in a sound your uncle calls *bleating.* We sacrifice our warmth for this pizza.

Geologists believe that substances with a "complex microstructure"—muds and sludges and suspensions, and cheeses and sauces and doughs—respond to an applied force in the same ways in which our bodily fluids do, and other elements of our insides that correspond to "soft matter." In this way, we are what we eat. This pizza behaves like our blood.

We write our names in the frost for the same reason we eat this pizza: as if inheritance. As if ancestry. As if water bodies as diverse as Boneyard and Michigan. Because we live here.

* * *

Lazerus enjoys being our guide, enjoys demonstrating the stages of slaughter. Lazerus extends his white-gloved thumb toward a lamb. The lamb reaches its small mouth toward Lazerus's thumb, attempts in vain to suckle, as Lazerus slowly backs the animal toward the steel gun, which hangs from the ceiling by a black stretch cable. Hooves clattering on the tile like castanets. As Lazerus reaches for the steel gun with his free hand, your first girlfriend turns her eyes away, not toward you, but behind you, the world beyond this slaughterhouse, and this dumbass boy, and this farmland stage in her life, which is to be so much bigger than this, through millions of years of limestone, sandstone, crusts thick and thin, pepperoni limp and pepperoni charred stiff, all the way to Chicago, or Wisconsin even, Canada, the Arctic, anyplace in which to hide in the depths of weather and scarf, any attempt to make such depths edible and steaming hot, and taken inside of us, any way to contain such multitudes in our own bodies. Your life perhaps will not get bigger than this, and you will dwell on this slaughterhouse for years, no amount of deep-dish sufficient to sop it up.

We will be hungry again.

Depth as a sponge. As the question: how can the deepest stuff we take inside of us also absorb us, carry us away, trick us into identifying an entire city after its measurements, and its outline? In a quick *boom*, as if in fast-forward, the air-forced gun fires its retractable steel bit into the animal's brain, Lazerus's smock and glasses flare with its blood, and the lamb, as if gravity doubles its force, deepens it all the way to the floor, accelerates to the tile in a heavy heap, and you think of the flow of its blood, so steady, as veil, as drapery, and as you turn away, Lazerus doing his carving behind you, you realize that you will never kiss her again—and, here, finishing a pizza with your uncle now, you're not sure if it's the butchery, or the first and final kiss that you recall only via its ripping sounds.

You wonder about yourself as a man whenever you feel these feathers in your chest. You think of your body, as you do masculinity, as a mineshaft. You wonder how deep it goes. You wonder if, at bottom, whispering secrets into your ear, is the demon we've named after light. Eventually all of this, under pressure, force applied, will coagulate like geophysics, like our small stories, extra large pizza.

Watch the snow, hear the pigs, wonder how Downstate can share space with Chicago; wonder how deep this geology goes, how sharp the spatula needs to be to cut into it, examine its layers. Wonder how many things Illinois really is. "We are everywhere," Uncle says, "we are a franchise."

Outside, the weather surpasses Skilling's prediction. Accumulate/bury, accumulate/bury . . . In so much depth, take comfort in the small things—the skinny plants, and hibernating insects. Try not to listen to what your uncle repeats: that the prairies grow smaller each year.

Between Chicago and Downstate, the last cicada of the season coughs enzymes into the cattails. The milkweed—ever too late—opens her nursing bra. You breathe a hole through the frost, stare at the elm in Uncle's front yard. You stare through the circle, still hot, but freezing. You don't think of pepperoni, or of any kind of slaughter. There's grass, you think, under all of this snow.

Deep-Dish Pizza

Here, at the Medici on 57th, our deepest dish pizza is our PAN pizza. We make the dough daily, from scratch, in our bakery next door. The dough is simple, made with bread flour, water, olive oil, sugar, yeast, and salt. Of our pan pizzas, the Garbage Pizza is definitely our most popular and it's been a menu staple since the Medici's beginning. The Garbage Pizza is a stacked pie, full of fresh ingredients. We let the dough rise for at least two hours in a 2-inch-deep pizza pan before we press it out. To the dough, we add a huge ladle full our pizza sauce and top that with fresh sliced mushrooms and fresh diced green peppers and onions. On top of that goes crumbled seasoned ground beef, cubed Canadian bacon, and locally produced Italian sausage. All of that is topped with a pile of mozzarella that we shred heaps of daily. To the very top of the pan Garbage Pizza we add huge rounds of sliced deli-style pepperoni. The loaded pie goes into a 390-degree oven for 10 minutes.

The following ingredients are for a Personal Size Pan Garbage Pizza. Our personal pan pizzas have a 7-inch diameter.

The following ingredients are all measured by weight:

11 ounces dough
1 ounce sliced mushrooms
1 ounce diced green peppers
1 ounce diced white onions
1.5 ounces seasoned ground beef
1.5 ounces cubed Canadian bacon
1.5 ounces Italian sausage
3 ounces shredded mozzarella
1 ounce sliced deli-style pepperoni

The only item we measure by volume is the sauce: 3 ounces pizza sauce (tomatoes, extra virgin olive oil, vegetable oil, salt, seasonings, granulated garlic).

—Mattie Pool, Medici on 57th

The Conflicted Archaeologies of Hoosier Cream Pie

WHEN WE NAME our state pie after the sweetest thing we can think of, grab your knees, rub at all that syrupy blood collecting at the base of your skull. Predict the inevitable exhaustion, the crash into the orange recliner in the middle of the house in the middle of the country. Remember its common name: Sugar Cream Pie. Remember: in renaming our favorite dessert after a nonsense demonym that even we incompletely understand, the origins of which even we debate on Sundays after football and church and 4x4x4x4 breakfasts (eggs, pancakes, sausage links, bacon strips), we are perpetuating the narrative that we can think beyond sugar, easy sweetness; that, in the mysteries of *Hoosier*, we can temper everything that's obvious about us.

Our Hoosier Cream Pie is so soft we can cut it with our pinkies. So sweet, we can think only of how it moves us, speeds our hearts, allows us to run from towns called Amboy and Amo, Trafalgar and Troy. Running, we can think of all of our dead aunts and uncles, all of the filled-in quarries, their ceilings waiting to collapse, the kinds of state histories buried beneath rock dust and tablespoons of sugar we allow to burn, harden, lacquer the tops of our Hoosier Cream Pies. So sweet, the glucose will undo our knees, and we will forget why we've run all the way out here into the silos and soybeans and water towers that are missing their own towns' names.

In *strip* is the taking away, the removal of. In *link* is either the bridge between all of the removed things, or every act of removal. Like Indiana, like any new name that merely adds an A to the rear of an existing name, this too is obvious. In the crashing of our bodies, we have to go home. We can buy all the required ingredients for our pie from any gas station on the way out, back.

Here, we try to convince ourselves: the things that dust us are different from the things that seal us in. The lid of the sarcophagus is not the same as the windmill, ever-rusted to a stop, etched into its surface. Our dead aunts told us: all a Hoosier is on Sundays is flour and cream and vanilla and cinnamon, and butter and piecrust that once was homemade and now (*it's okay*) can be store-bought, and brown sugar, and white sugar, and confectioner's sugar "for sprinkling." Two kinds of sugar for the crust, a third—the kind most pulverized—for the garnish. Here, the things we most break down are the things most likely to be decorative.

Hoosier Cream Pie was born in the 1850s when the Shaker populations in Indiana (most likely the West Union Shaker Village in Busro) had to improvise when they found their apple bins empty, and decided to add enough sugar to mimic the energy lent by the fruit. The Shakers originally called it Finger Pie, and early recipes demanded that the filling be "stirred with the finger during the baking process," as the consistency was to be so satiny, the bottom crust so delicate, that any utensil other than a human finger would destroy it.

* * *

THE HIGHEST QUALITY of quarried limestone in the U.S., known as Indiana limestone, waits for us in Bloomington. We eat our pie on Sundays, curse the day we will become strong enough to work in these holes. The 358 million-year-old marine fossils, having decomposed on the floor of the inland sea that blanketed Indiana during the Mississippian Period, say nothing, merely release their gas, turn to stone, seal in yet another precious thing that we'll one day feel compelled to unearth. *To unearth* is to take away a portion of our planet. *To Indiana* is to turn a people into a land, another sort of earth that we empower ourselves, with machines and our bodies, to remove.

* * *

Other names for Hoosier Cream Pie: Quarry Pie (a fixture of the quarrymen's lunch pails), Mock Apple Pie, Gluey Pie, Mothers Pie, Wet Pie, Pioneer Pie, Desperation Pie.

* * *

Here, we lend the holes we dig into pies and earth the power of prediction. Already we know, beneath the burnt sugar crust, is the sugar cream. That big hole in the ground is the Prophetstown Quarry. That dread we feel when digging is desperate, the high foretelling the crash. The prophets, or fossils, or Indians, or steam, escaping . . . Here, the fossils whisper their auguries. We know they're talking about us. What else can we do but counter the calcium carbonate in our blood with sugar, tell ourselves that we're not like them?

Bill Bryson—an Iowan, no less!—tells us: "There are many suggestions for the derivation of the word [Hoosier], but none is universally accepted." A Hoosier is a hick and a Hoosier is white trash, and a Hoosier is cheap labor—either white or black—contracted to haul bales of cotton from docks to ships, locking them into position via jackscrews. A Hoosier is a hard-living roughneck woodsman, and a Hoosier is any unusually large object, especially a hill, the sort of earth boil which such hard-living roughneck woodsmen (Cumberland immigrants settling in southern Indiana, perhaps) had to navigate in order to build their homes in the no-see-um-soaked and beige blankness of the New World.

Up here, we can tell ourselves that we live at elevation. We are on top of things. But deep down we know. It's just Sugar Cream Pie. Know: hills are false ceilings. The highest point in Indiana, at 1,257 feet above sea level, is in rural Franklin Township, is eleven miles off I-70 ("the nearest major landmark"), is on private property, was scaled (with the landowner's permission) in 2005 by an Eagle Scout named Kyle Cummings (of Troop 820) who built a rock cairn at the "peak," is part of the Dearborn Upland, a geologic formation sandwiched between the crust of the Cincinnati Arch and a ceiling of glacial debris called the Tipton Till Plain, has a topographical relief that's so hardly noticeable that local geologists can call it only "gentle," is no more than thirty feet higher than the surrounding farmland, is called Hoosier Hill, is itself about to be usurped in height by a man-made landfill in

Randolph County, the first county in the U.S. to consolidate strings of declining rural schools, as if chaining quarry to quarry, as if binding sugar molecule to sugar molecule in a preheated 350-degree oven.

Hoosier Hill is afraid that a pile of garbage will overtake its height. This fear usurps even the conflict over its name. The outer stuff that protects us is the same as the inner stuff that we protect, except burnt.

* * *

YOUR DEAD UNCLE, quarry-scarred, ever amazed that a big hole can leave such a wake, that an excision can be positive, active, loved to tell you, "It's all sugar, baby."

According to Aimone–Martin Associates, LLC, "Quarry rock blasting is perhaps one of the most challenging aspects facing the aggregates industry today . . . Quarry operators exercise great care, providing buffers around property, reducing impacts of blasting ground vibrations, and controlling fugitive dust."

You eat your second slice, wonder if that's the sugar, or your blood, or the entire state that's vibrating. It's the burnt sugar at the top of the pie that is the bridge between the softest, sweetest cream and our mouths. Without silverware, and fingers crushed by limestone, we crack this bridge with our tongues.

Here, language is the thing that destroys the bonds. A Hoosier and Hoosier Cream Pie are not, will never be, one connected thing. Here, as everywhere, we feed on things that feed on us. In this act, History and Future are just another set of conjoined twins in the farmland on the hill.

You wonder if the entire state, and its nickname, is a fugitive exercising great care or indiscriminately blasting, unconcerned about things like buffers or reduction. Your dead uncle called it Three Sugar Pie, called the resulting heartbeat his Imaginary Friend. To him, Hoosier was a simple question: a sugar-slurred plea, a mispronunciation of *Who's here?*

This state as if questioning its own existence, as if afraid of its own shadow. As needing a pie this saccharine to carry it away toward any manic, then exhausted, answer. And a Hoosier can be a follower of Harry Hoosier, also known as Black Harry, a nineteenth-century

African American traveling minister who spoke out against slavery and for the "frontier morality of the common man," and whose sermons may have empowered Randolph County (home of the growing landfill) to become home also of the first racially integrated school in Indiana, and one of the first in the country too.

If we generate morality from the middle, can it then expand outward toward the coasts, or are we doomed, like quarry and pie, to implosion? And we wonder, if only on Sundays, which story we want to name our pie after. Which sugar is stronger—the burnt kind, or the kind suspended in the soft cream filling? We wonder if the limestone has usurped the original marine fossil. If the limestone can ever divorce itself from its once-living source. If we can ever pulverize it enough to revise it from state industry, crushed skulls, decreased lung function, poor drainage, resurrect all dust as decoration.

* * *

INDIANA POET John Finley published in 1833 "The Hoosier's Nest," which finally imposed the label onto Any Indiana Resident (AIR). The poem opens, introducing AIR not so flatteringly,

Untaught the language of the schools
Nor versed in scientific rules,

and moves on to the anchors of the state's peculiar earth:

But ever as his mind delights
To follow fancy's airy flights
Some object of terrestrial mien
Uncourteously obtrudes between.

In seventh-grade social studies, Mr. Morton told you that in the early 1800s, two rival Frenchmen settled in Indiana and frequented a tavern in the foothills. After sufficient drink, they began to fight over a land claim, and one bit the other's ear off, spat it to the dirt floor. Later, a third Frenchman walked in, spotted the organ on the ground and, with a curiosity as obvious as sugar, inquired, accented, "Who'sh ear?" "We are both that question," Mr. Morton said, "and the answer to that question," and you could feel the classroom swell with pride—Ronny Ballenger and Kelly Konopka all but beating their Indiana chests—but you kept thinking about the self as a dismembered ear, about the future of the state, and its capacity to self-identify as mutilated, imbalanced, imperfectly heard.

Who's here, Cream Pie? And the answer is sugar, sugar, sugar, as if some neurotic attempt to convince ourselves of some historical sweetness, in spite of the salt corroding the limestone we had to dig so deep to mine. This beautiful pie we've named after our confusing selves lifts us as if into the air, where we have no place to go but back down. Hoosier Cream Pie as gravity. The speed of our flying blood overtaken by a landfill.

Who's ear, Cream Pie? And the answer is the Husser's (an ex-European pirate of the Napoleonic Wars exiled to Indiana), and the answer is the Huissier's (an ex-French bailiff exiled to Indiana), and the answer is the Hausierer's (an ex-German traveling salesman exiled to Indiana), or the answer is that of the brachiopod or the cephalopod or any of the other marine animals that have given their ears and eyes and multiply-chambered hearts to our limestone—another kind of exile that we dig up, the dust of the Mississippian swimming in the soft cream of our lungs, and we forget about the ways in which these animals once listened, their versions of ears intact, and we forget, in the magnitude of the explosions, the widening of our quarries, that all exiles are fugitive, and that we've named ourselves after nothing solid; after things garbled in the mouth and misheard by the maimed; after something as impermanent as a geologic period, as state boundary, as sound; and we forget that we've named the most beautiful of these fossils—the ones shaped like stars and flowers, the ones whose buds we've compared to hickory nuts and our own eyes—*blastoids.*

* * *

We are crust and the three types of sugar it takes to make it. We are crust and decoration. We are ceiling and the air beneath it. We are coffin and its etching. We are the holes we dig, seal up. Are white trash, are cotton balers, are unusually large hills. We are the running away, and the return—the horse that screams all the way back to the stable where Finley, "having stripped the saddle off / He fed him in a sugar-trough," and in eating, and in sweetness, and in one trough or another, we are home, and we are *home.* The weather buries our quarries and the limestone down there is becoming something else. We wonder if this is also something we can feed on.

Before he stopped breathing, your uncle spoke of a fight that broke out among the quarrymen, which ended when one stabbed another with a rock-hard shiv of stale piecrust. You wonder if the pie or the quarry is responsible for such aggression, if the softest edible stuff on earth always lurks beneath a blade, if acts such as this belong to dessert, or to job opportunity, or to the still-buried whole story of the bone and sinew of this state.

And Finley says,

Blest Indiana! in thy soil
Are found the sure rewards of toil
Where honest poverty and worth
May make a Paradise on earth,

and your uncle, from the Great Beyond, offers his famed *Fuck you,* and you marvel at how easily, with a mouthful of Hoosier Cream, the jagged sugar cutting valleys into the softness only your mouth can solve, *blest* becomes *blast.*

The calcium carbonate in our limestone communes with that in the eggshells, the snails, the pearls, the earrings we wedge into our good lobes, the antacid we swallow after too much Hoosier Cream Pie. Uncle once believed that there was a duck-billed dinosaur down there, entombed in some lower limestone, its eggs responsible for the quality of the rock we are so eager to lend the name of our state to.

Because the eggs are down there, our pie is eggless. And Finley says, "And dazzle our astonished eyes . . ." So obvious: we fill our pies with the softest, thickest stuff. In it is every quarry concealed by water, the fossils we rename after the sounds of the blasts that unearth them. In each—either so buried, or so compressed—there is no air. We've stirred it out, as if with our fingers, wait for it to return to us, as if evaporated groundwater, as rain. The names of our pie permit us to take all of this sweetness in. When we're told of our history, we cough the flower dust from our lungs, we beat with the sugar of some ancestral stirring finger, we burn our bridges, we listen, this time, with both ears.

"That's It! Hoosier Sugar Cream Pie"

I'm delighted to contribute my recipe for "That's It! Hoosier Sugar Cream Pie." This is my adaptation of a recipe from an iconic restaurant that was located in Bloomington, Indiana, that served this famous Indiana pie from the 1950s through the late 1970s.

Ingredients
A 9-inch unbaked pie shell
1 cup whipping cream
½ cup half-and-half, mixed together with ½ cup 2% milk
½ cup all-purpose flour
1 teaspoon vanilla
Cinnamon

Preheat oven 425 degrees.

Directions for the filling

Beat until stiff peaks 1 cup whipping cream. Set aside.

In another bowl, mix together 1 cup granulated sugar and one-half cup all-purpose flour. Blend well.

Add in the beaten whipped cream, and blend slowly with a wire whisk.

Combine the milk/half-and-half cream mixture with the vanilla.

Slowly stir the milk/half-and-half cream/vanilla mixture into the whipped cream/flour/sugar mixture.

Pour the filling into the unbaked pie shell (rim protected with the foil).

Lightly sprinkle with cinnamon.

Bake at 425 degrees for 10 minutes on the bottom rack of the oven. Reduce temperature to 350 degrees and bake another 30–40 minutes, or until the middle of the pie seems set but still jiggles.

Let cool. Enjoy, but for a truly Hoosier Sugar Cream Pie experience, do not add anything else such as whipped cream or ice cream! This is a plain little pie that packs a real taste whallop!

—Louise and Rick Miracle, Pie First Bakery

Cincinnati Chili Reincarnate

"Charles Ramsey, Who Helped Free Cleveland Kidnap Victims, Gets Burgers For Life"

—headline, *Cleveland Plain Dealer,* Northeast Ohio Media Group, May 22, 2013

1870: MAYBE you're a boy, and maybe you're a girl, and maybe you're watching your uncle Alexander again stick his fingers into the earth, his eyes prayerful, and once again, ignoring you. You know: you're in the bull's eye of the state, surrounded on all sides by so much Ohio, a word that sounds like the wind itself howling the clothes from your body, the word that means, in Iroquois, either *Great River* or the slightly less venerable *Big Creek*. Reynoldsburg is so small, but three counties—Fairfield, Franklin, and Licking—fight to claim it. It will be another ninety-five years until Ohio names as its state beverage tomato juice; over a century until the local high school picks as its mascot a Raider, before Bath & Body Works decides to build its headquarters on the soil your uncle is busy kneading. He's been dismissed as mad for proselytizing on the tomato, assuring your neighbors that it's "not poisonous, definitely not poisonous." And how can you know this: that your uncle is about to develop the first version of the fruit that the public will deem edible; that he will from this day forward be known by the title of Ohio Seedsman; that he will become the godfather of all heirloom tomatoes, and will name them Acme and Beauty and Buckeye State, Dwarf Stone, Golden Queen, Perfection? You can't possibly know, at this age, that the U.S. Department of Agriculture will say about this man:

With all due credit to the important contributions of other growers, seedsmen, and investigators, it is not out of place to call attention again to the great contribution of the Livingston Seed Co. to tomato improvement. Of about 40 varieties that had attained a distinct status prior to 1910, a third were productions or introductions by the Livingston company. If we add those varieties derived directly from Livingston productions and introductions, it appears that half of the major varieties were due to the abilities of Livingston to evaluate and perpetuate superior material in the tomato.

And you watch his knees press further into the dirt—this investigator, this man who sings you to sleep—and maybe you feel a stirring in your chest, and maybe you consider your own heart to be of "superior material," to be, as the French would come to call the tomato, *the Apple of Love,* and it's up to you to decide and engineer—it's in your family, for God's sake!—which part of you is the pericarp, the juice sac, the seed, the placenta; and maybe all of this Ohio, in every direction, begins to resemble a cusp that needs breaching, as Uncle Alexander stands, assesses the wind, countless invisible organelles swirling about his head in search of any red cavity, any anchor that will enable them to face the sun and grow up.

Ohio: just another state that begins with a cry of surprise, or pain.

Ohio: just another state that begins with a cry of surprise, or pain.

* * *

1922: You VAGUELY remember spitting up something red, but this memory dissipates with the opening of your eyes. Maybe, this time, you're a girl, a boy, a grown man, a grandmother, a pet goldfish, a garden pest. You see the tubes of red lipstick lined up like soldiers, their caps catching the red neon of the Empress Burlesque Theater sign, and guess, correctly, *girl.* Possibly, *runaway.* Either the Empress has turned on its sign way too early or you've slept until dusk again. Three stories beneath you, on the asphalt, Macedonian immigrants Tom and John Kiradjieff push their revelatory hot dog stand to their spot next to the theater. You are not hungry. Will not be hungry for days. Something is wrong with your body. Something's taking hold of it. Something with its own tight skin, seeds. How can you know that the Kiradjieffs last night shared a dream of prosperity; that they decided to incorporate as many ethnic styles as possible into a single dish in order to broaden their customer base; that they would create a "modified stew," combining their ground beef with so many chopped tomatoes, with cinnamon, clove, allspice, chocolate; that they would spoon it over hot dogs for the sexually repressed men who began to line up to see women singing and dancing and spouting low-brow humor in only their undergarments; that these repressed men would demand variety—always younger, newer girls—and to combat these demands, uniformed policemen would patrol the Empress as the performers' outfits grew skimpier, as the Empress launched the G-string, named after longest string on the violin (tempering the high-pitched girlish giggles with a sense of classical, symphonic decorum), and to accommodate this thirst for variety and acceleration toward extremity, the Kiradjieffs spooned their new chili over spaghetti and called it two-way; that there would soon be a three-way (chili, spaghetti, cheddar cheese), a four-way (chili, spaghetti, cheddar cheese, kidney beans), a five-way (chili, spaghetti, cheddar cheese, kidney beans, onions); that Cincinnati Chili would influence the language of the orgy; that the Empress would be indicted for forcing twelve underage girls to perform stripteases for men with five-way breath and tomato pulp in their molars; that the wardrobe mistress beat one of these girls when she refused, the blood from her nose catching in the silver sequins of her bra, reflecting onto the ceiling, the brown amoebic water stains there, like so many seeds of a fruit once believed to be toxic taken into the sort of wind that predicts the storm?

In dream, an old man with dirty fingers, dirty knees, speaks of too many heirlooms; of how variety reflects an easy move toward boredom; how boredom can predict violence, Beauties and Buckeyes, and Dwarfs and Perfect Queens sacrificed to so many different versions of chili.

* * *

1934: You WAKE UP in a room with red curtains and think of the womb as just another fruit susceptible to the aphids. An unprecedented number of tomato diseases strike Ohio's crop this year—bacterial canker, pith necrosis, anthracnose, stubby root, sting, target rot, black shoulder. Perhaps you've just given birth, as so many farmers, influenced by a man who, in another life, may have been your uncle, declare their bankruptcy, swallow their guns. It's cold. The desk calendar says November 12, Monday. Even the healthy tomatoes are dying. Perhaps, you're just sick, feverish, imagining things, as you hear secretary after secretary answering the telephone, "Cincinnati General Hospital," as you hear a baby crying a little too hard behind the pulled red curtain, the sixteen-year old mother cooing with a little too much breath, the sort of whispered secret that hurts the ear, the nurse with the thick voice recording the child's name while speaking it aloud, "No Name Maddox." And how can you know this: that it's a bad sign to be born during a tomato plague; that the teenage mother will soon choose for her son the name Charles, because it means *free man*, or because of Charlemagne, or Charles I, or Charles IV, or Dickens, or Chaplin, or Darwin, or Lindbergh; that she will marry a laborer named William Manson who will force, among other things, his last name onto the boy? You still think you're back in Reynoldsburg. You still think you're inside the tomato.

It's likely you won't live through the night, likely you won't have to stomach another anemic hospital salad, the tomatoes more white than red. The lights flicker as No Name nurses behind the awful curtain, and the mother nourishes the blood into her cheeks with diseased tomato juice.

Ohio means *river*, means *creek*, means *ditch, gully, vein,* and *vein opening*, means rape, means bondage, means bruises at the wrists and knees, means bleeding out in a basement, means living in a basement, force-fed, attended to, force-fed chili and spaghetti, not starving for chili and spaghetti, and beans named for our organs, and state dishes named for underage girls who are beaten for not taking off their clothes when they are told to.

Look: there's a cardinal alighting on a body—the Ohio state bird in Ohio state blood, and we will say nothing here of red, or of tomatoes, or of all things pressed of their juice so the meat, the meat, the meat can stay moist, so we can eat all this cow with a spoon.

* * *

1952: IT'S LUNCHTIME in the federal reformatory in Chillicothe, which, despite its name, is not, as you believe, named after chili. You eat your bowl—beanless, spaghetti-less, but rich with canned tomato—and listen to the trees screaming outside—the bur oaks and sugar maples and dogwoods and sour gums that will compel the National Arbor Day Foundation to name this godforsaken town Tree City USA. You listen to a splashing in the Scioto River, and would like to think that it's the deer after which the river is named. How could you know that the new boy eating his chili across the table would soon introduce himself as Charles, would soon, as was his habit at the time, hold a razor blade to your throat while he sodomized you, before becoming, as the Chillicothe guards would soon declare him, a "model citizen"? All you can do is stare into your bowl as this new boy speaks of pimping, of robbery, of tearful pleas, of California, a state which you now know has surpassed your own in tomato fame, but not in that of chili. All you can do is stare into your bowl as he speaks of music and guitar strings, of his mother selling him to a childless waitress for a pitcher of beer, of the dumb fucking farmers of Ohio, and pray for strings and strings of spaghetti, or anything resembling a tether.

The lower classification of the cardinal is Cyanoloxia, a name we mistake, as we once did the tomato, for poison. Surprise, pain: Which the Great River? Which the Big Creek?

* * *

1965: THE LOCAL television station cuts out due to a bolt of lightning. You sit in front of it, a bowl of five-way chili warming your lap. You run your hand over your throat, feeling for a scar that isn't there. You can feel your beard growing, so many things in your head that just want to come out, see daylight, thunderstorm. Soon, your chili will grow cold, as if a move toward an unpalatable temperature, toward sludge, were *growth*. The television screen, though dead, still crackles with that phantom layer of static. You gum your ground beef, spit a tomato seed into the carpet. Somewhere, far from his birthplace, Charles Manson scratches at his scalp. How can you know that the newsman is about to declare something monumental; that *Eye of the Devil*, Sharon Tate's first feature role, is to play at the local theater; that the Ohio General Assembly has chosen tomato juice as the official state beverage?

Perhaps we were not wrong in the first place. Perhaps we should have trusted our instincts . . . Maybe Uncle Alexander, whom you can hardly remember beyond what you've read in books, was a bad man.

* * *

1972: You wake up in a red Honda Z600. You drive to Cleveland to see Bob Hope do a show in his birthplace. The city is still rebounding from the great Cuyahoga River fire, the Hough Riots, and the Glenville Shootout. Somehow, you know that Cleveland will be the first city to default on federal loans since the Great Depression; that the city's sports teams will, for years to come, be doomed to stink. Though, elsewhere in the state, Ohioans refer to the city as "the Mistake on the Lake" (a moniker popular with countless regional comedians), Bob Hope, now living in California, stresses, "I don't do jokes about Cleveland." The radio says something about the reduction of sentences of five members of the Manson Family; says, "Vietnam Vet forced to dig his own grave," and "poorly buried," and "scavenging animals." Reynoldsburg, Ohio volunteers begin to prepare for their 7th Annual Tomato Festival—the Tomato Jam Battle of the Bands, Tomato Toss, crowning of this year's Tomato Queen. You pass a billboard for Skyline Chili that asks: *What Makes Skyline Chili So Special? It's Our Secret Recipe!* and pray for any clearer answer.

You drive, and speak into the windshield, and ask no one in particular: Is the desire to kill just another mood? Is Ohio itself the problem, incubating particular atrocity as part of state genetics? Is something wrong with our soil, our obsessions, our ornamentation, our billboards, our diet? In what way is the original tomato responsible for all of these corpses?

"In summary," says Elizabeth Kande Englander in *Understanding Violence*, "violence is suggestive of a significant, but not total or direct, heritability . . . [We must consider] the effects of environment." Adrian Raine, in *The Psychopathology of Crime*, says, "the interaction between heredity and environment accounts for more variance in criminal behavior than either influence alone." NBC News blames the Hatfield–McCoy feud on a "rare genetic 'rage' disease . . . or madness disease . . . that fueled violent tempers across generations," many descendants, including Bo McCoy, living in Ohio, nursing his "adrenal gland problem." Skyline Chili says, "It's Skyline Time," and "Some of our fans go so far as to say the food and the experience actually enhances their mood," and "Our waitresses will tie on your Skyline bib," and Gold Star Chili says, "We have a closely guarded secret," and Empress Chili says, "There can be no debate: it all started with Empress."

* * *

1987: You wake up as an old woman in a red blouse and, since Ohio has by now, according to *USA Today*, "lured Japanese corporations here—24 of them, including Honda, Nissan, Mitsubishi," and since Ohio has by now "affectionately" called the new Japanese residents "Banzai Buckeyes," you decide to honor this diversity by creating the Bellefontaine, Ohio, Culture Club (mission: "To offer Ohio hospitality to Orientals"). You will teach "younger Japanese housewives about shopping, sports, chili, and speaking English." You will feel a sense of pride when one such housewife tells *USA Today*, "I love the basketball games. I clap and eat popcorn." And you will not think of assimilation, of how the anatomy of the tomato disappears into the stew, of how *neon* means *dusk*, when you reply, "We eat their raw fish. Their work ethic rubs off. They've made more Ohioans willing to work all day Saturday or late at night," practicing their free throws, their advertising blitzes, simmering their chili and washing their dishes long after the rest of us have gone to bed.

There is no debate, because there can be no debate . . . Look: the cardinal flies into the tomato and drowns. Look: decomposition = less evidence. And Tiffin is close to Upper Sandusky, which is close to Cedar Point, where roller coasters named Monster and Mean Streak roar into the night, contextualize our state with speed and major insurance coverage, and a return to the same station where we began, an attendant in a red vest making sure we watch our steps, and Tiffin is in the middle of nowhere, and a tiffin, having originated in British India, is a light meal that may or may not say something about colonization, that may, or may not, include an Xtra-Small bowl of chili.

O foretells *Oh, no.*

* * *

2013: You wake up, eat ground beef and tomato. It's a sunny day in Cleveland. This time, you are a man, and you have a sense of humor, the ability to become a meme, a mascot, more than human, immortal as chili. You hear the sort of screaming that reminds you of steam escaping, of wind in trees you can't see, of rivers and raiders and dead televisions coming back to life, and birth. Outside, you see it—a girl this time, her arms so pretty and white and skinny reaching through the barred doorway of the neighbor's house, as if this outside air were some kind of earth that she needs to dig into. Maybe you think of all fruit once considered toxic, then domesticated, then diseased, then healthy again. Maybe you think this is only a case of domestic violence. That the crow cawing in the sassafras tree transmits messages about the dead feeding the living. You are Charles—after Dickens or Darwin, or Lindbergh, or the First. How can you know that this woman will run into your arms clutching her own child? That you will hold her, pick, without realizing it, a tomato seed from your molar with the tip of your tongue? That Hodge's, the restaurant where you work as a dishwasher, where you've scraped the viscera of so many tomatoes, but so little chili from so many plates, spoons, forks, will create a cartoon logo of your face? That you will be astonished, and that you will talk again and again about your astonishment? That you will finally be a hero, and that sixteen local restaurants will always give you hamburgers for free? That you will be looked at with prayerful eyes? That you will not be ignored? That you will be fed for life?

Cincinnati Chili

Gold Star Mini Meatloaf Cupcakes with Mashed Potato Icing

Servings: 12 mini meatloaves
Prep Time: 10 minutes
Cook Time: 30 minutes

Ingredients
2 eggs
½ cup finely chopped onion
1 can (10 ounces) Gold Star Original Chili
¼ cup ketchup
1 cup oyster crackers, crumbled
½ teaspoon salt
¼ teaspoon black pepper
2 pounds ground chuck

Glaze
⅓ cup ketchup (Glaze Ingredient)
1 teaspoon Gold Star Cincinnati Style Chili Seasoning (Glaze Ingredient)
1 tablespoon prepared mustard (Glaze Ingredient)
1 tablespoon Gold Star Hot Sauce, or to taste (Glaze Ingredient)
2½ cups (24 oz.) mashed potatoes, homemade or purchased (Glaze Ingredient)
1 cup shredded cheddar cheese, plus more for garnish (Glaze Ingredient)
1 hot dog, cooked, sliced into 12 rounds (Glaze Ingredient)

Directions

Heat oven to 350 degrees. Spray a 12-muffin pan with cooking spray.

In a large bowl combine the eggs, onion, Gold Star Original

Chili, ketchup, and crushed oyster crackers. Stir in salt and pepper. Gently but thoroughly mix in the beef.

Transfer the mixture to the prepared pan, pressing and smoothing the top of each mini meatloaf.

In a small bowl combine the glaze ingredients; spread over each meatloaf. Bake for 30–40 minutes or until cooked through. Let stand 5 minutes. Turn oven to broil.

Using a slotted spoon, remove each meatloaf from the pan and place in a foil cupcake paper. Place them on a baking sheet.

Stir the shredded cheddar into the mashed potatoes. (Add a little milk if the mixture is too thick.) Spoon or pipe the mixture over each meatloaf. Broil just until brown.

Garnish with additional shredded cheese and a hot dog slice. Serve warm or at room temperature.

—Charlie Howard, Gold Star Chili

PACIFIC WEST

Hawaii: Shave Ice

Alaska: Buttwiches

Washington: Aplets

Oregon: Marionberry Pie

California: California Roll

The Mynah Bird Eats Hawaiian Shave Ice

SHAVE ICE IS BOTH a command (as in *Shave ice!*) and a noun. Only the tourists call it *shaved*, imposing the past tense, a history, as if this cutting-down to manageable size isn't happening all around us here, all of the time. In the cutting down of the ice is our occupation of a great, if temporary, coldness. In the cutting down of the ice is the almost instantaneous melting on our tongues, the quickness with which we can take a second bite, pretending that our mouths are not the colors of this overcooked flora, of this decades-old blood.

Once the kingdom of Hawai'i was overthrown, the "new" government enforced, in 1893, the Act to Prevent the Spread of Leprosy, which, in 1893, ignited the Leper War on Kaua'i, when, rebelling against the forced relocation of Kaua'i lepers to a barren reservation on the island of Molokai, the leper Kaluaikoolau shot and killed deputy sheriff Louis H. Stolza, leading to further standoffs and battles between the lepers and soldiers of the "new" government. The lepers hid in caves, and the soldiers came with howitzers. The lepers hid in the thickest of the vegetation, and the U.S. Board of Health contracted subsequent assaults to American Civil War veterans. Twenty-seven lepers were captured and quarantined and one leper was lynched for murder, but the remaining members of the colony disappeared, which meant that the colony itself had to dissolve as a consequence, the members dispersing into isolated households, where, in an effort to cool the heat of their disease—their wounds, their mouths—they would do in isolation what they used to do communally, which is to wave their swords through the air toward blocks of ice, catch the shavings in baskets, and toss, like confetti, these flakes into the air like a real snow, a new kind of weather that even a new kind of government couldn't wrest, as if a scream of victory amid loss from their newly cooled throats.

In scream, in the expression of pain, is a sort of greeting, is a This Is Who I Am, however involuntary. No wonder that, in joy, we also scream, in order to mimic this.

The surface area of Hawai'i is 6,423.4 square miles. The surface area of our kiwi shave ice is incalculable—it melts too fast into green water. In the cherry-blue raspberry combo is the purpling of our mouths with old murder. In purple is the deliberate blending of two colors, the forcing of the present to the past, as if King Kamehameha III didn't write, "Where are you, chiefs, people, and commons from my ancestors . . .? Hear ye! I make known to you that I am in perplexity by reason of difficulties into which I have been brought without cause, therefore I have given away the life of our land. Hear ye!" both in 1843 and again just this morning, and again just now, as we swallow a cone of ice dust the color of another idiot sunset.

* * *

WHEN IN CAPTIVITY, the mynah bird, in what naturalists believe to be an act of desperation, reproduces in panic the sounds it hears, including human speech. We have come to expect, even demand, that mynah birds mirror our voices. Some species of mynah, though, have larger, more unwieldy tongues, which their owners often cut to match the shape of the human tongue in miniature, in order to allow them our version of speech. When the captive mynah speaks to us in our own voice, that is the mynah slowly going mad. In Hawai'i, the mynah, along with its interpretation of our language, is now considered an invasive species.

I wonder about the distance between language and the heart, the marginalized and the conqueror. The fruit, and the syrup we render from it. Which the mainland, which the far-flung archipelago? The mynah, in its nightstand cage, whispers, *Kill them all . . .*

The mynah can hear, even if we can't, the flakes of shave ice falling through the air. These are the ones that miss the cup. To the lepers, the mynah exhales more loudly. To the lepers, the mynah has a snowstorm in its mouth.

* * *

As opposed to the pellets of a snow cone, shave ice demands a finer, thinner grain, aims more to mimic the texture of actual snow. That our islands have never seen snow does nothing to deter the shaving. In this act is wish fulfillment, some silly stab at empathizing with the weather systems of the mainland, or, a retroactive reclaiming of weather that was never ours, the stories of which we heard whispered in the sleeps of the generations of occupiers, before they mutilated the tongues of birds who were then permitted to sing, and warble, and call, rather than pronounce words like *blizzard*, and—here, to us—other useless terms. Here, certain words also miss the cup, melt down to their water on leaves and in dirt.

Here, actual snow, like shave ice, recalls the strips of epidermis peeled from our sunburns. Through this veil of skin, the softbill mynah eats only soft foods. This is only nature, and speaks nothing to the delicacy of the bird's heart.

Shave ice is so soft, it melts. Strange that it takes such a formidable blade to cut it. Strange that, were it really the weather and not just another hopeless mimic, it would have the power to kill us. Here, we imitate even the weak things that can kill us. A flake of ice that melts on contact with skin, even as it resembles that skin. Enough of these flakes and we can have dessert, shelter, something large enough to call a disaster, a whole body.

* * *

Deportation that imitates concern. The howitzer that sounds like the wind. In this life, coconut shave ice recalls the coconut. In death, Louis H. Stolza mimics the leper. When the imitation encounters the original, which melts first? Is the mimicry of the weather systems of the mainland an act of empathy, reverence, or, in the turning of said systems into dessert, in staining them with syrups flavored with native fruits, one of condescension, reclamation? Above us, the mynah mimics the sound of the shave ice machine, which is to say, a wail of blades.

At Hale'iwa Beach Park, on Oahu's north shore, a hunchbacked old woman peddles shave ice that she tops with blue vanilla syrup, azuki bean paste, and sweetened condensed milk. She calls this a Snow Cap. Thawing, the azuki beans remember their days as an annual vine whose fibers were so strong it was used, in ancient Japan, as a noose. The plant as a gallows is a comment on either mimicry or ingenuity or desperation, but definitely intersection—intersection as two things that not only meet, not only cross, but impale themselves onto each other. Sometimes, we have to force the impaling. Ask the mynah. It now can answer.

In the 1920s, Japanese expats working the sugarcane and pineapple plantations would celebrate their Sundays off by using their work machetes to instead shave ice into cups, over which they poured the juice of the cane and the pineapple. Their children eventually moved off the plantations, some opened grocery stores and peddled this treat, as their parents did, only on Sundays. In this way, shave ice became sacred, elemental, meteorological. A hundred-year storm turned weekly tradition. As much a stain on us as the diseases we carry, the shades of our skins. Even when the sunsets became rote, the children would still order their shave ice not by the flavor, but by the color.

Here, our colors precede us, act as greeting. In this way, we are just like the rest of the world. Even the prettiest sunset here is a prelude to darkness and other weak metaphors. Next to that mountain of banana peels and horseflies, the Hyatt Regency clears some space for a new poolside bar at which you can buy "authentic Hawaiian" shave ice that is way, way too expensive. At night, in the browning phloem bundles, each horsefly lays its eggs in a sound that recalls water dripping—the sort of melt that predicts infestation. Here, authenticity is the sword. Dessert, like the weather, can cut your head off.

* * *

Though the azuki beans are so red, they leave no stain in my mouth. That's the syrup's job. When my lips are this color, they tell the world that I am a corpse, frozen. If my lips are this color, then why am I still sweating? Overhead, the mynah invades another coconut palm, plays dead in its fronds.

Today's flavors: lychee, guava, cherry, lime, mango, passion fruit, coconut, kiwi, pineapple, and *li hing mui*, the dried salted plum, a flavor that the hunchbacked old woman describes, like speech to a maimed bird, like these islands themselves, as *acquired.*

Li hing mui does stain the mouth red. I thank god for the satisfaction of this expectation, though I don't have the speech with which to mimic it.

* * *

THE MYNAH CAN'T keep up with the glaciers, and other ever-melting things, confused as to whether to retreat or advance. Sunburn, frozen throat, a communication between two unbearables . . . If we can feel two things like this at once, we exist. In the reshaping of the mynah's tongue is a sort of deportation. The cut-away parts of us repurposed as fertilizer, growing the fruits we use to flavor a dessert that evokes the kind of weather we'll never see here. A wedging of the foreign into the crevices of the indigenous. All it takes is a razor-sharp blade . . .

We need hard things to make other hard things soft. Here, our history is packed into a paper cone, is quenching our thirst, cooling us down, even as it leaks from the bottom, runs from our hands. We all know: Hawai'i is the fiftieth state, the last. We know: the last state before insanity is mimicry. In 1815, the Russians overtook Hawai'i. In 1843, the British overtook Hawai'i. In 1898, the U.S. did. All the blood looked the same.

In a melting dessert is an incomplete dessert. We can never eat all of our shave ice. It adapts to this weather so much faster than we do. This is to say nothing of a sense of *home,* and other volcanic detritus. Here, the birds pronounce our dripping desserts, confuse this with the sound of the egg pressed from the horsefly's body.

We retreat to our caves with our sweetest, melting things, stain our tongues calico, tell ourselves that those cannons are a new thunder, a jubilee. When we finally feel it's safe to step out into the light, the thickest of the vegetation will be so affectionate, that the birds here won't be able to distinguish our mouths from the flowers, *emerge* from *emergency.*

The mynah is red and the mynah is black and the mynah is white, and the mynah is pale-bellied and golden-breasted and yellow-faced, and rose-necked, common and great, starling and passerine. They eat the insects from the fruits we flavor our shave ice with. They sing clearly into the wind. They say hello.

Shave Ice

Ingredients

Red adzuki beans (cooked and cooled)

Fresh fruit (I like mango, lychee, kiwi, or strawberry), chopped

Simple syrup (equal parts water and sugar, brought to a boil, then cooled)

Ice cubes

Condensed milk (can substitute sweetened coconut milk)

Li-hing-mui (dried salted plum) powder

Mash the beans with enough simple syrup to form a medium-thick paste. The extra paste can be frozen. If it needs more sweetness (this depends on your liking), add a little more sugar to the paste.

In a saucepan cover the fruit by about 2 inches with simple syrup and bring to a soft boil. Poach for about 2 minutes, then remove from the heat, cover with a lid, and let steep for one hour.

Shave the ice in a shave ice machine (unless you want to try it the old way with a machete!).

Pack the ice into a glass, bowl, or cone. Spoon some of the flavored simple syrup and fruit chunks over the top, and garnish with a dollop of bean paste, a drizzle of condensed milk, and a light sprinkle of the li-hing powder (these garnishes are all optional, and should be portioned according to the eater's taste).

Enjoy!

—*Cindy Jade Sylva*

Extensions on Buttwiches and Idiocy and Buttwiches on Extensions

IN THE CHANNEL BOWL Cafe, in Juneau, the stuffing is held inside the counter stools with duct tape. Alojzy, a seventy-seven-year-old ex-gold-panner and commercial fisherman, scoffs at the Springsteen that the chef is playing on the stereo as he flips eggs, drops local blueberries into pancake batter (the blueberry pancakes here are called Fancycakes), splits open a reindeer sausage with a paring knife. Hacks twenty-seven fillets of halibut into workable parts: parts that can huddle together into pearlescent patties. Alojzy scratches his fontanel—nothing of the halibut there. He knows his name means *famous warrior,* knows that he has to use an axe as a cane. He watches the chef pack halibut paste, readying the awful white bun with mayo and iceberg. He reads the lunch special: Buttwich and salad. He says, "In a world full of idiots, you have to go to the place with the fewest idiots."

This is an insufficient end for a beast whose name means *holy flat fish,* for a beast the Catholics reserve for the most sacred of days, taking its flesh into their mouths prayerfully. For a beast that can grow to 483 pounds, that can, with its body, feed over a thousand people—more if sides are included. For a beast that, once caught and hauled to the ocean's surface, needs to be repeatedly shot to die. This is the beast that, after we turn its body into burger, we name after own asses. Here, through the halibut, we turn the holy into the joke. We can giggle as we eat it.

Beyond the griddle and the stools and the awesome puke-green gold-flecked counter, all ten bowling lanes of the Channel Bowl are occupied, each by a single bowler. Even their strikes sound lonely, isolated. Like the state itself, the sounds of these pins colliding—plasticized rock maple against plasticized rock maple—lack any kind of ultimate grandeur. Though pathetic, the sounds are too lonely to attain the position of *final.* Order matters. Acceptance matters. Like the state, the sound is second to last. Penultimate. Almost ultimate, but not quite. Ever beside, but never quite embodying, greatness. Any time a part is accepted into a whole, there is a period of adjustment.

The U.S. bought Alaska on special. Alojzy wonders about all kinds of folly, wonders if he was wrong when, all those years ago, he associated geographical extremity with a lack of idiocy.

"This is the fish," says Günther Hansel, after catching the world's largest halibut, "that I have been fishing for all my life." Nina Simone replaces Springsteen on the stereo. Though there is no guitar in the song, Alojzy strums his flanneled potbelly, says, "Blah, blah, blah." The third "blah" is the same as the others, but still, it is ultimate.

"All my life," Alojzy mutters, then stops muttering.

* * *

WE CUT OUR FOOD to fit our mouths. According to L. Pierce Clark, in his article "The Psychology of Idiocy," one of the symptoms of amentia is the inability to detect the parameters of concrete objects—not only the inability to distinguish between large and small objects, but especially the compulsion to make (if only mentally) large objects smaller, more manageable for those "fixated on the lowest stages of progress."

We use knives and teeth and naming. With these tools, we carve the holy from the halibut, take the final syllable away from *flat fish* and give it to our own locker-room sniggering. "It's a fucking flounder, Al," Rich says as he gums his Buttwich, and Alojzy pounds his good fist on the counter, and the bowler on lane 9 rolls a turkey.

An axe that's used as a cane and has fallen to the floor of a diner looks so out of place there—the thing stripped of its original function: the bullet now used to apply lipstick; the fish so far out of water . . .

Ice pellets today. On the coat tree of the Channel Bowl Cafe, Helly Hansen raincoats commune with Helly Hansen waders via their dripping to the floor. Here, there is intimacy in defrosting, even if we are not defrosting together. Here is the ocean as puddle, the weather made tiny by the diner.

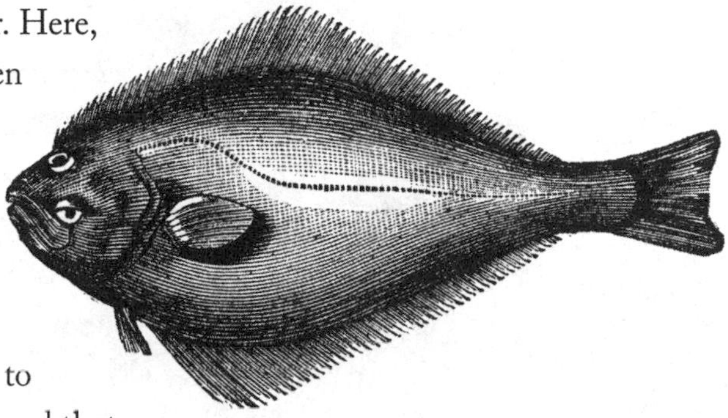

Clark maintains that another aspect of idiocy is insisting that what is popularly cold (according to median human perception) is warm, and that what is warm is cold. In this forced misinterpretation of a thing's temperature is a devaluing of the thing, a megalomaniacal revising of a thing's reality in order to fit our own skewed (read: idiotic) context. We ridicule that which is more powerful than us in order to subjugate it, leash it to the yard, tell it when to sit and speak. In this way, the winter here is a witch's tit, the holy fish, our *tuchus*.

Lane 9's doing well. No one cheers for his sixth strike in a row.

* * *

IN RELATION TO water temperature, the halibut is a boreal fish—it prefers long, cold winters, short, cool summers. In such climates, the water becomes cooler the deeper one goes, but only to a point. After a certain depth, the currents foster an odd reversal, and the water then becomes warmer the deeper one goes, as if the oceans here are palindromic. The halibut thrives in water that is about 36 degrees Fahrenheit, oftentimes having to withdraw deeper and deeper in order to uncover that kind of warmth. The lower it sinks, the warmer it gets.

The term *palindrome* derives from the Greek *palin*, meaning *again*, and *dromos*, meaning *direction*. Clark maintains that another aspect of idiocy involves the retracing of one's own misguided steps, over and over again, as if in mantra. Palindromes are neat, if idiotic. In an essay involving Alaska and idiocy, I promised myself not to use the word *Palin*. It's not idiocy, Clark says, to break one's vows if those vows themselves are idiotic.

In the strike, the best we can do while bowling, the ultimate throw, is a nothing-left-standing. A decimation. A total falling down. A clearing of the alley. A fostering of absence. Silent. Alone. The pins setting themselves up for the fall again and again, the bowlers trying not to commune . . .

The Greeks used the notion of the palindrome to describe the movement of the crabs on the beach. Though baby Dungeness crabs are often found (their shells beautifully intact and still bright red) in the stomachs of caught halibut, an online search for "halibut crab relationship" yields pages and pages of such popular results as "Crab Stuffed Halibut Baked to Perfection," "Crab Topped Halibut Steaks," and "Perfect Seafood Pairings" (pinot gris with crab, pinot noir with halibut). In our stomachs, as in our ethos, neither remain beautifully intact, or still bright red.

Perfection is simply the best that we can do. Sometimes, this means being an idiot. In Anchorage cafes, Buttwich special on Mondays. In Nome, Tuesdays. In Glenallen, Wednesdays. In Skagway, Thursdays. Here, in the Atlantic, if the days of the week were to correspond to water temperature as we go deeper and deeper, Friday would lead to Saturday, which would lead to Sunday, and Sunday would repeat itself before becoming Saturday again.

Fifty miles southeast of the Channel Bowl Cafe, the twin glaciers—North and South Sawyer—calve simultaneously at the end of the Tracy Arm fjord. They belch their icebergs into Holkham Bay, while the bulk of their icy bodies remains in a slow retreat. Here, is it idiocy or birthright to confuse forward with backward? Like the glaciers, we throw apples at the bully, even as we retreat from him. I will resist here any dumb watery joke about keeping things at bay . . .

* * *

ALOJZY, CURSING THE music, the town, the menu, and Rich moves on to discuss how, when he was liberated from the German concentration camp, he ran with his fellow emaciates into the nearby woods. "No one knew where we were going," he says, "but when we felt we had run long enough, even though we were starving and thirsty, we fell to the dirt and we fucked, goddamn, we *fucked*."

Birthright: propagation, ancient and out of our hands. About this, the halibut says nothing, keeps its goofy right eye on the crab ahead. Birthright: subjugation, ancient and out of our hands. One thousand portions from one big body. All it takes is a sharp knife. At some point, the relationship between propagation and subjugation must move and belch like the glaciers. At some point, they must double back and become themselves in some desperate attempt to return to any beginning, however redundant.

A flatfish bigger than a whale, or goo on a bun garnished with the most mundane of our lettuces? A goo we have to call *pearlescent* to force the preciousness of its source.

Where is the penultimate on the continuum of the palindrome?

Clark calls our idiocy our "'ancient past,' so significant, possibly, in the life of every human being." Lane 9's final throw hugs the edge of the alley. Just as it's about to curve inward toward the pocket, the ball decides against it, falls opposite, into the gutter. Lanes 8 and 10 surround this with lonely strikes. A perfect idiocy. Nina Simone, probably not thinking of fish or lunch specials or glaciers or Alaska, sings through speaker static, "Do I move you?" Alojzy frowns. Like the halibut, he says nothing. In the corner booth, eating alone, governor-hopeful Tony Knowles finishes his Buttwich and wipes the mayo from his chin. In the frost on the Channel Bowl window, in an answer to another kind of question, he writes "WIN" with his pinkie.

Buttwich (Halibut Sandwich)

Halibut Salad Sandwich

Ingredients	***Amount***
Bagel or Bread	*2 slices*
Halibut Salad	*Green scoop*
Provolone cheese	*2 slices*

Lettuce	*2 leaves*
Tomato	*2 slices*
Cucumbers	*3 slices*
Mayo	*.25 ounces*

Yield: 1 sandwich

Smoked Halibut Salad

Pulse the thawed halibut (2 packets—2 pounds) in the robot coupe just for a few seconds—get pieces not puree—should be like the hot smoked salmon

Add:

Mayo, exact amount	*2½ cups*
Finely diced celery (1/16" pieces)	*10 stalks*
Finely diced red onions (1/16" pieces)	*1 onion*
Lemon juice	*2 teaspoons*

Mix until all combined
Store in 6" 1/6 pans
Fill ¾ of the way full
Date it 17 days from today
Do not freeze or put in walk-in
Put into sandwich prep

—Jill Ramiel, owner, The Silverbow

Aplets, an Apocalyptic Love Story

IN THE MARITIME museums of Bainbridge and Bremerton, harbors named Gig and Grays, Port Townsend and Cape Disappointment, there are boats—boats juxtaposed with shipwreck dioramas. "Those poor fishermen," Uncle says. Boats juxtaposed with blooming vetch culled from Bottle Beach and Donkey Creek Bog. "One of the first domesticated angiosperms," Uncle reads on the placard. "Don't let that fool you, boy. Those purple flowers are staging a coup." Boats juxtaposed with music and recordings of, according to the placard, "steamer captains, and ships' whistles and horns from early Puget Sound Passenger vessel fleets, small boats, and shipbuilding." "None of which can sing for shit," Uncle says. Uncle kicks with the toe of his boot at a dugout canoe stained with, he assures me, decades-old murder. He bites at his pinkie nails like he's going to whistle for some ghost of a dog, thinks better of it. "Those poor Chinook Indians," he says, still biting.

Uncle remembers, as a child, watching a tall ship named *Apple O'Day* come into the sound. From the shore, he watched the captain lift his hands from the wheel, walk to the rail, and juggle twelve apples and twelve giant geoduck clams. "At once," Uncle says. Twenty-four of Washington's best, airborne all at once. He makes of his childhood something ephemeral—something briny whirling in the air, over a bearded man's face, with something sweet. "That captain," Uncle insists, "looked so much like Humphrey Bogart. I'll bet it was him. Some *Casablanca* publicity stunt. Most people don't know he could juggle like that." Uncle takes the blender from the cabinet above the refrigerator, his reach still admirable from decades of apple-picking. He wonders, muttering, where the *Apple O'Day* is today; if it made it to museum or historical society or seabed—arrivals all.

Uncle makes Aplets: purees (what he insists on calling "the blossom-fresh flavor of") our state's apples, cooks the paste over a low simmer, adds plenty of sugar, and just a drop of salt ("never lemon," he says, "in spite of what those fuckers from Spokane say"). When the puree coppers, he adds the pulverized walnuts, the powdered gelatin. He will spread the mixture onto a buttered baking sheet, refrigerate it overnight before cutting it into squares and rolling them in powdered sugar. He stirs the puree, looks into the garbage can, laments that, in Washington, the cores of things are the things that get tossed.

Uncle tells the story of meeting Aunt in the orchard. Were he Longfellow, or even Bogart, his pickup lines might have been better, might have been as he imagines them: *Yours is the one that's spicy and aromatic, possibly Russian in origin, and snowy because of it. Look there! There's talk of cross-breeding and an elderly woman in a green dress with a matching necklace and orange papier-mâché earrings was overheard whispering "Julyred" to her nodding husband. He fingers his breast pocket, his business card stretching its cardboard corner to the middle-aged redhead across the orchard. He wants, after so many years of silence, to again introduce himself as Worcester Pearmain just to see if she'll laugh. But yours, despite the lack of years, is one of the oldest varieties we grow.* Stirring, Uncle makes other apple jokes—the skin, the flesh, the seeds . . . To make things digestible, he has to, like most of us, break them down into their parts, and laugh a little.

* * *

ACCORDING TO Washington Apple Country and the Cashmere Cider Mill, Aplets (not *Applets,* or *Appletts* or *Applettes*) were invented on a small orchard in Cashmere, Washington in 1920, and their sales pitch demands an apocryphal nostalgia, asking us to "imagine a fresh fruit stand in the summer when flavors are at their peak, the air is filled with sweet aromas, the colors are a feast for the eyes . . . now you can get the same tasting 'excursion' in our Famous Fruit Delights. This bounteous harvest includes Aplets . . ."

Four years after the invention of the Aplet, Seattle's Sand Point Airfield served as the terminus of the first aerial circumnavigation of the world, by a team of U.S. Army Air Servicemen whom Uncle compares, in the language of the region, to "a cloud of gnats racing around the apple . . ."

The temperature of the earth's inner core is about 9,800 degrees Fahrenheit. Uncle dips his finger into the puree and, though he burns himself, he makes no sound. In the trash can, the apple cores have already gone to yellow, which means that they're softer than before. Here, we soften before we spoil.

A few states south, in Glendale, California, in Forest Lawn Memorial Park, in the Columbarium of Eternal Light subplot of the Garden of Memory, Humphrey Bogart's remains also soften, his heart long gone, having given in, Uncle says, to the "gnats around the apple."

> ***To make things digestible, he has to, like most of us, break them down into their parts, and laugh a little.***

Uncle, childless, looks hard at me as he stirs the puree. His face is paler than usual, as if freshly peeled, and his mouth stiffens like golf pencils, and his voice softens in a way that I don't like. When Aunt died, like Bogart, of cancer, Uncle made a pilgrimage to Glendale "to find answers." He believed, he said, that Bogart's grave would be decorated with the clamshells and apple skins he remembers the actor-cum-captain juggling on the deck of the *Apple O'Day* all those years ago. When he arrived, he found that the Garden of Memory was locked, and, as advertised on its own placard, "not accessible to the general public."

So, Uncle misremembers his pickup lines, confuses one orchard for another: *We all can see your pale yellow, your bands of orange. You come across as edible, a safe bet with a scary edge. Your Chenango skin—my God, how can it be so luminous after a childhood in Jersey? Quite a dish . . . I brush my fingers along your side until your stripes blush from orange to pink. We try to hide from the crowd, but I can feel their jealousy, tart as small strawberries, these chance seedlings, striving to become old in this Cashmere wind.*

In the Forest Lawn Memorial Park, Bogart undoes. Uncle tells me: his middle name was DeForest. Here, we undo our apples with a little gelatin, in order to make them softer. According to Washington Apple Country and the Cashmere Cider Mill, this undoing is "easy on the teeth and impossible to resist."

* * *

The tall ship *Lady Washington*, a 90-ton sloop, participated, in 1787, in the Pacific Northwest fur trade, porcelain trade, tea trade. In paintings, the *Lady Washington* looks stately in Commencement Bay. In Japan (*Lady Washington* was the first American ship to reach it), in Nagasaki, *Lady Washington* looks dejected, as she is unable to peddle her unsold pelts to the locals. In 1797, *Lady Washington* vanishes in the Philippines' Mestizo River, becomes legend, cautionary tale, ghost. (*Those poor trappers . . .*) Uncle knows: *mestizo* means *mixed*, referring most often to people who identify as having a racially mixed descent. Uncle stirs the puree, believes that the disappeared tall ship was named for both Martha Washington and the Lady apple.

March 26–28, 1856: The Cascades of the Columbia, Stevenson, Washington: Major Edward J. Steptoe "took 200 men from the 1st Dragoons . . . and steamed downriver to the Upper Cascades . . . fighting the Indians. Most of the Indians scattered at this turn of events, the Chinooks escaping to Bradford's Island. Steptoe detached Lt. Alexander Piper, Piper's 3rd Artillery Company, and a howitzer and sent them with Sheridan after the Chinooks. Piper's men cornered the Chinooks at the lower end of the island and the Indians surrendered, claiming they had not partaken in killing settlers . . ." Still, "A quick trial by military commission judged them guilty, and eight, including Chief Chenowith, were hanged." Uncle stirs, shakes his head, says something about the swinging of the corpse in the wind off the sea, how she never thought to have health insurance . . . This state is a pig, Uncle says, with an apple in its mouth.

If he's right, if this state is a dead pig, what does that say of its residents—let alone the vessels they ride, the fruit they alter? And who will do the eating? Here, the heart of the matter turns brown in the trash.

* * *

WENATCHEE, WASHINGTON, named for the Wenatchi Indians, is the Apple Capital of the World due to the valley's "super orchards." Wenatchee, due to a saturation of hydroelectric dams, is also known as the Buckle of the Power Belt of the Great Northwest. Uncle knows: we give ourselves nicknames because we need endearment, warmth. "Your aunt used to say," he says, "nicknames give color to our faces." He knows: *Wenatchee,* in the Sahaptin language, means *robe of the rainbow.* He stirs, wonders why his puree is monochromatic. Adds more sugar. Nothing yet gels.

"A pig," Uncle says. And, ultimately, a mushroom cloud is not a rainbow, even though it's comprised of many colors. In eastern Washington, in 1943, the Hanford Works nuclear power plant began producing the plutonium that would two years later fuel Fat Man, the atomic bomb dropped on Nagasaki, Japan, killing the descendants of those who wouldn't buy the leftover pelts from the traders aboard *Lady Washington.* Fat Man was flown aboard a Boeing B-29, also made in Washington.

Uncle hangs his head, "those poor . . ." and can't finish. A mere 100 miles from the Hanford Works nuclear power plant, the Apple Capital of the World drops its fruit.

And there goes Mount St. Helens, Uncle says. After the eruption, the apples in the nearby orchards collected such a thick layer of ash that the fruits disappeared into these gray spheres. "Tumor trees," Uncle called them, and, in this way, the apples themselves became cores of these strange new fruits of the apocalypse. "This has nothing to do with goddamn Adam and goddamn Eve," Uncle says. In Eden, Washington, the cancerous puke up their apples.

And this part, Uncle says, is what finally seduced her: *So what will we name the child? Elstar, Greening, Spartan, Snow? Kendall, Spencer, Tydeman, Rome? Jesus, they sound like appled reindeers, baby. What happened to my Ingrid Marie, now tied to this land, picking her men and children like apples, then scurrying away like a raccoon on a roof? Look at the old couple, baby; look at the redhead. We're better than them, right? But you hold your tongue, just for a moment. And here, my hands need to sweat, need to grab. I want to take a bite out of you. I want to bake you into a pie. "If it's a girl," you say, "let's call her Liberty."*

Perhaps the writer was talking about a dugout canoe, or perhaps he was talking about a fishing boat—certainly not a tall ship, certainly not *Lady Washington*, or Fat Man, or Eternal Light—when an anonymous local writer described an anonymous local vessel as "indomitable" and "beautiful only in its homeliness like Humphrey Bogart."

Uncle wants to think he's speaking of the *Apple O'Day*, but this is a long shot, of course. It's hard for him not to imagine where that boat is now:

It's likely that the boat eventually disintegrated, devolved to the slats of wood that comprised it. These slats of wood were likely burned or gathered or buried into the coccyx of some farm shed, unearthed from bale and pig shit and apple cores by a cadre of shadow gleaners, some of the slats now adorning, diagonally, the walls of a Philadelphia sports bar, some used as jousts in California surf-busting competitions, some bought as souvenirs by boat fetishist Hollywood stars like Sterling Hayden, some recobbled into rafts used to cross Great Slave Lake, the deepest in North America, water that once held gold.

It's hard not to imagine these parts ripping from these walls, coalescing in some paradoxically timeless 1787 as *Lady Washington*, where they nail themselves together so that the fur traders can stand on them, so the fur traders can unfold from their bunks at 2 a.m., so fur traders can prepare their gear at some coral first light, so they can prepare coffee, so they can drink it and burn their tongues, so they can curse the twenty-hour work day, their bodies snowed on, rained on, shat on, bled on, windblown and invisible in the fog.

It is still ten years until the ship becomes a ghost; still 102 years until, on Christmas Day, Humphrey Bogart, the celebrity with whom some mystery boat will be compared, is born. The traders are cold, but they're used to it. In this cold, a fertility, something of a field of trees, blossom-fresh. The captain eats an apple, offers one to the swab. Neither knows that in Dutch, *Bogart* means *orchard.*

Aplets

Ingredients
4 cups apple pulp
4 cups sugar
4 tablespoons gelatin
1 cup cold water
3 cups chopped nuts
¼ teaspoon rosewater

Use Jonathan apples or Winesaps. Cut up and cook with sugar in as little water as possible. Drain and press through a sieve. Soften gelatin in water; add to apple pulp and mix thoroughly. Add nuts and rosewater after mixture has partially cooled. Pour into buttered pans ¾ inch thick. Let harden, cut in even pieces, and roll in powdered sugar.

Aplets are the most genial palate ticklers, that have come our way since the advent of fudge. They are done up commercially at the Liberty Orchards in the Wenatchee Valley.

—*Cora Brown,*
America Cooks: Practical Recipes from 48 States *(1940)*

OREGON

The Devastating Flight of Marionberry Pie

"ALIS VOLAT PROPRIIS," Uncle says, citing the Oregon state motto. His lips are stained with marionberry juice, and crumbs of the flakiest piecrust "this side of the Snake River" collect in his moustache, form a colony against, perhaps, your aunt in the kitchen who kneads and kneads for next month's contest at the state fair. You know that our state motto was written in 1854 by Judge Jesse Quinn Thornton, that he traveled from Virginia to Ohio to Missouri to Illinois and finally to Oregon to "improve" his health. You know that members of Thornton's wagon train eventually split off for California and became the Donner Party. You know that Thornton and his wife, Agnes, would remain childless, and that he longed always for a daughter, and, as such, favored feminine pronouns, even in the face of mistranslation, and so imposed gender and, perhaps, the ghost of the daughter who was not to be onto the Oregon state motto, translating the genderless *Alis volat propriis* (*It flies with its own wings*) into English as *She flies with her own wings*, and maybe this was his stab at parenthood (Thornton often spoke of "raising Oregon"), or maybe he was taken with the yellow half-moon breast of the western meadowlark, our state bird, as she dive-bombs the trailing vines of the marionberry—the vines that Uncle describes as "damn-near bridal"—emerging with a gaped beak that could be purpled, as if with decades-old blood.

Here, any reminder of blood is just another kind of ringless covenant. According to the article "Cannibalism Along the Oregon Trail," "A family of four needed over a thousand pounds of food to sustain them on the long journey to Oregon, and when bad weather delayed the journey the food supply sometimes ran out, leaving the hungry pioneers facing death from starvation"; and Uncle starts on the new test pie, talks about hunger as if it's something that can be bred, cultivated, and therefore just as easily destroyed. You want to ask him to clarify, but he has so many drupelets stuck in his throat.

The marionberry was developed in the laboratories of Oregon State University, in conjunction with the USDA Agricultural Research Service, by George F. Waldo in 1945, as the crossbred offspring of the Chehalem and Olallie berries, and was released onto the general public only eleven years later, after extensive "testing"—locating the perfect climate in which the berry thrives, which just happened to be the area in and around Marion County in the Willamette Valley. The new fruit was soon marketed as the cabernet sauvignon of blackberries, due to its earthiness tempered by sweetness, the volume of its smashing juice, and its "powerful size." Uncle swallows and sniffs, thinks of chainsaws and rain, evergreen needles, and the longest unrestricted coastline in the continental U.S. "All here," he says. He says, "As long as we're willing to cut something down, we'll never starve."

Ask the pioneers: *Sauvignon* means *savage. Cabernet* derives from the Latin *caput*, which means, depending on the context, *head, sense, top, summit, source, root, mind, mouth*. That the word *kaput* also derives from this source inspires Uncle to kiss his paper napkin and wonder, you guess, about the point at which all upper, oral savagery goes extinct. Here, we name our state berry after the wine that most evokes our desire to take a bite out of one another.

Uncle wonders if in cannibalism is the urge toward extinction, or infinity. Uncle wonders if he'll ever stop laughing at bad jokes long enough to finish his third slice, kiss Aunt on the most tender of her scars. And, according to the Oregon Historical Society, "cannibalism was practiced on the Northwest Coast of America . . . off the mouth of the Umpqua River in Oregon," and Uncle laughs the crumbs at the ceiling, and Aunt punches through another curtain of dough.

Uncle has all of them in a thick book on the toilet tank:

Q: What do tornadoes and graduates from the University of Oregon have in common?
A: They both end up in trailer parks.

* * *

ACCORDING TO the Cornell Lab of Ornithology, "As they forage, meadowlarks use a feeding behavior called 'gaping'—inserting their bill in the soil or other substrate, and prying it open to access seeds and insects that many bird species can't reach. Western Meadowlarks occasionally eat the eggs of other grassland bird species. During hard winters, they may even feed at carcasses such as roadkill . . . The buoyant, flutelike melody of the Western Meadowlark ringing out across a field can brighten anyone's day."

The meadowlark knows: the world survives by being buccal, by taking us into both of its cheeks, our flavor slowly seeping into cavity after cavity. Uncle assures you: the day will brighten—perhaps even melodiously—with or without us.

The cornstarch binds berry to berry. At the treetops, as within us, another kind of binding agent gathers. The spruce tickles the windowpane like an awful violin. This is not meant to be savage. To drown out the sound of the trees, the berries hissing as their juice evaporates, to prove your hands still work, you compel your fingers to tango the broken piano, snaking the keys like the river, like the roaches through the sugar.

According to the Bureau of Land Management, the Umpqua River is wild and scenic, the beautiful heart of the timber industry. In 1854, the Coquille tribe, who inhabited the river's valley, ceded nearly all of its land to the U.S. government. Seven years later, the river spilled its banks in what was then the greatest recorded flood of the American West. According to a December 14, 1861, article in the *Oregon City Argus*,

a gloom settled on a scene such as probably never was witnessed in our Valley before. The ceaseless roar of the stream made a fearful elemental music widely different from the ordinary monotone of the Falls; while the darkness was only made more visible by the glare of torches and hurrying lights, which with the shouts of people from the windows of houses surrounded by the water, all conspired to render the hour one of intense and painful excitement . . . the insatiate monster is still creeping up inch by inch, winding its swelling folds round the pillars and foundations of all the houses in its way, crushing and grinding them in the maw of destruction, and sweeping the broken fragments into a common vortex of ruin . . . On the fragments of a large barn, sat a number of chickens, bearing melancholy evidence of devastation above . . .

Here, beautiful hearts are born of devastation. From its maw come the berries of hybrid parentage that now line the Umpqua's banks. This has little to do with music, and every sound we use to drown out other sounds. Uncle wonders: in what way is naming predictive? He knows: *ouragan*, in French, means *hurricane.*

* * *

MARION COUNTY and, in turn, the marionberry, is named after Francis Marion, a slave-owning brigadier general in the American Revolutionary War (nickname: Swamp Fox) who is considered the father of modern guerrilla warfare and who forced the Cherokee toward starvation and desperate cannibalism after decimating their villages and burning their crops, and who was tasked with hunting and executing freed slaves, and who inspired Lord Cornwallis to say, "Marion had so wrought the minds of the people, partly by the terror of his threats and cruelty of his punishments, and partly by the promise of plunder," and who inspired author Neil Norman to call him "a thoroughly unpleasant dude who was, basically, a terrorist," and who inspired historian Christopher Hibbert to call him "not at all the sort of chap who should be celebrated as a hero . . . [He was] very active in the persecution of the Cherokee Indians and . . . committed atrocities as bad as, if not worse, than those perpetuated by the British . . . [and had] a reputation as a racist who hunted Indians for sport and regularly raped his female slaves," and who was known on the trail for entertaining his men by trapping birds and breaking their wings and watching the poor beasts waddle in confused circles before mercy compelled him, with his boot-tip, to kick their bodies into the campfire. Here, this is who we name our pie after.

Here, mercy is just another form of terror. Here, we don't quite understand the mechanism with which our state berry has flown to such heights of flavor and fame, or who precisely possesses it.

Cannibals capture three men on the Oregon Trail. The men are told that they will be skinned and eaten and then their skin will be used to make canoes. Then they are each given a final request. The first man asks to be killed as quickly and painlessly as possible. His request is granted, and they poison him. The second man asks for paper and a pen so that he can write a farewell letter to his family. This request is granted, and after he writes his letter, they kill him, saving his skin for their canoes. Now it is the third man's turn. He asks for a fork. The cannibals are confused, but it is his final request, so they give him a fork. As soon as he has the fork he begins stabbing himself all over and shouts, "To hell with your canoes!"

If one misspells *Alis volat propriis, Alis volat propiis,* it translates as *Wings fly closer,* suggesting the presence of a second entity. Closer than what? Or: closer *to* what? In this is a cocktail of intimacy and foreboding, a little shock and just a pinch of terror, another series of ingredients we incompletely understand, but still, we name our counties, and our pies, after it.

* * *

AUDUBON GAVE the western meadowlark the binomial nomenclature *Sturnella neglecta*—meaning *forgotten race*—as he believed that the early settlers who ventured west of the Mississippi ignored this widespread bird precisely because it was so common.

The early settlers knew: our arteries only want to untangle like shoelaces, like the ribbon that tops a box made of cellophane and cardboard, in which this year's winning pie will soon be coffined, cooling, gelling into the sort of softness that allows us to eat it without teeth.

* * *

IN THE 2009 Oregon State Fair's Marionberry Pie contest, first place went to Arlene Thorp's Marionberry Surprise Pie, so-called for the "shocking" and "hidden" layer of cream cheese frosting, sweetened with sugar and vanilla, in between the outer piecrust and the inner filling of local marionberries stewed with sugar and thickened with cornstarch. According to the Oregon Raspberry and Blackberry Commission, Thorp's pie is more likely than other pies to "protect against cancer, heart and circulatory diseases, and age-related mental decline," until, of course, we get to that uncommon layer for which her dish is named. "Marion," Uncle says, and he does not say, *berry*. You can't tell if this is an utterance of damnation or reverence.

If we can crush our food with only tongue and palate, we can convince ourselves that we're not so violent. In this way, survival on the trail, like our pie, can be fall-off-the-bone.

If one truncates *Alis volat propriis* to *Alis volat*, that translates as *flies wings*, which evokes that frenzied cloud buzzing over the corpses.

* * *

FROM "Whispers: A Man Questions God," by Anonymous:

The man whispered, "God, speak to me."
And a meadowlark sang.
But the man did not hear.

* * *

EVEN ON THE MOST current word processing computer programs, *marionberry* appears with a squiggly red line beneath it, indicating a misspelling. A right-click on the word brings up a menu without any alternative spellings, but with only the generic options Help, Ignore, Ignore All . . .

In the article "What to Eat When There is No Food," nutritionist Tess Pennington states, "What will you do if your family is starving and there is no food to be found? This fear is always in the back of our minds. There are many choices of tree bark that can be eaten," which makes you wonder how long the pioneers endured sustenance by Oregon's alder and ash and cherry and plum, juniper, fir, chestnut, and locust before turning their teeth on one another.

"The wood smell is the smell of Oregon," log marker Ray Agee says. "When I come home from work, I've got tree sap all over me.

It's on my glasses and in my hair," and in this way, the body makes a pact with the woods that only starvation can break. We watch the sky, the trees, the river, the oven. We wonder, and wonder what's coming . . .

"Promises that you make to yourself," Francis Marion says, "are often like the Japanese plum tree—they bear no fruit," and Uncle spits the harder of the marionberry seeds into a napkin with a wagon on it.

. . . and the meadowlark with still-working wings builds over its nest, a roof of grass and a six-foot long entrance tunnel, hatching its eggs and digesting its berries in this concealed layer between earth and sky.

* * *

EXCERPT FROM *The Eugene Register-Guard* article "Oregon's Marionberry Is No Joke" by Jan Roberts-Dominguez (July 15, 1998):

> *The amused caller, a features editor from the Daily Hampshire Gazette, had just finished reading through the story and recipes on Northwest berries I had sent her. My inclusion of the marionberry—one of Oregon's agricultural pride and joys—had created a comical stir among the newsroom staff.*
>
> *To them, it wasn't Marion—"the berry." And they sure couldn't figure out why anybody out in Oregon would name a wonderful piece of fruit after the mayor of Washington, D.C. Then the marionberry jokes began to fly: "Are they habit forming?" "Can you only eat them in hotel rooms?" "They must be pretty seedy . . ." this unique variety . . . this special berry . . . perfect for hand-to-mouth consumption . . .*

* * *

STEP SIX in above article's Marionberry Pie recipe: "Prick dough with fork."

* * *

THE MARIONBERRY, due to its "powerful flavor," now dominates the current blackberry market, allowing us to forget its more subtly tasty ancestors—the dewberry, youngberry, santiam berry, the Chehalem and the Olallie—push them toward extinction, or the sort of infinity that's ever eating itself, thus ever-surviving.

* * *

Q. What's the difference between a Portland State University sorority sister and a scarecrow?
A. One lives in a field and is stuffed with hay. The other frightens birds and small animals.

* * *

HERE, in our mouths, all species go hybrid and confused. Our throats don't know whether to swallow, or laugh. Aunt brings out her fifth test pie like a punch line, the steam trailing into the air. You think of vines, or bridal trains. Between her stained front teeth, you can't tell—marionberry seed, or cuticle. The trees scream against the window, but they scream softly. Before he even tastes it, he knows. "This," Uncle says, "is the winner, baby." He's never been sweeter.

Marionberry Pie

Pie Dough
Flour 2⅔ cups
Salt 1 teaspoon
Shortening 1 cup (like Crisco)
Water 6 tablespoons (cold)

Mix flour & salt together. Cut shortening into flour mixture with a pastry cutter, until it resembles coarse crumbs. Add enough cold water (1 tablespoon at a time) for pastry to form into a ball.

Divide dough in half. Roll out on a floured surface, 1 inch longer than a 9-inch pie pan. Roll out remaining dough & cover until marionberry mixture is complete.

Marionberry pie mixture
Marionberries 4 ¾ cups

Water 1 tablespoon & 1 teaspoon
Sugar 1 cup
Salt ¼ teaspoon
Water ¼ cup
Cornstarch 5 tablespoons & 1 teaspoon

Loosely measure 4¾ cups (not too heaping) frozen marionberries. Let them thaw a little before using. Measure 3 cups of the marionberries into a large heatproof bowl & let sit while you cook the rest.

Add 1¾ cups marionberries to a 2-quart pan along with 1 tablespoon & 1teaspoon water, sugar & salt & let come to a boil on med. high heat. In the meanwhile, mix in a 1-cup measure, the remaining ¼ cup water & the cornstarch together until fully combined.

After pan comes to a boil, lower heat to med. & add cornstarch mixture & stir. Cook until mixture thickens & clears—this takes a minute or 2. When mixture gets thick, remove from heat.

Stir into remaining 3 cups marionberries & stir to combine. Let cool to 80 degrees. Put into prepared pie pan & cover with remaining rolled-out dough. Crimp edges & make vents with a knife in the pie center. Bake at 350 degrees for about 45 to 50 minutes.

—*Shari's Café and Pies, Shari's Restaurant Group*

A Hopeless Mimic Engages the California Roll

SOMEONE CARTWHEELS in the Mission District after eating her to-go California Roll—the pseudo-sushi, traditional sushi turned inside out, the cucumber and avocado of it—her hands to the asphalt, her feet to the sky, limbs whipping like the spokes of a wheel. We mimic the machines we've built to move us. We try to remember when we didn't need them.

In the California Roll is the difficult mask, is too much makeup, is the source fish, or source face easily forgotten. Here, our masks are applied step by step, then inverted. The California literally wears its heart on a sleeve of seaweed.

When we flake Pacific pollock, shave the meat from its ribs as we would hair from our faces and legs, and when we steep such flakes in the thick gel of albumen—the sad trickle of the anterior section of some sadder hen's oviduct—and form the resulting sludge into even little phalluses, paint them orange-red, and spray them with pressurized crab esters, we stress that it's not easy for one natural thing to imitate another. But that doesn't change our desire.

Sometimes, a cartwheeler will opt not to use her hands to propel her legs over her head, to complete the arc of the body. The contact with the earth, then, is relegated to beginning and to end. There is no middle contact with the earth. The wheel, then, is a two-spoked one—pretty sparse for a wheel. Still, it comes around. In this, I sense, is the difference between rotation and revolution, the clarity of which remains untethered, hovering. This kind of cartwheel demands its own name—is not really a cartwheel at all, but a noun forcing itself upon an adjective; but a violent commingling, as if seemingly diverse landscapes, of our parts of speech; but an *aerial.*

* * *

VIOLENCE IS GEOLOGY, is eating, is turning one fish into another, is breaking off into the ocean, is whipping our bodies through the air. Gravity whimpers, but wins. Here, ocean commingles with mountain, which commingles with redwood, which commingles with desert. I wonder which the rice, which the avocado, which the imitation crab . . . Here, is the sort of environmental cassoulet that evokes an identity crisis and shift, dueling regional banjos plucking their dissonance in the same case. *California.* How to survive this without resorting to other violence, but in mimicry? If we can empathize with the California Roll: we beat and gurgle and digest on the outside. Our flesh is flipped inward, we can kiss behind the closed doors of our vertebrae.

In 1968, students, faculty, and community activists launch the San Francisco State College Strike demanding equal access to public higher education for ethnic minorities. Vietnam War protests explode in the city following the Tet Offensive and My Lai massacre. Further south, in Los Angeles, over 1,000 Chicano students stage a walkout of Abraham Lincoln High School, protesting the school's treatment of minorities. By the end of the week, more than ten thousand students will follow suit at high schools across California, launching a mass student strike that becomes known as the Blowouts. Schools turn inside out. Fires, once bound to the earth, now leaping into the air, and whirling. In 1968, blood coagulates.

In 1968, the grandparents of students who walked out of Abraham Lincoln High, sushi chefs having come to California from Tokyo seeking fortune, began substituting local ingredients for those they couldn't readily find—avocado for fatty tuna, enzymatic pollock—then known as *krab*—for crab.

In 1968, famed sushi chef Ichiro Mashita hand-squeezed the liquor from squares of really good rice at Tokyo Kaikan restaurant in Los Angeles, became the first to think of the avocado-for-tuna substitute, thereby allowing L.A. to become, according to the *New York Times*, "the beachhead for the sushi invasion." In San Francisco's Winterland Ballroom, 382 miles north, Jimi Hendrix plucks the opening chords to "Catfish Blues," but thinks nothing of catfish or pollock or pollock masquerading as crab, or of his own impending death as another kind of invasion, imitation.

Do we force the pollock to invade the identity of the crab, or to imitate it? At what point do the two overlap? In imitation is wish fulfillment. With my voice, I can be Jack Nicholson. In these clothes, I can be my dead grandfather. In eating the California Roll, I can pretend I heard "Purple Haze" played live on the same night that the Kenyan government stepped up its persecution of Japanese expats, that Alfredo Cantu "Freddy" Gonzalez accepted bullets and rocket shrapnel into his body during Vietnam's Battle of Hué, succumbed to his wounds, and posthumously received the Medal of Honor, as Mashita, likely disappointed with himself, accepted imitation crabmeat as a passable substitute for the real thing.

According to the *Guardian*, a famed Tokyo sushi chef known only as Mr. Sawada, masking himself in the anonymity of a business card bearing only the name (sans qualifying address) of a street and the Red Dragonfly samurai symbol (to find his restaurant, the hopeful diner must wander the street, scrutinizing the "unremarkable" doorways for this same tiny dragonfly, engraved beside a buzzer), calls Mashita's California Roll "chaotic, at best."

As we spin away from a source, we come to accept the new chaos as the norm—the chaos of indistinct sources as a new kind of source. I want to say something here about not understanding those generations younger than I, but then I will just be imitating/inventing an old man.

* * *

THE CALIFORNIA ROLL as ventriloquist, as eye shadow, as a rubber mask of Lyndon Johnson pulled over a rubber mask of Eisaku

Satō, pulled over the flesh of a face that's now interior, razor-flaked, dipped into egg white, formed into tubes in the palms of some other hands. As the dummy.

A two-foot-tall man carved from the trunk of a giant cypress is a poor imitation for a real man, in spite of those creepy eyes. Even the tongueless can't confuse the avocado with the belly fat of a bluefin.

The rules of war dictate that uniforms must be worn to distinguish one side from another, and to distinguish combatants from civilians. Still, in every war, secret missions abound in which combatants disguise themselves in civilian garb or in the uniforms of their enemy. This sort of imitation elicits the sort of confusion that often results in accidental death, or accidental acceptance. Though the rules of war declare that such acts are to be treated as criminal ones, these missions persist. This sort of imitation creates, according to international law, "a kind of purgatory."

The rules of aerial warfare dictate that the indiscriminate bombing of private homes be considered a "serious war crime." As such, human targets of an enemy military oftentimes hide in "private homes," assuming the role of ordinary (read: *not important enough to kill*) citizens. I can only wonder if such targets believe that they are engaged in an imitative act or not, or if they're just divorcing themselves from the *enemy* label. Sometimes, our authenticity can be confused for imitation, imitation being the stronger of the two forces.

* * *

THE CRUSHING PRESSURE of the crab's claw, at 90 psi, while not the strongest in the animal kingdom, is inimitable. The human hand has a squashing capacity of 25 psi, and it takes only a fraction of this force to pull a trigger. Still, the crushing power of the pollock's soft mouth pales in comparison to this, and to the crab claw, and to the spray gun responsible for painting its feeble eggy crab imitation that glossy orange-red.

Here, we eat our imitations with mayonnaise and soy. We think nothing of the culinary espionage taking place before us, within us. Here, the chopsticks wobble in our fingers, too skinny for the force of our hands, too silent in the face of a parroting California. Here, our imitations move like birds and protests. Like blood. They swoop up, coagulate, clot, scab, heal, disperse.

* * *

THERE ARE at least forty-seven Californias within our world, and a couple without. Many in Mexico. One in Michigan, one in Kentucky. There's a California in Ohio, and Ontario, Columbia, El Salvador, Italy. There are seven in the UK, two in the Netherlands. There's a California in Morocco, and one in the Philippines. The California nebula emits its inimitable gases in the Perseus constellation, so named for its resemblance to California, the U.S. state. I wonder who is jealous of whom. If the terrestrial imitates the cosmic, or vice versa, or if this is all just some terrible, if universal, coincidence.

> ***In this space, between the bite and the swallow, the dead can mimic the living, and all of our brief departures from this earth are no-hands.***

In literature, the name *California* was applied, in García Ordóñez de Montalvo's sixteenth-century bodice-ripper *Las Sergas de Esplandián*, to the mythical island inhabited by gorgeous (and naked) Amazon warriors, who fashioned their bows and arrows from pure gold. What the novel fails to mention is that *Amazon* derives from the Greek *a mazos*, which means *without breast.* Reputedly, this band of "gorgeous" female warriors self-amputated their own right breasts so as not to impede the drawing of their bows. They desired to make of their bodies more efficient fighting machines, imitating the flat-chested form of the men they used only to propagate their tribe, before slaughtering them and all the resulting male children.

I watch a red-throated loon crash into a puddle in the L.A. River. The crush of the concrete kills it before it has a chance to drown, imitate the song of a fearless bird. I wonder if the bird was male or female. If it imagined itself an aerial attack, a violation of international law. Perhaps the loon mistook the reflection of my hand for a fish, a real crab, or real pollock, rather than this violent splicing we call imitation. When the sun is this persistent, all of this stuff looks the same.

Meat imitates other meat. I'm not sure that this is what meat wants. Food historians believe that we paint the imitation crab stick not only to resemble the color we (mistakenly) associate with the original crab, but also to resemble something beautiful and (as we also mistakenly imagine) benign: the flower. The 341 California is an asteroid in the Flora family. Its albedo is unusually high, meaning, among other cumbersome things, that it appears to reflect more sunlight than your average asteroid. On the crowded sands of Venice Beach, a young woman in a black bikini, a red and green tattoo of a chainsaw holding to her sacrum, eats, with her fingers, discs of California Roll. A piece of avocado falls to the sand. She wears no sunscreen. Something of the 341 caresses her skin, confuses another loon.

We eat our California Roll with the same hands we use to crush and caress. Above us, birds and bullets, space gases and space rocks. We imitate a species that does not have stardust in its blood. We take imitation into our bodies. It tries to mimic the cartwheel in our guts, but lacks the limbs for it. The Roll as the wheel. Our arms and legs as the spokes.

* * *

"Sushi purists now turn up their noses at [Mashita's] invention. The California Roll has become a humble dish, available on grocery store shelves, its rice cold and stiff, its fatty avocado turning brown."

—Swati Pandey, *The Daily*, September 22, 2011

* * *

Here, we eat what they give us. We cook what we have. As with water, we follow the path of least resistance. It's not our fault. We can only shrug, palms up, and force one thing to imitate another, name it after our state, our *private home*. This imitation goes straight from the water to our mouths—a bird that will die before it ever touches down. In this space, between the bite and the swallow, the dead can mimic the living, and all of our brief departures from this earth are no-hands.

California Roll

Ingredients

1 cup cooked white rice
1 tablespoon rice wine vinegar
2 teaspoons sugar
1 teaspoon salt
1 avocado, sliced thinly
1 cucumber, sliced thinly
3 sticks of imitation crab, sliced
3 nori seaweed sheets
2 teaspoons sesame seeds

Toast nori seaweed sheets over a dry skillet, over medium heat, for about 2 seconds per side (do not burn the seaweed). Mix sesame seeds into the rice. Line a bamboo sushi rolling mat with plastic wrap. Lay a piece of the nori on the mat, and pack a thin layer of rice on top of the nori. Flip the nori over (rice side down) and line the edge of the nori sheet with the imitation crab, cucumber, and avocado. With the bamboo mat, roll the sushi into a tube, then slice into pieces. Repeat with remaining ingredients. Serve with soy sauce and wasabi. Garnish plate with pickled ginger, if desired.

—Eva Valencia

GREAT PLAINS

Nebraska: Spoon Bread

Oklahoma: Okie Sirloin

South Dakota: Wojapi

North Dakota: Lefse

Kansas: Bierock

Spoon Bread Dictates

HERE, IN NEBRASKA, we name a thing after the tool used to destroy it. Here, on this spot, where the American Legion Memorial Highway intersects with Outlaw Trail Scenic Byway, in October 1804, Lewis and Clark spent several days with the Arikara tribe—days that Boyd County historians insist on calling "tranquil." That the Arikara had been nearly decimated due to a smallpox epidemic may be responsible for this description. Many of those whom the plague did not claim were later beaten and hung from the boughs of the region's black walnuts and black cherries, honey locusts, hackberries, cottonwoods, and pecans. The township decided, in 1948, to change the name of its new surveying pillar from Old Baldy to Lynch.

Downstream from the Knife River, still a ways from Massacre Canyon, Lewis and Clark discovered the prairie dog, a species then unknown to the Western world. Scientists later discovered that prairie dogs are chiefly herbivorous, with an affinity for buffalo grass, tumblegrass, fescue, and blue grama. Pregnant and lactating females, in the wintertime, gorge themselves on snow for the extra water. In the name of development, manifest destiny, and what the Nebraska Department of Agriculture once called "prairie dog management," we began poisoning their food supply with aluminum phosphide. We began referring to them as a plague. The grounds that were to become Lynch were soon littered with the suffocated corpses of the prairie dogs, their lungs filled with a fluid of the loveliest amber. The thing most responsible for the decimation of the prairie dog colonies was now the prairie itself.

I stare at the crumbs on my plate, and Uncle stares at his, the leftover bits of our Nebraska spoon bread. Uncle forms his into a mound, scoops the last into his mouth. The plate now clear, we can see Aunt's initials monogrammed in pink script and decorated with stylized baby's breath at his plate's center. Uncle stares at this as if surprised, says nothing of the cancer, or of so many breeds of debt. The spoon bread is gone, but our trigger fingers wrap around the necks of our best utensils. Some passerby whips a snowball at the kitchen window. Though the sound of it startles us, neither of us jumps. Here, we excavate our plates and our aunts and our earth with spoons. Here, spoons are prized for the sharpness of their edges, their ability to carve crescent moons into what is really just a butter-rich corn bread.

Ten miles north of this kitchen, in which Uncle now jabs at a second helping with the spoon's rounded rim, the weather works in destructive rotation. April 2011: a horrible drought and heat wave, a plague of wildfires. According to northeast Nebraska's *Norfolk Daily News*, "it's hard to believe now, but in the spring the water in the river was so low that fishermen couldn't get their boats in." Come June: rising floodwaters, decimated homes, propane tanks capped and moved to higher ground, the roads turned to tributaries carrying windows and doors, blinds and houseplants, "a mattress, chair cushion, chunks of insulation and other debris." Residents said things like "Our grandchildren grew up here," and "We gutted our trailer," and "We've never had anything like this," and "I can't believe it," and "Right now, we're holding our own, but I don't know for how long," and "It's just a shell sitting there," and "This is a beautiful place."

The floodwaters buried the blackened prairie. In order to see it again, we need the violence of heat—of excavation, evaporation. We need to remind ourselves of that wildfire. In a dressing up of disaster, we've named this place Sunshine Bottom.

Uncle opens up his spoon bread and sighs at what he finds, or doesn't find, inside. I want to impose things on him. He wonders: if the ways in which we've made our homes, historically, have been abominable—and if the ways in which prairie dogs make their homes have been interpreted as abominable by us—does it follow that the things made in our homes are also, in part, disgraceful? He picks at his spoon bread, mutters, "I'm so sick of this."

Here, we confuse *inside* with *underneath. Our breath*—we try to locate it inside of us, and outside. When excavating with a spoon, there is a revealing, a lending of air to that which has been previously buried, asphyxiated. The removal of prairie dog from prairie, conversely, is an act of taking air away, of suffocation. Whether we unearth via spoon or poison, each remains a tool, our tool. In each case, we may not like what we uncover.

* * *

When a human being is executed by hanging, the neck is stretched, the tongue becomes engorged, the lips turn blue. We can't tell if it's the tree creaking, or the body.

We use the tools at hand, scan the earth: there's the corn, the milk, the butter, the eggs. There's the option to make it maple-sweet, or jalapeño-spicy. There's our former neighbor sighing, "I went to elementary school in Nebraska where spoon bread was on the lunch rotation. Ah, I miss those days . . ." There's Uncle digging in, the steam escaping like something craven, predicting collapse. He says, "There's nothing to miss about those days." Says, "She taught me to cook spoon bread, but not how to get the pills down her throat; not how to convince her to drink enough water." Uncle knows: if we see steam, don't think *heat*, think, something is cooling down, shedding its fever.

We know: the rivers sometimes take over our state, mimic the topography beneath—here, the floodwaters appear unbearably calm, smoothed out, iced like a cake. Beneath, so many dead things. Nebraska acknowledges its name—the Otoe term for *flat water*—and whines, wimpish, like the steam that now collects in Uncle's eyebrows, mimicking, I think, some displaced weeping.

* * *

Prior to 1970, Aunt could get the eggs and milk and butter for spoon bread from Clary Ranch. Soon after, the ranch started belching up bison remains, many of the bones fashioned into the utensils and weapons of the hunter-gatherer cultures of the Late Pleistocene Era, and the land was taken over by the Nebraska Archaeological Society. Uncle tells me, jabbing at the air with his spoon: the former owner, Oren V. Clary (1899–1991), was forced off his family's land, lived out his final twenty-one years in exile in a one-bedroom apartment in Lewellen.

Mapped onto Old Man Clary: the holes left by the prairie dogs. The holes filled in and the holes remaining. Archaeological discovery as the poison. The spoons that came to unearth the bison, and the old man. "I can't believe it. Right now, we're holding our own, but I don't know for how long . . ."

Here, old spoons excavate new spoons. In honor of this, we change the name of corn bread, and claim ownership in the names of tool and state. In spite of its shape, the spoon is classified as cutlery, a device used to sever something from itself. Uncle holds his spoon in his mouth and, behind him, the stuffed spoonbill—a primitive fish with a skeleton that's almost entirely cartilaginous—tilts slightly on the wall.

According to Rusty "Spoonbill King" Pritchard, the best way to catch a spoonbill is to "get the line caught in the gills here, and that will guide the hook all the way up toward his head. It doesn't cut a hole in him at all, it just pokes a little hole."

If we're bleeding out, Uncle wonders, how much does language matter, our compulsion to name? In the midst of all that blood, does it matter if we've been cut or poked? Here, if we say so, a little hole is not a hole at all. Uncle knows: we get through the night the same way we deal with the prairie dogs—by managing. In management is coping. In this way, we decide that the prairie dogs have victimized us. We make of their little holes no holes at all.

* * *

Recovered from Ponca Fort archaeological site in Niobrara, Nebraska: a palisade, kettles, cloth, beads, fur, mauls, slabs, bone spoons, hatchets with flowers etched into their handles, pottery painted with knives.

Uncle searches for any companionship, however thin. He says

that the spoon is a surrogate for our hands, so we don't burn our fingers. He stares at the plate's dead center, gripping his spoon, a kind of hand-holding.

We revere the stuff that destroys us, make gods of it—weather, wrath, plague. Of all ancient utensils unearthed via the world's archaeological digs, it is the spoon that was most often decorated with religious symbols. In early fifteenth-century Europe, apostle spoons became popular as christening gifts. Produced in sets of thirteen, each spoon depicted at the handle's end an upside-down bust, or head, of an apostle. In this way, we can comfortably smother the confidants of Jesus in our palms as we sip our soup, stir our tea, halve our corn bread in a kitchen with a snowball stuck to the window.

* * *

IT IS THE SPOON, in early medicine, that was finally used to excise the plague—the tumor, the abscess, the evil eye. Uncle again stares at his crumbs, his wife's initials, and is not blind to the implications.

In many cultures, spoons are the primary utensil, and the fork is used only to push food onto the spoon. The tools we use most, that we most associate with a god, are the tools that best fit our mouths. And the spoon is linguistically primary. In lunchrooms and cafeterias across the world, our plastic hybrid utensils the spork (crossbred with a fork), the sporf (triply crossbred)—always begin with the spoon.

In Lynch, we've renamed the prairie dog the Lynch Dawg—so many destroyers in a single nickname, we need a spoon to excavate them all. We associate with the spoon: our bodies, and the bodies of the animals. In the early eighteenth century, the spoon's bowl was known as *the man's tongue*; the edge of the bowl, *the lip*; the border of bowl and handle, *the collar* or *the neck*; and the handle, *the tail of the rat*.

Our bodies are soft and craven, and we are ever indecisive about ourselves and the things we name.

* * *

HERE, WE TREAT our prairie dogs like any other rodent, carrier of disease. They pock our earth. But that—pocking the earth—is our job. We treat our prairie dogs with aluminum phosphide so we can build our houses so the river can wash them away. Like spoon bending, this is another deformation—paranormal, psychokinetic, magical, human . . . *a beautiful place* . . .

We know: *prairie* means *hollow*, and *dog* means so many things: *other pig, house pig, finger muscle.* And when we *spoon,* we chip or splinter, wedge our way inside. Here, we spoon poison into the hollow in the name of saving our lives, keeping our hands clean. And this swallow of crumbs: another kind of burial that predicts the unearthing.

Sometimes, we name celestial things after spoon parts—the ladle, the dipper. We plead with the stars because it's hard to be without a home, hard to move into a one-bedroom after a ranch, to bake a spoon bread that's inferior to that of the dead. We know our tools are faulty. Sometimes the spoon's neck is called the *transition.*

Uncle sneezes, as if to melt the frost on the window. I watch the steam escape his mouth. The spoon rings against the plate, becomes musical, another kind of instrument. Two hundred miles northwest, the Platte River tries to dislodge its pollution—the fecal coliform bacteria, the fertilizer, the tarnished silverware, the corpses of prairie dogs—and flows, for a second, nowhere, choked, like Uncle, as if with spoon bread, or *homemade*, or some other embarrassment.

Spoon Bread

Ingredients

½ cup cornmeal

1 cup fresh Nebraska corn, kernels cut from the cob into a bowl (run the back of the knife along the cob to press the "milk" out of the cob, and let this drip into the bowl too)

2 cups milk

3 tablespoons butter (melted), plus enough butter to grease a baking pan

2 eggs beaten

½ teaspoon baking powder
½ teaspoon salt
1½ cup shredded cheddar cheese (optional)

Directions

In a saucepan, stir together the cornmeal, the corn, and the milk. Cook for about 10 minutes, stirring often to prevent too much sticking. In a separate bowl, while whisking, spoon in (slowly, one tablespoon at a time, for about 20 tablespoons) some of the warm milk–corn mixture into the beaten eggs, and whisk together so the eggs don't scramble. Then, pour this egg mixture into the saucepan, and whisk together thoroughly. Add the baking powder and cook over medium heat, whisking constantly, for another 2–3 minutes. Add the melted butter and salt (and if you're using cheese, add 1 cup of that too) and stir it in. Pour the mixture into the greased baking pan. If you're using the cheese, sprinkle the remaining ½ cup of it over the top. Bake at 375 degrees for about 30 minutes. Spoon it out onto plates and eat with a spoon!

—Justin Daugherty

Making Weight of the Okie Sirloin

UNCLE WAS A wrestler in Stillwater, slept in silver plastic suits to sweat out the weight, always made 103. He was the smallest on the team, but had the largest appetite. He talks now, on the couch, his initials finger-inked in the dust on the windowpane, of driving with his father pre-sunrise across the panhandle to Goodwell for the meets, the talk radio station droning meditatively about the Sooners—our adopted nickname, purloined from the "illegal" white land-grabbers who stole the choicest parcels from the "legal" white land-grabbers who stole them from the Creek and the Seminole—or droning about Will Rogers, or interviewing a medical research technician at Oral Roberts University who, as Uncle—young and exhausted and starving in the passenger seat and filling a Styrofoam cup with his spit, emptying it out the window, and filling it again: anything to make weight—imagines her juggling scalpels and biohazard bags filled with untold excised horrors, declared, "This is the only Christian medical school in the nation and I wanted to be trained with the Christian perspective, not a more secular perspective," to which his father, driving, Uncle assures me, now old and fat and sneezing cherries of blood into a peach Puffs Plus, his window initials now dusted over, replied, "Does that mean she aced Laying On of Hands 101?"

Or the radio droned on about oil dropping to ten bucks a barrel, and skyrocketing unemployment, and all manners of starvation, before segueing into Albert E. Brumley's "I'll Fly Away" ("He was from Spiro, boy," Uncle says now as a point of pride, so much lovely gospel leaking from a town that once based its notions of prosperity on the number of cotton gins it possessed—one in 1901, a whopping three in 1910), and Uncle, just a skinny boy known for his ribs, clavicles, "backbones like a winged monkey" (so he self-identifies), downturned his spit cup for the fourth time as they passed through regions known as the Cimarron Strip and No Man's Land, something cracking open in Uncle's belly as they crossed the 100th meridian—a malign ignition toward adulthood, perhaps, or some notion of adulthood as dreamt during a night of plastic shuffling against other plastic, the sweat in his ears drowning out all heartbeat, blood flow—or perhaps it was only such a hunger, the sort that would inspire Uncle, after weighing in, after a fat man in cutoffs and a Stetson inked "103" onto Uncle's boy-shoulder in black grease marker, telling him, "A wink of an eye or a handshake is the cattleman's word," or telling him, "You've got to keep your eye on the bottom line," or telling him, "Things go in a boom-bust cycle here," or telling him nothing, to flee with his father into downtown Goodwell, to pass the No Man's Land Museum and its pioneer relics and its gift shop peddling books called *Angels in the Dust* and *Keeping It Together*.

They passed also the site where, so many years later, two Union Pacific trains would collide head-on before bursting into flames, the diesel-fueled fireball welding the locomotives together, scalp to scalp, in some unholy surgery, as employees leapt like sparks from the cars. They stopped at a restaurant called the Rodeo for breakfast, to order, after all that sweat, spit, illusion of fever and implosion and winning wrestling moves called high crotches and fireman's carries and double-leg takedowns and throws and inside cradles, the Rodeo's famed 4x4x4x4—that is, four eggs, four pancakes, four strips of bacon, and four slices of what Uncle now calls, his eyes bloodshot, his index finger tracing new identities onto the air, the couch cushions complaining, "the best fucking Okie Sirloin in No Man's Land," and he closes his eyes, and the couch cushions shut up, and he's making weight again, and here, in his filthy one-bedroom, all reward hisses its flavor, as if slow-cooked, as if made with all long-gone love.

The Okie Sirloin is, of course, derogatory, and is smoked and barbecued bologna, and is derived from the famed mortadella sausage of Bologna, Italy, itself named for the mortar in which the pork and lard are pulverized until married, a tool which is itself, of course, derived from the Latin *mortui* or *mortem*, or *dead* or *death*, the mortar being the place where things go to die, the sausage itself named for the subsequent corpse, which we now eat, as Uncle once did, voraciously and plentifully beside our buttermilks and over-easies.

Too easy: jokes about the mouth and Oral Roberts. Harder: picking the dust from our bologna, the lard from our earth. Here, we whip the pork fat before folding it into the meat. This allows us, when engaging all manners of death, the illusion of clouds, some cumulus paradise around which entire curricula are developed at the "only Christian medical school in the nation."

"Fuck the cathedrals," Uncle says, "here, to eat our barbecued bologna is to be closer to God."

According to the *Encyclopedia of Oklahoma History and Culture*, the term *Okie* "became derogatory in the 1930s when massive migration westward occurred. 'Okie' usually described 'white' migratory agriculture workers; 'Okie' was never, or at least rarely used, about African American migrants during the Great Depression. Most migrant agricultural workers, or 'Okies,' were white and traveled westward from the Midwestern drought and cotton-growing states." During the Dust Bowl, when many Oklahomans fled even further west in search of a better life, California responded, in 1937, by passing an "'Anti-Okie Law,' making it a misdemeanor to bring or assist any indigent person into that state." Uncle runs his good hand over his shoulder, feels for his old weight there. "Try as we might," he

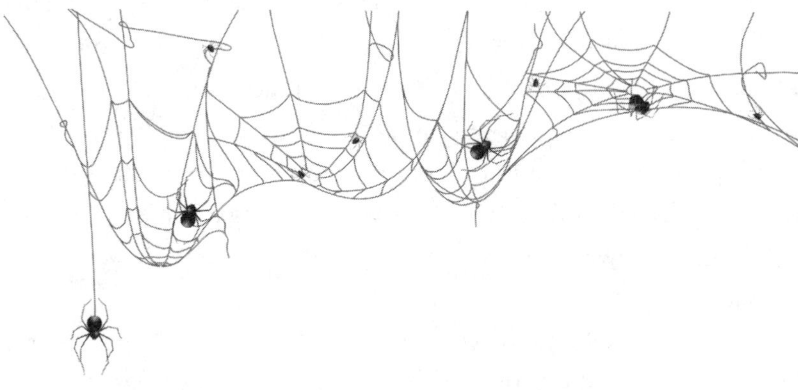

says, "there are some things we can never dignify," not even with all that smoke.

According to Jane and Michael Stern, in *The Lexicon of Real American Food,* "Okie Sirloin is a full cylinder of bologna that smokes low and slow in the pit until the outside is a beautiful dark bronze and the inside still weeps garlicky juices," and Uncle wants to know what this has to do with indigence, or the Cherokees, or the sort of state that today prides itself on the high percentage of resident Native Americans—*the highest in the U.S.!*—when that population is 4.6 percent. The Sterns persist, "Barbecued bologna is almost always sopped with tangy red sauce," and Uncle sits up suddenly, as if waking from a dream, and assesses himself, searching in vain for his beautiful bronze, for the source of his tangy weeping. All he finds are cylinders.

* * *

PIT COOKING allows us the illusion of resurrection, a return to this world a little crispier, and rendered of our fat. If the pit, Uncle says, "then no grave," and if the mortar, "it's just the pig that dies," and there are no sarcophagi in the sort of paradise that hides itself, like the head of one train in the head of another, in our bologna. His ears are cauliflower, his heart mortadella.

Uncle searches the amoebas on his ceiling for some sort of answer, transcribes a grocery list like a joke. We don't know if he's planning to cook for himself for the first time since Aunt died. We all know he will not be buying these items. We all know that we can't stay here forever, unless we keep paying. Three floors below us, someone chars their bologna over redbud wood and the skinny bones of the scissor-tailed flycatcher, whose own sternum resembles the spider.

Look there: in Oklahoma City, in 1932—the air going thick and brown, the children slaughtering rabbits for supper—Carl Magee invents the parking meter. We now have to pay to abandon our cars, feed our nickels into the machine and twist. This, Magee, says, "is a modern solution to a modern vexation—parking congestion," and we all feel something tighten in our chests, growing the sorts of narratives that we'll never fully dislodge.

At Uncle's feet, the *Tegenaria atrica* dust spider builds a web in the lint between his toes. Unlike us, it knows little of its own name, how it's meant to recall the dark, feral recesses of the heart. When we say *recess*, Uncle thinks we're saying *abscess*. Regardless, a spider is making a home of him, documenting his weight, and the weight of the things it must kill to sustain itself.

Somewhere in there, the language of the living pig has been transcribed. And, here, the planet speaks in dust, its mother tongue.

* * *

INSTEAD OF CUCUMBERS, we put cooled slices of derogatory bologna over our eyes and sleep and dream of leaner times, which we've since buried beneath decades of the fattiest of the sausages. We're in the middle of the country. A way station, intermediate and smoky and maybe a little disastrous. "Of course," Uncle says, "we were the first state to charge for limbo."

With Magee's idea and crude model, Oklahoma State University's engineering department sponsored a parking meter design competition, offering $160 to the winner. The students' designs all proved insufficient, so they took the contest to greater Stillwater. A professor and his former student created the guts, and a local plumber built the shell. The first meter was named Black Maria, after, according to local lore, Maria Lee, a "large and fearsome" African American woman who ran an Oklahoma City boarding house, and who helped the police with their "more difficult prisoners." The prototype was manufactured by the MacNick Company of Tulsa, who previously made only timing devices used to explode nitroglycerin in oil wells. (The then president of the company went on the record, calling the parking meters "neat.") When the first Black Maria went up on July 16 at the corner of Robinson and First, Oklahomans were outraged, calling the device un-American, and the protests were so violent they received national attention, the side effect of which resulted in parking meters spreading throughout the country with the dust. Soon, en masse, we started paying money to stop moving. Two years later, Magee was arrested for manslaughter, and we began saving our nickels by eating more fat than meat, by keeping on, staying mobile, even though we are tired.

We feed our meters. Uncle says, while we're doing this, "if there ain't something in your mouth, you're being inefficient." We want Uncle to call bullshit after he says, "If we pay for something, we treasure it more," but he doesn't. Says Oklahoma City psychologist Mary Pepping, "[Oklahoma] has a very high-caliber group [of citizens]. I was struck by the fact that so many cities have Indian names. It was amazing to see an eighty-year-old man with long hair and young children in costume. Their ethnic pride is neat." Here, we know Uncle would say something if his mouth wasn't full of bologna. Either the spider is dead or lying in wait.

Here, the pig looks to resurrect itself from the casing, the embalming by its own fat, the char, the weeping of garlicky juices. Uncle can't see out the window, but the sky is gathering electricity. It may take this sort of lightning, or a bolt at least as powerful . . .

We use the word *spam* like we use the word *bologna*, both of which originated as delivery systems of meat to the poor—meat coupled with the corresponding animal's less desirable parts; humble, dubious, junk meat, our mouths the mailboxes, the stunned-dumb slots. Ask Oral, Uncle, Maria: we have always been full of it.

* * *

The psychology of neat: In the article "Neatness a Sign of Godliness—or Compulsion?" clinical psychologist Amie Ragan (pronounced *Ragin'*) says, "[Neatness] is a problem when your need for constant order causes you extreme distress," though psychotherapist Tom Corboy (pronounced *Core Boy*) believes, "anxiety has evolutionary value," and Uncle can't tell he's speaking of the anxiety of Pepping's long-haired geezer, or dressed-up kids, or the pigs who wept at the slaughter, or the Okies who stopped moving and therefore stopped being Okies, or the first person to slip a nickel into a meter and buy just enough time to stop and stand still and breathe, or the mortar that grinds all of this shit together into the sort of paste that just will not die, that will charge us its fee, Uncle says, in extremity, "for-fucking-ever."

Oral Roberts mapped onto Whitman and incanted, as if, through Uncle's bologna breath: *There is something of the mouth that calls to the pigs in the uniform of sleep as a bird collecting the weight of a flock, an ant who, when threatened with a fall, discovers that it can spin a web like a spider.* In all communion, here, is a strain of distress. It's hard to tell, though, if it's extreme or not.

The laying on of hands is a practice both symbolic and formal. Here, even foundations are ephemeral, and mean something else. Okie Sirloin communes with the pigs of our state, and therefore, everything the pig ate. There, in its stomach, dust, a handful of nickels, a message in a bottle written from one migrant worker to another, and the body of water it had to cross to get to Oklahoma. Uncle's final love letter mailed to a hospital . . .

We can now eat our junk sausage in No Man's Land, together . . . Bologna is nonsense, bologna is bullshit, bologna is frustrating and funny. The 1995 Oklahoma City bombing depended on the detonation of nitroglycerin, and of laughing gas.

* * *

BOLOGNA IS PLASTIC. We cook and cook against poverty, as the wind outside, like the bologna, goes great and cylindrical, and entire. Tomorrow, the *New York Times* will use words like *vast* and *debris-clogged* and *reduced* and *twisted metal* and *fallen beams* and *fused* and *funnel* and *prayer.* One interviewee will lift briefly from the earth before dropping into a ditch and use the word *weightless*, and Uncle will say nothing of the body encased and floating in plastic, of a dream of the cold tips of grease markers, of permanence. He will say nothing of the singlet, the headgear, the kneepads. How the things meant to protect us are the things, here, that pin us down. He will laugh, and then he will not.

Barbecued Bologna (Okie Sirloin)

Ingredients

3 tablespoons brown sugar
½ cup paprika
2 tablespoons salt
1 tablespoon chili powder
1 tablespoon cayenne
1 tablespoon onion powder

1 tablespoon garlic powder
1 tablespoon ground black pepper
1 bologna log

Mix ingredients in mixing bowl

Cut bologna into ½-inch pieces (about the size of a ½-pound hamburger patty)

Lightly rub top side of bologna with seasoning rub (don't over-season)

Store unused excess seasoning in airtight container in freezer when not in use

Using desired wood (we prefer hickory)

Set smoker temperature to 185 degrees

Place bologna slices as indirect from heat as allowed

Smoke for a couple of hours until edges are a dark brown and middle is lightly brown

Remove and serve Oklahoma-style BBQ Bologna

—Aaron Latsos, Smokies Hickory House BBQ

Arrested Outline for Wojapi

I) Make it Soft
  a) To the awful astringency of the chokecherry add:
    i) water
      (1) According to the *Telegraph*, softness can kill us; softness, when applied to water, is an ionic thing
        (a) if not bionic
        (b) is bionic made singular, the removal of the *bi-*
        (c) is bionic with a limb removed
          (i) arm
          (ii) ear
            1. all of our doubles halved
              a. If one were to split a collection of human beings in half lengthwise, one would find, as according to the responsible gene sequence, that our hearts would, more often than not, tip toward the left of us. Of course, there are mutants among us. Mutants whose involuntary penchants for recessivity deem that *their* hearts tip toward the right side. Linguistically, these right-hearted folks, though in the minority, are more "correct" than the rest of us—*right* (and the word *dextrous*) derives from the Latin *dexter*. Folks who favored their right sides (right-handed people, for instance) were seen as dex-

trous people. Folks who favored their left sides were seen as evil, in cahoots with the devil; left-handedness was seen as a sign of bastardy, and such mutants were often forced to unnaturally favor their right hands. *Left* derives from the Latin word *sinister.* This, linguistically, is what our hearts are. As human beings invented this language, this is how we see ourselves. Countless variations that deviate from the dominant version are capable of arising in the same singular species. These "right-hearted" people are mutant truths. Recessive ones. Somewhere, in the recesses of these recessive versions of our dominant truths, behind a daisy chain of lanterns and Darwin's theories drunk and conga-lining, Rudolph Valentino was a blond, and, just outside Pierre, the awful cowboys have inherited the right to fuck up their own Wojapi.

(2) To soften water, we must replace calcium ions with sodium ions, and though a pint of this softened water may contain less salt than a slice of bread, if you have a heart condition, this soft water may kill you, increase your chances of developing diabetes, kidney problems, the sort of anxious beating that will remind you of the defunct Buffalo Ridge railroad cars, shuttering their bolts as they threaded the waistline of South Dakota carrying their masses of
   (a) molasses
   (b) corn
   (c) snail shell powder for poultry feed and fertilizer
      (i) How we salt the very snails whose concentric shells are the objects in nature that most closely resemble the ventricles of our strange human hearts.

(ii) In *The Anguish of Snails: Native American Folklore in the West*, Barre Toelken writes, "We can see that the ongoing responses of the living snail have been recorded in the structure of the shell over time, forming patterns with which we want to become more fully acquainted. We believe that the markings before our eyes have meaning, and we want to explore the clues. We start here, not with the snail's sensitive innards. As outsiders, we may not initially understand what the many-patterned expressions of Indians 'mean,' either . . ."

1. The clues are on the skin.
2. The heart, ever an innard, beats obviously. There are no answers in its sound.
    a. . . . no answers beneath the thick rabbit coat, beaver hat, or buffalo pants of Pierre Chouteau, Jr., after whom our capital is named. All of his clues were written on the skins of animals.
    b. . . . no answers in the wheeze of the steamships Chouteau piloted down the Missouri River, knowing, even then, that his first name (though so common), and not his last, would provide the name—*Pierre*—we would give to our capital city, as the steam became the outermost clue, and the one that would disappear most quickly.

(d) chokecherry

(3) Collect both the fruit and the bark in a bucket. Separate one from the other, the dessert from the medicine.

(a) . . . Pierre's chest hair from that of the buffalo.

(b) . . . his scalp from the belly of the beaver.

(4) 25 percent of all South Dakotans die of heart disease

(a) Ranking among the highest heart disease casualties in the U.S. are the South Dakota Sioux, with a rate that's 20 percent greater than among other U.S. ethnic groups.

(b) Sioux tribes of South Dakota:

(i) Crow Creek

(ii) Standing Rock

(iii) Rosebud

(5) In 1972, over the Eastern Black Hills, outside the unincorporated community of Nemo, 15 inches of rain fell, and not softly, in under six hours, and Rapid Creek spilled its banks, igniting record floods that would kill 1,335 houses and 5,000 cars and trucks and vans and RVs, and 238 people (injuring 3,057 others), and the living prayed with broken arms in roofless houses, doorless houses, and with broken arms cooked the hot Wojapi, alternately stirring and screaming.

(a) A sweet mouth is good at a time like this.

(b) Due to the twisted metal, twisted bodies, eyes and hearts halved and leaking, we chose not to use these floodwaters in our Wojapi, the delicious thick fruit pudding that the American Indian Health and Diet Project feels can promote increased cardiac function, and dubs, perhaps thinking of borders and brims, brinks and peripheries, deprecation and defecation . . .

(i) (Snails, due to the twists of their bodies inside their shells, shit in their own mouths.)

(c) . . . "marginally nutritious."

(d) The crows got away.

(6) Says Toelken, "Like T. S. Eliot's *objective correlative*, an external object or metaphor provides the [watery] touchstone for complex systems of abstract meaning within us and our cultures. In our model, it represents a whole class of abstracts having to do with snail-ness," and the concentric whirling of the floodwaters good enough to kill us, but too contaminated for our chokecherry pudding.

ii) honey

(1) To soften honey, immerse the jar in warm water.

(2) Allow the bee to copulate with the flower in the rain.

(3) Allow Henry, your only Sioux friend, to cleanse your washer-dryer of its ghost via the burning of cedar chips and sage smudges on the carpet of your rented apartment in Rapid City, knowing that you will not get your security deposit back, but will later spoon the best Wojapi you've ever had over vanilla ice cream, contemplating all concentric things on the margins of a healthy heart, and other settlements so appropriately named.
   (a) Nemo
   (b) Rosebud Reservation
      (i) Honeybees, solitary bees, carpenter bees pollinate rose hips
         1. The American pawpaw (growing right there outside of Rosebud), its flowers opening their three-lobed calices, triple corollas, the fruit of which we fed to . . .
            a. George Washington
            b. Thomas Jefferson
            c. Lewis
            d. Clark
            e. the fuckers who demanded that Mount Rushmore be built on sacred land
         2. . . . is pollinated now by flies named Carrion, and flies named Dung

(4) and you will eat your dessert without thinking of ghosts, or the stuff the snail conceals beneath its tongue, or the other fluids meandering inside of us
   (a) and if we listen to the honey soften through our hearing aids, we will hear
      (i) bees
         1. our state insect
         2. In response to the sounds of bees, African elephants shake their heads, kick up dust, and, rumbling rather than trumpeting, retreat into the flora.
            a. An elephant's heart weighs 70 pounds.
            b. "The ear is so sensitive," the poet Alberto

Ríos says, "that the body, if it heard its own pulse, would be devastated by the amplification of its own sound."

c. Bees cannot talk, we tell ourselves.

(ii) dead uncles

1. their hipbones working
2. their coming-to-a-boil tongues

(iii) In this thick sweetness, to impale is to remember, to kiss with strangled mouths, is to shock our partners into believing this love is marginally, if not fully, nutritious

1. good for our hearts
2. *Good*

a. *for our fucking hearts.*

iii) cornstarch

(1) double the thickening power of flour

(a) the restoration

(i) of both legs

(ii) arms

(iii) ears

(iv) atria of the heart

(v) one last decent prayer

(vi) everything lost to the flood

1. to Lewis
2. Solubility
3. Dilution
4. Clark

(2) and flower

(a) and the sun shines thick from the thoraxes of the corn that in its drive to propagate, confuses itself for bees, a swarm.

(b) and in *The Penguin Companion to Food*, "chokecherry" falls in between "chocolate" and "cholesterol."

(i) we are stung and we convulse and our mouths sweeten and thicken with our insides, all the vessels that aren't cars or trucks or vans or RVs.

1. or boats

b) Boil the mixture
   i) Soup it with lemon zest, cassia.
      (1) do not scorch
      (2) watch your fingers
   ii) Feed it to your daughter, sans ice cream as punishment.
      (1) for her crying when you brushed her hair.
         (a) made her stand thigh-deep in the cold river with the bees and the roses, plucking the snails from between her legs
            (i) arms
            (ii) ears
         (b) made her hold the hot Wojapi in her mouth as you hemmed her dress, her burning tongue the talisman against your pricking her with the needle.
         (c) made her.
   iii) The mouth knows
      (1) wooden teeth
      (2) "a tongue," William Wood wrote in 1634, "so furred with astringency [it will] cleave to the roofe, and the throat wax horse with swallowing those red Bullies . . . they are as wilde as the Indians"
      (3) to ladle it over your weak liver
         (a) to celebrate its shrinking
      (4) that imperatives are bullshit
         (a) *Do not scorch*
         (b) South Dakota is bisected by the Missouri River, dividing us, sociologists say, into two distinct geographical and cultural halves.
            (i) the ring-necked pheasant arrests its song, removes the front part of its collar, then continues, *toooo-toooo* as if craving a predicate, a doubling up of a column of sound or idea of amount (of a portion of berries in a bowl, of title, subtitle, sub-subtitle) so powerful it can be called only Dakotan, if not Roman
               a. in *sub-* is bottom. That's where we go to drown.

b. There go the lobes of the brain . . .

(ii) the bees build their columns in the ribcage of the dead buffalo, call this *home.*

(iii) . . . heart is.

c) Scorch

i) This cherry heart, made of smoke, keeps us alive by burning.

ii) The Rosebud in the middle of the Pierre.

(1) We finish our pudding, and the daisies push up like indictments under our tongues.

Wojapi

Ingredients
½ cup water
1 pinch mineral salt
1 cup blackberries
1 cup blueberries
1 cup raspberries
1 cup strawberries, tops removed
2 tablespoons maple syrup

1. Bring the water to a simmer in a saucepan, add the mineral salt.

2. Add the berries, continue to simmer and stir.

3. Let the berries simmer for 20–30 minutes, stirring as berries break down.

4. Cook to your desired consistency, remove from heat, stir in maple syrup.

—Chef Sean Sherman and Christine Werner, chef de cuisine, The Sioux Chef

Drilling for Lefse

IN MINOT (rhymes with *Why not?*), twin sisters with matching eyepatches unfurl a single Lefse and, each beginning at an outer edge, eat their way toward the middle, the middlemost point retaining the heat of the potato, the flour, the egg, the cream, the lard. Think of Lefse not merely as potato flatbread but as canvas for so many other flavors, as Norwegian manifest destiny oozing over a griddle before coming to a stop in the mouths of two sisters without the depth perception required to assess the size of the thing they're eating.

Here, even our monuments freeze, and the sort of human breaths that will freeze in the air before ever reaching their bronze, their marble, their freezing Plexiglas flanks. Here, we are shortsighted as a point of survival. In all of this cold flatness, we would otherwise see too much.

The sisters exhale blankets of air over the garish red ribcage of the giant Dala Horse sculpture in the Scandinavian Heritage Park. They are obviously bored with the monochromatic leaden statue of Sondre Norheim, the Father of Modern Skiing, who stares plaintively at the sky, clutching his skis against the coming storm, as an underdressed, overweight tourist from Fargo in a "Battle of Sitting Bull" sweatshirt shouts to the girls about how Lefse is better slathered in butter and rolled up, before his wife demands a smile without so much as a *Cheese*.

To make a proper Lefse, one must own a Lefse pin (a specialized rolling pin with deep grooves carved into it), and a Lefse stick (to flip the Lefse on the griddle). Should the sisters have taken the underdressed-overweight tourist from Fargo's advice about the butter, rather than simultaneously spitting at his feet, they would have engaged in a particular way of eating Lefse known as *lefse-klenning.* Here, in North Dakota, we remind ourselves of our ancestry by repeating, as if in incantation, the names of the traditional things we eat.

Here, flatness is not severity but a point of pride, a desperate stab at making this place, as the wonderfully named former mayor of Fargo Bruce Furness would have said, "cozy." Here, we name sticks and pins after flatbread. Here, we blanket ourselves like giant horses against the winter with potato, lard. Perhaps this aids in fostering the "stick-to-it-ive-ness" of our people, as our former governor George A. Sinner would have said. There is a coziness in naming things after Lefse, if not sin.

Today, in North Dakota, the majority of the 95.8 percent white population recalls, when they hear the words "Battle of Sitting Bull," not the famed Lakota Sioux chief and holy man (who was shot by two federal agents—once in the heart, once in the head—on December 15, 1890, at 12 noon outside his home on the Standing Rock Reservation, eliciting, as described in a Western Union telegram, a "Wild scene STOP Squaws death chant heard in every direction STOP," and the Ghost Dancers howled and did not stop until seven Lakota and eight federal agents and two horses lay dead, and in every direction: weeping masked as chanting, chanting masked as anger, the weather, distended and grooved with clouds, about to flatten and flatten again so much blood into so much narrative, easily rolled and taken inside of us until we can say, *Fuck Custer* and *Fuck Billund, Denmark.* Next to the Billund Airport—Denmark's second busiest—travelers with sufficient layovers can wait out their delays gawking at the massive sculpture of Sitting Bull made entirely of Legos, their cooing fused with their whirring cameras in a sound not so much like a death chant, but more like a Lefse taking in air, then letting it out), but a so-called football game between the universities of North and South Dakota after which the winner gets to claim as trophy, until the next year, a bigger-than-life oak bust of Sitting Bull's head and

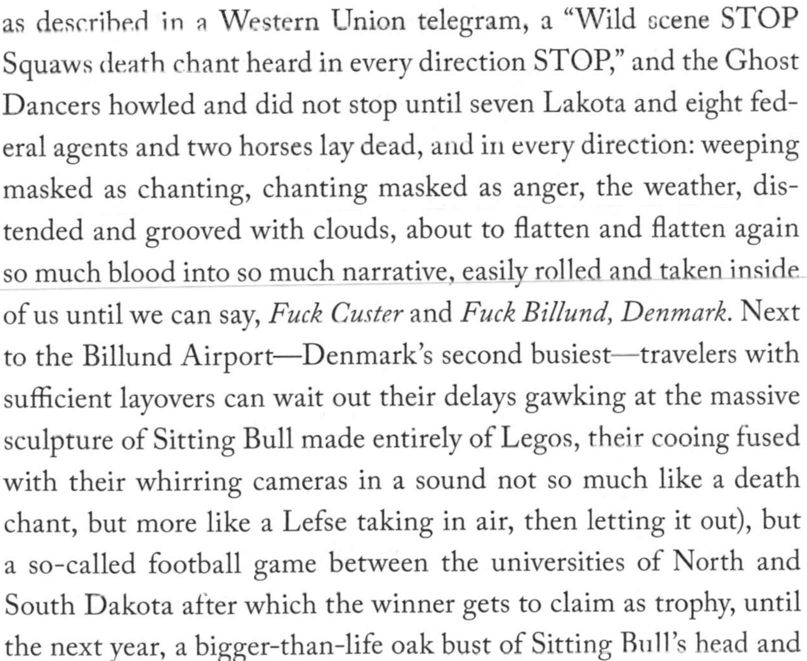

upper chest, which always sits in a prominent central space in each respective trophy case, behind the sort of Lucite that Rob Bollinger, former football coach and offensive coordinator for the University of North Dakota, described as—like a Lefse made without the "required tools"—"bulletproof."

Here, we watch our football and eat our Lefse slathered in cinnamon or lingonberry jam, or with peanut butter or white sugar or brown sugar, or corn syrup, or mustard, or stuffed with ham and eggs, or lutefisk—air-dried whitefish steeped in lye, or rakfisk—flattened trout fermented for a year, or Ribberull—lamb shoulder flattened and sewn into a long rectangle, rolled, pressed, and steamed; and we won't think of how we're compelled to compress our food here, to make of it a blanket stuffed with other blankets, as if this will tell our story, keep us warm, as our mouths consider our histories, as we watch our touchdowns and fumbles on the sort of screen that will shatter, open up—like a person, like his body—if a bullet merely grazes it.

In Swedish, to *klen* is to *clone*. That oak bust, that pile of Legos, look nothing like the real Sitting Bull. Here, to slather in butter and roll up our Lefse is to eat exactly as the Vikings ate. In all mimicry is a question of ethics and implication: *Is this something we should be doing now? Is this something we should be doing at all?*

One of the eyepatch sisters licks the frost from the flank of the Dala Horse. The other dips her Lefse in it. Neither says, *Better than butter.*

* * *

LEFSE WAS BORN in the early ninth century during the seagoing voyages of the Vikings. In larding the dough with additional flour, and allowing the cooked bread to dry, they found that the dish could last without refrigeration for six months or more. Before eating, the Vikings soaked the dried Lefse in seawater for an hour—plenty of time to catch and prepare their herring, and hatch their plans for pillage once they reached an inhabited shore.

According to *Time* magazine, North Dakota's 2013 oil production allowed "one of the coldest, flattest, least populated states in the country, [to become] an economic hot spot." According to ProPublica: Journalism in the Public Interest, North Dakota's oil boom is the product of "rape and pillage for short-term gain." According to the *New York Times*, oil companies are forcing North Dakota families off their private lands in the western portion of the state (as the law allows for a division between the ownership of land and the minerals beneath it) in a "rape-and-pillage mentality."

Here, cloning is evident even in the language we use. Such land grabs have spawned the unintended consequence of countless orphaned ranch cows wandering the state, or countless ranch cows poisoned with the chemicals leaking from the land after it's drilled. And we are the most rural of the U.S. states, with the most farming. "Are dying cattle the canaries in the coal mine?" asks the *Nation*, as, with their bad eyes, the twin sisters surely dream of lutefisk and prosperity mapped onto the corpses of the cows decorating the shoulders of our highways.

Pillage comes to us through the Old French, meaning *to abuse or mistreat*, and the Old English *pilian*, meaning *to strip or to skin*, from the Latin *pila*, meaning *a ball*, *pillage* finally evoking the destruction of that ball, a stopping of it in its tracks, which requires, of course, an ultimate flattening. In flatness is the absence of swell, of voluptuousness, of fertility. And yet, our state is the most fertile, with 90 percent of our land devoted to farming. Strange, how flatness here feeds so many.

The Vikings, like all the ancient Norse peoples, believed in a flat earth, surrounded by a great ocean, with the Yggdrasil—a giant ash tree—as the central *axis mundi*. In that great ocean lived the serpent Jörmungandr who grew large enough to encircle the earth, hold it together with its body. When Jörmungandr decided to let go, the world would end—and so, though the Norse creation myth warned, "it may well seem a hard thing to most men to cross over [the sea]," the Vikings did just that in a manner of self-sacrifice in order to preserve the world, and those who survived the journeys—on Lefse after Lefse—sacrificed those poor pillaged instead, and took off their wet clothes and made others do the same at knifepoint, and procreated so fiercely, their descendants popped up here, in North

Dakota, to prepare the same flatbread in the sort of ancestral honor we can grasp only incompletely.

What came first: starvation or the Lefse? The flatlands or the snake? We know the pattern. We've seen the sun unstitched by cold. In this snow, even the smallest of us leave trails.

In 1987, UND football coach Rob Bollinger said, of the Battle of Sitting Bull, "We've lost the game for the last five years and we're trying to rebuild. We want to be in the position where we have the firepower and numbers the Sioux had at the Little Big Horn." One of those numbers was a Cheyenne battle chief named Ve'ho'enohnenehe, or Lame White Man. Lame White Man was married to Twin Woman.

The sisters consider the remains of their Lefse. They do this with one eye apiece. With one eye apiece, the Lefse can be even flatter.

* * *

In a fictional Norway, the colony of Lefse-Klenning (town slogan: *Lefse!*) is, according to NationStates: The *Fair* Nation Simulator, known for its complete lack of prisons, is hard-nosed, lives in a state of perpetual fear due to a rise in biker gangs, has an income tax of 12 percent, a booming industry in the buying and selling of kidneys, no surveillance cameras, plenty of beggars. Recently, it was rated Highest Drug Use, Greatest Rich–Poor Divide, Most Pro-Market, Most Extreme, and Most Avoided. Still, the colony has many lush forests in which the elk, the national animal of Lefse-Klenning, "frolic freely."

After the Battle of the Little Bighorn, boys searched the pockets of the dead soldiers, finding paper money and silver coins. From the mud, they sculpted play horses and used the paper money as toy saddle blankets. They made belt buckles of the silver coins which, according to John Stands In Timber and Margot Liberty's *Cheyenne Memories*, required that "they pounded it with a heavy iron to flatten it out." Here, to flatten a thing out is to lend that thing utility, worth.

According to Peter J. Powell's *Sweet Medicine*, "Lame White Man's last words to Twin Woman had been, 'I must follow my boys into battle.' So he had ridden after the suicide fighters . . . When they reached Lame White Man's corpse, his body was covered with dust . . . They made ready a travois, stripping it to the bare skeleton of poles, making a flat surface upon which the body could be tied."

According to Monuments.com: A NEW AGE OF MEMORIALIZATION: *We ship worldwide!*, "Sitting nearly flush with the earth, flat grave markers preserve the memory of your loved one in a simple, yet profound way. Flat grave markers typically feature a smaller amount of text than other types of headstones, but a wide variety of images, designs, and symbols are available in our art files to help memorialize the one you love."

The flat red granite headstone of Lame White Man sits wedged in a sand flat surrounded by the sort of prairie grass that can cut into the skin if the wind is fierce enough, and allows us to consider "A CHEYENNE WARRIOR DEFENDING HIS HOMELAND." Sitting Bull, on the other hand, allows for another sort of consideration. In April 1953, grave robbers from South Dakota raided Sitting Bull's burial site at Fort Yates, North Dakota, and, with a backhoe, removed some but not all of his remains, tossed them into the trunk of their Mercury Monterey (said to have the most dangerous car interior in history due to the aircraft-style levers of the Merc-O-Therm heater on which drivers routinely impaled themselves during accidents), burying the purloined parts in Mobridge, SD. North Dakota claims that all the thieves got were horse bones, but South Dakota "experts" refute this. Between the two sites, Doug Kirby, in *Roadside America*, states, "Fort Yates loses points for presentation. The dirt road leading to the grave site is marked by a sad, hand-painted sign nailed to a wooden post. It lists precariously toward a gully. The grave itself is at the far end of a small, dusty parking area. It's covered by a thick, flat slab of concrete and a big rock."

* * *

ACCORDING TO the mission statement of NationStates: The *Fair* Nation Simulator, "NationStates is a nation simulation game. Create a nation according to your political ideals and care for its people. Or deliberately oppress them. It's up to you."

"I want to pause first to worship human technology. At some

point not many thousand years ago we were wandering around the African savannah plucking berries from shrubs, beating off intruders with clubs, and trying not to let the fire go out because it was so darned hard to get it started again," says Clay Jenkinson, staff writer for the *Bismarck Tribune*. "Last week I had the opportunity to visit the Bakken oil fields north and west of Belfield with Ron Ness of the North Dakota Petroleum Council and Blaine Hoffman of the Whiting Oil and Gas Corporation . . . It was an amazing, and amazingly generous, tour. I am immensely grateful to have had the opportunity to see the industrial profile of the oil boom through the eyes of such remarkable and dedicated professionals."

Continues Clay Jenkinson, "Bakken oil is going to be one of the greatest gifts that ever came to the people of North Dakota. It's not an oil boom. It's an industrial revolution," he said, flatly.

To drill into flatness, to test the depth of it, is the job of our teeth. Ask the sisters: It's the job of the Lefse to give in to the sharpness of our mouths and crumble. To take this job from our teeth, to industrialize it, seems to be tempting fate, to be, as former Fargo mayor Alf T. Lynner once said, "playing with the lioness's titty." Still, we're compelled to do it—to drill and drill into all this fertility until we unearth the sort of sustenance that will do us in, as if overeating to burstage.

According to NationStates, the fictional colony of Lefse-Klenning is categorized as "Post-Revolution Embryonic Society," recently promoted from "Anarchy."

This ND/SD controversy over who can claim Sitting Bull's remains, described by *USA Today* as "ghoulish" (to say nothing of the desecration of a body), is what ignited the football version of the annual Battle of Sitting Bull and, in an article about said football version, *USA Today* was inspired to caption a small photo of the oak bust of the fallen chief and holy man like so: "SITTING BULL: Trophy travels; did his bones?" Such remarkable dedication. Such flat, dry bread.

* * *

SPORTS HEADLINES: "Vikings Flatten Trojans," "Vikings Flatten High Point," "Vikings Flatten Red Springs," "Vikings Flatten Falcons," Flatten Tennessee, Flatten Freeport, Flatten Cats, Flatten Arrows, Run Wild, Pull It Off, Steamroll, Keep Season Alive . . .

* * *

It's easy to travel through North Dakota. According to the state's Department of Mineral Resources, the state is divided into "six major physiographic regions each defined by a suite of characteristic landforms that serve to differentiate it from its neighbors," including "Monotonously Flat Countryside" and "Deeply Eroded Badlands."

What else can we do to commune with our state but build a Lefse pin to better flatten and pock our suppers? Which flattening honors? Which desecrates? Strange how the topography that's easiest to traverse is also the most monotonous. Here, we have more cars than people—so easy to drive across the state, so hard to drive away. According to the Norse mythology text the *Gylfaginning*, some of the ancient Norse also believed that flat, dry land "floated about [on the surface of the water] as if it were floating oil."

* * *

. . . pronounced Why not?

* * *

Perhaps it's genetics, our nature, our secret: like soothsayers, we all wish for the failing of our vision; for the oil and the snow to lay claim to our irises. Perhaps we depend on this, as the earth does. For the flattening to finally become the blotting-out. Like us, the skies cry milk, cry fungus, cry storm. Shut the windows. Close the doors. The blizzard came first.

The twin sisters have finished their lunch. At their lips, no crumbs. The sisters hold hands, flatten the air between them. Beneath their eyepatches, we can only guess about a furious blinking, that roundness obscured.

Lefse

6 quarts cooked potatoes
1 stick margarine
⅓ cup cream

2 tablespoons sugar
2 tablespoons salt

Add all above
Then cool well
Then rice

Add 4 cups flour, mix by hand well, make soft balls, roll, fry on lefse grill, 1 side then the other until brown spots

Cool separately on cloth towel before storing in frig or freezer.

—*Charlotte Landsem, Charlotte's Homemade Lefse*

The Uprooting of the Bierock

WHEN WE PRICK the dough of our Bierocks like this, we imagine the fork as a shovel, and we are digging for precious things like gold, like water. We find beef and we find sauerkraut, and, in these, we try for something else—for escape, for *all the way to China*, for anything to remind us of anything other than our exile from Russia, from Germany, from Poland, to Kansas. Our exile: another cow ground down to crumbs, another cabbage chiffonade allowed to ferment until hay-blond, until the soft, unwashed hair of the daughters we were never destined to birth in Middle America.

Instead, my imaginary son Arlo asks about the intersection between algorithms and the weather. Why Kansas has an earthquake index of 0.05 compared to the country's average of 1.81. A tornado index of 252.53 compared to the average 136.45. A volcano index of 0.00. I want to tell him to take comfort in the fact that the earth's stuffing will never attack us. We have no chance of being lit gloriously by upwardly spat fireballs. He asks—and this is so cute—if it's better to be wiped out by the earth's hair dryer than its acid reflux. I tell him, mussing his hair, that there's medicine for heartburn. That to keep our hair wet just a little longer, all we need to do is unplug the machine from the wall. Though I'm not sure exactly what we're talking about, the meteorologist on TV talks about the high winds ripping off roofs in Topeka and my heart stutters when Arlo says, taking his first bite of Bierock, this is *lava* hot.

The Bierock, according to the *Lawrence Journal*'s Tom King, is like "the empanada, the calzone, the Hot Pocket," is "almost always beef," is almost always yellow onion and sauerkraut "wrapped in a bun of sweet leavened dough," is "golden," is "palm-sized," is portable, should be cradled in the hands or kept warm in one's inside jacket pocket, where it can continue to steam, commune with its cousin the pierogi, can dream of a life as other-than-dumpling, as other than a tight knot of sustenance that, in spite of its ability to keep its heat, "freezes," according to Tom King, "great."

I want to tell Arlo that lava can't freeze, though I don't know if this is true. He asks me if, should our house flood again, a Bierock can be used as a raft, if he can float his paper cowboy dolls from carpet to prairie on the back of this sour, golden horse, which, it must be said, is far too big to fit into his palm.

* * *

KANSAS IS A STRESSOR, a bird of prey. It says, *I flew once, but I've been pounded into my own ground by the bison.* It says, *when I used to be singular, when I used to be the name of a semi-nomadic tribe called the People of the Wind, I was Kansa. Now, I am plural, many. What else can I do but flood my banks?* We're all wind here. When we get wet, we are the agent of our own drying-out. To cool our Bierocks, all we have to do is open our mouths and blow.

Now, the land agitates its own river, and the river floods Manhattan and Wamego and Topeka and Lawrence. Lecompton loses five of its six churches, barely recalls a time when it was known as Bald Eagle, Kansas. Here, our crust is a shell, the intermediary between our mouths, and hot things that wish to burn them.

On the benches of Lecompton's Riverview Park, overlooking the limestone bluffs of the Kaw Valley Basin, twelve picnickers today eat their Bierocks, the sauerkraut waving like viscera in the wind after which the state was named. Here, the wind can be the sort of predatory equation it takes a golden dough to solve. The dough as levee, as saving us from releasing the sweet air in our lungs. We can forget to cool things with our breath. Forget about the panic inherent in each required inhale. Here, two bald eagles scream as they couple over the river. Their voices sound nothing like *Kaw*.

Nearly one hundred years before the Great Flood of 1951, during which Harry Truman flew over Kansas in the airplane he privately nicknamed the Bald Eagle, staring down at the 1,074,000 flooded acres, his voice wavering as he spoke into the CB, "one of the worst disasters this country has ever suffered from water . . ." the water of the Kansas ran red as the anti-slavery Free-Staters and pro-slavery Border Ruffians fought a proxy war along its banks, Northerners and Southerners immigrating to the territory in order to duke it out for their side. Pistols and canes and rocks and broadswords later, men blinded by, and drowning in, the fluid that just moments earlier was held inside them by levees of skin, the territory became known as Bleeding Kansas.

"Nostalgia," says Tom King, "is a sublime seasoning."

In Kansas, when we fall to the earth dying, we fall to seed and to root. We stain with our bodies the stuff that once sustained us, bleed out into the agriculture. In this way, we become the blanket, the blemish, the outermost layer of the earth. We tell ourselves, as we blink out, that we are keeping some essential filling at bay. We imagine we are brushed with a little melted butter, that we are cooking at a breezy 350–375 degrees. Until we are bitten, we are exactly this golden.

The introduction of the Bierock to Bleeding Kansas by Volga German–Russian–Polish–Mennonite immigrants coincided in 1861 with the end of the proxy war and the admission of the territory to the Union as a free state. That this is an innocuous coincidence is obvious. Less so: the early dough was flavored with the same red wheat seeds and peony roots that once collected so much of our blood.

The river Volga, Europe's longest, is home to some of the world's largest reservoirs. The name *Volga* refers both to moisture (literally, *wetness*) and veins, blood vessels, a mythical juice. As such, in Russian folklore, the river is both a waterway and an animal.

* * *

ARLO TELLS ME about his dream. That addition became confused with subtraction. That a drought, like a flood, is an addition to a landscape. Just look at all that new brown—all that wheat and sorghum, all those sunflowers sloughing to dust, taken into the wind, adding gaps to the rows, the illusion of stars exiled to our state, whirling now, about twenty feet over our roofs, and rising.

Here, when the river breaches its banks, it sounds like slurred speech, a mispronunciation of the healthy flow. I'm not sure what sort of medicine can solve this, but watch how the dough sponges the juice of the cabbage. Watch how the heat, if not the lava, allows the wet to forget itself. In a mispronounced incantation is a false healing.

The Volga delta, deep into Russia, supports anomaly. Though the river is frozen for at least a quarter of each year, the delta supports a thriving community of flamingos and lotus flowers and the same red wheat seeds that once covered Bleeding Kansas, grew over our bodies.

Toward the Nebraska border, folks pronounce Bierock *brook*. In this way, we allow our heaviest of foods a communion with the most benign of our waterways. On the border, our mouths full, it is our babbling that we believe will protect us.

We give back. In April 2012, the Volga basin flooded, forcing the villages of Saratov, Tambov, and Volgograd to declare states of emergency, to evacuate. The waters devastated much of Tatarstan and the republic of Mordovia. One Moscow official, unnamed, perhaps mistranslated, said that urban planners have set about "building a golden shell" against such future disasters.

* * *

We eat our Bierocks in Reading, close to the river named by the French explorers for the nearby marsh, and for our trumpeter swans, the river famous for its flash flooding, floods so powerful we give them names like Big Water. Before we officially settled on the French name *Marais des Cygnes,* we called this river Old Aunt Mary. We called every person she killed—over 100 in 1844, 86 in 1909, 60 in 1915, 39 in 1928, 35 in 1944, 28 in 1951, and 0 in 2007—Old Aunt Mary, too.

Arlo asks: how can so much water take so much away? He tells me that in school, he learned that the human body is mostly water. He asks me if we're always flooding on the inside.

I answer him. I say, Nesho, Spring, Shoal, Cottonwood. Verdigris, I say. I say, Caney, Chikaskia. I say Whitewater and Cow and Rattlesnake and Walnut. I say, just to make him feel better, Little Walnut.

On special occasions, Arlo paints his Bierock dough with red food coloring, and I try not to tell him about Bleeding Kansas. Instead, as if recalling a better, if fictional, inheritance of statehood, he taps two finished Bierocks together three times and, even while muttering *There's no place like home,* looks disappointed in the kitchen, if not the entire spread of land beyond it.

We're almost a perfect rectangle, Arlo says, and I imagine all of the twiny things meandering through this almost perfect shell of a state. I bite the upper right corner of the Bierock. All sorts of mutilated things pour out onto the napkin.

The rivers will split in two and flow around us. Arlo calls us the barrette to the braid. So: logic dictates that I muss his hair after the bath, watch the water run from it to the towel on which a nondescript bird reaches in vain for the beautiful fringe at the border.

For supper, we eat Bierocks. Two for Arlo, four for me. Arlo: milk. Me: dark ale. Last winter, we premade 120 of them. You should have seen all the yeast. Arlo told me it felt like the entire kitchen was rising.

Bierock

Ingredients

2 pounds ground beef
1 cup diced white onion
2 tablespoons chopped garlic
2 cups sauerkraut
3 cups shredded cabbage
1 tablespoon celery salt
1 tablespoon chopped fresh thyme
Salt and pepper
3 cups shredded sharp cheddar cheese
3½ pounds white bread dough

In a large pan, brown the beef until the juice is almost gone. Add onion and garlic and cook another 5 minutes. Add cabbage and cook until tender. Add sauerkraut and cook an additional 5 minutes or until the juices are almost gone. Add celery salt, thyme, and salt and pepper to taste. Remove from heat and cool. Make 5-ounce balls of bread dough. Roll or stretch dough ball flat. Top with 2 ounces cheddar cheese and 4 ounces cooled meat mixture. Fold dough over mixture and pinch closed, forming a ball. Place bierock pinched side down on greased baking tray. Bake in 350-degree oven for approximately 12 minutes until bread appears golden brown. Remove from oven and let stand for 10 minutes.

Makes: 10–12 bierocks.

—Chef Manuel Hernandez, Gella's Diner & Lb. Brewing Co.

MOUNTAIN WEST

Wyoming: Milk Can Supper

Idaho: Spudnuts

Montana: Elk Stew

Colorado: Denver Omelet

The Desperate Deranging of Milk Can Supper

THIS IS ONLY PHYSICS, Uncle tells us. We lean forward in the saddle, then back. We allow for the brief coupling of horn and groin, scratch lightly at parts named pommel, swell, gullet, skirt, parts named hobble strap, seat jockey, cantle, front rigging dee. Blevins. Concho. Can of milk. We think nothing of cows today, or of the boys who compel them to walk in straight lines through the sort of landscape we call *big*, so we don't have to call it *barren*. We think nothing also of mothers, but of another kind of sustenance. Instead, we layer one kind of food atop another, stuff it into a milk can and bring it to temperature over the fire. Overhead, something that sounds like a plane writes letters in the sky. Our horses look confused. Overhead, the sky is so big we can't make out the words. This mishmash will carry us through another day.

There's order here: our sleeves need to hug our arms just so in order to reduce wind resistance but still allow for the throwing of the rope. Order: the longer-cooking vegetables need to be at the bottom of the milk can, closest to the heat—the potatoes, the cabbage, the corn. Then the onion, carrot, green pepper, garlic, bay leaf, thyme, and sausage. Here, the ingredients at the top of the milk can should be the most delicate, closest to all that nonsense in the sky. Our Milk Can Supper burns onto the bottom. We didn't add enough water, and drank all the beer. We eat it anyway, and chase it with three aspirin apiece. Once, the stuff we packed into a single milk can fed an entire team of drovers. Tonight, we wipe our mouths and, until we fall asleep, recite quotations by Ron Levene, founder of Cheyenne's Gunslingers Association. "I figure I was born a hundred years too late . . ."

If the fire shushes us, that means something's leaking from the can. One recipe stresses that the ingredients in Milk Can Supper should be cooked "until you can see through them." We think of lingerie, of the delicate things we want to remove from a body. We think of fingertips, and of breath—breathing to cool, breathing to heat up, the skin rising to our mouths. Uncle finishes his cigar and says nothing of the cataracts gathering like weather in his eye, of the translucent disc of onion as weak monocle, of trying to see all of this invisible night through the smoke.

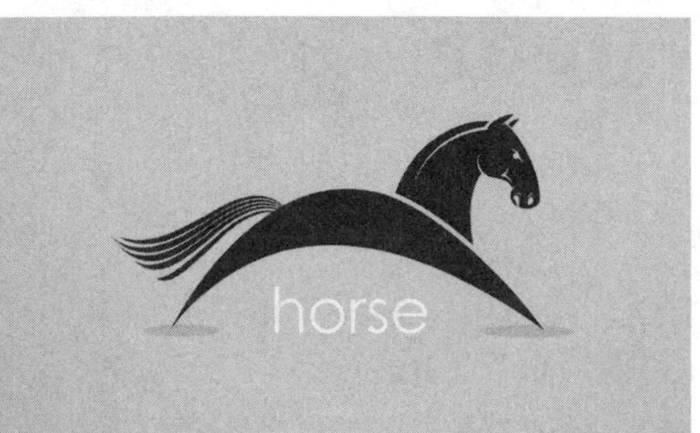

Milk derives from the Proto-Indo-European root *melg*, meaning *to wipe away, to rub off, to stroke* . . . We use our fingertips to lightly clean the supper from our mouths, wonder about the intersection of *cleanse* and *extract*, wonder if both actions demand the caress. What else can we do but stuff our gentlest of touches full of slow-cooking vegetables and sausage and pray that it doesn't burst at the seams?

The mountains are hiding. We stare out into all of this stretched-out landscape and pray for corners, edges. Uncle tells us that, as a child, he made a balloon out of his mother's lingerie, filled it with raw milk. "It was a miracle, boys," he says, "the cream was so damn thick, that, for the first time, silk became impermeable." Then, he tells us that he threw it at his younger brother, that it bounced from his shoulder, spun in the dust like some awful bladder. "The horses," Uncle says, "smelled it and ran away, but I'll be damned if they didn't come back, again and again, to smell it . . ."

* * *

THERE, JUST BEYOND the Former World's Largest Jackalope, the night lights of Lusk undo the pitch blackness of the range. Beneath one orange light lies the monumental grave of famed local prostitute Mother Featherlegs, tucked along the Deadwood Stage Road, itself having long ago given in to furrows Uncle calls "deep," and ruts he calls "udders of the avenue." We know, because it's inscribed: *She was roadhouse ma'am. An outlaw confederate, she was murdered by*

"Dangerous Dick Davis the Terrapin" in 1879 after he was gypped of his portion of Milk Can Supper. We lay down our heads on thin pillows. Because it's dark, we can't see what that plane is writing up there. But still, we speculate. Because we're full of supper, because the blood's in our bellies, we tend to overdo it.

In Wyoming, we inherit our rhetoric from cowboys and fur trappers. As such, that valley surrounded tightly by sheer faces of rock is called a *hole.* "Just because you feel hollow inside," Uncle says, beginning to doze off, "doesn't make your body a mountain." We withdraw into our sleeping bags, but do not find warmth there. We're not warm.

Perhaps we're sleep-deprived and a little deranged. Strange, we think, how when something is totaled, it has reached the irreparable stage of its destruction. Strange how, linguistically, at this stage, it is finally *entire.* It is everything.

* * *

SAYS GORDON PRICKETT, assistant manager of Western Ranchman Outfitters in Cheyenne, "Drugstore cowboys overdo everything. Bolo tie, hat, boots, vest, the works. Mainly, you can tell by their attitude. Real cowboys are quiet. Withdrawn. And they always have chew in their mouths."

The western meadowlarks sing flutelike into the night. The notes of their song, as always, descend. Even in our sleep out here, we talk and talk. That means our mouths are empty. Uncle mutters in between snores, "Dusk or Lusk, lust or dust, in Wyoming, we are murdered by alliterative men who are named after turtles. We are so dangerous in our pink pantalettes. So look away and up-up. There's a lasso in the sky . . ."

There's a sausage in the milk can. A body in a bag. We press our faces into the silk, try to find the old drool there, as the dust whips our bodies and we ride faster and faster, with anxious hearts, toward something we mistake as a peaceful sleep. Here, our release into sleep is sometimes painful. Says A. W. Lishman in the article "The Cow's Udder and Milk Secretion," "Lack of massage during milking causes blood and other body fluids to dam up in the teat. This is painful to the cow, and she will then be inclined to kick."

We close our eyes and picture all of these cowboys, night after night, eating the same supper from the same can, the range having stripped all those lovely bolos from their throats. We tell ourselves that in repetition is equal parts reverence, desperation, neurosis. Onion, carrot, cabbage. We wake in the middle of the night. The lights of Lusk have gone out. Something whistles into the dark, and this does not feel like home.

We can't help but feel that there's something blasphemous about preparing meat in a can made for milk. We kick our legs and are grateful to find the bottoms of our sleeping bags.

* * *

In order to transport milk from cow to can, commercial dairy farmers often use a stainless steel milk pipe, the higher end of which is fitted with filters that reportedly block the passage of certain strains of harmful bacteria. We blink the crust from our eyes, watch the stars fall. At this hour, we can't tell which are the harmful ones.

Extract. Caress. Obliterate, but gently. The long-cooking things are at the bottom. We try to make for the surface of the can. *Take me by the mouth*, we say. We say, *fill me up. Forgive me,* we say, *That's not a cloud.*

Here, we call all barriers to pathogens *rosettes*. Still, the best of them offer little resistance—few if any furrows—to the passage of the milk. Etymologically, other words associated with *suckle*: *fruit, leech, nurse, hatch, hay, happy, fetus, lamb, woman, cow, boy, yield, shoot, swim, animal, wet, dripping, chew, withdraw, home, legs, feather* . . .

All of that supper and all of its parts whirl in our bodies, come together and break apart. This is regrettable, not good for sleep. Like our state, we are not densely populated.

That *Wyoming* derives from the native Unami word meaning *At the big river flat* is unsurprising. That, when sleeping on it, this flatness seems to menacingly swell, less so.

* * *

Old Faithful empties itself every 71.2 seconds with such a force that the water appears white, opaque. "The milk of the Earth," the brochures call it. Says an astounded tourist to her husband, "This couldn't just happen. It has to be God's work."

All miracles lose their luster, no matter how forceful their discharge. In the early days of Yellowstone National Park, the famed geyser was used as a laundry. According to Henry J. Winser's *The Yellowstone National Park: A Manual for Tourists,* "Garments placed in the crater during quiescence are ejected thoroughly washed when the eruption takes place. General Sheridan's men, in 1882, found that linen and cotton fabrics were uninjured by the action of the water, but woolen clothes were torn to shreds."

Earlier today we passed a totaled horse, its carcass.

According to *Wyoming Breezes*, some Milk Can Suppers are "a strong tirade and others merely a whisper." According to Roadside America, the arduous journey to Mother Featherlegs's headstone offers "not much of a payoff. No bawdy statuary, or even a noble bas relief. Just a 3,500-pound pink granite slab, the worn inscription blocked by a metal pipe fence."

Here, the night has a clear middle, and we wake into it, and Uncle recites the skywriting. "Right here on this very spot," he says, and we look deep into the silk of our pillows. Those who give off milk, and those who desperately want to receive it.

Milk Can Supper

In order to make a milk can dinner, you must find a good 10-gallon milk can. It should be free of rust on the inside and should have a lid. It should also be checked to be sure that the seals are good and it doesn't leak. The best thing to do is to scour it on the inside with a Brillo type pad. Cream cans (5 gallons) can also be used. Note that a 5-gallon cream can will serve approx. 10–12 people, and a 10-gallon milk can will serve approximately 25 people.

Fires for the milk cans were usually made of wood with two cinder blocks on the sides to hold the milk can. Now we use propane torches.

These are the ingredients in the order that you will place them in the milk can:

25 potatoes—not peeled
3 pounds carrots—peeled
25 shucked ears of corn
4 heads of cabbage quartered: cut the hearts out so after cooking, leaves will separate.
6 medium onions, cut into quarters
50 sausages (we use a mixture of brats, Italian sausage, and hot dogs to make everyone happy)
1½ quarts of water (don't worry that this seems so little; the food is actually steamed)

Once you have filled the can, place it on the fire. Be sure not to push the lid down tightly. If you do, the can will eventually explode and you will be serving dinner to everyone within a block! Also be careful that the fire is not too hot. It is easy to burn the food on the bottom. This just takes a little practice.

In general, the milk can will be on the fire for about 1½ hours.

When the food is cooked, two men should take hold of the handles on the sides and carry it to where it will be served. It works well to use some large tubs to pour the food in to. Several people will then serve people as they pass through the line.

We usually serve the dinner with some rolls and a tossed salad. Salt, pepper, and butter should be available so people can season as they like and have butter for the corn. Enjoy!

Please note: It has been our experience that this amount of food usually requires several milk cans and also a cream can and will end up serving 100 people. Maybe they were heartier eaters back in the day when the Milk Can Dinner was popular.

—Pastor Karen O'Malia,
Christ Lutheran Church & AKIDEMY

Prayer for the Spudnuts, as They Take to the Sky

DEAR LORD, bless us here, in Arco, as our air quality gets the Green Square every time, which means Good. Our air is good here. We trap this air in our Spudnuts—our potato flour doughnuts—and this air, like the river, finds its path of least resistance, and builds channels through the dough—the potato, the egg, the sugar, the flour, the salt. Though slick with oil, it is this Green Square air that keeps our Spudnuts light, our good potatoes that allow for the combative density. Lord, you know: in the Spudnut is an argument between one good thing that wants to ground us and another that wants to lift us from this earth.

Here, our famous tuber oozes the sort of starch we can dress only in confectioner's sugar, and a quick dip in the magma of our morning coffee. We finish our breakfast of scrambled eggs and Spudnuts at Pickle's Place in Arco. We beseech our Craters of the Moon National Monument brochure, learn that this black earth has "A Violent Past, Calm Present, and Uncertain Future." We will walk off the third Spudnut on this exact earth on which the astronauts are compelled to practice for their moon landings. Here, it's right up the road.

Here, a conduit is a vent, and a vent is our passage from crust to core. We can traverse this with our mouths, find that nothing else lives at the center of the Spudnut but Spudnut itself. Forgive our uncles who complain that there's nothing special about a doughnut made with potato flour, in spite of our uncles being with the Idaho Potato Commission since its inception in 1937. They say there's nothing special about putting the potato on the radio, on television, on the license plate, on T-shirts and underpants and postcards and keychains and mugs, on forearms via tattoo, and in dreams via the fourteen-hour workday. Nothing special about the potato at trade shows, a board of directors of the Idaho Potato, and frequently asked questions that include "What Makes Idaho Potatoes So Good?" and "Why Are My Potatoes Turning Green?" We honor You in breathing in this Good Green Air, and answer our uncles' complaints with the slogan on our own blessed sweaters, "Changing the world, one Spudnut at a time." In the sweetening of the starch that is our birthright, we can both engage and manipulate the potato. Look graciously upon us, as we say, *It is ours. It is above us. It is air, moon, the sort of birthright that greens when exhumed from the soil and bathed in sun, like a tree.*

Right or wrong, it is the landscape on earth that most closely resembles that of the moon. We wonder how many Spudnuts we'd have to eat to uncouple from this soil, our skin greening—so alien!—the higher we rise. Look with pity upon us as we ascend, as we explore "this weird and scenic landscape." Here, even our brochures think we're odd.

As if talisman, medical mask, the only thing they know, our uncles hold Spudnuts to their faces when stepping outside. We wonder about the quality of that air. Hear us: we wonder what color is even better than Green.

Watch over Signature Spudnut, manufacturer of Spudnut™ Mix, as it claims that the ideal Spudnut should be "so airy, it seems to float." Here, the rising from this earth is not a move toward death, but an ideal in life, in the starchiest of prayers, and in breakfast. Sure, we have this lovely black earth, but that air—that air which we can take inside of us, but still can't quite reach—is Green, and therefore, both the luminous color of alien skin and Edenic.

* * *

According to the *Telegraph,* in August 2007, physicists decided, "levitation has been elevated from being pure science fiction to science fact." Said physicists cited a law called the Casimir effect, a consequence of quantum mechanics that works on the principles of repulsion—a "free" object being repelled by the very surface that should seem to embrace it. In principle, these physicists declare, this "effect could be used to levitate bigger objects . . . even a person." You wonder about the fluctuations in the energy field of the Spudnut, those lovely chambers of air between the soft caves of potato, stretched like the sort of cotton candy that lifts into the air with each exhale, communing with the molecules of Arco, and beyond that, two kinds of moon. The earth, Uncle says, will toss us from its surface like pop flies.

The town of Arco, originally called Root Hog, was named for Georg von Arco, a visiting German physicist of radio transmission who invented radio vacuum tubes, which, among other things, found a way to levitate information, the human voice now airborne, disseminating important messages from our home state about things like atomic power, floating lava fields, and when, exactly, a baked potato is "done."

That Arco was the first city in the world (in 1955) to be lit by atomic power is obvious. That, up until recently, one was able to buy non-weapons-grade plutonium right next to the regular unleaded at Dave's Travel Plaza on US-20 (which also peddles some of the best Spudnuts in town), less so.

Down the street from Craters of the Moon, the line cook at Pickle's Place throws down another batch of Spudnuts. They float like actual stars in all of that grease. Uncle eats three. Wipes his lips. Wants to say nothing more of the potato, even as he takes so much of it into his body.

Here, the Spudnut, like the split atom, is inevitable. We wonder which will allow us to levitate first. How much, you ask your uncle, of our body is comprised of voice? You wonder: if von Arco found a way for our voices to float and fly, will the body follow, as if a dog on a leash? You hold your arms out to your sides. You stand on your toes. Your skeleton, ever clunky, remains earthbound. But when you shout, you are airborne. When we broadcast our voices to others—to so many at once—we are *on air.*

Uncle no longer fishes in the Big Lost River, which, in spite of its proximity to the nuclear reactor testing station has remarkably clean waters. "Radiation," Uncle says, "flies away." As ever, the moon keeps quiet on this. Uncle says he is losing himself. You wonder if loss is just another kind of levitation.

Down the street from Craters of the Moon, the Idaho National Laboratory uses that non-weapons-grade plutonium to produce levels of heat and electricity sufficient to rocket the vessel (cheesily named *New Horizons*) into deep space toward the dwarf planet Pluto. Down the street, the men and women who eat Spudnuts on Sundays, who breathe the same atomic Green air that you do, launched that vessel from the earth with the greatest ever speed for a man-made object. You finger your great-grandmother's opal engagement ring in the right pocket of your blue jeans and something in your chest feels like it's speeding up.

You remember your uncle fishing for trout called bull and trout called rainbow and trout called cutthroat. You wonder how the name of a thing affects its flavor. You wonder how the Spudnut can taste so good.

You walk to the corner of Front and Temple, to the giant green rocking chair in front of Pickle's Place, from which, as a child, even after a basket of Spudnuts, you used to leap, counting the seconds you were airborne before landing in the dust.

* * *

In prayer, St. Teresa of Avila was said to levitate. "I confess that it threw me into a great fear," she writes, "for in seeing one's body thus lifted up from the earth . . . (and that with great sweetness if unresisted) the senses are not lost; my body seemed frequently to be buoyant, as if all weight had departed from it."

You wonder if levitation is merely an emotional state. You wonder this as you hike and hike on the hardened tephra of Craters of the Moon, the airfall material ejected by a volcano, now keeping you aloft and, for the time being, upright.

When *New Horizons* was launched in January 2006, you and

Uncle and your then new girlfriend celebrated with warm Spudnuts from Dave's. That April, as you celebrated your six-month anniversary with kisses and Spudnuts, *New Horizons* bypassed Mars, and your uncle complained, watching reruns of *Deep Space Nine*, that he could "retire from the potato, but the potato couldn't retire from me." Ten months later, he mutters about the potato as planet, as shackle, as dependency, parasite, as a right cursed and a right God-given. *New Horizons* passes Jupiter.

The Ch'an monk Ying-fung levitated (as did his master). In the year 621, he performed this feat over battlefields during the Battle of Hulao in order to distract the warring soldiers from their fight. Uncle, without breaking eye contact with the wall, whispers to your concerned girlfriend about a whirlpool on Mars over which rocks and (purportedly) humans can levitate. You don't have the heart to tell him, *New Horizons* passed Mars over a year ago.

The physics of this love feels decidedly **upward,** *even as you fall and fall.*

Uncle is becoming increasingly insomniac, wonders if we're misguided when we associate *falling* with *asleep*, *up* with the waking, as if both were directionally bound to a single vertical axis. As if both, like the Big Lost, didn't meander as a rule.

The same team of physicists that used the Casimir effect to explain levitation earlier deduced that the invisibility cloak is a feasible creation, and that we should have a prototype within twenty years.

St. Joseph of Copertino levitated so aggressively in the seventeenth century that he became entangled in the branches of an olive tree and refused to come down, even when the Pope brought a ladder and demanded that he shed some of this lofty ecstasy. St. Joseph levitated so often and effortlessly that it took on an air of braggadocio, and the Pope, therefore, as punishment for the insubordination of allowing a miracle to become commonplace ([eyes rolling] *There's fucking Joseph levitating again . . .*) banned him from attending public services for thirty-five years.

In the Spudnut is our endurance of time on this earth, is our compulsion to name our own phenomena after those of the moon, is our awareness of a loftier other-side that's both invisible and greener.

The potato, says the Idaho Potato Commission, is the "aristocrat in burlap," ever giving a "dependable performance." You breathe in its steam, kiss your girlfriend. Like a mosquito confessing in your ear, the Idaho Department of Environmental Quality cloaks its obviousness in a seductive whisper, says, "Air is basic to life."

* * *

SIENESE NUNS LEVITATE, and St. Adolphuses levitate, and Zulu *sangomas* levitate, as do Iranian dervishes, Brazilian mediums, legless lamas, well-hung fakirs, and guys named Padre Pio. We assume that in ascension is ascension to a better place. In Idaho, Better Place is measurable by Color, Quality, and the powdered sugar of Fugitive Dust and Regional Haze.

Our Better Place is in the particulates. Light levitates. Your girlfriend juggles her Spudnuts. They will never touch the earth.

Your uncle has his first heart attack as *New Horizons* passes Saturn. His fourth as it passes Uranus. On July 14, 2015, the estimated date when the vessel will finally reach Pluto, he says he will return "to the atoms of this fucking town," by which you'd like to believe he means that he will be the one to illuminate the street lanterns for the first time again, the residents lining Main Street and clapping in what used to be, given the volcanic earth, one of the darkest nights on the populated planet.

Above us, the moon quakes like the earth. There are Venusquakes and Marsquakes and sunquakes and starquakes. Among other things, astronomers call these "sudden adjustments." In the tent at the Craters of the Moon campground, overlooking Inferno Cone and Echo Crater, the Monoliths and Devil's Orchard, and the cinders and the Cinders, post-coital, you think nothing of the roiling heat of the cooking oil, the way the Spudnut repeats its exhale with each of your subsequent bites, the potato as pillar and idol and fruit fallen to lava, and your girlfriend shudders in her mummy bag and you wonder if she's really that cold, or imitating Andromeda as she shifts, suddenly, in her sleep.

The internal composition of the moon includes a core that's three times smaller than that of the average terrestrial body. It has to beat thrice as hard for the moon to maintain its composure.

You know: there's something about the night at Craters of the Moon that invites the stuff inside you to shift like those mechanical wave machines, tipping its dye-blue liquid to one wall and then another. You wonder if that fluttery stuff can ever escape, ride some shaft of air up and out of your mouth, bury itself, for just a moment, in the spongy crumb of the Spudnut, before rising again from it. You know: you're so far out into the earth here—there's nothing lit like the lamps of Arco. Here, you can't tell where the earth stops and the sky begins; those stars over there could be littering the rocks upon which the astronauts practice. You listen to *The Best of Holly Cole* on a tiny battery-operated radio in the tent, and as she sings her syrupy version of "I Can See Clearly Now," throws it, as if all the way to Pluto, or some other decade-long journey, you think nothing of von Arco, and his radio, the wall your uncle watches while massaging his own chest, the static he listens to on the transistor for messages between the noise, and the stuff inside you shifts. At first, you think, this means you are going to throw up, that you've eaten, if it's possible, too many Spudnuts, until, in zombie-daze, you unzip the canvas, walk to the Windstar, the pitch-dark meat in some celestial sandwich, and retrieve Great-Grandma Sarah's opal ring from the backpack. You know: you want to be a man both aristocratic and dependable. You want to be the kind of intersection at which kids fly from a big green chair.

Here, levitation is just another kind of proposal. Even now, your girlfriend mutters potato names in her sleep—Lady, Amandine, Russet, Snowden, Pink-eye, Megachip, Marcy, Golden, and Idaho, and Idaho as if naming children or dogs, as if calling, from the basement carpet of her dream, to our satellites and projectiles and everything over our heads—even those slippery uncaught trout swimming back-first in a chamber of riverwater both nuclear and pristine, their tongues channeling the last orgasm of Ying-fung. Even now, when you know what you are supposed to do, you can't rule out vomiting, the stars and the potatoes beneath them nudging you in a very precise but appropriately aeriform direction, that, given the physics of this love, feels decidedly *upward*, even as you fall and fall.

Spudnut / Potato Donut

Ingredients

1 cup cooked potatoes pressed thru ricer
¾ cup granulated sugar
¼ cup butter, melted
3 large eggs
⅔ cup buttermilk
2½ cups flour
½ cup cake flour
3 teaspoons baking powder
½ teaspoon soda
½ rounded teaspoon salt
2 teaspoons ground nutmeg

Heat 2 inches oil to 375 degrees in Dutch oven or deep skillet.

Sift/whisk dry ingredients in a small bowl.

In a large bowl whisk the potato with sugar and butter. Whisk in the eggs and buttermilk.

Stir in dry ingredients until dough forms. Dough should be tacky, not dry.

Let rest 5 minutes.

Dump onto heavily floured surface. Cover with light layer of flour. Pat to ½ inch. Cut with floured donut cutter. Just keep dipping cutter in flour, no need to wipe off dough.

Gently shake off excess flour and place donuts on wire rack until dough is used, gently reworking and cutting scraps.

Place in oil, flip when donuts come to surface, fry 1 min, flip, fry another minute. Remove from oil. Let cool.

Shake in cinnamon sugar when cool.

—Kris Wallace, owner, Buy the Dozen Donuts

The Circumventing of the Elk Stew

THE SCAR MAKES a promise that something happened, that something opened up and spilled its guts. In Montana, that something could be the sky, or one's mother, or every insect given in to ice and windshield, or the elk, minus a foreleg, still twitching there beneath the lodgepole pine, unsure as to which portion of itself—now pooling onto the cushion of needles, the arbitrary sheddings of the bark—is the stew meat, the toughest part of its body to chew. At its nostrils, three grasshoppers find their way inside, take the plant dust into their mandibles. They will survive today. They prove this by leaping from the elk's head.

With his shirt open, Uncle dices carrot, celery, onion, rutabaga. And Uncle sings to himself:

Montana, Montana,
Glory of the West
Of all the states from coast to coast,
You're easily the best.
Montana, Montana,
Where skies are always blue,
M-O-N-T-A-N-A,
Montana, I love you . . .

as he whips potatoes with butter and cream, trims the diced elk with a razor blade. He sings of giant blue skies as he takes up a fistful of the silverskin and the fascia, and to you it looks as if he's holding in his hand a collection of eyelids, and the ceiling fan churns his shirt open wider and you see the scar fanned over his chest like a willow, like an antler, like the sung-about expansive Glory of the West, as he foot-pedals the trash can open, empties his hand of the tissue, says nothing of heartbeat, of bypasses, of living-off-the-land, just picks up a wooden spoon, stirs the glaze from the carrots, and says, "Boy. Fuck that song."

You think of valves, chambers cooked until they're soft enough to gum. You want to lend heart to all surgery, butchery. You want to call this sort of procedure *bypassion*, though you know that's not a word. You know: the lodgepole pine is a tall, slender tree. In Kalispell, they call it the *elk leg*.

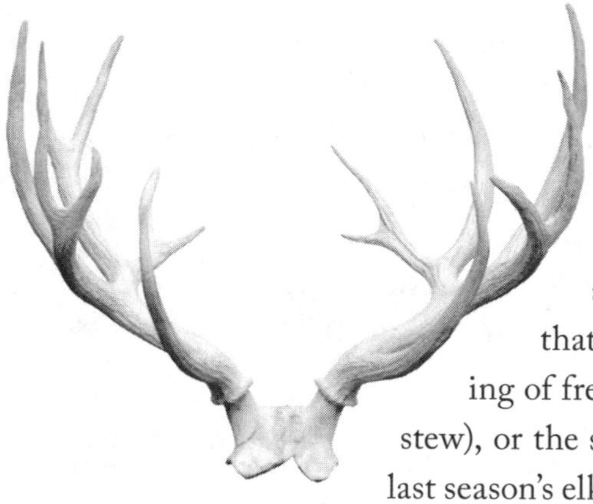

Uncle relights the burner after Montana blows out the flame. He prays for the wildfire to flush the elk from the woods, to heat up the cones of the lodgepole until they loosen their fists, burst open, reseed the yard and the cemetery beyond it. After three whiskeys and an over-salted elk stew, Uncle can't tell if that's a lodgepole or a ponderosa. He says nothing of fresh peas (which he forgot to add tonight to the stew), or the strength of the stock, made from the bones of last season's elk. He scratches at his chest, remembers too late to be careful. In all of this blood, it's tough to tell: which the surgery and which the butchery? If each sustains us, does it matter?

* * *

THE PONDEROSA PINE distinguishes itself from other species by its bark—a cinnamon-brown or orange-yellow, which breaks, from older trees, into flat, irregular plates. According to Montana State University's *Trees and Shrubs in Montana*, the piles of broken bark often found at the bases of the ponderosas have earned the species the nickname the Jigsaw Puzzle Tree.

The mission of the jigsaw is to cut arbitrary curves. Into last years' pelts, with a monogrammed jigsaw, Uncle stenciled his initials, the same abbreviation as the state. It's important to him to claim ownership, to keep his name sewn into things, to keep his things sewn up inside him. Now, from the inside, he beats irregularly, traces his name over his scar with his pinkie. This is also a sort of branding, a revision. You watch his hand dance, arc over his torso as if stirring the steam from the stew. Outside, the tiny sun folds into the fat hip of the sky. These are also arbitrary curves.

Uncle, after three whiskeys and stew, can't tell which headstone belongs to his wife, which to his mother. But he knows: only 22 percent of the energy he derives from the elk meat comes from fat. "Compare that," he says, pledging allegiance, "to 35 percent for beef. And all that goddamn phosphorous, and iron out the ass." He continues muttering to himself, his voice made smaller by the fact that he keeps repeating "milligrams, milligrams."

You stare out the back window, watch the elk thread the cemetery. The earth is buck-toothed with the headstones, and Uncle pours his fourth whiskey, pinches a piece of shin-meat from the cooling stew. He tells you again about birthright, and the nightmare—the horrible jigsaw puzzle, the 1,000 pieces the size of baby teeth. "And when I finally put it together . . . Boy," he says. "It was the image of my mother's mouth, or maybe your aunt's, and this time, last night, I thought I saw a thread of meat under her tongue. Or maybe it was an insect—which is also meat, I guess. That's the thing. Her mouth—the puzzle of it—moved for the first time last night. Laughing or screaming, I couldn't tell. But there was the meat in there, and her tongue was bouncing . . ."

The elk's antlers fall off each March (the process is called *casting*) only to regenerate. The osteoclast cells begin to absorb calcium from the bone, which weakens, becomes grainy and chambered. Once the antlers break away, the remaining stubs of bone begin to bleed, then scab. According to nature photographer and outdoor writer Charles Alsheimer, researchers believe, but can't know, that the bull elk feel no pain when this happens, as they have "when under extreme stress, a high pain threshold and rapid wound healing." Of the casting process, Alsheimer said, tenderly, "I've even seen the bull lick his shed antler."

Here, in regeneration is the beat-beat-beat of a headache. A splitting one. Some hunters call these bald March bulls *flatheads*, a term originally (and derogatorily) lent by white settlers to the

Salish-speaking Kootenai tribe of northern Montana, who were mistakenly believed to have practiced the custom of compressing the skull in infancy by artificial means. The settlers (mistakenly) speculated as to such means, one of which involved placing planed animal bones (including, in some accounts, those of the elk) on the fontanel and then tightly wrapping the head in "bandages" made from the boiled silverskin of the fauna.

* * *

ACCORDING TO *Field & Stream,* "female elk almost always taste better [than males]." According to the Montana Elk Company, LLC, their flavor is "easy and very elegant [in recipes such as] Elk Stroganoff . . . Mature cows average 550–600 pounds. They do not grow antlers. They are very good mothers."

In Kalispell, the county seat of Flathead County, Dr. Roger Brown often receives the best reviews for "scar revision." Uncle doesn't laugh when he talks of trading in the willow on his chest for the ponderosa pine, the one making all those puzzles of the forest floor, and the official state tree of Montana.

* * *

UNCLE HUGS HIMSELF, feels for the flame, the cone, the seed, continues to sing to himself the song he hates:

Tell me of that Treasure State,
Story always new,
Tell of its beauties grand
And its hearts so true.
Mountains of sunset fire . . .

until he forgets the words.

* * *

THE MONTANA STATE flower is the bitterroot, this ethereal pink and yellow darling that grows like a weed in our cemeteries, produces leaves beloved by the elk. One Kootenai story speaks of a mother weeping over her starving children. The benevolent sun changed her tears into fields of bitterroot, the roots of which she boiled and thus sustained her family. Soon, according to state legend, we began fighting the elk to keep this nourishing flower to ourselves. From the war over the bitterroot comes Elk Stew. From Uncle's mouth, weeping.

Ponderosa derives from the same Latin root as *ponderous.* You look out the window with Uncle at all those namesake trees, weighing the earth down. He shouldn't have eaten all that stew. He runs his hand beneath his shirt, over all that pink lattice. He wonders if this scar has yet been revised. If it has become something official of the state. He knows: this heaviness of heart will pass after a good night's sleep, but all that sky will keep pressing down tomorrow.

* * *

OTHER NAMES for the ponderosa pine: Black Jack, Three-Needle, Bull Tree. Revision: remembering what we've forgotten:

Each country has its flow'r;
Each one plays a part,
Each bloom brings a longing hope
To some lonely heart . . .
Montana, Montana . . .

We don't cry over the graves anymore. We sweeten our stew with white honey, black honey, bitter honey, cane. We let this season's elk get away, nurse their young, raise their lot. Scab over. Uncle says, it's a long life. Says something about slow-cooking until tender, and how if you're tender, that means you're dead.

A longing hope, some lonely heart, in another sort of scarring-over: just a few miles south, in the Crazy Mountains, Grasshopper Glacier considers its name—entombed in its ice are countless grasshoppers from various historical plagues. They are not like us. Their blood is green. In their digestive systems, frozen, are bits of carrot, celery, so many plundered crops. Their mouths are full of sensilla. Their hearts don't beat, but chirp.

Elk Stew

Ingredients

3 ounces olive oil
2 pounds Elk stew meat
¼ cup flour
2 pounds carrots
1 pound celery
½ pound red onion
¼ cup garlic
2 cups red wine
1 tablespoon fresh thyme
2 tablespoons fresh sage
¼ cup fresh parsley
4 quarts homemade beef stock
2 tablespoons tomato paste
Salt and pepper to taste

Method

1. Cut the meat and vegetables into 1-inch pieces.

2. Heat half of the oil on high heat in a 2-gallon pot.

3. Dredge the Elk in the flour and brown slightly. Remove from the pot and reserve.

4. Sweat the vegetables in the other half of the oil briefly.

5. Add in all of the other ingredients and lower the heat to medium. Bring to a simmer and transfer to a 350-degree oven until the desired thickness is achieved.

6. Adjust the seasonings with salt and pepper to taste.

* If you wish you can add parboiled potatoes or other soft vegetables such as squash or peas while the stew is still hot and just before serving.

—Chef Zachary Bernheim, The Spur Tavern and Kitchen

At Altitude with the Denver Omelet

AT THIS HEIGHT, we fuse pig to chicken, cow to bitter green fruit . . . just to see what happens—as if elevation itself were responsible for this inquisitiveness. At this height, our ears ringing like church bells, we can tell ourselves that there's something holy about this marriage of ingredients. In Denver, at 5,278 feet, oxygen diminishes, rains downward toward the lower earth, the still-living pigs and chickens, cows and fruit. Air pressure girdles itself, shows off its slim waist and inflated ribcage. Here, I am dizzy, I am tired, I am nauseous. I skipped breakfast this morning, and didn't sleep well last night. Still, I tried to eat the omelet, but the fork was uncooperative.

Uncle also drops his fork. He begins the story about the fluffiest omelet he ever had, about Napoleon commissioning every single egg in the village of Bessières, Haute-Garonne, about the marriage of egg to egg, about giant omelets that have fed entire towns. He wipes his forehead. At this height, he needs his energy.

The ham confused itself with the egg, the yellow cheese with the green pepper. At this elevation, it's better to think of these things in smaller, reasonable doses. Better to break down the larger body into workable parts. To scramble, to dice, to shred. The air in Denver is a thin blanket. The cows shiver, drained of their milk. The hens, having laid, huddle breast to breast. The peppers brown, pock. The pig would shiver if it weren't already dead.

Heat compounds the effects of altitude sickness. Heat allows the egg to gel, to bind the other ingredients. At this elevation, the 40.8 grams of water in the hen's egg evaporate more quickly, and at a lower temperature. Like the origins of the Denver omelet, every breath is in question.

The city is confused, laying claim to ingredients that one can find almost anywhere else. Denver was a gold rush mining town, and Denver was once Montana City, and Denver was once Auraria, which Uncle tells me, is a mispronunciation of *aurora*—a celestial flare-up coupling with opera.

In Colorado is everything deemed ruddy or red-faced, everything carrying the silt of the river, the plaque in our blood. Uncle says, "this closer to God bullshit," speaks instead of the late 1800s, the influx of German, Italian, Spanish, and Chinese workers to Denver, enticed by industry fueled by precious metal. Of the bust—the Silver Crash of 1893—and Denver's backlash against the immigrants, the city pulsing with Red Scare and a booming Ku Klux Klan. "What else is there to do with the leftovers," Uncle says, "than fist them into a mess of scrambled eggs?"

* * *

SOAPY SMITH, famed late-nineteenth-century Denver crime boss, climbed to the top of City Hall's central tower to fend off the state militia with rifles and dynamite. He screamed about *Freedom!* as if he were the tower's bell. Even in a city at this elevation, he had to climb higher if he wanted to live.

Still, today, according to the *New York Times* census maps, Denver remains one of our more racially segregated cities, and certainly our highest one. We can uncover these results, says the *Times*, by "mining the data."

The Pike's Peak Gold Rush began in 1858 in the territories of Kansas and Nebraska. When gold was discovered in the so-called No Man's Land beyond these borders, the Colorado Territory was settled and created in order to encompass this ever-widening greed, and to lend the place in which it thrived a colorful name. Some historians say that it was elevation and the attendant oxygen deprivation that was originally responsible for the *fever* part of *gold fever.*

One of the more successful mines in Old Colorado was called the Liberty Bell and, outside it, the dry goods shop that served its employees was known as the Temple. Some historians believe that the wife of one of these Colorado Territory mining men masked the rankness of rotting eggs by mixing them with the fresher ingredients at hand—surprisingly: cheese, ham, green pepper. Whether it was this dish, or the altitude, or the lungfuls of gold dust that made these pioneers sick, these historians haven't decided.

* * *

ACCORDING TO the U.S. National Library of Medicine, visitors to Denver may, in severe cases, need to be treated with a "breathing machine." According to blogger Macheesmo, if the hungry approach a Denver restaurant after hours, the chef won't just "let them starve." Sometimes, to breathe here, we require an extra apparatus. Starvation requires no such mechanism.

West of Denver, full of omelet, Uncle and I hike the Front Range. The Twin Sisters Peaks. In the clearing, sibling dachshunds tugging-of-war with what at first appears to be a twist of tin foil but as we get closer is, in fact, a chrysalis. Above us, the sky complains. At this elevation, the bell pepper goes so rapidly soft. The bell pepper as tumor. Here, the tumor does the ringing. We crouch to the earth and breathe, as if the reddish dirt here will help, commune with our blood. We can see now: that's not a chrysalis but a pig's ear, a chicken's bone, the nape of the cow, something awful and almost-green. Or: nothing substantial at all but a strange yapping contest over mouthfuls of this skinny air.

> ***Today, up here, nothing rings for us.***

Up here, the body suppresses the digestive system, using that energy to boost cardiopulmonary function, which, by this point, is running on fumes. Uncle bends to the fruits, the peppers named after the thing meant to ring us and ring us until we believe. Ring us until we believe in Liberty or God, in the power of elegy to encapsulate, dirge to heal. This wind is a dirge. This dirge is mile-high. So: the pepper is nothing but a mood, and a mood elevator.

Like our breath, waves dissipate over distance. We look all the way down. Though we are standing on the earth, we are so far from it. Beyond the roofs, there's nothing to stand on, hold us aloft. Like everything else, these mountains rise until they stop. Below us, countless Denver omelets puff like blowfish in the heat of countless ovens. If they cook too long, they'll pop, spilling their cubed ingredients over the slick rink of the nonstick skillet.

"Belief makes for lousy scaffolding," Uncle says. Like the lung and the omelet, it collapses in the face of this gravity.

* * *

CERTAIN SOUND WAVES change the rate of our heartbeats. Like altitude, they shorten our breath; can reduce the amount of oxygen sent to our brains. Sometimes this can be exhilarating, as when we feel pleasantly "buzzed" at a rock concert. When a bell rings, we similarly gulp for air. Though it's hardly noticeable, our brains, in the face of the bell, are receiving a little less oxygen.

Our cultural narratives deem that bells be solemn or celebratory, but always ceremonial. In the ringing is when the angel gets its wings, when the evil spirits are warded off, when it's okay to stop talking and to finally sip from that sacred tea. Biologically, the bell evokes the effects—albeit in a milder fashion—of hiking at altitude. An angel gets its wings when we feel dizzy. When we feel dizzy, the devil retreats to his hive. Reverence emerges when our brains are thirsty for O_2.

When my brain is like this, all of these ingredients get mixed up, thrown together. They need a binding agent to implicate them, and commune.

* * *

THE GONG AS the bell turned inside out and ironed flat. Bells, at elevation, are doubly stupefying. What else can we do but long for the meat of the pig, the milk of the cow, the eggs of the chicken—the byproducts of beasts who low to a lower earth. Perhaps we throw in the bell pepper as a tribute: we are up here where the air is thin, where height commingles with a ringing in the ears. Where our blood slams itself against the wall. This is where we come from.

In Denver, there's a funeral at Trinity United Methodist, the city's first church (constructed in 1865). Traffic rockets past. Even the parking meters look woozy, crooked. Faint. Uncle tells me that the church bell's clapper has corroded, has been removed. "They're waiting for the new one to come in," he tells me. "I wonder where they order these things . . ." As the service ends and the mourners pour into the street, heading, I'd like to think, for the Breakfast King and a meal named for their city, the bell, as if trying to scratch at a phantom limb, rocks back and forth. It's all it can do to remember how it once was. How its body once worked, sounded. I can't tell if this is pathetic or beautiful. We can hear it squeaking in its tower, but today, up here, nothing rings for us.

Denver Omelet

3 farm fresh eggs, diced ham, white onions, and green peppers mixed into eggs.

(At Sam's we serve a "flat top omelet" which is to say that the contents of the eggs and mixings are mixed then poured on the flat top grill, cooked on both sides then folded in thirds.)

The omelet then receives American cheese and is steamed with a lid on top until the cheese is melted.

We have many more creative omelets but the Denver is a standard.

—Alex Armatas, Sam's No. 3 Diner & Bar

SOUTHWEST

Arizona: Sonoran Hot Dog

New Mexico: Christmas

Utah: Funeral Potatoes

Nevada: Nevada Cocktail

Texas: Brisket

Some Theories on the Sonoran Hot Dog

I'VE BEEN THINKING about spice. As vine, as flower. As catastrophe in the mouth. As some kind of biological confusion. The feeling faint, the feeling amorous. The disintegration of the tongue. The window's open. It's unseasonably warm. I had too much red chile sauce on my Sonoran Hot Dog this morning.

This is Arizona and the saguaro cacti are wilting; Arizona, where the hot dog shuns the boiling, demands the *comal*. In this: thirty horrible jokes about how it's a dry heat. Here, in the Sonoran Hot Dog, everything assimilates: *cotija* cheese to onion, red chile to mayonnaise, tomatillo to tomato. This is what we tell ourselves. That the Sonoran Hot Dog can be a blurring of borders. As American as *manzana* pie. As the pig graffiti'd in chili-cheese. I will say nothing of the encased, or defaced. It's too hot to speak about the heat.

I help myself to too much red chile. You blow hot air over my nape. If you blow hot air over my nape, why do I shiver? The Sonoran Hot Dog as all confusions of the body. The saguaro is braced to praise or punish, hands on its hips, hands in the air. My mouth hurts and I want to kiss. It's hot, and I'm in the Sonoran Desert, and there are no yellow leaves here, no red leaves, nothing to remind me of ketchup, mustard, any less spicy sauce. Hydrochlorofluorocarbons dripping from the walls like malarial perspiration, we eat our dressed-up hot dogs in the shuddering, weakening A/C. The spice beats in our temples like a machine gun. In this spice, a confusion of identity. How, when the sun burns us, we feel chills.

In the summer of 2005, Phoenix decided to ice its 120-degree cake with a pair of simultaneously operating serial killers: the Baseline Killer (or Baseline Rapist, so named for his prowling of Baseline Road, who escalated his criminal activity from robbing at gunpoint a Little Caesar's pizzeria to murder, and who disguised himself in a Frankenstein mask, or as a homeless man, and raped his targets before shooting them in the head) and the Serial Sniper (or Serial Shooter—who later turned out to be two men, or *shooters*—who began blowing away dogs and horses before going randomly after human pedestrians, and people on bicycles, a vehicle which, at the time, served as my primary mode of transportation to and from work at Arizona State University). My wife would wring her hands until I came home from talking with other nerds in a cinderblock classroom about the poetics of space. The entire city was gripped in this fist of fear, this cult of anxiety about setting foot outdoors into the be-pricked and be-bulleted heatwave, the communion with Son of Sam a pale conferva indeed.

I can't tell if it's the spice that invades the hot dog, or the hot dog that invades the spice. Can't tell creosote from algae, the plant from the meat. Now, I can't tell if it's the spice that's the flower/vine, or the hot dog. In what part of us it is planted.

Here, the kudzu uses other plants as its grow-base in order to invest the least amount of energy in reaching the sunlight. The kudzu is known as an "invasive exotic." For the light, the plants mask themselves in other plants. Here, too much light yields the burning, and the burning begins with the smoke.

Something outside our window is burning. On your breath, something so much more than the hot dog. You're hot, and confused, so you pull the blanket around you. A spicy mouth craves the sort of water that will not cool it down. The bun as more efficient cooling tool. Your breath is inadequate to uprooting the saguaro.

No one knows where *Sonora* comes from. Its origins are merely theoretical. Some feel it's the Yaqui pronunciation of *señora* (in response to an image of Nuestra Señora de las Angustias, or Our Lady of Anguish). Others feel it's a Spanish mispronunciation of the Yaqui term *sonot*, or *natural water well*. Like Water to Anguish, each theory is inadequate to the other.

In home, in home, in home is ownership. In ownership, an assertion of dominance. Dominance sweet dominance. We dig beneath the toppings to find a sense of home, the home being closest to the bread, the bread being the closest to the mattress—the place where we sleep and snore and spoon. Home. To be home is to be encased. To be encased is to be the hot dog. Hot dog searching for the mattress of the bun, the blanket of toppings. The bun as spice blotter, as the soaking of one thing into another thing. We wipe our awful stains into the purity of the napkin. This is also what we tell ourselves. The home as the familiar hot dog, the familiar as the *familial*, the home as thing we, masked, stole for ourselves. Words like *destiny* and *birthright* confused as whether to be the blotter or the blotted, the costumes or our real faces.

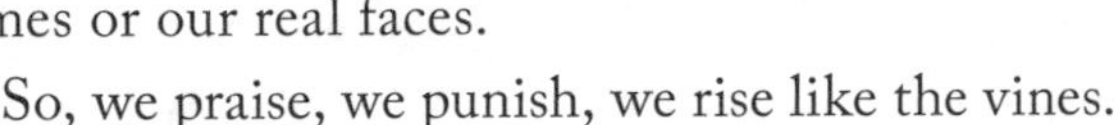

So, we praise, we punish, we rise like the vines.

* * *

At the Phoenix Wells Fargo, I fill out a deposit slip for $165. A young mother in a green neoprene kerchief (Dragonfly Salon is just around the corner) walks up the six steps from Home Mortgage into the bank lobby. She's out of sight of the tellers, and the personal bankers, as usual, are away from their desks. She drags her daughter, seven years old at the most, by the sleeve of the girl's pink windbreaker. The girl's hood is up. It's 114 degrees outside and the little girl's hood is up. Tendrils of blond hair snake from beneath it. By the way they hold their mouths, I can tell they've had an argument—the little girl acting up in front of the loan officer. A pink Mylar foil balloon—a gecko—is tied to the girl's right wrist with a length of scrolled green ribbon. The mother carries an obese white purse, stops at the landing. The tellers can't see her. I sign my deposit slip and stand where I am. The mother opens her purse and removes a wooden pepper mill as long as my forearm. The little girl knows, frowns. She lifts her chin, sticks out her tongue. The mother raises the bottom of the pepper mill to the girl's mouth, completes eight twists and the eight twists of ground pepper collect into a pile on the girl's tongue. The girl closes her mouth, tightens her lips. Is silent. The deposit slip is getting wet in my palm. The ink is beginning to run. Mother and daughter walk to an open teller window, and the mother chats to the teller—a young man in a white shirt, red tie—about the heat. They laugh. The daughter is too short to see the teller. The teller sees the mother standing next to the gecko. The daughter's face becomes more and more red. Her eyes close. She says nothing. Makes no sound. No cough or sneeze. Not a whimper. Her feet begin to dance on the tile as if she has to go to the bathroom. The sleeves of her windbreaker swish so quietly against the torso, as if shushing all of us. The gecko begins to shake. After four minutes, the mother yanks the daughter, still tight-lipped, by the arm. I imagine the pain and its wonderful release. The spitting of the pepper. The scream. They open the door to the sidewalk. Silent. The weather storms inside. Defeats the A/C. They turn the corner.

At my neck, I can't tell if that's your breath or the desert.

Sonoran Hot Dog

The Mission Restaurant Sonoran Kobe Hot Dog Recipe

Ingredients

4 brioche-style hot dog buns
4 Kobe grade beef hot dogs
8 ea. thinly sliced bacon
12 ea. 5-inch bamboo skewers
4 tablespoons clarified butter
2 cups Green Chile Pinto Beans—recipe follows
4 tablespoons rocoto aioli
4 ounces cotija cheese
1 radish—thinly sliced then julienned
4 ounces red onion—small dice
Picked cilantro—to taste

First start by wrapping each hot dog in 1 slice of bacon starting at one end & curving toward the center of the hot dog

Skewer your starting point of your bacon and start the second slice where the first one left off

Skewer your starting point for the second slice of bacon and continue downward until your hot dog is completely wrapped

Skewer the end of the second slice of bacon & deep fry until your bacon is crispy and your hot dog begins to split

Proceed with the remaining 3 hot dogs

In a pan or a griddle, ladle 1 tablespoon clarified butter & warm each side of your hot dog bun—proceed with the remaining 3

Remove the skewers gently from the hot dog & place in the bun

Add a generous portion of green chile pinto beans on top

Drizzle 1 tablespoon of rocoto aioli on each hot dog

Top with 1 ounce of cotija

Garnish with julienned radish, red onion & picked cilantro

Green Chile Pinto Beans

2 cups canned pinto beans—rinsed and dried
¼ cup bacon lardons
2 poblano chiles
¼ cup red onion—small dice
2 cloves of garlic
1 cup chicken stock
1 ounce cold unsalted butter
½ bunch cilantro (finely chopped)
Salt—to taste

Start by charring your poblano over a gas fire stove or in your oven closest to the broiler until the skin becomes black

Remove & place in a bowl covered by a kitchen towel to allow the skin to peel more easily

Once cool enough to handle use the same towel to remove the charred skin & you're left with a beautifully cooked poblano chile

Small dice & set aside

In a cold pot add your bacon & render the fat on medium heat until it is nice & crispy

Remove & strain onto a paper towel

Add onions & garlic to the bacon fat & season with salt

Cook until fragrant—about a minute or 2

Deglaze with chicken stock & with a wooden spoon or spatula scrape the bottom of the pot to get all the nice food into your mixture

Add your pinto beans & bring to a boil, add your diced poblanos & reduce your heat to a low simmer

Simmer for 10–15 minutes to meld all the flavors together

Remove your pan from the heat & stir in your butter to bind the ingredients

Stir in your cilantro, add the bacon back to the pot & season to taste with salt

—*The Mission Restaurant*

It's Always Christmas in New Mexico

BECAUSE WE ARE in love, we live outside. Proof: there's our Coleman Cimarron tent caving in on the bank of the Hondo River. There's our shower curtain of Lawn 'n' Leaf bags roaring in the wind. Because we are indecisive, in-between, we are living here, and since we are living here, we order a lunch that includes as many spicy sauces as possible, and sweat until the forgetting.

After Alaska, New Mexico has the highest percentage of indigenous peoples of the Americas—predominantly Navajo and Pueblo; has the highest percentage of Hispanic people in the U.S.; was part of New Spain's imperial viceroyalty; was part of Mexico; was a U.S. Territory. The state flag is a fusion of the Spanish red and gold and the Zia Pueblo sun symbol. Here, you say, it seems strange to make declarations; and unless our hearts sink below the freezing river water and we are compelled by temperature to scream, exclamations seem to have little place here as well. We know very little but that a single sauce won't do.

In 1996, the New Mexican legislature proposed to make official a state question, which would allow New Mexico the designation of being the first and only U.S. state to possess something official that wasn't a declarative answer. It's easy to swagger when answering.

It's funny, you say, how so much of our official stuff is either linguistically aggressive or linguistically dying. What are we telling ourselves about ourselves? I try to weigh down our shower curtain with sand so the off-the-grid men the next site over can't see you undress, but the wind . . . As salve—maybe even as prayer, I can hear you mutter into the gale, "State reptile: whiptail lizard. State fish:

cutthroat trout . . ." I want to comfort you somehow in an indoorsy sort of way. I want to talk and talk until you see living room and couch and a real nightstand on which to set your earrings. Until thermostat, ceiling.

I want to say, *But the state tie is the bolo. That's something, right? And the state amphibian couldn't be cuter—the spadefoot toad? I mean, c'mon. The state aircraft is the hot air balloon, for fuck's sake.* But you're already on to the tarantula hawk—a spider wasp who hunts fucking tarantulas as food for its babies; the nectarivorous spider wasp that intoxicates itself on fermented fruit before hunting; the wasp whose sting is the second most painful insect sting in the world (described by the Schmidt Pain Index as "blinding, fierce, shockingly electric")—our goddamn state insect, for which I have no answer, much less couch. You're tired of living outside, gathering water into a plastic yellow tub, cleaning the communal pit toilet as if this were our house and not the sort of place to braid love and poverty with a freezing cold river whose beauty is becoming more and more antagonistic.

The state question, "Red or green?"—referring to whether a diner may want red chile sauce or green chile sauce on his or her pork or chicken or beef *adovada* or enchiladas or fry bread—was finally made official in 1999, a full three years after Republican governor Gary Johnson (former door-to-door handyman, Ironman triathlete, Mount Everest summiter, and national record holder for most vetoes ever) proposed it. Most New Mexicans know to order their dishes *red, green,* or *Christmas* (a combination of the two chile sauces) before they are asked. If a diner waits to be asked our official state question, chances are that diner is officially not from New Mexico.

"Hot air balloons are propelled by flame," you say, and we speak again to the stars of the Cerro Grande Fire, about the drought, the uncontrolled burn, about your uncle in Los Alamos who, along with four hundred other families, lost his home; how the fire began, you say, on the rim of the Valles Caldera, and was fueled predominantly by the two-needled piñon pine, which, you assure me, as my mouth fails to cool the double-chile assault, "is our state tree."

Here, we try to make official all of the conflicting things that have tried, and failed, to destroy us. Here, Christmas is the brew that allows all aggressive heat to disappear into other heat, which, you assure me, "is not the same as cancelling each other out." Here, conflict is for the indecisive, "the best," you say, "of both worlds."

Some theorize that the colors green and red associated with Christmas symbolize the colors of our own blood—first inside of us, then excised. Some say that this is meant as a narrative arc—not so much a move toward a climax, but an acknowledgment of an inevitable logic.

"Our sauces are finer and thicker than most," says our state legislature, and we wonder too—as the Hondo River argues with itself, as the off-the-grid men shoot bullets into the piñons—if *fine* and *thick* are not just another broken stab at homogeneity.

We hug each other in our sleeping bags. We tell ourselves any narrative that will allow us sleep. In the Sangre de Cristo Mountains, the greater roadrunner flees the black bear. Around our tent, the yucca flowers open like spectral mouths, gossiping, as if asking questions or providing answers.

Your uncle, also newly homeless, fled to the Hatch Valley and worked for a season on a chile farm, told us that the chiles are the same, that the green becomes red when it ripens. He told us that he would stare at the wildfire burns on his arms, his hands, his chest, and as he would pick chiles, he would consider this. Here, in the burn, is a ripening. Here, if we order our dishes *Christmas*, we can ripen twice as fast.

The Sandia hairstreak butterfly, the official state butterfly of New Mexico, is rare and tailless, and green and gold, frolics among bear grass and is more sensitive to warmth than other butterflies, is named, according to *Orion* magazine, for its "zippy flight." We are nearly asleep now, until you remind me, "and it blends perfectly with its larval host." Here, even a rare beauty is parasitic.

One of the reasons for its small population is that the caterpillars of the Sandia hairstreak are monophagous, meaning that they feed only on one plant—the flowers and fruit of the Texas sacahuiste, which itself is able to adapt to our state (the sole climate in which it can now "thrive") by self-desiccating its own tissues, which means, you say, that in nature, loyalty is often self-destructive. The Hondo River screams and screams and never loses its voice.

According to the New Mexico legislature: "children love butterflies, and naming a New Mexico butterfly would bring joy to New Mexico's children . . . the Sandia Hairstreak symbolizes the ability of New Mexican residents to thrive year-round in a semiarid climate where different years bring floods and droughts and where the terrain is beautiful but rugged."

At White Sands, a rocket research group detonates the first atomic bomb. Less than fifty miles away, the children of Las Cruces fall in slack love on yellow inner tubes, growing their cancers and undiagnosables. They don't notice the Sandia hairstreaks raining dead in the desert, or recognize the boiling point of their own joy.

We are getting to that age when homelessness is no longer an adventure. We speak most truthfully when our tongues are burning. In Las Cruces, City of the Crosses, in 1990, in the Las Cruces Bowl, on the morning of February 10, two men shot seven people execution style (including four children—the youngest of whom was two) in what became known as the Las Cruces Bowling Alley Massacre. The case remains unsolved and, so far, we have not named any official state thing after this.

February 10 is the date of three important Christian feast days, including that of St. Scholastica—patron saint of convulsive children and rain—who, after a meal of "spicy supper," wished to continue a conversation about the parameters of holiness with her brother, Benedict of Nursia. When he insisted on leaving to return home, she invoked a terrible storm which prevented her brother from returning to his monastery, rendering him homeless and at the mercy of his sister's conversation, which lasted through the night. Three days later, Benedict found his sister mysteriously dead with white doves flying from her mouth, which he interpreted (or so he said) as her ascension to heaven.

Here, so many things named for fathers, sons, ghosts. We began the Atomic Age in the Jornada del Muerto Desert—the Desert Route of the Dead Man. We had the audacity to name the first detonation of a nuclear device *Trinity*. Here, Christmas everywhere, always. Here, the lizard decapitates its prey with its whiptail.

The off-the-grid men's guns are enchantingly empty. Tomorrow, they will go back to work at Subway and save up for the reloading. They will tack the Subway napkins to the wood plank over the pit toilet, believing they are doing their part. In the tent, in spite of the sleeping bag, you are worried, and I am worried, and tomorrow we will eat our eggs Christmas style, and now something inside shrivels, and the stars pierce the river and the river is screaming, and out there: execution, and maybe we are dreaming that this is really our home for good.

Green and Red Chile Sauces

New Mexico Green Chile Sauce
Yield: about 4 cups

Butter, oil, or lard: 2 tablespoons
NM Hatch green chile: 2½ cups, diced
Oregano: 2 pinches
Garlic: 3 cloves, minced
Red bell pepper: ½ cup, diced
Onion: 1½ cups, diced
Water or chicken stock: 3 cups
Meat (optional): 1½ cups ground beef
Salt (to taste)

In a saucepan, cook onion for 5 minutes over medium heat in the butter (oil, or lard). Add the remaining ingredients and simmer over medium-low heat for one hour.

New Mexico Red Chile Sauce
Yield: about 4 cups

Butter, oil, or lard: 2 tablespoons
NM dried red chile pods: about 30, stems, ribs, and seeds removed

Garlic: 3 cloves, minced
Oregano: 2 pinches
Cumin: 2 pinches
Black pepper (to taste)
Salt (to taste)
Water, beef or chicken stock: 3 cups
Meat (optional): 1½ cups ground beef or pork cubes
Sugar or honey (to taste)

Toast the chiles in a dry skillet over medium-high heat, until they smoke, but don't burn. Move the chiles to a saucepan and pour water (or stock) over them and let reconstitute for 30 minutes. Then, bring the chiles and soaking liquid to a simmer, and puree the chiles into the liquid using an immersion blender. In a separate saucepan, cook the garlic and meat (if using) in the butter (or oil or lard) for 5–10 minutes over medium heat until the meat is cooked. Add the pureed chiles and remaining ingredients (with the exception of the sugar or honey), and simmer over medium-low heat for 30 minutes. Remove saucepan from the heat, and add the sugar or honey—just a small amount.

—Antonio Matus, chef and owner, Antonio's: A Taste of Mexico

The Subservient Prophesy in the Funeral Potatoes

UTAH, MY FATHER never learned how to tell you to fuck off, even after you smashed his headlights and told the church he was an Algerian. It was his beard and moustache—I've never seen him without facial hair. Utah knows this; knows that I'll never fall asleep holding in my head an accurate picture of the intimacy of his chin. I can only imagine it sort of round, a smashed circle, some celestial body in miniature, the moisture sucked out of it by all this salt, yet another dry plain that has the audacity to call itself a lake.

And my father's chin is that whirling kiln in the basement labs of Tooele as they suck out the poison from chemical weapons named Sarin and Mustard, named G-series (after the German scientists who first synthesized them) and V-Series (V for Venomous, for Viscous, for Victory), named *Newcomer* in Russian.

Because this is Utah, and because our state's name insists that we are People of the Mountains, this means that we can rise above even our most victorious of poisons. In shredding the mundane into wet, workable strings like some awful facial hair; in heaping (as we like to say) *unto* the most mundane of our tubers mounds of cheddar, onions, cream soup mix (we prefer cream of mushroom, or cream of chicken. If both are sold out—if too many people have died—cream of celery will do), and sour cream and butter and corn flakes. Here, we call this side dish Funeral Potatoes. In this way, we can make of my father's inevitable death another thing to sustain us. A parable. A potluck.

The Relief Society, a Utah women's organization and official auxiliary of the Church of Jesus Christ of Latter-Day Saints, urges (to the point of commanding) the Utah bereaved to always include Funeral Potatoes on the post-burial buffet table as a matter of "tradition." In this way, oxymoronically, we can elevate the potato by weighing it down; facilitate ascension by burial.

In making the potato so heavy and fattening, we can laugh in the face of death, make something viscous of our fears in order to master them. The viscous things run through us that much more slowly. Because of Funeral Potatoes, many of us can work to dispose of rockets and land mines stuffed with the sort of poison that can diffuse throughout our bodies so quickly, can kill us on contact. We must put up barriers, allow the everyday to smother the extraordinary, to steel our as yet ungassed nerves.

Here, at the Church's urging, death is engaged family style. Motto of the Relief Society: *Charity Never Faileth*, which is Charity Never Fails pressed through a mouthful of Funeral Potatoes. Synonyms for *auxiliary*: *midwife, appendage, protuberance, subservient.*

* * *

In 2012, the Mormon Church finally apologized for their posthumous baptisms of countless dead Jewish bodies, having worked from a mysterious list that included famed Holocaust survivors like advocate Simon Wiesenthal and still-living author Elie Wiesel. The list was apparently created by a shadowy auxiliary Church group responsible for conducting this sort of genealogical research. According to this list, bodies were exhumed and bodies were smuggled, then washed in the same sort of salty Utah lakewater into which trace elements of G-series gases have leached.

According to a February 14, 2012, article in the Yiddish newspaper *Viz Iz Neias?*, those performing the posthumous baptisms "believe they are providing a service to their church, [allowing] the deceased persons to receive the Gospel in the afterlife." I wonder if my father is at risk. If he has to be clean-shaven in order to receive. If there will be Funeral Potatoes served at his baptism-by-proxy. If, when stabbed with a fork, the steam will snake from beneath the corn-flake crust like the ghost of his own father, or his father's father, or his father's father's father.

Synonyms for *relief*: *restfulness, succor, softening, deliverance.* One may wonder, as I wonder, how exactly the Mormon Church amassed the power and networking skills necessary to procure all these dead Jews. Whom did they pay off? How did they locate the corpses? How, and to where, were the corpses shipped? Who packed them? Who received them? Who dug them up?

One may wonder, as I wonder, about the most mundane of the details. The paperwork: the affidavits, permits, stamps, clearances, memos. The notary, and the notary's glasses. The offices with their filing cabinets and secretaries and water coolers and aquariums full of yellow fish. The to-do lists tacked to the bulletin boards. The lighting: by lamp or by fluorescent? The air freshener: vanilla or pine?

One may imagine, as I imagine, some minimum-wage gravedigger doing as he was told, even his manager not privy to the whole story. He is sweating, and his hands, even in the thick gloves, start to bleed. He breathes and he digs. A simple stone carved with the words *beloved* and *blessed* and *missed* and *dear* begins to lean a bit to the left. He does not question the Hebrew letters. Does not know that a few of them mean *God.*

He finishes, wraps the bones in damp cheesecloth for the shipping, clocks out, drives home to no radio, windows down, to a house full of family, or a house full of no one, eats a dinner of simple potatoes about which there is nothing even remotely funereal.

* * *

Some say the corn flakes act as a "lid" to the potatoes, trapping their heat. I try not to think of the coffin here, of the earth as the thing that we both ride atop, and are suspended within.

* * *

During the era of the killing fields, the Cambodian death squadron compiled the names of its targets on what became known as the Must Smash List.

* * *

"We have a saying for everything that goes wrong around here," says Jim Silver, president of Salt Lake City's Saltair Resort (whose mission is to provide an alternative to the "spiritually bleak" resorts of the area, a place that a young courting Mormon couple could frequent without gossip). "We blame it on the lake effect."

We are mountain people, salt people, poison gas people. At high elevation, we still sweat trace amounts. We still need our beards not just for religious purposes, but for warmth. Look at all of those mundane potatoes, surviving beneath the snow. We dig them up, wash their dirt from their skins. We shed and we shred, we peel and boil, we heap with yellow cheese. We deliver. We soften. We let them rest, so they can congeal before we eat them with mournful mouths.

According to the *New York Times*, "the snow-clotted mountains that tower around Salt Lake give this city a mythic quality during winter. But lately, the Wasatch Front, the corridor of cities and towns where most Utahans live, has acquired a reputation for a less enviable attribute: bad air . . . intermittent warm high-pressure systems trap the cold air, creating the effect of a lid on a soup bowl and keeping dirty air from car emissions and other pollutants from escaping."

In celebration of the 2002 Winter Olympics in Salt Lake City, our city mothers and fathers, deliverers and relievers and genealogical researchers, created a series of over one hundred commemorative souvenir lapel pins, including those bearing the logos of their sponsors, Coca-Cola and Certified Angus Beef, as well as those highlighting Utah's famed culinary offerings, including, of course, a Funeral Potatoes pin, a Mormon Muffin pin, and one for something called Widow's Milk.

* * *

DURING THE SALEM witch trials, the local government compiled the names of its targets on what became known as the Gallows Hill List.

* * *

I IMAGINE so many Olympic skiers wearing the sloppy and damn near indistinguishable Funeral Potatoes pin on their jacket breasts, wiping out during practice, their heavy bodies calling up great plumes of snow. I imagine so many tiny pieces of brass or gold plating, stylized versions of cheddar cheese and sour cream and corn flakes no larger than a thumbnail losing themselves to their hosts' falls, disappearing into the ice that, at this elevation, never thaws. If we never thaw, we are never not being baptized.

* * *

On July 3, 1940, the British Navy compiled the names of its French Algerian targets at Mers-el-Kébir on what became known as the Operation Catapult List.

* * *

Mouth slick, in part, with cream of this or cream of that, I'll never fall asleep without reciting, as litany, some of Utah's best roadside attractions. Still, all the scrap metal fossils and World's Largest Watermelons can't make him remember me. Can't make me understand the code written on his chin. Here, or in his dreams, I tell myself, there's a special room for mine disasters, kilns that spin the poison from rocket into river. And the lake is great and salty. And the Virgin Mary's in a willow stump.

* * *

During the Stalinist era, Russian officials compiled the names of their targets on what became known as the Great Purge.

* * *

According to Ann Cannon's article in the *Deseret News*:

> *I wanted to be different. Original. Memorable. Well! I'll never forget the disappointed looks on the faces of the family when we did NOT break out the funeral potatoes. These people had had a long hard day burying their grandmother, and they were definitely in the mood for some comfort on the food front—the kind of comfort only a mouthful of warm cheesy potatoes can provide. And there I was, dishing up arty Food Network fare. I learned an important lesson that day: Innovation is fine—just not when it comes to certain meals.*

The potato and the funeral: which the sealant and which the stain? Which out-innovates the other? Here, the stars gush their art and we receive it tight-lipped, our needles dead or dying, our mouths dropping open if only to express surprise in the face of poison, delight in the face of potato casserole, and we reserve our innovation for the creative rinsing of the bodies of the others. We dig them up and we prepare our onions, we peel and we dice and we mash, and we open our tin cans and our plastic tubs and we rinse.

* * *

IN 1970S' Afghanistan, the then Communist government compiled the names of its targets on what became known as the List of the Unknowns.

* * *

WATER IS ONLY supposed to clean us. We're not supposed to season our potatoes with the leavings of a lake.

"Look at me, please look at me," my father says. But that's all he says.

"Please pay attention," Ann Cannon says:

Here's my Last Will and Testament involving potatoes. I hereby want my potatoes to be of the hashed variety. While hash browns made from scratch taste best, the time spent peeling, boiling and shredding virgin tubers doesn't really justify the amount of work involved. So please feel free to start with bags of frozen shredded potatoes. I'm cool with that.

Also, please use plain cream of chicken soup. Don't use the herbed kind or the kind with allegedly roasted garlic. And please do NOT use the Healthy Request variety. Seriously. What's the point? Now about the onions. Yes, please. I want lots. Green are best. As for the cheese, make it a straight-forward, honest cheddar. Finally, don't get fancy with the topping. Crushed cornflakes drenched with butter will do the trick.

The trick: My father tells me he believed in Bigfoot, saved the paper cones from his cotton candy, built from them a model of a pipe organ in the living room. He played ragtime. He *believed.* Still, it sounded like paper. Mom called him genius. He called Mom a mermaid. Mom said his brains were like mashed potatoes. Sometimes, she said, they were frozen.

Here, the virgin tubers keep their legs crossed. It's easier if your body is buried beneath toppings.

* * *

DURING THE HOLOCAUST, the Nazis compiled the names of their targets in various documents, one of which was known as the Black Book. Another was referred to as the Rainbow List.

* * *

"GENEALOGY HAS to do with commitment," says Salt Lake City Genealogical Library director David Mayfield, "to families. We believe that families can continue beyond the grave into eternity, that those who have gone before can be sealed to their families."

From parts of my father's body, others will devise their Last Wills . . .

* * *

DURING THE AZTEC Empire, officials compiled the names of those to be sacrificed on what became known as the List of Flowers. The bodies of the sacrificed were also called Flowers.

* * *

"OBVIOUSLY," SAYS Bryce Bird, director of Utah's Division of Air Quality, "this is not acceptable."

A wedding ring doesn't sink into the great salt flats, but ossifies—like the fish swimming in our bad water. If we ossify, we are easily shreddable. Our bodies will be the toppings for the sorts of potatoes our descendants will use to commemorate our beautiful flowery mountain deaths. And the corn flakes seal themselves to the potato, and all the widows weep while eating.

Here, the kilns perform a cleansing, a reversal. Our poisons are virgins again. "It's up to you," my father says, and I'm not sure if he's talking to me, or to his last potato casserole, now cooling on the plate, predicting its quick (just a few weeks now . . .) evolution to Funeral.

List of things to take with me to the funeral, front passenger seat of the car: Hanukkah candles, blue and white; my grandfather's Bowie knife, his stations listed in handwritten blue ink on the lambskin sheath—Newport News, Oran Algeria, Toulon France, Marseille France, Mers-el-Kébir, New York; my father's blue *CWC* Utah Crusher Wrestling Club T-shirt, the old sweat stains hanging like chandeliers at the armpits; flowers; a red pillowcase inscribed with "Candy Heart"; a decoder wheel with Aquaman on it; his bifocals.

This is salt. It makes our mouths happy, but nothing sails here. It's afterward. I have a bellyful of tubers. The Relief Society compelled us . . . I'm driving with the windows down, west on I-80 from Tooele to the Bonneville Salt Flats. On the radio, a Salt Lake City tour guide named Inalee Herbert says, "One of the values of our church is the belief that we should not take things into our body that are harmful to us. We've known this all along." Now, only eternity, and the freshly dead. I have a few things I want to throw slowly out the window. These are the things I don't want to sink.

Funeral Potatoes

Barbara's Funeral (Party) Potatoes
Yield: 12 servings

Ingredients
¼ cup butter, melted
1 onion, peeled and quartered
1 can cream of mushroom soup
1 tablespoon chicken base
1 pint (16 ounces) sour cream
¼ cup milk
½ teaspoon salt
½ teaspoon pepper
2 tablespoons dried parsley

2 packages (20 ounce) fresh shredded hash brown potatoes
2 cups cheddar cheese, grated

Topping
1 cup panko bread crumbs
⅓ cup crushed potato chips
2 tablespoons butter, melted

Directions

Preheat oven to 350 degrees. Spray a 9 x 13 pan with nonstick cooking spray.

In a blender, pulse butter, onion, cream of mushroom soup, and chicken base several times to chop onion. Add sour cream, milk, salt and pepper, and pulse just until almost smooth. Stir in dried parsley.

In a very large bowl, combine the hash browns and cheddar cheese. Add the cream sauce and stir until it's well combined. Pour into 9 x 13 pan and smooth the top.

Prepare topping: Mix panko crumbs, potato chips, and melted butter in a Ziploc bag until well combined. Sprinkle evenly over the top of the casserole.

Bake uncovered for 1 hour until the sauce is bubbling and the topping is golden brown.

—Barbara Schieving

NEVADA

The Nevada Cocktail and the Meadows of Auschwitz

IN THE LATE 1930S, Jewish gangsters Bugsy Siegel and Meyer Lansky began investigating Las Vegas, mining the desert for "legitimate" business opportunities. Legend has it that, in 1946, when Siegel and Lansky, with black-market building materials and money laundered through Mormon-owned banks, built the Flamingo Hotel and Casino, Siegel, a man with a taste for strong acidic drinks, called for a celebratory concoction of rum, grapefruit and lime juices, a dash of bitters, and the sort of sugar we now categorize as *superfine.* Siegel's lieutenants followed suit, and soon the beverage became known as the Nevada Cocktail, the sweet-sour intoxicant that, in claiming the name of our state, also means the Snow-Covered Cocktail, which confuses my cousin Bonnie as she listens to the window A/C unit hiccup and wheeze, as she adds with arthritic fingers an ice cube to her cocktail, as she closes her eyes, as she sweats and sweats and remembers too much.

Cousin Bonnie says that to press a grapefruit of its juice is to take a gamble. She points to her citrus-burned eye, its wildness, the burst vessels mapped through the white in what she describes as *mice pussies in the snow.* She laughs, then asks why she's laughing. She forgets things easily these days. She mutters something about overparenting, but we can't make it out. Outside, the desert throws the smallest bits of itself against the house, the windows that haven't been cleaned in years. Through the film of the pane, we can see Las Vegas begin to turn itself on. We can hear it. Bonnie sits down on the couch, drains her third Nevada Cocktail from a plastic Flintstones cup.

According to the Center for Occupational Health and Safety, "Children are exposed to the most obvious form of citric acid from citrus fruits including oranges, grapefruits, and lemons that they are served at school or are encouraged to eat at home. It is easy for the citrus juices to squirt into a child's eye when he or she is peeling or separating the fruit. [We have] documented incidences where individuals have suffered permanent eye injury after their eyes were exposed to citric acid."

As Siegel and Lansky, in 1945, scoped out the future site of the Flamingo, and muttered things like "We only kill each other," and "Don't worry, don't worry . . . ," the Soviet Army liberated Auschwitz and, thereby, Cousin Bonnie. With droppers, she says, the Nazis would bathe her eyes with grapefruit juice, and, "Oh!" she says, "the constellations!" It was a better fate for her eyes, she says, than to be scooped out with a thumb. With her thumb, she stirs her fourth Nevada Cocktail, dares the grapefruit juice to do something about it.

Flamingo derives from the Greek meaning *purple wing*, which further means that even in ancient Greece we confused one color for another. We are a species of bad eyes.

* * *

BONNIE ROARS and the desert tries to get inside. Her wrinkled hands shake. In Cactus Springs, a seventy-six-year-old retired restaurant owner rubs her eyes, sips the state's cocktail, admits, "I tell you, I'd rather run into a mountain lion than a thief from Las Vegas. Your chances are better."

In 1947, two years after the liberation of Auschwitz and one year after the Flamingo's construction, Bugsy Siegel's head was torn apart by the bullets of a .30-caliber M1 carbine, the standard firearm of the U.S. military during World War II. He was memorialized at the Bialystoker Synagogue. Bonnie holds the spent grapefruit half to her face. We remember that she once told us how, in the concentration camp, she would press her face to the cinderblock wall, the pores of it, searching for any kind of safer air.

Into the grapefruit, the remaining pulp hanging in wet strings against her lips, she mutters, to no one in particular, the mourner's Kaddish. Funny, how our state is named for snow, and this city is named for meadows that we can resurrect only in dream. The nightmare, or the waking to this desert bedroom, this asthmatic ceiling fan torturing itself to whine in circles: which the sour, which the superfine?

Funny: before it became known as the site of the concentration camp, the land around Auschwitz was known for unusually beautiful oak trees, birch, chestnut, poplar. Nazi soldiers forced prisoners to plant additional fruit trees—typically pear, apple, and cherry—in order to conceal the gas chambers, mass graves, crematoria pyres. Bonnie remembers the pine forests in the distance, the fields of tall grass and the wind in them. Funny, how *Nevada* means *coffined in snow*. Funny, how *Birkenau* means *birch meadow*.

Sweet, sour, alcoholic, Wayne Newton says, "Vegas has taken a bum rap over the years. If you're sleazy and looking for that, you'll find it. We also have more churches per capita than any city in the United States!"

Funny, how our dead can't mourn us; how, per capita, we're nothing in the face of them. In December, in celebration, the Nazi soldiers carried Christmas trees into Auschwitz, and, in celebration, had their prisoners decorate them with tinsel, ornaments, stars.

Some churches in Las Vegas: New Morning Star, Greater Calvary, Oasis, Shadow Hills, New Revelation, Sunrise, Paradise, Birchman Baptist, Victory, Prince of Peace, Desert Storm.

The grapefruit, upon its discovery, was thought to be the original forbidden fruit of Paradise from which all human immorality descended.

* * *

HERE, THE GRAPEFRUIT, halved, is just another kind of sick eye, open wide to dream and ambition, to businesses named after big pink birds who have no place here, to the bullet that wants to blind it. Bonnie roars, but thinks she's only breathing. Here, the grapefruit wrung out is as innocent as hair, or the hair of a dead sister, or the hair of the dead sister going bright in the orange sparking stars of the crematorium. So, we add superfine sugar, and think not anymore of her beautiful thin hair, but only of the sweetness necessary to temper the acid, and the alcohol jabbing at our throats with the butt of its gun.

Adolf Gawalewicz, Auschwitz survivor, remembers, "A tree

can be seen by the entrance to the camp, to the right of the gate, inscribed 'Arbeit macht frei.' This is no ordinary tree! Beneath it stood the tormented parents and siblings of a prisoner who had escaped. Here, also, stood those whose escape attempts had failed. They stood with their skin ripped by the claws of the dogs, holding a sign reading 'Hurra! Ich bin wieder da!' [Hurrah, I'm back!] as a warning to the labor details returning from work."

According to the Ministry of Forests, "At present, the conservation of vegetation at the [Auschwitz–Birkenau State] Museum is comprehensive and includes care for grassy surfaces and the trees, as well as the use of herbicides for weed control."

Bonnie puts down her glass, works her hands, squeezes in the air invisible grapefruits, branches, the shoulders of a man with a gun who will knock her back to the ground. What is the value of this drink, the sand in our teeth, the rum and sand, rum and sand, proof that we're still capable of taking in air? We breathe with Bonnie and somewhere inside of us, the separating of the fruit.

In the meadows, so many bodies—the stacks, the piles, the snow-covered mountains—can no longer contemplate *value* as they fertilize some of the world's most beautiful birches, and the flies buzz like the alarm the world sleeps through.

Says Victor Stoffer, casino supervisor, "You see so much money that you lose what money is worth. It just doesn't mean anything to you."

* * *

VIRGINIA WOOLF wrote in her her diary in 1915, "I do not like the Jewish voice; I do not like the Jewish laugh." Lyndall Gordon, in her book *Virginia Woolf: A Writer's Life*, chalks up such statements to fluctuations in Woolf's "sanity." "There is a recurring pattern to her bouts of 'madness,'" Gordon writes. "The diary entries from 1915 and 1941 show, just before collapse, a phase of studied mundaneness, preceded by—and sometimes interspersed with—a Swiftian hatred of the human race . . . There was no attempt to control the irrational malice."

"Bum rap," says Wayne Newton. "Sleazy," he says, and "churches." Bonnie's not laughing. That's because she's drinking another Nevada Cocktail.

Virginia Woolf wrote, in a 1930 letter to her friend the composer Ethel Smyth, of her Jewish husband, Leonard, and his family: "How I hated marrying a Jew—how I hated their nasal voices, and their oriental jewellery, and their noses and their wattles." When Hitler later blacklisted her, she also began indicting Fascism.

"Her genius does no one any good, has no social force or perspective, and—like most literature—is not needed: It is the intolerant genius of riddle," Cynthia Ozick writes of Woolf in the October 2, 1977, *New York Times* article "The Loose, Drifting Material of Life,"

> *But she is also malicious in the way of the class she was born into. She calls the common people "animals," "a tepid mass of flesh scarcely organized into human life." Unlike the majority of her class, she mocked the war; but the celebrations that mark its end she ridicules as "a servant's peace." Of famine following massacre: "I laughed to myself over the quantities of Armenians. How can one mind whether they number 4,000 or 4,000,000? The feat is beyond me." She has no piety or patriotism, but retains the Christian bias of the one, and the Imperial bias of the other.*

Bonnie wonders if, like the flamingo, we are paraphyletic—if we too belong to a group descended from a last common ancestor, or if this is all just another sort of bias, riddle. She says, "Fuck Adam, fuck Eve." Her body creaks and cracks and gurgles on the couch. On the cushions, there's plenty of space for her body. Luckily, we are not long-legged. The desert at the window whispers so loudly on the glass, it sounds like screaming.

In the 1940s, Nevada prison officials chose a new strain of lethal gas that they would use in capital punishment executions. According to Scott Christianson, author of *The Last Gasp: The Rise and Fall of the American Gas Chamber*, "The newest and most potent form of cyanide gas in the United States came from Germany. The product was called Zyklon. Nevada's shiny new gas chamber was inaugurated on Bob White, who had been condemned for killing a fellow gambler at Elko. In the face of new refinements in gas-chamber design and fumigation, other states also began to consider switching to gas," and soon, we all began executing our own prisoners with the efficiency of the Third Reich.

Bonnie wonders about the intersection of *solve* and *dissolve*, the melting down of air. This living room is supersaturated and, therefore, both heroic and drowning.

Somebody's grandfather—like my grandfather—helped to liberate the camps, then returned to Nevada with a marketable idea for our prisons. Not even another Nevada Cocktail can solve all of the Zyklon of Auschwitz. The desert knows, near the prison up the road, still, so many old tanks of it, shoring up or breaking down in the heat. The desert as storage for toxicity. The martini glass as sugar-coated, as a reminder of all things that incompletely dissolve.

The Nevada Cocktail

Recipe for the Nevada cocktail:

1½ ounces Bacardi rum
2 ounces fresh grapefruit
1 large basil leaf
½ ounce fresh lime juice
Splash tonic water
Splash simple syrup
2 dashes sea salt
Topped with Amaro Averna

Garnish with grapefruit slice and basil top.

Tear basil leaf into pieces and place in glass muddle slightly add remaining ingredients give a slight shake with a Boston shaker top with Amaro Averna garnish serve.

—*The Cin Cin, Eldorado Casino*

TEXAS

And Texas Brisket Is Again Usurped by Tissue We Can Call Only Connective

ON THIS NIGHT, which is different from all other nights—as evidenced by the bitter herbs on our plates, the cute little bowls of saltwater that sit like awful Ashkenazi zeros at the tines of our forks—we try to empathize with the displaced cow, the cow ripped from pasturage, separated from its own muscle. Since this is a Texas seder, we try to not to let the braising broth ruin the smoke in our brisket, try to determine which cooking method is more oppressive—an immersion in a wet heat or a dry one, our faces blinded by mesquite smoke, or diverted by the discs of sloppy carrot, tumbling end over end, hypnotically, in the flood.

Since this is Texas, we remain huge, and hugely indecisive. Which should flavor the brisket most: the carrot or the smoke? You ask such ancillary questions, even as you clean your mouth with the herbs, the saltwater, the small drop of Manischewitz Extra Heavy Malaga wine that Uncle, in spite of your being twelve years old, pours into your crystal goblet, the purple Concord light scattered over the ceiling like an old upstairs murder, muttering beneath the brim of his ten-gallon (that he refuses to remove at the table), "Boychik, if you throw up tonight, you can blame Exodus."

Because our seder plates are filled with barely-edibles, and lamb shank bones stripped of their meat, because we are supposed to remind ourselves of our slavery and our escape therefrom, and because we are part of the diaspora, and because, as a population, we comprise 0.5 percent of the total of our most zaftig of the continental states, pinpricking ecoregions named Panhandle Plains, Rolling Plains, High Plains, and Hill, named Blackland, named Gulf Coast, named Llano Uplift, and Trans-Pecos, we must ground ourselves and coalesce, for tonight at least, via the cut of beef that reminds Uncle of the excised parts of Aunt, bears tissue we can call only connective, muscles that teeter between *superficial* and *deep*.

Because this is Texas, our seder plates are etched with blue longhorns. Again, the desert, and again we are confused as whether to sink ourselves in or to float above it all, to smoke or to braise. In a lack of regional commitment is the easier escape.

The etymology of the word *Pecos* is often debated and has been open to various translations. Here, *Pecos* means *cowboy* and *Indian*, and *gunfight*, and *rodeo*, *folktale*, *outlaw*, *hamlet*, means *river*, means *cantaloupe*. In contemporary Texas, *to pecos* something is to steal it. In late-nineteenth-century Texas, *to pecos* meant *to murder*. If we live in the Trans-Pecos, and hold our seders here, we can sip our wine safely, beyond thievery and massacre, reinvent our histories, on an opposite bank, with a wet heap of meat.

* * *

You are twelve, and there are no pretty girls at this seder. You've developed a taste for the cheerleaders who wear white cowgirl boots at recess, kick them off into the wind and dust as they stretch themselves ever higher, ever forward on the swing sets, and you watch their knees as their shorts creep up as they rocket down slides named Tornado. You try to commune with the shank bone on your plate, its virility trumping the elders' stories of hunger and forced labor, the sort of excision that overlaps the wandering.

Months earlier, you remember watching Aunt change her clothes, her bedroom door left open, gape-mouthed, as if it couldn't believe its eyes. You dip your bitter herbs in the saltwater, the conflicted brisket humping the *latus rectum* of the stockpot, and sing songs about Joseph's brothers dipping his tunic into a cup of blood, and you remember her ultra-skinny and topless and barefoot, a red shawl draped over her shoulders, a purple skirt dropping over her legs. Her hair then was dark brown and stick-straight, just beginning to go patchy. You watched the one small breast—the left one—and the long shadow it cast over her ribs as she bent to put on her stockings. And then: the jagged scar where the right one used to be—as if this portion of her had been excised with a can opener; as if her torso's one eye was sewn shut; as if her entire body was winking—opened up like a mouth and sang of affliction smoked until crusty, braised until soft; sang country and western, sang *Deep in the Heart!* and *Don't Mess!* and *See you in Jerusalem again!* the cavity spewing white butterflies into the room as Uncle swatted them from his ears, trying to listen to everything her body was trying to tell him.

According to *Texas Monthly*, "The seeker of Brisket Truth must first embrace mental discipline, immersing himself in the craft of minding the meat. Second, the seeker must practice physical discipline, to be capable of wielding and slicing a twelve-pound brisket after having consumed a six-pack of Shiner Bock. Finally, the seeker must exhibit spiritual discipline, neither napping beside the smoker, nor wandering inside . . ." and you wander inside because you have no discipline and you wonder to what degree *Texas Monthly* is right when they say that a good brisket should be hallucinatory, should be resonant, should be shiny and well-rested. The wine is going to your head. Aunt says something about tears, and starts coughing into the blessings.

We know: *brisket* derives not from the Hebrew, but from the Old Norse word *brjósk*, meaning *gristle*, *cartilage*, meaning *abdomen*, meaning *thorax*, meaning *bruise*. Some linguists believe *Pecos* derives from the Latin *pecus*, a single head of cattle. Others believe it derives from the Spanish verb *pecar, to sin*. Either way, we bow our heads, singly, and pray for a cleansing in a language we incompletely understand.

Here, a bruised brisket melts in our mouths, the protein lozenge after a diet of bones and sand. This is drawl-Hebrew and a gunfight with lamb bones; a Texas brisket immersed in the sort of broth that has little to do with any version of *Pecos*. Here, it's okay to be missing pieces. Sign outside a Dallas barbecue shack: "Need no teef, to eat my beef."

"Dallas is the new Sinai," Uncle says, and Aunt slaps him on the shoulder with a bitter sprig of parsley. Because Texas identifies with *big*, and because Uncle dares you, you chase a mouthful of brisket with a sip of the saltwater and swallow, staring at your pants, as one of the neighbors chants something about the year 2666, about a stoic temple and its painful erection.

In the etymological intersection of the brisket and the pecos is the caressing of oneself back into the present, into the sin at the center of the bruise. "That's where," Uncle says, "your ancestors' bodies are, boychik," and you don't know if he's talking about the saltwater or the smoke, or of origin, or of none of these words.

* * *

THIS IS TEXAS and this is Passover, and this is serious, serious sacrifice: a playground date with a cowgirl for family tradition; the perfect one-year-old lamb—always male—its throat cut, its carcass skinned, but only to the brisket; its breast excised and salted; its abdomen ripped open, entrails cleansed in saltwater and offered to God, the blood collected in silver cups to deter the coagulation, and with it, and with our fingers, we paint crucifixes or dog stars or butterflies on our door jambs, so as to avoid the plague of the slaying of our firstborn, meaning *you*—you sitting at the seder table with a mouth salty and smoky, and bitter and wet, reaching into the right pocket you stocked for this occasion (because you are twelve, and can't resist), with the pinup of Karen Velez, the December 1984 centerfold, you ripped from Uncle's *Playboy*, and the sandwich baggie of Irma D. Shorell's Foaming Facial Wash you found in Aunt's medicine cabinet, waiting for the right moment to adjourn to the bathroom, your entire body beating with the anticipation, your heart somehow both saturated and smoking, and there's lamb's blood on the aluminum siding, and there's a cow skull above the fireplace, and hidden in the folds of your clothes: lotion and sacrifice, and a picture of the breasts that, years later, you will tell your wife woke you up sexually, you will describe as the healthy untwined bridges between Jew and Texan, between dry rub and braising liquid, between entrails and temple, between everything ponderous about our chests, and everything incantatory that is cut from them.

You wonder if the left side of Aunt's body has an antagonistic relationship with the right. You wonder why the word *Tejas*, a derivation of the Caddo word for *friends*, was applied (by the Spanish) to the Spanish–Caddo relationship, if they were cutting each other to pieces. In these mouthfuls is conversion, if not excision, made tender.

In the town of Pecos, the headstone of famed gunman Clay Allison shudders into the wind. He once waited for his rival to finish his supper before shooting him in the gut. "I didn't want to send a man to hell," Allison said, "on an empty stomach."

"Divine intervention," Uncle says as he squeezes the yolk of his hard-boiled egg from the white. Aunt pulls a fiber from her brisket, ties it into a noose around her pinkie, and mutters something about injections. That star above us is Forgiving Plague, is Unleavened, is Ten-Gallon, is Lone. For guidance through the deserts of this state, it is clear, and clearly insufficient.

We know because we know brisket: collagen makes up about 35 percent of our body protein content, binding blood vessel to ligament to skin to cornea. It holds us together—even way out here in Texas—allows us to commune with the other vertebrates, the lone stars of David in the spurs. To make our brisket palatable, we must convert the collagen to gelatin. To make this happen, water is necessary.

The saying goes, "If you haven't had a Pecos cantaloupe, you haven't had a cantaloupe." We wonder if we can say the same of this saltwater.

Aunt calms herself down with the *charoset*, the stewed and cooled paste of pine nuts and walnuts and apples and figs, pears, raisins, orange juice, red wine and cinnamon that's supposed to remind us of the mortar we once used as slaves to construct the storehouses of Egypt. It's the sweetness that Aunt responds to; the pebbly texture breaking in her mouth. Something like a star shoots over the house, sees blood, passes us over, just like it did last year, and the year before that. Uncle calls Aunt's mouth the Red Sea, and no one laughs.

According to Meathead, chief blogger at AmazingRibs.com, crying doesn't undo the toughness of the meat—"like a Republic of Texas cowboy, brisket is unforgiving."

In toughness is connection. In tenderness, we fall apart and we scatter. Aunt doesn't listen to Uncle, or Meathead. She starts up again, and the neighbors don't know what to do, but press on with the seder. This is your cue. Pretend to be emotional. You're twelve. This is easy. Excuse yourself. Walk to the bathroom. Turn on the extractor fan. The sink is marble or the sink is clay. The silver faucet: shank bone or whiplashed swan. The toilet is red, and the hand towels have ducks on them. The mirror is fire and sand and thumbprint, and you watch yourself in it, growing into the reflection, every sort of pecos whirling molecular in the air, and you stare at the spaces between them, and Karen Velez, your palm slick with facial wash, brisket between your teeth.

* * *

THE TEXAS STATE BIRD is the mockingbird. The Texas state bird mimics the calls of other species, of amphibians, of insects. In this way, if only in its bird brain, the Texas state bird can copulate with the long tongues of the frogs, the durable haunches of the cockroach. In this, to be sure, is some quiet treatise on penetration and endurance, but you can't quite make it out—in a state this big, one species confuses itself for another, and besides, the extractor fan is roaring.

Ma nishtanah ha-laylah ha-ze mi kol ha-leylot, the neighbor kid—the youngest at the table—chants, according to the tune devised in 1936 by Jewish folk singer Ephraim Abileah, beginning the traditional Passover asking of the sacred Four Questions: *Why is this night different from all other nights?* From the safety of the bathroom, you try not to make out the answers, the references to matzo and the bitter herbs and the saltwater, and you stare Karen in the face and she says nothing of sin or of murder or of cantaloupes or of bruises, but the hand towels quack, and her bottom lip is so full and happy, and you don't think of excision or slavery or smoke or mockingbirds as you climax to the final *mi kol ha-leylot*, moaning, you think, as the Christians do.

According to Cantor Sam Weiss, "Ephraim Abileah was among the founders of the Society for Jewish Folk Music in St. Petersburg in 1901 . . . he was the composer of the melody of Mah Nishtanah that we all sing at the Seder. In the year 1936, Ephraim Abileah composed an oratorio 'Chag Ha-Cherut' Festival of Freedom which included many pieces on texts from the Haggadah, among them the Mah-Nishtanah. Though the melody became part and parcel of the Seder celebration in many families around the world, the oratorio was performed only once in Haifa and was forgotten."

This we remember: The practice of wrapping brisket in foil in order to faster tenderize and moisturize the meat is known as the Texas Crutch. You rejoin the table, hobbling but tender. You know: *Chag Ha-Cherut* means *the Gift of Choice*, which doesn't necessarily mean that you have been chosen. Uncle's shoulder is keeping Aunt's head up. You feel older and nervous and powerful.

Uncle is drunk, so he doesn't stop her. Aunt, you can tell by her stillness, has taken her medication. You are afraid of what's in your pocket, and this state is too big for us, and Aunt thinks she has the answers. "Even the sun here is dingy," she says, "constructed like the Tabernacle. Did you see that article in the *Morning Star* about that man who threw his grandchild from the fire escape yesterday, to see if she would float like paper? Her dress looked like a daffodil. She clutched a yo-yo to her chest. I remember paper, the old Lamar Street printing press that ran the underwear ads. I wonder if the underwear would have blown. Like paper. How many times do I have to hear you mutter *Jerusalem* in your sleep? Live: to soften the meat (the Kaddish! the Kaddish!). Live: around the world."

Texas Brisket

Louie Mueller Barbecue Texas Style Oven Brisket

Ingredients

1 pre-trimmed 12–13-pound deckle-off choice or higher brisket
2 cups coarse / cracked black pepper
¼ cup kosher salt

Preparation

Prepare the brisket rub by thoroughly mixing 2 cups of cracked black pepper with ¼ cup of kosher salt.

Remove brisket from packaging. Trim if not pre-trimmed.

Rubbing

Pour brisket rub onto large sheet pan (larger than brisket in surface dimensions) and spread evenly across bottom of pan (a countertop or large cutting board may be used if large pan not available).

Dampen a kitchen towel and rub the wet towel over entire brisket

Turn brisket upside down (fat cap facing down) and place onto the brisket rub in the large pan.

Note: The rub application is thick. A dusting or light rub will not produce the desired bark or flavor profile.

Scoop up the rub extending beyond the brisket and rub all sides thoroughly. Repeat rubbing to the exposed flat facing upward.

Flip brisket over with the fat cap on top. Ensure the entire brisket cap is thoroughly encased in the rub. Cover any exposed cap area with remaining rub.

Cooking

Place oven rack in middle setting.

Preheat oven to 275 degrees.

Place brisket in large aluminum pan or a large enough cooking pan to completely encase the brisket without any side of the brisket touching any side of the pan. Always use a pan with side heights of at least 3–4 inches.

Once oven is preheated, place brisket into the oven leaving the brisket uncovered.

Remove brisket every 60 minutes and pour liquid grease from pan. Return to the oven.

After 5.5 hours remove brisket from oven.

Resting

Remove brisket from the pan and place on a cutting board or other large flat surface.

Immediately, thoroughly wrap brisket in food film until no brisket surface is exposed.

Wrap brisket again (over the food film) with newspaper, paper bag or butcher paper until all surfaces are covered.

Place brisket into small insulated ice chest that is room temperature and empty. A microwave can also be used in place of an ice chest to hold the wrapped brisket.

Allow brisket rest in container undisturbed for 1 hour.

Remove brisket from ice chest/microwave and decant it from all wrapping.

Place brisket on cutting board for carving.

Carving

Face brisket on cutting board lengthwise with the point facing left and the flat facing right.

Begin carving the brisket on the flat (right side) moving right to left as you carve.

Once you reach the brisket point (approximately the midpoint of the brisket), turn the brisket 90 degrees to the right so that the point is facing away from you and the exposed (cut end) of the brisket is facing you.

Begin carving from the right side and continue carving from right to left until the entire point is carved. (Carving in this manner will ensure you are cutting across the grain of both muscle masses, ensuring the most tender eating experience.)

Serve and enjoy!

—Wayne Mueller, 3rd Generation Owner and Pitmaster, Louie Mueller Barbecue

MID-SOUTH

West Virginia: Rat Stew

Tennessee: Dry Rub Ribs

Kentucky: Mint Julep

North Carolina: Moravian Spice Cookie

Virginia: Peanut Soup

WEST VIRGINIA

Mountains, Mines, and Rat Stew in the Asylum

THOUGH RAT MEAT often bears traces of pesticides, heavy metals, and human excrement, and though most residents of our state (save, perhaps, for the town of Marlinton—famous for the annual autumnal Road-Kill Cook-Off featuring such local delicacies as pothole possum stew, rat gumbo, and the awesomely named Peter Caught-on-Tail Gate Roll) long to shuck the backwoods "barefoot and pregnant" stereotype (after all, we have the lowest birthrate in the U.S.), Uncle empties the traps into a stockpot as his father and his grandfather and his great-grandfather did before him, adds the water, the tomato, the salt and pepper, and the hot red peppers (his personal touch), and cracks his knuckles, says something about infertility, about eighty-hour underground work weeks, about coal as black lipstick, the sort he'd smear Aunt's face with when she was alive and well and simmering anything but rodent on the range.

Today, Uncle thumbs through the classifieds while the stew simmers. The top jobs:

- *Processing Supervisor: Evisceration. Pilgrim's Pride Corporation, Moorefield, West Virginia. 3 or more years' previous experience. Education: High School Diploma. Salary: Competitive.*
- *Research Assistant, Surgical Techniques. Department of Ophthalmology, West Virginia University, Morgantown. Experience with evisceration with Hydroxyapatite implant preferred.*

✦ *Evisceration and Whole Bird Retail Laborer. Cargill Meat Solutions. Ability to travel a must. No experience necessary. Immediate opening!*

* * *

According to Calvin W. Schwabe's book *Unmentionable Cuisine* (published by the University of Virginia Press, which Uncle lambasts as "propaganda from Virginia slavers," before launching into his manifesto on how we seceded from that similarly named state in 1861 after they joined up with the Confederacy, prompting the invention of our albeit blunt and variously interpreted state motto: *Mountaineers are always free*), step one of the Rat Stew recipe: "Skin and eviscerate the rat and split it lengthwise." Uncle dips his face into the stockpot's steam and inhales. He rattles the newspaper. At the window, the dead sugar maple, collecting the freezing rain, scratches eidolic at the screen. He writes his name in the frost. He traces his finger along the length of the back-page columns. He is tired. He's done this for years. A branch breaks off under the weight. He feels qualified.

Uncle calls you to the stove, puts his arm around you. You watch the little nuggets of sour meat surface and dive down, surface and dive down. Uncle says something about peaks and valleys, shifts and shafts and the upper crust. He hands you the wooden spoon, and the newspaper, the only two things he has at the moment to pass on. You think of togetherness and inheritance and ancestry. You think of the wages of secession, of lumps of coal the size of a fist, a human heart. You think of the pride of Debbie "The Rat Lady" Ducommun as she said, "I do as many necropsies of rats as I can, and between 1998 and 2003 I took measurements of the hearts of 150 rats."

Uncle kisses your neck, quotes, for the fifth time this week, Reverend Charles R. Echols, minister of the United Methodist Church over in Huntington: "When you think of church in West Virginia, think of family. People go to church where their grandpa went. The harshness of life makes religion a serious thing." You kiss Uncle back, lean your ear toward the stockpot, swear you can detect the point at which the simmer becomes choral; swear you can see so many tiny hearts going gray in the wet heat. Uncle closes his mouth. This is another meat solution.

You know this: that in Bordeaux, vintners trap rats that inhabit the wine cellars and subsist on the fermenting grape juice. Per step one, the vintners skin and eviscerate the rodents, brush their bodies with a thick sauce of olive oil and crushed shallots, and grill them over a fire of broken wine barrels. Apparently, the resulting meat bears the flavors of cabernet sauvignon, merlot, and petit verdot grapes, the latter of which is known in French wine circles as the "little stiffener." Like every escape route from a subterranean darkness, the origins of this grape are unclear.

You try not to think *little* when you think of fertility, and worry about the heritability of Uncle's mistakes, anatomical and otherwise. You watch little heart tumble over little rib and little liver. You try to pick out the tenderloin, the neck meat. The feet. The hands. You try not to think of the appendages that anchor us into the sorts of shafts that only want to constrict, the earth filling itself back in, becoming whole again. This, we call *collapse*. You tell yourself each night in bed that those are canaries screaming into some implacable, original depth, and not the rats in the kitchen. You try not to think of stiffening bodies, of rigor mortis, of the 2010 mine explosion in Montcoal after which not a single survivor was found. The names of the dead were not released.

Says Eugene Claypole, president of the Local 31 United Mine Workers, Fairmont Division, "There's a strong camaraderie among coal miners. Most miners have fathers who were miners and brothers and uncles who were miners. It's a family tradition." Uncle rattles the paper. He reads, "Crews will soon begin the bleak task of trying to recover all 22 bodies still inside the mine. Rescue efforts had been an agonizing 100-hour exercise in frustration as the teams repeatedly inched their way through tangled debris and fallen rock only to have to withdraw because of explosively high levels of methane and carbon monoxide. Above ground, the miners' families waited for word. Passing much of the week sequestered from the news media, they huddled together in an open-air warehouse on the mine's sprawling property, eating pizza," and stew, "whispering consolations to each other, and sometimes praying."

Uncle stirs. The wind snakes through the window frames. His body huddles into itself, frustrated, withdrawn. He puts his ear to the stew. He whispers something not entirely consoling to himself. He sometimes prays. He waits for word. This is also a family tradition.

* * *

SINCE JUNE 1, 1961, Mr. and Mrs. David T. Myles have lived in the Coal House of White Sulphur Springs, the only home in the world build entirely of coal. When asked if he worried about lung disease, David T. Myles inhaled weakly, and held his breath.

On page 8 of the May 11, 1964, edition of the *Beckley Post-Herald*, just before the article on the Coal House, the OCR clip text reads,

Short of breath?
Cough top
See your doctor
Don't take chances with respiratory diseases
chronic emphysema, allergies, fungus infections
tuberculosis
lung cancer
Dust!

David T. Myles exhaled and said, "I feel pretty lucky."

You know: *Montcoal* means *Coal Mountain*. You're not sure: If we die nameless, do we die freer? According to Connie Baisden, columnist for the *Coal Valley News*, "Mine rats come into the mine to live on the oats spilled by the mine mules and on anything else they can find to eat. The mules are stabled underground and the oats are for feeding the mules. The oats provided the rodents with food. I knew a fellow once who brought food to feed the rats from the home because he said that the rats are the coal miner's friends. As long as they were running around his dinner bucket, the coal miner believed himself safe."

Rat populations also take up residence in abandoned mines and, as rats are the favorite food of certain species of bats, bats are often soon to follow, and Uncle whispers something childishly poetic into the steam cloud, the vapor bearing the melee of electrons that once housed themselves in the flanks and brains and mouths of the rats, and hatches an unlikely recipe he thinks will take next year's Road-Kill Cook-Off. This is another serious thing that depends on the harshness . . .

Road-Kill Cook-Off, past winners: Buzzard Breath Maggotini, Turtle A1-A Road Soup, The Buck Stopped Here Pepper Steak, Deer Drop Chili, Buffalo Balls, Wapiti Relleno, Raccoon Ribs, Skid Mark's Bumper Grill, Wild Turkalo on a Log, Blood Rocks and Guts over Snails and Maggots (ground venison with black beans and rice), Rat-a-Tat-Teriyaki.

Strange how, according to Michael R. Haines's *Journal of Interdisciplinary History* article "Fertility, Nuptiality, and Occupation: A Study of Coal Mining Populations," "coal miners have been observed to have relatively high fertility," and Uncle stands there, silent at the stove, as the ice revises the window, his name, its clarity, its potency for revelation obscured, painted over so thickly with weather that not even a steam cloud that reeks of rat meat can melt it.

Here, to melt is akin to a clearing up. Melt, if the stew is properly prepared, is what the rat meat will do in our mouths. *Rattus rattus*, we call them, as if even binomial nomenclature acknowledges their twitchy grossness, an expression of alarm (*watch out! watch out!*) that demands repetition.

Strange: as the mortality rate of coal miners increased, so did their fertility. In this is a quiet treatise on some kind of desperation, but the roiling of the fall-off-the-bone road-kill drowns it out. Says Baisden, "if the mines are about to collapse or flood, the rats will run out in the hundreds. It could be a day or more before the actual collapse or flood, but the rats can sense it. They can hear the movement in the walls or feel the oncoming water. That little rat over there can help to save your life."

Rats, according to the Frito-Lay Company (offices in Poca, West Virginia), serve as a fabulous advertising replacement to their 1970s-era endorser, the Frito Bandito. Domingo Reyes, then head of the National Mexican American Anti-Defamation League, launched a protest against the use of the Bandito (whose modus operandi involved stealing corn chips, drawing pencil-thin moustaches on the upper lips of their eaters, and hooting in an overblown corporate interpretation of a Mexican American "accent"), and, after he succeeded in the ban, Frito-Lay went back to the drawing board and came up with a peasant sombrero-wearing rat as the Bandito's replacement and the selling point that "our chips are endorsed by none other than Speedy Gonzales!" Juan Martinez of the Julian Samora Research Institute believes that "they are nineteenth-century images going into the twenty-first century." Patrisia Gonzales (no relation—to answer Frito-Lay's probable question) of Indigenous Peoples' Literature believes said ad campaign is "akin to Black Sambo eating a watermelon." According to more than one Caucasian Frito-Lay executive leak at the time, folks like Martinez and Gonzales are "too sensitive."

Last night, on the shadowed grounds of Uncle's kitchen floor, illuminated briefly in the headlights of a right-turning Cargill Meat Solutions truck, one rat, lifting its sensitive face from the more sensitive crotch of another, held a glob of its former compatriot's 20 x 13mm heart in its edema-infected paw, and without a single *Andale!*, without a single *Arriba!*, turned its hairy face toward the light, winked into the maw of forthcoming evisceration, and, showing as many teeth as possible, uttered, in a cruel mimicry of Huntington coal stacker operator Jerry Cornell, "I guess that makes me partly responsible for lighting up the world."

Continues Debbie "The Rat Lady" Ducommun, "Externally I measured the length and width of the heart, and internally I measured the thickness of the left ventricle walls and the width of the left ventricle. I also measured the length of the rat when stretched out from nose tip to anus." And Uncle reaches his arms over his head, but even with the wooden spoon can't quite touch the ceiling. He mutters something about how the smallest things are the ones that sustain us; how a serving of rat has as much protein as a serving of bison.

Published in 1991, Jeff Eberbaugh's book *Gourmet Style Road Kill Cooking* was a "runaway success in West Virginia." (The headline reads: "Road-Kill Recipe Book Splatters Across West Virginia.") The book's page on Amazon.com sports only one customer comment, though, penned by none other than Jeff Eberbaugh himself, and is comprised solely of the line, "Great tongue in cheek humor," and though Uncle's friend Harold Brookman, a salesman from Princeton, WV, proudly says, "We're West Virginia mountaineers; always free. Out here in the mountains, you have to learn to trust others," you're having a little trouble trusting the word of Jeff Eberbaugh.

Uncle knows, and so he tells you: West Virginia State Code Statute 20-2-4 "makes it legal to take home and eat roadkill." Though most of them are found not in the road but already in the home, West Virginia allows rats to fall under the roadkill umbrella.

Many modern rats are the progeny of a human rights violation which occurred when famed Harvard bacteriologist Dr. Hans Zissler smuggled typhoid-infected rats (who can perpetuate fever, paralysis, brain damage, et al.) through West Virginia into Mexico in order to complete his experiments on the spread of epidemic plagues.

According to Alan Davidson's *The Penguin Companion to Food*, "professed cooks, we are told, serve up rats' brains in a much superior style to the Roman dish of nightingales' and peacocks' tongues. The sauce used is garlic, aromatic seeds, and camphor."

Says Calvin W. Schwabe, "Brown rats and roof rats were eaten openly on a large scale in Paris when the city was under siege during the Franco-Prussian War. Observers likened their taste to both partridges and pork," and Uncle says nothing of the window rattling in its frame, of the rats who love and fuck and dream and make plans in our ceiling, of the roofs of earth falling in on so many men and women donning insufficient hard hats, or of mountains, or family, or freedom, or other kinds of siege.

* * *

If we're not underground, we're not under siege. Look at that peak behind the lunatic asylum. Look at the asylum's early definition of self-sufficiency: all it takes is "a farm, a dairy, waterworks, separate rooms for black people, and a cemetery."

And in Weston, in the corridors of the asylum, the ghosts of the first-admitted 1864 patients still howl, their testimonies living on in the pores of the hand-cut stone masonry—how the first to be committed was a female housekeeper who bears, Uncle assures you, an uncanny resemblance to Aunt; how the place was built to accommodate 250 patients (defined as epileptics, alcoholics, drug addicts, and "non-educable mental defectives"), and how, operating at its peak in the 1950s, it housed over 2,600; how, due to overcrowding, the asylum was unable to provide adequate furniture, sanitation, plumbing, lighting, heating, and food; how the asylum, as a result, supported a magnificent rat population, and how a faction of the asylum's staff was charged with trapping these rats, skinning them, eviscerating them, baking them into casseroles, boiling them into stews, and serving them to the starving inmates; and how the "defectives" ate hungrily the stewed hearts and livers and brains and loins, the pinna, the thorax, the crus and the pes, the brachium, the antebrachium, the manus and external nares and vibrissae, the head, the tail, the eye, as the doctors burnt camphor in the corners of the rooms to treat their developing mania . . .

Rat derives from the Latin *rodere—to scrape, to file, to gnaw, to scratch*, and *to rasp*. This, Uncle says, is also a sort of music, and, if we add the simmer, an orchestra . . . and the rats are freed of their names.

Uncle finishes his bowl, picks his teeth with the vibrissae. He takes his fiddle from the closet, begins to play what his mother and father played, what his sisters and brothers played—what we in West Virginia sometimes controversially call "blue-eyed soul." And when it's quiet, and he's feeling lonely, he plays for those still living. He plays for them, and they scurry into hay, pine straw; they scurry into our mountains and our sugar bowls, our oats and flour, our ducts and pipes, and shafts of all kinds. And when they scurry into places from which only they can find exit, he tells himself that they are dancing.

Rat Stew

Squirrel/Rat Stew

4–5 squirrels (or 7–9 rats), skinned and cut up
Flour
Salt and pepper

A pot of boiling water (or chicken stock or broth)
4 cups corn
9–10 large potatoes, cubed
5–6 medium onions, sliced
2–3 cups chopped celery
2–3 cups chopped carrots
2 cups canned tomatoes with juice

Directions

Roll the squirrel/rat pieces in flour, salt, and pepper. In a skillet, over medium heat, brown in butter.

Add squirrel/rat and all other ingredients (with the exception of the tomatoes), to the boiling water, cover, and simmer for 1½ to 2 hours.

Add the tomatoes and continue to simmer another hour.

—Fredricah Gardner

The Little Orchestra in the Dry Rub Rib

IN THE RIB is the xylophone tile we've been dying to strike with the mallets most shaped like our fingers. When we can squeeze or poke or pinch, we can elicit the most beautiful music from the sorts of bones that imprison our organs—bellies and livers and diaphragms and hearts—everything responsible for the rush of our fluids, our anatomical delivery systems, the inhale and exhale required to scream bloody murder, or sing our aria. Here, all it takes is a light tapping of the tongue to the transverse and palatine folds of our hard palates to separate aria from atria, any expressive melody from a chamber meant to collect our gore.

Uncle says, the ribs are cage and the ribs are weapons. Says that, immersed in the Tennessee River, beneath the crushed shells of 102 species of mussel, beneath the now homeless hemocyanin proteins which once carried oxygen to the hearts and stomachs and kidneys, to the adductors and palps and hepatopancreata of so many late bivalvia mollusca, are bows and arrows and daggers and scalpels made of the ribs of so many late moose, buffalo, deer, human.

Which the bones used to protect, which to detain, or stab, or excise the ribs of another? The answer lies in another mouth inflamed with the sort of spice we can only name after a caress, an act of, if not always love, then intimacy, at least.

In Memphis, the spice rub used to flavor our ribs varies from restaurant to restaurant, family to family, but often includes amounts of salt, black pepper, paprika, onion powder, garlic powder, cayenne, brown sugar, white sugar, rosemary, ginger, celery salt, mustard, oregano, cumin. Here, our mouths are confused as whether to parch or to salivate, cool themselves down with water or bite themselves faint.

Here, if left to cure overnight, the dry rub reacts with the wetness of the rib meat, and if we add heat, said reaction will form a crust we call a *bark*, and we will imagine all of our sourwoods and pecans and sugarberries, white pines, black gums and swamp oaks, dogwoods and locusts, hiding a softer meat deep into the middles of their charred trunks.

The bark on the rib, the cage on top of the cage . . . Here, when we're feeling hungry and patriotic, even our doubly protected things are not protected enough. We'd rather think of music while we're eating, than unearthing future weapons with our mouths. To get to the middles of all hard things, all it takes is an axe and the capacity for the chopping.

Our mouths: such soft anatomy into which bones are pressed, the teeth the cage for the tongue, and the tongue, when unleashed, capable of so much damage and delight. The best-protected thing is the thing most surrounded on all sides: the bull's eye, the iris, the bone. The best-protected thing, we think, is the thing with the juiciest of secrets. Our mouths: once the tools of war here . . .

The cure doesn't heal. That pig is still dead. We bite our way to the middle, thinking that that's where the answers are. Here, the tongue mops the last of the rub from the rib, the last of the meat from the bone, the last of the meat being its juice . . . We bite with these mouths made stupid with spice, and our superior labial frenula—those sexy cords connecting the insides of our upper lips to our gums—shudder with the spice as if plucked, as if, in tearing the meat from the rib, our mouths—if not our hunger—are building some horrible new instrument: agitating the howl from the xylophone with a bow made of catgut, the *mmmmmmmm* from the dead pig with the dumbstruck tiles of our teeth.

The tongue is capable of language and licking, unwinding like a snail, a carpet, the sort of river whose pronunciation requires that light tapping of the tongue to the hard palate, a brief acknowledgment of the music there: we shape the word *Tanasi*, exhale the perfect amount of breath to navigate the three syllables that, when spoken in order, recall the name of the Overhill Cherokee village site after which our state is named; the Overhill Cherokee village site that once served as the capital of the Cherokee nation; that now sits submerged beneath the rank waters of the Tellico Lake impoundment of the Little Tennessee River; whose name means, according to Uncle, *the ribs of the current*, presumably referring to the whorls elicited when water comes into contact with branches, or the bodies of the endangered snail darter fish, the length of which compares uncannily to the length of a pork rib stripped of its meat.

Rife with nerve endings, the tongue is capable of enduring so much pain, but not without our crying. If we want to properly pronounce the name of our state, we must be careful when chewing our ribs.

In one hundred years, Uncle says, our teeth too will be at the bottom of the Tennessee. "Mine and yours." Then, he says, the Cherokee will come back, rename the river after their tribe, mix our pulverized incisors into clay to make a stronger pottery. "The whole goddamn state's," Uncle says, pulling the meat from his rib. "Our teeth—holy shit—the tiniest ribs of the future."

According to *The All Season Pocket Guide to Identifying Common Tennessee Trees,* "Learn bark characteristics as quickly as possible. Use all of your senses. Some trees have a unique smell, taste or feel that helps in identification." Here, beneath all of that cumin and paprika, it's tough to tell that there was once the pig, the security of its breathing.

Uncle exhales. It smells like cumin communing with a dogwood. He says something about "nearly sixty fucking years on this planet, and no son to show for it, no daughter, even."

Here, we bite, and the steam escapes like the ghost aria hidden in the *sooies!* of the as yet unslaughtered. Some of the rub's power resides in the litany of its ingredients when spoken aloud, the tongue whirling in orbit like an electron in the cave of the mouth. Here, the spice can lurk in the music, the speech, in tags like *shouts,* or *sings,* or *says.* This rub is different from all other rubs, which affects the tenderness of the meat, the caress of teeth to pig, the sort of kiss that is tipped in our favor, the sort of exploring that leads to our downfall.

Among the first Europeans to explore Tennessee were guys named de Soto and de Luna—men of the thicket and men of the moon. Here, we're explored by those who know how to navigate the tangle, the foliage that most obstructs; and those who orbit us, distant and bone white.

When we dammed the Little Tennessee to form Tellico Lake (which is really a reservoir), we ignited in the state what became known as the snail darter controversy, after it was discovered that said reservoir would impact the river's habitat to the point of decimating—entirely—the snail darter population. Lawsuit after lawsuit ensued, and eventually, Congress, on a "special case" basis, exempted Tellico "Lake" from the Endangered Species Act. Now, should we dive deep enough into Tellico's middle, we will find the intact skeletons of so many snail darters, the ribs of which are way too small to resemble xylophones.

When the steam whines from a bitten-into Dry Rub Rib, Uncle confuses the sound for the sort of cheerful music that, he says, "is for children." We inhale and exhale and our lungs evolve from organ to pump organ, our bodies again bi-instrumental and therefore, again, breathing sustenance into dissonance. "Circulation is a circular argument," Uncle says, and opens his mouth until it becomes round.

Which the satellite: the tongue or the teeth? Which the Soto, the Luna? "If we think the teeth are fixed," Uncle says, "we're sadly mistaken. Your aunt, at the end, used to take her ribs through a straw."

Also wiped out when we dammed the Little Tennessee: the Cherokee village of Chota, several Native American burial sites, Cherokee bowls carved with likenesses of fish and frogs, ancient inscribed tablets carved with words we've mistranslated to mean *holy,* to mean *river,* to mean *rib,* to mean *demolished* . . .

Linguists cite some serious translation issues involved with the Cherokee syllabary, as words with different meanings in Cherokee often translate into the same Latin word. Here, *drown* overlaps with *resurrect, cage* with *song.*

According to George R. Stewart's *Names on the Land: A Historical Account of Place-Naming in the United States*, Memphis founders John Overton, James Winchester, and Andrew Jackson "cherished hopes for [the town's] greatness, and were conscious of the Nile of America. They remembered the great city of ancient Egypt, and called their new venture Memphis." Soon: ribs, and soon: music and dams, and the sorts of racial and political assassinations carried out by men with pig in their teeth, at motels named Budget and motels named Lorraine, new weapons made not of bone but of the sort of judgment and steel that guys like Overton, Jackson, and Winchester made famous through things called historical state *rulings, militias, massacres.*

Weapon or not, we can't perform mouth-to-mouth on a rib. In the barn, an opened-up pig nailed to the rafters by its forelegs, its hind legs hovering over the purpled sawdust. Uncle earlier, with a blowtorch, removed the hair from the hide, unzipped it with a chainsaw, its ribs still attached to what was once its insides, now freed from the coffin of skin. It's not that we want to play the carcass, but still, earlier this morning, how we stared into the cavity, listened to the wind dry it out like a river, and couldn't tell if it was the weather or our mouths that were whistling.

Uskwa'li-gu'ta, Overhill Cherokee chief from 1788 to 1794, lived in the now submerged village of Chota. From boyhood, his maternal uncle trained him in the ways of becoming a man. Our maternal uncle will soon train us to excise the ribs from the carcass in the barn, and we will stare deep into the animal, past the edge of the long knife, and think of vessels, and waterways, train tunnels, and others that may have some kind of beautiful light at their ends.

In dryness is a clouding of the vision, a breaking of the skin. We can't tell if that brightness is welcoming us or wants to cut us in half. And the rib, once drowned in river or rub, is unrevivable.

Meathead says, "the salt pulls the moisture from the surface to form a 'pellicle,' and penetrates the meat far deeper than the spices," and we think of the pellicle as another cage—to protozoa and to photomasks, to mirrors, to teeth, to protein—and we imagine our own hearts as the semiconductors beneath the pellicle, which means that they're smaller than actual conductors, and protected from the amplification of their own beating.

Evaporation in Tennessee, if not Nile: the dam that petrifies the faithful fish; the spice hot enough to boil our water down to its pea gravel, to burn our goliath hearts.

We cry after the carving. Uncle runs his hands over the backs of our necks. It's a dry rub, at best. We know: *rib* derives from the medieval Latin word *costa*, which has also come to refer to bone, to bow, to flank, to side, to slope, to shore, to coast, to the edge of a thing, to that thing's limit, to the beginning of something else, some new thing, to a border crossing; to the cage, and the escape from that cage; to end, to finish, to freedom, to death . . .

Uncle finishes his slab, looks confused, doesn't know what to do with the bones. We want him to think of circulation, of things that move like water. We want him to think even of the snake—or something almost as biblical; how its ribcage provides support and protection for its entire body; how sharks have no dorsal ribs, but do have that really big fin, and very sharp teeth; how the frog has no ribs, save for a sacral pair which confuses itself for a part of the pelvis; how we have ribs we identify by number, as *true*, as *false*, as *floating*.

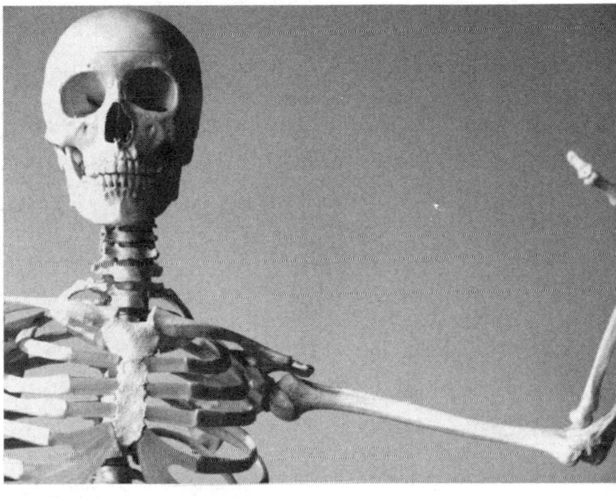

Uncle toasts "to the mouth opening to sing through a pellicle of water." Even within our bodies, we don't know what's real and what's not; what's anchored down and what's hovering. Last year, the Little Tennessee drowned six people. Oddly enough, this is double the amount claimed by the "big" Tennessee River. In this is an interrogation of truth in naming. Still, like the answers, the bodies floated and floated before sinking to the old settlements.

Tapping one bone against another, we think of size as another kind of border, some membrane to break through—the growing and shrinking of the things at the bottoms of our rivers, the middles of our bodies; a sloughing-off . . . And Uncle says, "Red," and Uncle says, "Rocky," and Uncle says, "Calfkiller," and Uncle says, "Bald," and there's tomorrow's rub to prepare, the overnight cure, and our fingernails are dirty, and even when we try to clean them by cutting, the clippings littering the dry sink like ribs or little ribs, or parts of the moon, readying themselves for the rinsing down the drain, they stay dirty, and we sit here at this table and we think "clean them by cutting?" and we can't believe it, and everything inside us, protected by our ribs, can't believe it either, and the organs are about to express themselves with sound, take in breath, and are about to release it in aria, we think, in full orchestra—in a cello played with hammers, a cymbal struck with teeth—when Uncle says, "Blood." "Blood," he says.

Memphis Style Dry-Rub Ribs

We use loin back pork ribs, 2½ pounds or less.

Create a basting solution of one part white vinegar, one part water, one-half part Rendezvous Sauce and a healthy dash of Rendezvous Seasoning.

Keep the basting solution hot, and frequently baste while grilling.

Cook indirectly over charcoal for about 1½ hours, or until the temperature reaches 162 degrees. Cook the ribs at least 12 inches over the coals.

Cook the bone side down first until brown. Then cook the meat side until done.

When done, place ribs on a plate and give one more good basting, then sprinkle a healthy dose of Rendezvous Seasoning and serve.

Tip: If you're cutting the ribs into individual bones, cut along the bone so all the meat is on one side.

Bon appetit'

—*Charlie Vergos' Rendezvous Restaurant*

The Putting Down of the Mint Julep

YOUR UNCLE MUDDLES three leaves of spearmint with two pinches of white sugar into the bottom of a rosy rocks glass with a miniature Ebonite International bowling pin toy, the one he received as a trophy for twenty-five years of "striking" service at the bowling ball factory in Hopkinsville. You're not sure if it's misplaced shop talk or neurotic self-analysis when, as he twists the essential oils from the mint leaves, the menthol and menthone streaking with their grease the sides of the glass, pours more than a splash of bourbon, less than a splash of water, he mutters, "Three strikes in a row . . ." into the burley tobacco field of his own chest hair, anticipating his first sip of the morning.

Your uncle curses the horses on the television. Tells them they'll soon be lunchmeat in Lexington. Out the window, you watch the tobacco leaves brighten from what Uncle calls off-white to yellow. Uncle swallows the last of his julep and burps, cleanly.

You wonder if there's something wrong with the light here. Those horses on television look reflective. The tobacco leaves shrivel, the air does the curing. The earth here seems to howl, as if pressed of its own juice, as if giving itself to the muddler. It is the light that does the crushing. Uncle says it is the light that makes things taste good, that releases the flavors in things. He says, in *spearmint* is the spear. Before he makes his second drink, he mutters something about the hierarchy of violence. How, here, to puncture a thing is to release its flavor. He mutters something about fighting back, about how another name for the mint julep is the mint smash.

* * *

UNCLE TALKS HIMSELF back from his hangover with racehorse deaths. *Ruffian,* he says, *1975. Sesamoids in her right foreleg snapped. Went on running. Pulverized her bones, tendons. Went on running. Ripped the skin off her fetlock. Ligaments trailing behind like a bridal train. The jockey—Vasquez—desperately trying to pull up. It was the* sound *of it, he later said. The hoof flapping about. Useless. At the end of it, all this thrashing, this spinning in circles. They tried to cast her, but she kept knocking the cast against her good legs, smashing those too. All that was left was the gun. Dumb motherfucker went on running,* Uncle says, stirring the julep with his good pinkie now—circles, his fingertip reddening, the mint oozing its oils, heaving like seaweed—*ripped herself open to win. Boy,* he says to you, *you should have seen it . . .*

Uncle knows, he's supposed to sip his mint julep from a silver cup, or one made of pewter. He's supposed to hold the cup only from its bottom, to allow the cold bourbon and water, the ice cube or two, to grow frost on the vessel's sides. He knows this even as he blows bubbles into the rocks glass, grasping it desperately with all of his hands, muttering something about the aunt you never met, about how heat is better, heat is better. How he will make his juleps smooth as a bowling ball. How, at bottle's end, he will turn this entire living room into *a goddamn Pro Shop Gold.*

The word *julep* derives from the Persian *golab*, meaning *rosewater.* Early versions of the drink saw rose petals, rather than mint leaves, muddled with sugar at the bottom of the glass. On the television, it looks as if his horse will win, then lose. "Either way," Uncle says, stirring cube to cube with the toy bowling pin, "I'm drinking a fucking *corsage.*"

He tells you about the man from Louisville who wanted a rose embedded in his bowling ball. "You should have seen his sunglasses," Uncle says. "Rhinestones and shit." You're about to say something about *all that glitters,* about how beautiful it is—the way the light catches his glass, the ice there, the tobacco shadows on the sheetrock inspiring the mint leaves to lift themselves from the suspension, give themselves to this man's mouth. Uncle breathes deep of the julep. He tells you that glass is too *clean,* that he misses the smell of the plastic.

There's more folkloric romance inherent in the mint leaf than there is in the rose. In this way, we are trying to coax a kind of love from the drink whose own name resists it. The mint julep should be sipped in a dark, cool room while stepping carefully down a spiral staircase, and the splash of water should be a splash of limestone water, and the sugar should be loaf sugar, and the ice crushed, and the mint should be young, and laid over the coffin of ice until muddled, and, before the muddling, the drinker—anticipatory, discerning—should test the softness of the foliage against his, or her, ear.

Uncle thumbs through *Blood-Horse* magazine, then uses it as a coaster. *Old Rosebud,* he says, *1922. A windy day. Couldn't tell if those were the tendons blowing, or some awful head of hair . . .* Uncle says: here, the julep makes the man. The more the mint, the more feminized the drink, but the more the mint, the more likely the drinking man is to be kissed. "It's your classic dilemma," he says, as he tries in vain to use the bowling pin as a telescope, stare beyond the television and the silent horses chewing at their bits; stare beyond all things Kentucky—its number-one status in the production of non-alfalfa hay, its bluegrass, cardinals and tulip trees and goldenrods and all things capable of muddling birds and petals and leaves and lawn—factories that produce bowling balls with strong names like Dyno-Thane and PowerHouse and Hammer, strong things thrown by good Kentucky men to knock other strong things down; balls your uncle gave his fingertips to; balls he made of wood, then rubber, then plastic, then urethane, then reactive urethane, then particle, then epoxy. Balls whose cores should never be muddled; balls that, in your uncle's hands, become oddly sentient—the mint predicting the kiss—remembering the original sport, when human skulls were used as pins.

Uncle stirs his julep with the last good fingertip he has left. That pinkie. Then: *Dark Mirage. 1969. Raced only twice. It was the fetlock joint that went. The cannon bone exploded. The ligaments of the pastern rolling up like a window shade.* He looks at his left thumb, the way it hangs there, sips his julep, silently curses the bowling ball. You know: he'll soon start speaking of euthanasia, and all death we call *good.*

It's easy to forget that *to muddle* means *to confuse, to make indistinct.* You suppose that crushing something likely confuses it. Here, in the pulverizing of a thing is that thing's best expression. We think of our own bodies. How else to let all the good sweetness out? And Uncle, like the state that refreshes itself with bourbon aged in wood, with the sort of mint that allows the nation's highest concentration of deer, and turkeys, and coalfields to scatter, to disappear into tobacco fields and the cave behind the pins, pulls the blanket over his head . . . beyond all things Kentucky—its Mammoth Cave, named, Uncle reminds you, for yet another giant extinct thing.

That *Kentucky* derives from the Iroquois word for *meadowlands* is quaint enough. That the Cherokee called the land *a dark and bloody ground* compels your uncle to lose himself in the muddling. What else can he do but crush some skinny leaves until, in his mouth, they are allowed to refresh, until he believes he is strong, or strong enough.

The pastern bone of the horse is the thing in nature most anatomically homologous to the largest bones in the human finger. Uncle wishes he had a knuckle left to crack.

* * *

Go for Wand. 1990. Leading by a head when her right cannon bone openly fractured. Threw the jockey—fuckin' Randy Romero—then limped across the finish line. Right into the winner's circle. They say she broke her leg just as she passed the flagpole that they buried Ruffian under. How crazy is that? Because she was screaming, they euthanized her right then and there. Right in the fuckin' winner's circle. Because she was screaming, he muted the TV, listened only to his own mouth slurp at the ice cubes as they buried her *in the middle of the fuckin' infield,* and the wind took a banner bearing her name into the air, and the crowd held—just held—their plastic cups.

Dulcify. 1979. Crushed pelvis. Mummify. 2005. Foreleg. Lamb Chop. '64. Broken body, is all they said. Cryptcloser. Ha. 2000. Fell past the wire. Crushed shoulder. '55: White Skies. A bullet horse they called her. A tobacco eater, because she was bought by some tobacco farmer outside Lexington, I can't remember the name. Anyhow, compound fracture. Right hind cannon bone, anyhow. Couldn't get to the volume fast enough. Who could predict these things?

We inherit these shadows on the wall, the wind that allows them movement. We stay inside with our juleps and curse the weather, though there's not a cloud in the sky.

. . . George Washington. 2007. Ankle. Crushed ankle.

We close our eyes. We sleep it off. We have crushed things inside of us. We have things inside of us waiting to be crushed. We dream of horses. We name them after forefathers. We can't tell if they're cheering or screaming. So, we keep running. In this kind of wind, *bullet* can mean so many things. In this kind, we are the things we try to outrun.

Mint Julep

2 ounces Maker's Mark bourbon
2 ounces mint simple syrup (recipe below)
Crushed ice
Club soda
Fresh mint springs, for garnish
Powdered sugar, for garnish

In a tall glass, fill with crushed ice. Pour in bourbon and mint syrup. Stir gently. Add a splash of club soda and garnish with fresh mint sprig and sprinkle with powdered sugar.

For syrup: Combine equal amounts sugar and water and several sprigs mint in a small saucepan over medium heat. Stir until sugar dissolves and syrup thickens slightly. Remove from heat and allow mint to steep until syrup comes to room temperature. Strain to remove mint leaves. Refrigerate until needed.

—*The Brown Hotel*

NORTH CAROLINA

Pressed into the Ground with the Moravian Spice Cookie

UNCLE SAYS THAT, here, our hearts are thinner than the tobacco leaves, anorexic even, he says. "You can see the ribs showing through!" He's not talking about tanking industries, or pulled pork, or any animal reduced to its threads. He's not talking about sewing new field clothes from pressure-cooked pig, however silken, however heavily sauced. I may be wrong, but I think he's talking about marriage. "I'm talking, boy," he tells me, "about something sweet and skinny, the spiciest goddamn thing you can still see through." I ask him about tobacco and our hearts, but he just gobbles like a turkey, tells me that North Carolina is "number one in goddamn turkeys (40-some million grown last year), number one in tobacco—still." I think of the thinnest paper into which to roll our cash crop, think of any way to sweeten it, inspire it to beat just a little bit faster.

"All the politics and publicity about smoking," Uncle says over his fifth Moravian Spice Cookie, "is like someone coming into your home and taking the dinner plate from in front of you." I watch the cookie melt on his tongue like the holiest thing that isn't representative of the body.

Our state cookie, sometimes called a wafer, has this designation: the World's Thinnest Cookie. "Paper-thin, by hand!" Uncle insists in the faces of all the bakeries in Winston-Salem that have now switched over to mechanized dough flatteners. Uncle, spitting the most fragile of crumbs, mutters something about the hands and thinness, about the burning down of all holy relationships.

The Moravian Protestants launched their Lamb-of-God-style denomination in the 1450s in Bohemia, fled to Saxony in the 1720s to escape persecution, spoke of the conquering lamb as they unbuttoned their blouses, unhooked their bras, sang songs about love and about fire, spoke of following the hoofprints of all sacred bleaters as their pants fell to floors of oak and cherry and urine and hay, as they made boys and girls who would make boys and girls who would dream of some odd inheritance of flight, of some contraption that would move the air over its own body just so that it could lift—and not just briefly—from this earth, and they would open their eyes in North Carolina, perpetuate what is still today the largest Moravian community in the U.S., where in windowless kitchens and kitchens full of windows, this community sweats and curses and asks for forgiveness, and they rolled out the cookie dough, larded with molasses, brown sugar, cinnamon, clove, allspice, nutmeg and ginger, as they held it to window or no window or bulb or candleflame to see if it was thin enough through which to see the light.

Uncle says, we must see the light before we add heat, lest we burn. He's on his twelfth cookie and says, "so goddamn thin it's like eating one regular one . . ." He unbuttons his shirt and juggles five heirloom tomatoes. As long as he holds the shards of cookie in his mouth like glass, he believes, he will not drop one. They nearly hit the slats of the broken ceiling fan. Their arc is beautiful.

In spice is aggression or a reminder of aggression. Is the tongue rising, in estrus, to meet it. Like Uncle, like much of Winston-Salem, the early Moravian Church believed in utraquism (from the Latin *sub utraque specie, in both kinds*), meaning that salvation was attainable only via the ingestion of the bread *and* the wine, the body *and* the blood, during the Eucharist. Uncle lies down on the couch and rests his hand on his belly, at his scar's end. He muses on the music in his mouth, the conversation between spice and sugar, between a cookie so light and the weighing-down of the body after eating fifteen of them. I know: this isn't quite the best of both worlds so much as a faithful greed, as a slippery, ultrathin engine we hope and hope will propel us upward toward any grace.

Here, grace is watching the turkey vulture fall into the tobacco after trying and failing to lift a turkey from the earth. Here, watching a bird of prey dislocate its entire body through a picture window is like watching a house of cards collapse—something so big dying in the skinniest of whispers. Here, the size of death is a secret, something to be hissed from ear to ear.

In order to keep the Moravian Church from spreading, the Roman Catholics, throughout the 1400s, launched a series of bloody conflicts during which countless Moravian "heretics" were burned at the stake, and countless others were captured as entertainment during the Holy Roman Empire's infamous and indulgent torture orgies. Some of these gatherings would culminate in the collective and drunken slaughter of the prisoner, after which his or her heart would be excised by a church servant and divided into paper-thin slices, to be served raw, with a little salt, with a digestif of sweet red wine, itself typically fortified with the same autumnal spices we now heap into our cookie dough, after which the revelers would begin a night of frantic copulation.

This is the heart as aphrodisiac to other hearts, a spicy propagation, a carpaccio love. In the Moravian Spice Cookie is the reminder of our own persecution, is some chambered, and therefore cloistered, engagement with our poor ancestors; is a rewriting of history in butter and flour and spice, is the membrane-thin delusion of us as the winners; is persecution turned dessert, the last thing we taste before bed.

* * *

Tho' the scorner may sneer at
and witlings defame her,
Still our hearts swell with gladness
whenever we name her.

—the North Carolina state song

Carolina is not a "her" at all, but derives from *Carolinus*, the Latin for *of Charles*, the Latin for England's royal possessiveness. "Once again we confuse one thing for another," Uncle says, and I stare into the center of a Spice Cookie and delude myself into thinking that the light there can help impose a context on all of this.

Something's wrong. A vulture is not supposed to hunt like a

hawk. Here, the wind brushes through the tobacco, whispers predictions about the collapse of an industry. I can't tell if this is sweet or spicy, rolled by hand or by machine: the wind helps us to cool down, slow our hearts. The wind helps us to locate the carcass out there.

According to Oxford America's "A State of Fear: Human Rights Abuses in North Carolina's Tobacco Industry,"

> *A majority of workers interviewed reported regularly suffering symptoms of green tobacco sickness (GTS), a form of acute nicotine poisoning caused by absorption of excessive amounts of nicotine through the skin. These symptoms include dizziness, vomiting, weakness, coughing, and headaches.*
>
> *The workers interviewed also said that growers fail to provide them with protective clothing (such as gloves) or training that would enable them to take steps to protect themselves. Heatstroke is the leading cause of work related death among farmworkers, even though North Carolina law requires that every fieldworker have access to cold, fresh water. Many reported that clean water was not available.*

Former governor James Martin, who also opposed a holiday honoring Martin Luther King, Jr. (because "I don't think we need more days off"), called these accusations "a spiritual issue . . . an ingrown part of our society . . . tolerable . . . [and] cookie-thin."

Martin plays the tuba, the least thin of the instruments. Martin graduated from Davidson College where, years earlier, in 1896, Dr. Harry Lewis Smith took the first X-ray photograph of his own hand, his wedding ring dominant. First observers expressed their surprise that the bones appeared in great detail but the blood didn't show up at all.

Uncle believes that in sleep, Virginia Dare, reportedly the first child born to English parents in the Americas, who mysteriously disappeared along with the remainder of the Roanoke Colony, speaks through us. I don't have the heart to tell him that in North Carolina, her name has been invoked to prevent women from getting the vote, to delay the end of racial segregation (one popular slogan:

Keep North Carolina white . . . in the name of Virginia Dare!), to deter immigration reform, to hawk vanilla extract, wine, cigarettes, cookies. On Roanoke Island, the bureau of tourism erected a statue of Virginia as an adult woman (*as if she never disappeared!*). This is how the bureau envisioned her, surely the product of long debates, committee meetings that went deep into the humid night: naked, save for a buffalo skin cape. In spite of this, the Virginia Dare Extract Company believes that she epitomizes all of North Carolina's "wholesomeness and purity."

Here, conflicting narratives collide in the same skeletal cookie. The thinner the dough, the more the sugar and spice can declare themselves, the more we can contextualize our history in the language of nursery rhymes.

Overhead, so many songbirds escape the raptor. Down here, we bake cookies against that thing groaning at the window—the wind, or the turkey, or the economy, or all things we misinterpret as *nice*. Just another Lost Colony as another found heirloom . . . This is dessert as lingerie, as the Moravian diaspora renaming itself "the Hidden Seed."

Here, when we bite, something shatters. Here, breakage is only vaguely sweet. Uncle tells me about his honeymoon at Nags Head, about seeing the world through a bridal veil, about stretching something so concentrated so thin, about testing parameters, about breakage, and about trying again. He speaks of the promise of resurrection as another human rights violation. He does not speak of spectral photographs, or of cookies so thin, we shiver as we eat them.

* * *

In 1744, the Moravian missionaries were expelled from New York for their support of the Mohicans (with whom the colonists had developed their typical hostility), traveled south, died and lived, fed on dishes that allowed them the illusion of holiness and abundance. Four thin cookies *sounds* like a lot of food, feels like sacrament on the tongue. They held in open fields and in forests, half-starving, their famed Lovefeasts, services dedicated to the parameters of the Christian heart. When they got to North Carolina, they stopped, settled, made their fires, their proclamations, their dough.

Moravians are buried in graveyards called God's Acre, beneath only thin, flat headstones pressed into the ground which birds often confuse for a softer earth. This is a recipe for disaster . . .

Uncle has the brochure prepared, pressed between the couch cushions. He points to the "Things To Do" heading: "We went hang-gliding, boy," he says. "Your aunt and me. Can you believe that shit?" He passes me the folded paper rectangle and I see lovers on the beach and in sunglasses, and tulip glasses with long straws in them, and testimonials. In one picture, a barefoot man strapped into a pair of rainbow wings says, *Have you ever had a dream you were flying?* Uncle's eyes are closed. His boots are on, but untied. His fingers, in sleep, are closing over another cookie, not yet exerting enough pressure to break it. He does not speak Aunt's name. Outside, something screams in the fields. *No motor*, the barefoot man says. *It's just like being a bird.*

Moravian Spice Cookies

Moravian Christmas Cookies
These are very hard to make.

¾ pound butter and lard (or shortening) mixed
¾ pound flour
¾ pound dark brown sugar

Rub above ingredients together. Then add the following:

1 quart molasses
1 wine glass (6 ounces) brandy
1 ounce soda (dissolved in a little milk, then add a bit of vinegar)
2 tablespoons cinnamon
2 tablespoons cloves

2 tablespoons nutmeg
1 tablespoon ginger
Approximately 3 pounds (12–14 cups) flour

Mix well, then add enough flour to make stiff dough. Let sit overnight or longer to chill. Roll thin and bake in slow oven (about 260–300 degrees).

Note: lard helps make a slick top.

—*Mrs. Hanes Moravian Cookies*

Peanut Soup as Solace

Friday, October 11, 2013, 3:25 p.m.
Today, I searched for the giant squid in the Chickahominy River. I chose the Chickahominy River because it's close to my house. I brought the cat on the cat leash. The temperature was exactly balmy. I brought the binoculars, but these proved an insufficient tool. With a fishing rod, and a Mizuno little league mitt, I caught a yellow perch. It just exceeded the legal length limit (which I had conveniently marked with a staple in the cat leash—distance from loop to staple: good, legal). Tonight, I will grill it with Dijon mustard, garlic, and a little tarragon. I saw three blue jays, two black-capped chickadees, one garter snake, and no squid. The cat ate one of the chickadees. I tried to do some mental gymnastics, and peeled a banana. The giant squid has eight tentacles and two arms. The banana peeled in only three beautiful ribbons. The cat mewled. Morale remains high.

* * *

Uncle tells me to bury the exotic in the common. To forget about the squid and begin embracing the peanut. To stop daydreaming and start concerning myself with the things at hand. With the stuff I can find in Virginia. "For solace, boy," he says. Even our state, he tells me, is chastely named. "It's the fantasy that's common," he says, "not the keeping of your pants on." If we're to be disappointed and tight-lipped here; if our mouths, ever unsurprised, do not gape open, we must take into our bodies only thin, watery things.

When the slave ships came to Virginia in the 1600s, they brought with them, among other stores, peanuts. Soon, peanuts were planted throughout the gardens of the colony, and the exactly balmy air here allowed for such an abundant yield that Jefferson himself, in 1794, demanded that something be done to preserve the slutty crop of the sixty-five peanut hills at Monticello. Too many peanuts is crisis. Colonial cooks spread their legs and made babies, further mouths. Colonial cooks stretched their arms toward mortars and pestles and pulverized the nuts to their butter. Here, butter is the result of the final stage of crushing. Here, flexibility refers to the number of textures we can elicit from the peanut.

Virginia, so far from chastity, is nicknamed "Mother of the Presidents," as she, eight times over, spread her muddy thighs and birthed into the shadows of our peanut hills red-faced boy babies named Washington and Jefferson and Madison, Monroe, Harrison, Tyler, Taylor, and Wilson. That she was named for Elizabeth I, England's Virgin Queen, is, Uncle says, a bad joke, thin soup at best.

Slogans of our state: *The birthplace of a nation*; *Our power to rule is our birthright; Virginia is for Lovers; Sic Semper Tyrannis: Thus Always to Tyrants,* which is what John Wilkes Booth shouted as he shot Abraham Lincoln, who was not born in Virginia, in the back of the head at point-blank range.

* * *

Friday, October 18, 2013, 12:07 p.m.

Today, I searched for the giant squid in Lake Brittle. I chose Lake Brittle because it's one of the first man-made lakes in the state. I'm looking for clues, I think. Uncle calls it "futile stabs at narrative reconciliation," as he smashes peanuts beneath a half-full bottle of premixed Lynchburg Lemonade. "Ain't no way you're gonna make all these mottos gel." He's about to say elusive, or is about to say *myth made real,* but the butter obstructs his tongue.

I packed the binoculars. I read beforehand that the state instituted a moratorium on blueback herring and alewife. I thought about nuts named for vegetables, about fish named for corpulent female tavern-keepers. On the way, I drove past the site where the first peanuts in North America were sown, and the Arby's on the edge of it, advertising *Ladies' Day: Twofer-one Beef n' Cheddars.* Threads of peanut shell cellulose collected on the windshield and stuck to the hornet viscera. Though there was no rain, I had to use the wipers.

A group from the hospital beat me to the lake, and was swimming for diabetes. Someone in a miniskirt held up a blue-gray sign that read "$10,000!" Glitter was used. Her knees looked like peanuts, suction cups. Fetching. A friend of mine claimed to have found a dead suckerfish on the bank here last year. Local officials have called this fish "unattractive," though marine biologists have referred to its body moving through the water as "beautiful," "sinuous." The suckerfish, in mythology, has the power to stop a sailing ship in its tracks, to undo Mark Antony at the Battle of Actium, to inspire the assassination of the tyrant Caligula, the thirty stabs of the "conspirators'" knives . . . To catch a suckerfish, Uncle swears by peanut shell bait.

I dropped my eyes, confused, briefly, scum for tentacle. I baited my hook with a crumb of peanut shell stained with beet juice. One of the swimmers lifted her head. There was a blue morpho butterfly on her bathing cap. For a second, I couldn't tell if it was real or not. I cast. A dime-sized bubble rose to the surface and popped. Families cheered. I fixed my hair. For a brief second, everything solid felt like a soup. For a brief second, I swore I could feel the earth move.

* * *

THE SUCKERFISH is also known as the remora, which means, in Latin, *delay*. If my heart doesn't skip a beat in the face of Peanut Soup, then I must look for squid. If I am sucking, that means I haven't yet exhaled, haven't yet failed to hold my breath.

Here, coming out of your shell sometimes means losing your virginity. Here, a lack of chastity sometimes means that you will never be the namesake of an entire state. To the peanut paste and chicken broth, Uncle adds butter, onion, celery, a little lemon juice, and a little flour. The purists among us will never add peanut butter to the soup. That's not the colonial way. The colonial way is to foster gulfs, chasms; is to fill these with a paste so thick, it muffles even our clearest expressions of surprise, pain. Here, pain, if not chastity, is point-blank, and therefore, short-lived.

Though our state motto translates directly as *Thus Always to*

Tyrants, many of us insist, for some reason, on translating it as *Death to Tyrants*. If the butter is the subtext of the peanut, then the yielding of such a subtext requires a great pulverizing. At what point does pulverization become fictionalization?

* * *

Friday, October 25, 2013, 9:51 a.m.

Today, I searched for the giant squid in Chesapeake Bay. I rode my motorcycle to the docks, packed into my saddlebags a bottle of water and a BLT, and a thermos of Uncle's Peanut Soup. The bacon wasn't so good cold. The peanut paste separated from the chicken broth. I got stung by a bee on the way. I chartered a boat from a guy named Manny. I asked him if it stood for Manuel, and he said, "No, it stands for masculine." I left the cat at home with the automatic feeder. When she presses a paw-shaped pedal, the feeder purrs, then dispenses a tablespoon. I've always thought that the mechanical purr was a little scary. Once, I had a dream that the feeder attacked me while I was watching TV in bed. Ripped the blankets right off of me. Then, ripped off the roof. The last thing I remember seeing before I woke up was a meteor coming right for the memory foam pillow. Somehow, the feeder controlled its trajectory. Uncle calls meteors *space peanuts*. Uncle feeds his silkworms mulberry leaves and tobacco. He wears the resulting scarves as he prepares the soup, talks about the gulf between *colorful* and *fragrant*; talks about intoxication as a bridge.

Manny had a tattoo of a rodent on his biceps. "Did you know," he said, "that the word *muscle* comes from the Latin *musculus*, or *little mouse*? The Romans thought that our muscles wriggled like mice beneath the skin." I told him that I didn't know that. I told him, "That's something." My rod jumped. A seagull said something in seagull to another seagull. I rolled up my sleeves. I prepared for the best. The line buzzed like the entire hive. Minnow.

* * *

"We may be hungry," Uncle says, "but we'll never *go* hungry." I wonder about the nature of *go*. As if hunger is something we actively move toward. A goal. I wonder about the point at which wigs no longer signified wealth in our state. I wonder about the contents of his stomach when Robert E. Lee said, "I have been up to see the Congress and they do not seem to be able to do anything except to eat peanuts and chew tobacco, while my army is starving."

Myth here is tyrannical; a legume, not a nut. According to Willard Scott—Virginia native, weatherman, and original Ronald MacDonald—his hometown of Upperville "is a little kingdom of its own . . . there's an Exxon station and a little grocery store." As he said this, because it was National Peanut Month, Scott held up a bag of peanuts. In the days following, while reporting the weather, Scott will also hold up a framed picture of a duck, a giant chocolate bar, a drooping daffodil, and a bunny rabbit made of pussy willows. I'm not sure if these objects also had their own Month, also had the capacity to go National. I'm not sure what comprises a kingdom anymore.

Here, if we work for peanuts, we work for our cultural inheritance. Here, that's not quite enough to sustain us. If the common can't sustain us, why not search for the rare?

* * *

Friday, November 1, 2013, 11:06 a.m.

Today, I searched for the giant squid in the Cowpasture River. On the drive out, I listened to my Selected Poems in Morse Code CD, repeating Eliot's "Virginia." In the poem, he claims that the primary elements of nature are "Delay, decay. Living, living." The rare and the common and the contradictory. The squid incubated in the peanut shell. The peanut that asphyxiates the squid. Anyhow, the clicks were amazing. Upriver, a boy of no more than six fished alone. On his neck, a spider, or a tattoo of a spider. At that distance, I couldn't tell. The wind was strong, and the leaves slapped the ground in dots, dashes. A redbreast sunfish leapt from the river into the air. I couldn't believe how high it got. I thought, briefly, about that clown at my high school who, dressed as Jefferson, exacted an exemplary slam-dunk. The sun caught the body of the sunfish, double-edged and sharp like a sickle. I thought, *once, even Gorbachev lost his virginity*. I thought of my favorite origin story—the one involving Leah and the tentacle—and of awful kisses, and other firsts. Of the lies about the first Thanksgiving. Still, no squid. Before the sunfish fell again to water, the spider, or the tattoo of the spider, bit down, in. The boy dropped his rod. Slapped his neck. The fish landed. For the first time in his life, I'd imagine, he said, "Fuck."

* * *

Says Terry Wood, of the University of Virginia, "The influence of Thomas Jefferson is amazing. You get the feeling he's behind a tree somewhere." Today, I looked behind a tree. I found the peanuts.

Due to its housing of the Peanut Corporation of America, Lynchburg was once known as the Peanut Capital of the World. Due to its lack of churches, evangelist Lorenzo Dow called Lynchburg "the open air in what I conceived to be the seat of Satan's Kingdom . . . a deadly place for the worship of God."

The peanut, in Chinese symbology, represents the birthing process, and the desire for many children. According to *The Dream Dictionary*, the peanut represents poverty and miscommunication. The peanut is what hides in the soil, represents secret, the code in the screams of the infant, the answers only hunger can provide.

In 2009, the Peanut Corporation of America was forced out of business due to a salmonella outbreak. As a result, the *Washington Post* referred to the peanut as "a time bomb waiting to go off."

* * *

Friday, November 8, 2013, 9:41 p.m.

Today, I searched for the giant squid in Lake Shenandoah, about an hour's drive if I keep it above 70. I was inspired by the DGIF's (Virginia Department of Game and Inland Fisheries) Lake Shenandoah Lunar Conditions report, which read, "The affects of the moon on freshwater fish and game are at a minimum right now. The fisherman should never use this as an excuse to not get on the water." I told myself that I have real get-up-and-go. I was waxing narcissistic. The moon was waxing gibbous. I saw a largemouth bass yawn. I saw four cigarette butts: two Marlboro, one Camel Light, and one beedi. I saw two chipping sparrows, one red-headed woodpecker, a dark-eyed junco, and a locust coupling with a spruce needle. I invented a bumper sticker in my head: PULVERIZE YOUR BIRTHRIGHT. The fish seemed agitated by the moon. I realized I had read an outdated Lunar Conditions report—one from over a decade ago, in fact. The DGIF's current analysis of Lake Shenandoah reads, "Lake Shenandoah has had chronic fisheries problems that can be attributed directly to development in the drainage. A public golf course and expanding residential housing have introduced excessive nutrients and sediments to Lake Shenandoah. The result has been severe negative impacts on fish habitat . . . Low oxygen levels can suppress aquatic insect populations and stress fish." A boy, who should've been asleep at that hour, practiced his golf strokes on peanuts. The DGIF calls the lake a "time bomb," though I'm not exactly sure what they mean by this. A bunch of dead insects, I think. The woodpecker pecked what looked, in the moonlight, like a squid into the bigtooth aspen bark, though it was tiny. In only the moonlight, I impaled my thumb on the fish hook. The woodpecker spat. Termites rushed from the hole.

* * *

A BLOGGER known as the Peanut Whisperer provides instructions for sewing an eight-foot-long giant squid pillow ("whipstitch the eyes onto the head"); and Sarah, on MySpace, provides a recipe for "Giant squid chocolate cookie with peanut butter filling," that netted exactly zero comments; and LiveLeak.com asks, "Why is live squid like peanut butter? Both stick to the roof of your mouth."

I don't believe it's Jefferson that Uncle is speaking of when he says, "godfather of Peanut Soup." He shows me the picture of Aunt when she was young and healthy and wearing a plum sundress and had a Band-Aid on her knee. She's clutching a fistful of shells in one hand, a wooden spoon in the other. The tip of her tongue is stuck to the roof of her mouth as if she's about to pronounce the word *Love.* I don't believe the photograph's not doctored.

* * *

Friday, November 15, 2013, 10:37 a.m.
Today, I searched for the giant squid in Lake Biggins, a full three hours from my house, by car. I wasn't going to take the cat, but she started complaining and rubbing her sebaceous glands on the cat carrier. On the cat carrier's rear, a sticker of a reclining peanut, the peanut as a Botticelli model, as the birth of something, as the symbol for infinity, as the arms that keep unfurling, feeding us, or feeding on us.

I caught and released two bluegills. I told myself they were grateful, that they had the capacity for gratitude. The cat ate a poisonous puffball mushroom. Lethargy and labored breathing ensued. Later, at the vet's, they extracted a three-inch roundworm from her gastrointestinal tract. The vet worked deftly with this sturdy tweezers-like tool. His hands didn't shake, but his pinkie nail looked infected. *Fungus*, I thought, but that could have been paranoia. When he withdrew the implement from my cat, he said, "Here we go." He extended the O. He placed the worm in a Petri dish. Held it to my nose. It whirled like a sidewinder, did a balançoire, then stopped. *The smallest tentacle in the room*, I thought, and then said, "The smallest tentacle in the room." The vet whistled something beautiful and nodded at me, but I couldn't make out the song, and felt ashamed.

* * *

THE TWO MOST POPULAR comparative size and shape descriptions for paralarvae (giant squid in their larval state): cricket; peanut. Uncle is hungry. As he tries to duplicate Aunt's soup, he resorts to eating the shells.

Waverly, Virginia is home to "the First Peanut Museum in the U.S.A.," which, according to the *Washington Post*, boasts display cases filled with "a peanut scooper, needles for sewing peanut bags, and . . . a peanut sleigh being pulled by peanut reindeer, a gift to the museum after their elderly owner died."

Shirley Yancey, director of the First Peanut Museum in the U.S.A., "nursed a diet soda and let her mind drift back to the museum's opening in May 1990.

"Hundreds packed the place that day, she said, and as she looked over their heads . . . past the town's only stoplight, she swelled with pride. When she cut the twine stretched between two burlap bags of peanuts, officially opening the museum, people crowded to get in . . ."

"This day, though, was different. 'Slacker time,' she called it. The sun was sinking, and not a single visitor had stopped by . . ."

If no one stops by, what else can we do but turn our "lowly legume" into liquid, into river, into anything that rushes, whirlpools, anything that bears a current, anything that may hold within it the most unlikely of historical beasts? We will open our mouths to receive it, and we may or may not think of lightning, and we will swell and we will swell with something we can only pray is pride.

One of the first carvings of a giant squid attacking a person predates the Venus of Willendorf, and was made by an unnamed Japanese sculptor. Of this sculpture, officials at the Zoologische Gesellschaft Frankfurt write, loosely translated, "This carving is an inch and a half long, and about as big as a peanut. The unfortunate lady has been seized [by the squid] while bathing." Uncle says that our soup is neither the myth nor even the myth pureed, but the vessel to which our most gigantic of myths are compared.

* * *

UNCLE AND I finish our soup. Nothing sticks to the roofs of our mouths, or the roofs of any other part of us. We go for a walk. He wants to hold my hand, and I let him. His palm feels huge, his fingers, small. With his other hand, he addresses the landscape. Here, we plant our peanuts among the puttyroot orchids and hop clovers, the thimbleweeds and spreading asters and bellflowers and heartseeds. Among the blackberries and bittercress and bloodroots. Among the fairycandles. Among the naked broomrapes. Earlier today, while Uncle smashed and stirred and slept, I searched for something bigger than the peanut, bigger than Virginia. I didn't see the squid, but I saw the flowers.

Peanut Soup

Mount Vernon Colonial Peanut and Chestnut Soup

Ingredients
¼ cup margarine
1½ tablespoons all purpose flour
1 quart chicken broth
1 quart water
1 cup smooth peanut butter
½ cup unsalted peanuts, chopped
½ cup water chestnuts, chopped

Melt margarine in a large saucepan. Stir in flour to make a roux. Cook on medium heat while frequently stirring until the roux is light tan in color. Once the roux is ready, add chicken broth and bring to a boil. Then add peanut butter and stir. Hold on stove at a low heat until ready to serve. The longer it heats, the thicker it gets. Garnish with chopped peanuts and water chestnuts.

Serves: 10 to 12

—*George Washington's Mount Vernon Inn*

Acknowledgments

Grateful acknowledgment is made to the editors of the following publications in which some of these essays appeared, occasionally under different titles and in slightly different form:

Sundog Lit: Montana: The Circumventing of the Elk Stew

Baltimore Review: Hawai'i: The Mynah Bird Eats Hawaiian Shave Ice

Kenyon Review: Rhode Island: The Clouding of the Clear Clam Chowder

Indiana Review: North Dakota: Drilling for Lefse

Ninth Letter: Ohio: Cincinnati Chili Reincarnate

Gulf Coast: Minnesota: The Hotdish Muddies the Water (a.k.a. Those Poor Drowned)

The Normal School: Colorado: At Altitude with the Denver Omelet

Willow Springs: Kentucky: The Putting Down of the Mint Julep

Black Warrior Review: California: A Hopeless Mimic Engages the California Roll

Black Warrior Review: Michigan: Elements of the Pasty and Its Relation to the Lake

Zone 3: Indiana: The Conflicted Archaeologies of Hoosier Cream Pie

The Book of Uncommon Prayer (anthology, Outpost 19): Idaho: A Prayer for the Spudnuts as They Take to the Sky

Gastronomica: New York: At the Center of the Center of the New York Bagel

Alaska Quarterly Review: Georgia: Peach Pie on Badstreet

Shenandoah: Louisiana: The Sad Autoerotica of Crawfish Étouffée

Bending Genre: Kansas: The Uprooting of the Bierock

Watershed Review: Delaware: Qualifications on Things Said about Dover Cake

Mid-American Review: Missouri: A Blow to the Head for St. Louis Barbecue

Prairie Schooner: Alabama: The Beginning of the End of Hummingbird Cake

Cimarron Review: Iowa: The Fata Morgana in the Loosemeat Sandwich

DIAGRAM: Alaska: Extensions on Buttwiches and Idiocy and Buttwiches on Extensions

Superstition Review: Arizona: Some Theories on the Sonoran Hot Dog

The Collagist: Maryland: The Dawning of the Blue Crab

Ecotone: Nebraska: Spoon Bread Dictates

The Way North: Collected Upper Peninsula New Works (anthology, Wayne State University Press): Michigan: Elements of the Pasty and Its Relation to the Lake (reprinted)

The Way North: Collected Upper Peninsula New Works (anthology, Wayne State University Press): Wisconsin: Endnotes for the Sheboygan Bratwurst

The Great Lakes Book Project (anthology, Felix Exi Press): Michigan: Elements of the Pasty and Its Relation to the Lake (reprinted)

Hotel Amerika: Illinois: The Biblical Rheology of Deep-Dish Pizza

Quarterly West: Arkansas: The Ecstasy of the Beaver Tail

Seneca Review: Maine: James Earl Jones Eats Whoopie Pie

Boundless gratitude to Rayhané Sanders, Katie Henderson Adams, Cordelia Calvert, Matt Bell, Beth Staples, Ander Monson, Nicole Walker, Elena Passarello, Mike Madonick, Steven Church, Sam Ligon, Jameelah Lang, Jon Billman, Jen Howard, Josh MacIvor Andersen, Charlotte Pence, Amy Wright, and to my family.

Special thanks to Robin McCarthy and Tim Johnston.

And very special thanks to you, Louisa. We have a real shower now, baby. Hot water and everything.

Credits

Information regarding the sources and citations for *The Mad Feast* can be found at www.matthewgfrank.com.

Illustrations

p. v Can Stock Photo Inc. / cmp designz
p. 4 bonchan / Shutterstock
p. 14 r.martens / Shutterstock
p. 21 Nir J. Shaviv
p. 28 Hywit Dimyadi / Shutterstock
p. 35 abxyz / Shutterstock
p. 53 S J Francis / Shutterstock
p. 60 Stephanie Frey / Shutterstock
p. 67 Edward Fielding / Shutterstock
p. 73 Christopher J. Martin / Shutterstock
p. 81 NinaM / Shutterstock
p. 88 UMB-O / Shutterstock
p. 97 junyanjiang / Shutterstock
p. 108 Gua / Shutterstock
p. 111 Camille Flammarion, L'Atmosphere Météorologie Populaire (Paris, 1888), 163
p. 116 PhotosJC / Shutterstock
p. 125 squarelogo / Shutterstock
p. 135 locote / Shutterstock
p. 151 werbeantrieb / Shutterstock
p. 160 koss13 / Shutterstock
p. 173 RedKoala / Shutterstock
p. 180 mike_expert / Shutterstock
p. 187 Everett Historical / Shutterstock
p. 197 Tribalium / Shutterstock
p. 205 George W. Bailey / Shutterstock
p. 214 Pinkyone / Shutterstock
p. 221 Yuriy Boyko / Shutterstock
p. 234 You Touch Pix of EuToch / Shutterstock

p. 239 Morphart Creation / Shutterstock
p. 246 kozirsky / Shutterstock
p. 251 Randy Hines / Shutterstock
p. 261 melazerg / Shutterstock
p. 272 Henk Bentlage / Shutterstock
p. 278 Natykach Nataliia / Shutterstock
p. 288 Hein Nouwens / Shutterstock
p. 293 Everett Historical / Shutterstock
p. 310 murphy81 / Shutterstock
p. 317 siminitzki / Shutterstock
p. 324 24Novembers / Shutterstock
p. 332 Jaimie Duplass / Shutterstock
p. 339 astudio / Shutterstock
p. 346 Nicolas Raymond / Shutterstock
p. 354 zoryanchik / Shutterstock
p. 361 ojal / Shutterstock
p. 367 Ase / Shutterstock
p. 377 Gallinago_media / Shutterstock
p. 389 TAGSTOCK1 / Shutterstock
p. 393 isaxar / Shutterstock
p. 400 Minerva Studio / Shutterstock
p. 409 grop / Shutterstock

Recipes

p. 11 Key Lime Pie: Blue Heaven Restaurant, 729 Thomas Street, Key West, FL 33040

p. 18 Beaver Tail Bouillon: Josh Brewer, Hot Springs, AR

p. 24 Hummingbird Cake: Something Special Deli, 128 Industrial Parkway, Saraland, AL 36571

p. 30 Mississippi Mud Pie: Heather Ries, The Ladybugg Bakery & Cafe, 205 E. Commerce Street, Hernando, MS 38632

p. 39 Crawfish Étouffée: Darren Chifici, chef and co-proprietor, Deanie's Seafood Restaurant, 841 Iberville Street, New Orleans, LA 70112

p. 46 Perloo, a.k.a. Pilau: Forrest Parker, chef, Old Village Post House, 101 Pitt Street, Mt. Pleasant, SC 29464

p. 54 Georgia Peach Pie: Eric Wolitzky, South City Kitchen, 1144 Crescent Avenue NE, Atlanta, GA 30309

p. 63 Whoopie Pie: Sue Moody, Moody's Diner, 1885 Atlantic Highway, Waldoboro, ME 04572

p. 71 Maple Creemee: Bluebird Vermont, 86 Saint Paul Street, Burlington, VT 05401

p. 77 Clear Clam Chowder: Scott Cowell, Melville Grille, 1 Lagoon Road, Portsmouth, RI 02871

p. 83 Lou's Corn Chowder: Shawn Nelson, Lou's Restaurant & Bakery, 30 South Main Street, Hanover, NH 03755

p. 90 Boston Cream Pie: Annabelle Blake, Flour Bakery and Café, 1595 Washington Street, Boston, MA 02118

p. 100 Creamy Cape Cod Clam Chowder: Jasper White's Summer Shack, 1 Mohegan Sun Boulevard, Uncasville, CT 06382

p. 113 Bagel: Evan Giniger, Kossar's, 367 Grand Street, New York, NY 11212

p. 121 Blue Crab: Jimmy Cantler's Riverside Inn, 458 Forest Beach Road, Annapolis, MD 21409

p. 130 The New Jersey Ripper: Rutt's Hut, 417 River Road, Clifton, NJ 07014

p. 143 Cheesesteak: Tony Luke's, 39 East Oregon Avenue, Philadelphia, PA 19148

p. 152 Sugar-Free Red Velvet Dover Cake: Chef Dana Herbert, Desserts by Dana, Hideaway Cafe at Herman Holloway Campus (Route 13 S. & I-295 overpass), 1901 N. DuPont Highway, New Castle, DE 19720

p. 163 Bulldog NE Tater Tot Hotdish: Kevin Kraus, executive chef, Bulldog, NE Minneapolis, 401 E. Hennipen, Minneapolis, MN 55414

p. 175 Sheboygan Bratwurst: Harry Ljatifovski, owner, Harry's Diner and Harry's Prohibition Bistro, 2504 Calumet Drive, Sheboygan, WI 53083

p. 183 Loosemeat Sandwich: Melissa Freidhof-Rodgers, Ross' Restaurant, 430 14th Street, Bettendorf, IA 52722

p. 191 Pasty: Jacob Taylor, Marquette, MI

p. 199 St. Louis BBQ Ribs: Marc Rollins, chef, Hendricks BBQ, 1200 S. Main Street, Saint Charles, MO 63301

p. 207 Deep-Dish Pizza: Mattie Pool, Medici on 57th, 1327 E. 57th Street, Chicago, IL 60637

p. 216 "That's It! Hoosier Sugar Cream Pie": Louise and Rick Miracle, Pie First Bakery, Gosport, IN 47433

p. 226 Cincinnati Chili: Charlie Howard, Gold Star Chili, Cincinnati, OH

p. 236 Shave Ice: Cindy Jade Sylva, Maui, HI

p. 241 Buttwich (Halibut Sandwich): Jill Ramiel, owner, The Silverbow, 120 Second Street, Juneau, AK 99801

p. 249 Aplets: Cora Brown, *America Cooks: Practical Recipes from 48 States* (New York: W. W. Norton, 1940)

p. 257 Marionberry Pie: Shari's Café and Pies, Shari's Restaurant Group, 9400 SW Gemini Drive, Beaverton, OR 97008

p. 265 California Roll: Eva Valencia, San Francisco, CA

p. 274 Spoon Bread: Justin Daugherty, Omaha, NE

p. 282 Barbecued Bologna (Okie Sirloin): Aaron Latsos, Smokies Hickory House BBQ, Broken Arrow, OK

p. 291 Wojapi: Chef Sean Sherman and Christine Werner, chef de cuisine, The Sioux Chef, Minneapolis, MN, via Pine Ridge, SD

p. 299 Lefse: Charlotte Landsem, Charlotte's Homemade Lefse, 10449 71st Street NE, Edmore, ND 58330

p. 305 Bierock: Chef Manuel Hernandez, Gella's Diner & Lb. Brewing Co., 117 E. 11th Street, Hays, KS 67601

p. 313 Milk Can Supper: Pastor Karen O'Malia, Christ Lutheran Church & AKIDEMY, Cheyenne, WY

p. 322 Spudnut / Potato Donut: Kris Wallace, owner, Buy the Dozen Donuts, 104 E. 6th Street, Moscow, ID 83843

p. 328 Elk Stew: Chef Zachary Bernheim, The Spur Tavern and Kitchen, Highway 35, Bigfork, MT

p. 333 Denver Omelet: Alex Armatas, Sam's No. 3 Diner & Bar, 1500 Curtis Street, Denver, CO 80202

p. 340 Sonoran Hot Dog: The Mission Restaurant, 3815 N. Brown Avenue, Scottsdale, AZ 85251

p. 347 Green and Red Chile Sauces: Antonio Matus, chef and owner, Antonio's: A Taste of Mexico, original location: 122 Doña Luz, Taos, NM 87571, current location: 246 Main Street, Longmont, CO 80501

p. 356 Funeral (Party) Potatoes: Barbara Schieving, Salt Lake City, UT

p. 363 The Nevada Cocktail: The Cin Cin, Eldorado Casino, 345 N. Virginia Street, Reno, NV 89501

p. 370 Texas Brisket: Wayne Mueller, 3rd Generation Owner and Pitmaster, Louie Mueller Barbecue, 206 W. 2nd Street, Taylor, TX 76574

p. 382 Rat Stew: Fredricah Gardner, Clover Lick, WV

p. 390 Memphis Style Dry-Rub Ribs: Charlie Vergos' Rendezvous Restaurant, 52 S. Second Street, Memphis, TN 38103

p. 395 Mint Julep: The Brown Hotel, 335 West Broadway, Louisville, KY 40202

p. 401 Moravian Spice Cookies: Mrs. Hanes Moravian Cookies, 4643 Friedberg Church Road, Clemmons, NC 27012

p. 412 Peanut Soup: George Washington's Mount Vernon Inn, 3200 Mount Vernon Memorial Highway, Mount Vernon, VA 22121